The Americas Revealed

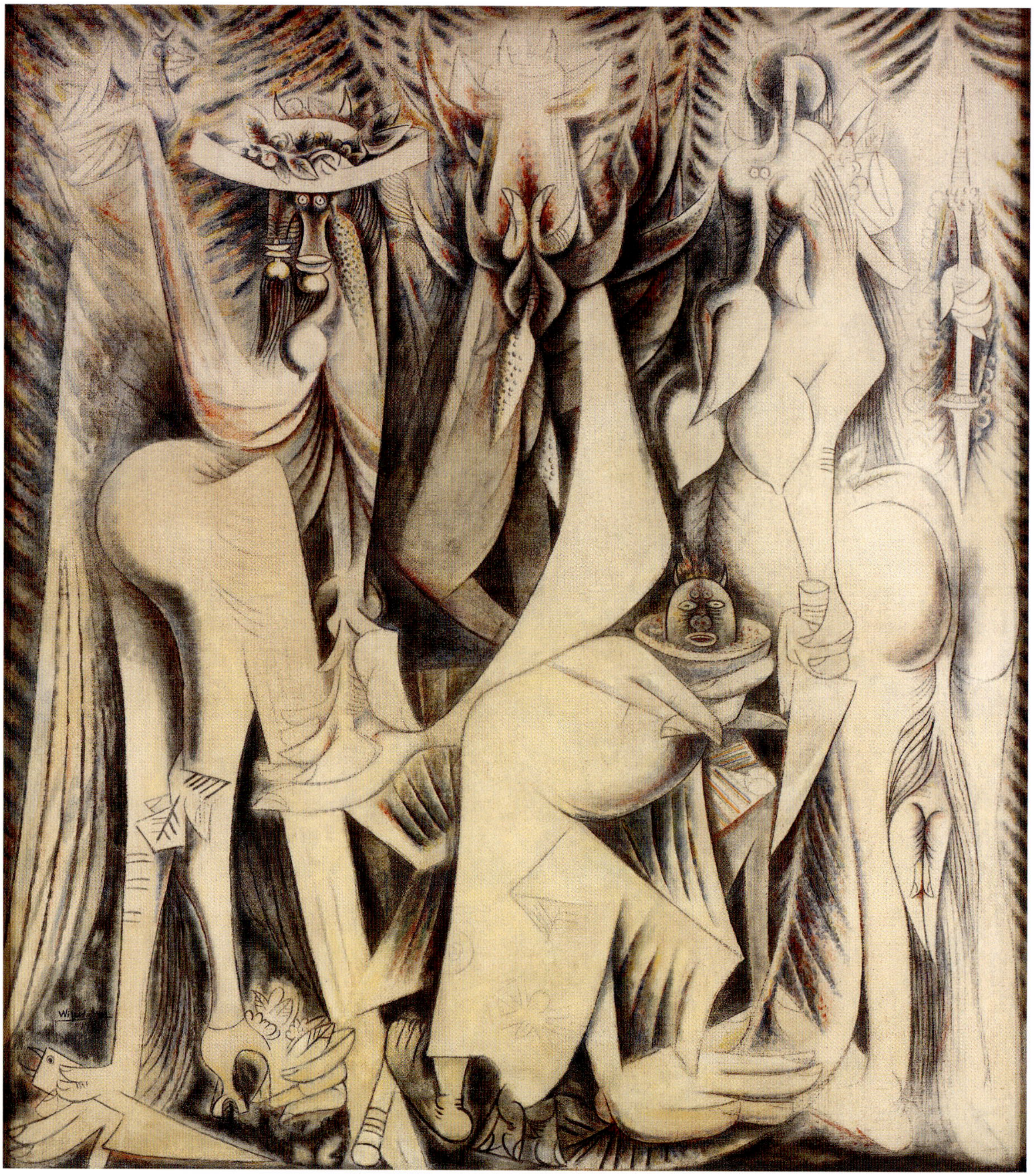

The Americas Revealed

Collecting Colonial and Modern Latin American Art in the United States

EDITED BY EDWARD J. SULLIVAN

THE FRICK COLLECTION
THE PENNSYLVANIA STATE UNIVERSITY PRESS
UNIVERSITY PARK, PENNSYLVANIA

This book evolved from a symposium organized by the Center for the History of Collecting that was held at The Frick Collection on May 16 and 17, 2014. The symposium was made possible through the generous support of the Institute for Studies on Latin American Art, Isabella Hutchinson and Diego Gradowczyk, Tanya Capriles Brillembourg, and Diana L. Beattie in memory of Walter Eberstadt.

Library of Congress Cataloging-in-Publication Data
Names: Sullivan, Edward J., editor.
Title: The Americas revealed : collecting colonial and modern Latin American art in the United States / edited by Edward J. Sullivan.
Other titles: Studies in the history of art collecting in America ; 4.
Description: [New York, New York] : The Frick Collection ; University Park, Pennsylvania : The Pennsylvania State University Press, [2018] | Series: The Frick Collection studies in the history of art collecting in America ; fourth volume | "This book evolved from a symposium organized by the Center for the History of Collecting that was held at The Frick Collection on May 16 and 17, 2014." | Includes bibliographical references and index.
Summary: "Explores the formation of public and private collections of Spanish Colonial and modern Latin American art throughout the United States, and the impact of the ever-changing political landscape of Latin American countries"—Provided by publisher.
Identifiers: LCCN 2017045209 | ISBN 9780271079523 (cloth : alk. paper)
Subjects: LCSH: Art, Latin American—Collectors and collecting—United States—History.
Classification: LCC N6502 .A494 2018 | DDC 709.8—dc23
LC record available at https://lccn.loc.gov/2017045209

Printed in Korea
Published by The Pennsylvania State University Press,
University Park, PA 16802-1003

The Pennsylvania State University Press is a member of the Association of University Presses.

It is the policy of The Pennsylvania State University Press to use acid-free paper. Publications on uncoated stock satisfy the minimum requirements of American National Standard for Information Sciences—Permanence of Paper for Printed Library Material, ANSI Z39.48–1992.

Frontispiece: Wifredo Lam (Cuban, 1902–1982), *The Eternal Presence (An Homage to Alejandro García Caturla)*, 1944. Oil and pastel over papier maché and chalk ground on bast fiber fabric, 216.5 × 195.9 cm. Providence, Rhode Island School of Design, Museum of Art. Nancy Sayles Day Collection of Modern Latin American Art, 66.154. Artists Rights Society (ARS), New York.
Page v: Detail, Mario Carreno, *Afro-Cuban Dancer*, 1943 (fig. 38). San Francisco Museum of Modern Art. © 2009 Artists Rights Society (ARS), New York / CREAIMAGEN, Santiago de Chile.
Pages vi, ix: Details, Diego Rivera, *The Flower Carrier*, 1935 (fig. 24). San Francisco Museum of Modern Art. © 2016 Banco de México Diego Rivera & Frida Kahlo Museums Trust, Mexico, D.F. / Artists Rights Society (ARS), New York.
Page 1: Detail, María Fernanda Cardoso, *Woven Water: Submarine Landscape*, 1994 (fig. 42). Houston, The Museum of Fine Arts. Courtesy of María Fernanda Cardoso.

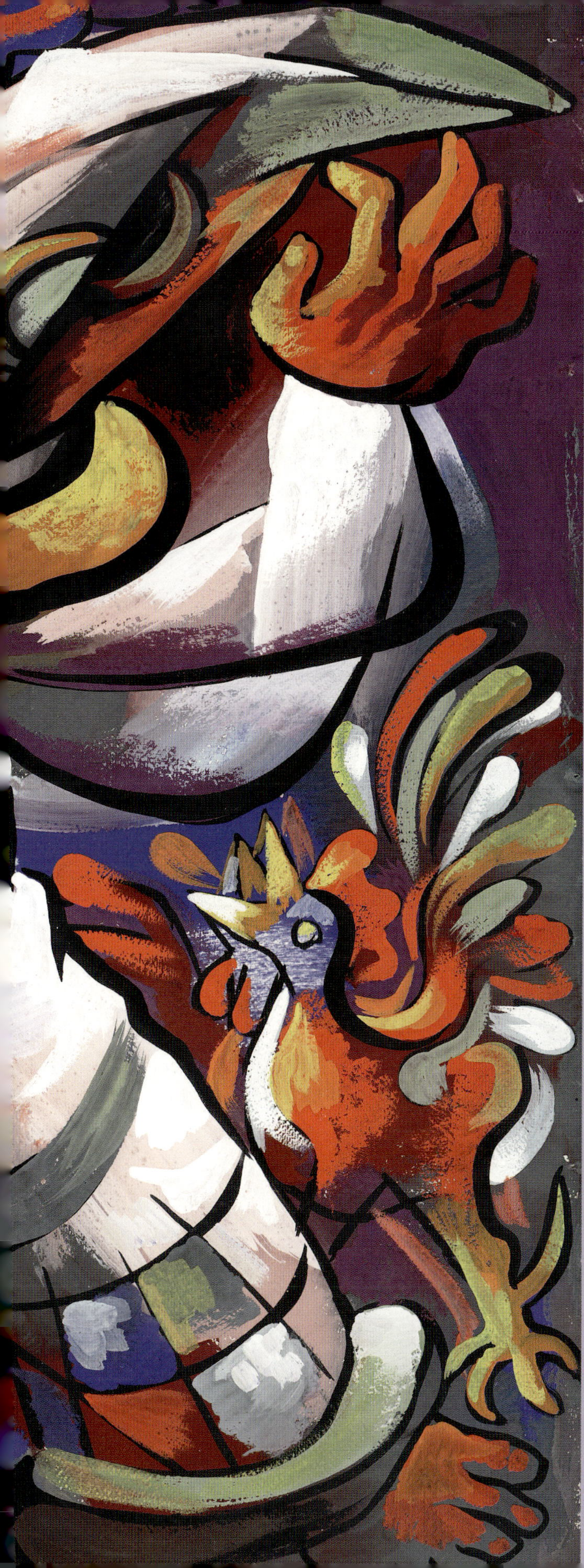

The Frick Collection Studies in the History of Art Collecting in America

SERIES EDITOR: Inge Reist

This is the fourth volume of Studies in the History of Art Collecting in America, a series conceived by the Center for the History of Collecting at The Frick Collection. The Center, established at the Frick Art Reference Library in 2007, is a research institute that focuses on an expanding area of study within the fields of art and cultural history. It encourages and supports the study of the formation of collections of fine and decorative arts, both public and private, in Europe and the United States from the Renaissance to the present day. An important element of the Center's mission is to add to the scholarly literature on art collecting both through its own publications for this series and through its support of authors who benefit from the Center's fellowship program.

Other Volumes in the Series

Quodbach, Esmée, ed. *Holland's Golden Age in America: Collecting the Art of Rembrandt, Vermeer, and Hals*

Reist, Inge, ed. *A Market for Merchant Princes: Collecting Italian Renaissance Paintings in America*

Bowron, Edgar Peters, ed. *Buying Baroque: Italian Seventeenth-Century Paintings Come to America*

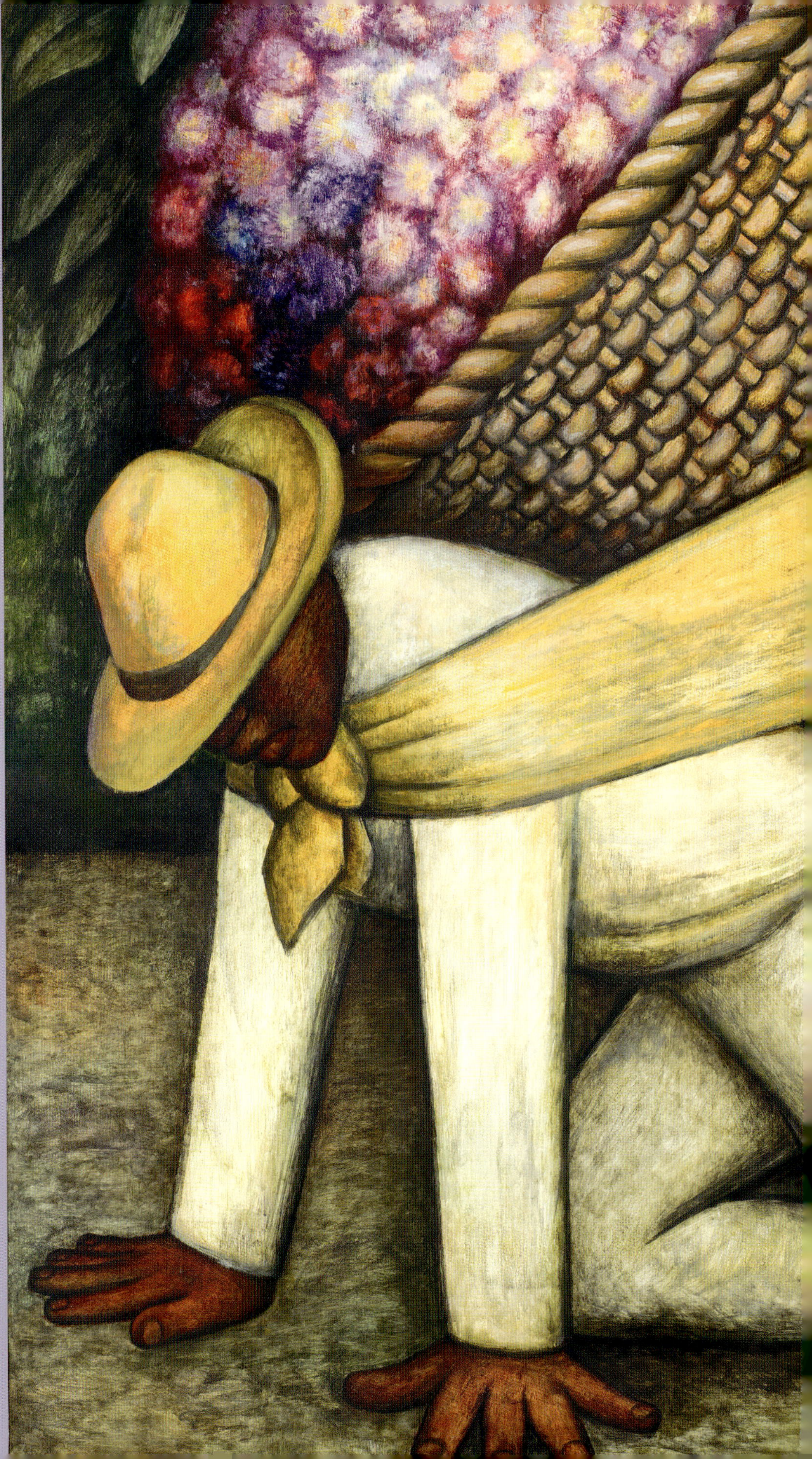

Contents

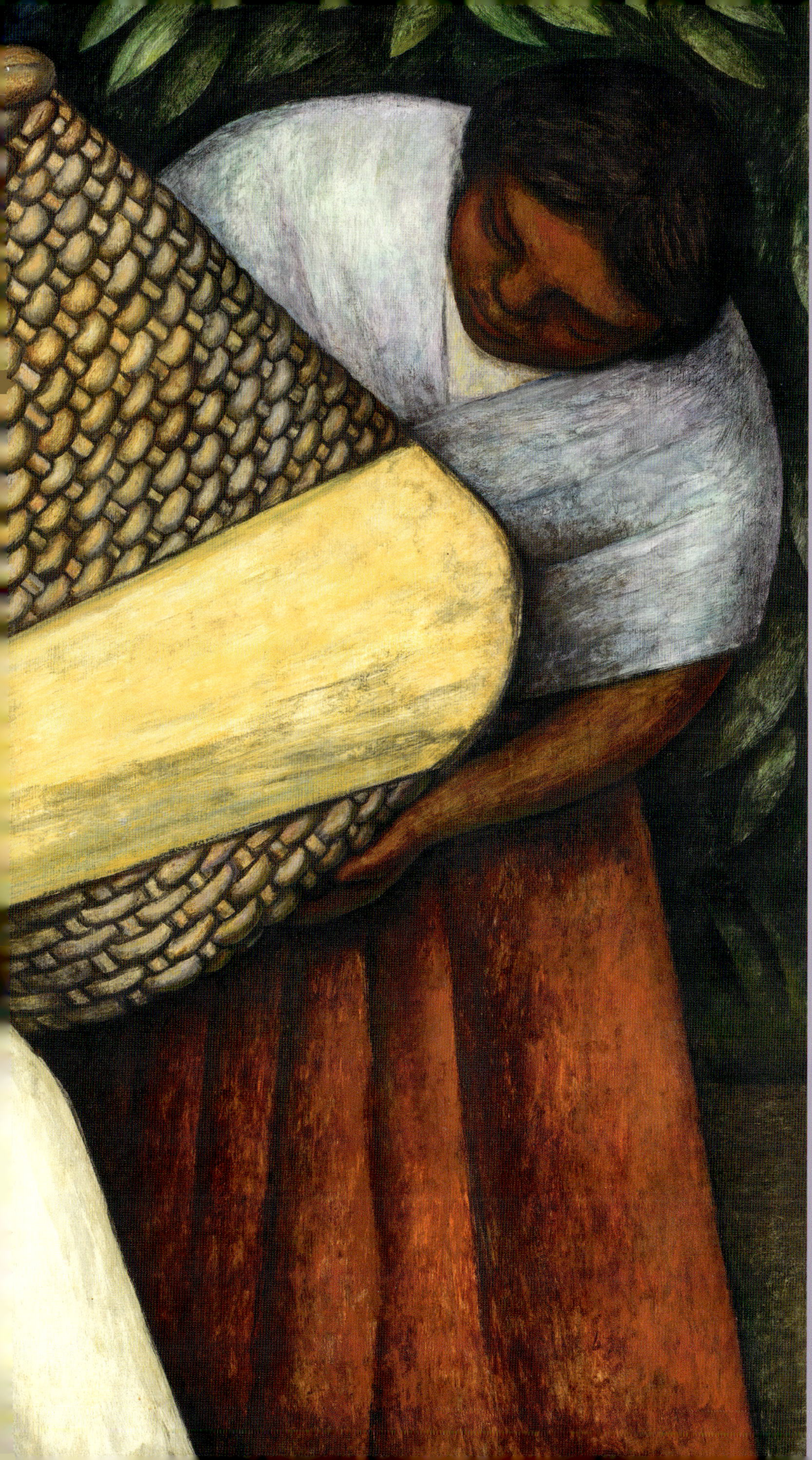

Illustrations

Foreword

Whether the subject is politics, language, or art, people who hail from the countries south of the Rio Grande have long criticized some of us who live in the United States for viewing the cultures of Central and South America monolithically. We citizens of the United States often even refer uniquely to ourselves as "Americans" while everyone to the south bears the appellation "Latin American." Fortunately, in recent years, and perhaps due in part to the growing number of U.S. residents whose heritage is Central or South American, our country has gradually awakened to the rich variety, both artistic and literary, that the cultures of Central and South America embrace and celebrate. Thus, today, we refer to an artist as Venezuelan, Argentinian, Brazilian, Peruvian, Colombian, and so on rather than as merely Latin American, finally aligning our view of art from the nations to our south with the way we think about "European art," appreciating it for qualities that are decidedly "French," "Italian," "Dutch," "German," or "Spanish."

Just as our clearer understanding of the nuanced differences among national styles in South America was slow to come to the United States, so, too, was an interest in collecting colonial and modern Latin American art. Not surprisingly, then, publications focused on collecting in this area are few and far between, making a volume of essays so intently focused on the formation of private and public collections of Mexican, Central American, and South, and Caribbean art a necessary and significant contribution to the burgeoning field of the history of collecting.

With the publication of this, the fourth volume in the series The Frick Collection Studies in the History of Art Collecting in America, we reach for the first time beyond the categories of European and American art associated with The Frick Collection. However, since its founding by Helen Clay Frick in 1920, the Frick Art Reference Library has collected materials on Latin American art and artists. For example, the Library holds unique copies of early twentieth-century exhibition catalogues, including a 1928 catalogue published for Weyhe Gallery, *Paintings and Drawings by Diego M. Rivera*, and a sixteen-page booklet for a Wifredo Lam exhibition held in 1946 at the Lyceum in Havana. Thus, it seems only fitting that our first venture in publishing a subject not directly connected with the collecting of Henry Clay Frick should be one that has been supported for decades by the library his daughter founded, as she apparently recognized, before many of her peers, that Latin American art is in every way as much a part of the Western tradition as the European art her father (and she) so keenly admired and sought to possess.

In his elegant and all-encompassing introductory essay, Edward Sullivan takes us back to the beginning, to the moment of "contact" between the Europeans and indigenous peoples, when collectors began to develop a curiosity about art created in their "Western" tradition in Latin America. Theodore de Bry (1528–1598) and much later Alexander von Humboldt (1769–1859) are examples he points to of men of astounding intellectual depth and curiosity who dedicated significant time and energy to understanding the cultures of the Americas, during a time when the constant transfer of precious goods back and forth between the New World and the Old fueled the interests of less intellectually refined individuals as well. From the United States, traveler artists such as Frederic Church also nourished an appreciation of the imagery and art ema-

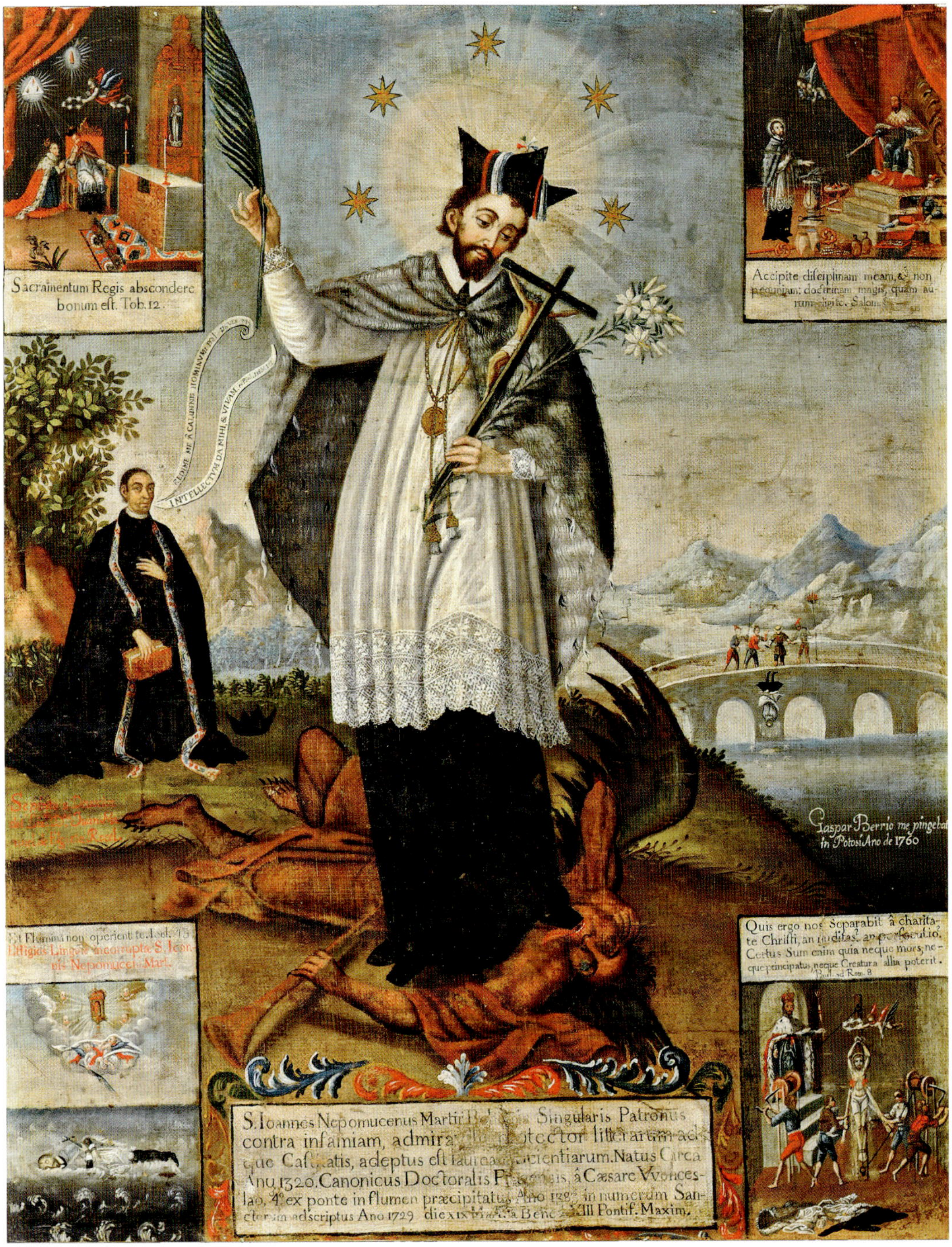

1. Gaspar Miguel de Berrío (Bolivian, 1706–1762), *Saint John of Nepomuk*, 1760. Oil on canvas, 103 × 82 cm. Collection of Roberta and Richard Huber. Promised gift of the Roberta and Richard Huber Collection to the Philadelphia Museum of Art. Courtesy of the Philadelphia Museum of Art.

nating from Latin America, as both Sullivan and Berit Potter explain in their essays.

In assessing the developing interest in Latin American art, one cannot help but notice that politics almost always plays a role, whether relating to curious shifts in taste in viceregal capitals of New Spain, reactions to the assertion of "American exceptionalism" as promoted by the Monroe Doctrine, and, in a somewhat different way, by the "Good Neighbor Policy" encouraged by Nelson Rockefeller in the 1940s, or even aesthetic biases found within the government-sponsored art academies in Mexico, Rio de Janeiro, or Havana. Yet ultimately, once collecting art from Central and South America, as well as the Caribbean, took hold in the United States during the nineteenth century, the role of determined individuals led to the situation we know now in the twenty-first, with art from Latin America highly sought after by private collectors and regarded as an essential component of any encyclopedic public collection. Robert Lamborn (1835–1895) in Philadelphia; Emily (1851–1942), Robert (1848–1931), and Lockwood (1850–1932) de Forest in New York; Grace Louise McCann Morley (1900–1985) in San Francisco; Abby Aldrich Rockefeller (1874–1948) and her son Nelson (1908–1979), Lincoln Kirstein (1907–1996), and René d'Harnoncourt (1901–1968) in New York; and in our own time, collectors and philanthropists Diane and Bruce Halle in Phoenix; and, in New York, Roberta and Richard Huber, Patricia Phelps de Cisneros, and Estrellita Brodsky, can all claim credit for giving Latin American art, both colonial and modern, the place it deserves in the eyes of specialists and the general public alike. The chapters in this volume celebrate those individuals as well the energy and passion of countless museum professionals and academics, such as Dorothy Canning Miller (1904–2003), Alfred H. Barr, Jr. (1902–1981), Barbara Duncan (1921–2003), and more recently Mari Carmen Ramírez, who nurtured the collectors' interests and carried forward their legacies.

Earliest among these driven individuals was Robert Lamborn, whose collecting activity is central to the essay by Joseph Rishel, who credits Lamborn's 1892 donations with "putting Philadelphia on the map as an institution with interests in Spanish Colonial art." Fortunately, the Philadelphia Museum of Art continued to enjoy the fruits of energetic personalities who cared deeply about Mexican and South American art in a succession of curators and, above all, in its director from 1982 until her untimely death in 2008, Anne d'Harnoncourt (1943–2008), daughter of MoMA director René d'Harnoncourt, who infused her with his own passion for Latin American art, which had resulted from his years spent in Mexico from 1926 to 1933.

The pivotal role played by the Museum of Modern Art beginning in the 1940s and steadily strengthening into this century is explored by Miriam Basilio and Delia Solomons, while Ronda Kasl sheds light on how early patrons and curators at The Metropolitan Museum of Art such as the de Forests boosted the arts of Mexico. Kasl's concentration on the dedication of the Museum's early patrons and curators to Mexican art cannot help but point to a dwindling commitment at that institution in later decades. The balance is only slowly being redressed now with a full-time curator dedicated, as of 2013, to Latin American art.

No book on the collecting and patronage of Latin American art in the United States would be complete without a full treatment of how Diego Rivera (1889–1957) and other Mexican muralists captured the attention of so many collectors. Anna Indych-López's contribution to this volume probes into the reasons behind the appeal of quasi-folkloric imagery to U.S. collectors on both the East and West Coasts, specifically to the Rockefellers and Albert Bender (1866–1941).

Mari Carmen Rámirez, Berit Potter, and Vanessa Davidson have all contributed essential chapters to this book, delving into the formation of important collections in Houston, San Francisco, and Phoenix. Ramírez underscores the vital role of special exhibitions (as do, admittedly, other chapters of the book). For Potter, the force of an individual—Grace Louise McCann Morley—is paramount, as Potter allows us to learn about the collecting climate in San Francisco during the 1930s and '40s through Morley's own statements, as recorded in the archives of the San Francisco Museum of Modern Art, and introduces us to the collecting personality of Albert Bender through many of his letters to personalities such as Frida Kahlo (1907–1954).

The last three chapters of this volume are dedicated to collectors of Latin American art who are still active today, and thus offer personal accounts of rare immediacy. These collectors all participated in the 2014 symposium that gave rise to this publication: Roberta and Richard Huber offered reminiscences of their collecting adventures on day one, Estrellita Brodsky presented her personal story on day two, and Edward Sullivan's interview of Patricia Phelps de Cisneros concluded the proceedings. Suzanne Stratton-Pruitt, who wrote and edited the book that accompanied the Philadelphia Museum of Art's exhibition of the Hubers' collection in 2013, *Journeys to New Worlds: Spanish and Portuguese Colonial Art in the Roberta and Richard Huber Collection*, chronicles the couple's abiding interest, over more than four decades, in the art produced not only in Central and South American colonies of the Iberian empires, but also farther afield in the East Indies. Gabriel Pérez-Barreiro, Director of the Colección Patricia Phelps de Cisneros, elegantly presents how the Cisneros collection has grown from its modest beginnings in the 1990s to the formidable size it is today, and how, through the Fundación Cisneros, it has taken on a role far more extensive than most private collections, as it supports the art of Latin America through grants, loans, and involvement with academic and major museum programs. In the final chapter in this book, Estrellita Brodsky rounds out the section about present-day collectors of Latin American art with a beautifully written memoir that candidly offers the author's own view of how her taste for certain artists developed; how her own research, both for her advanced degrees and for exhibitions she has curated, influenced her appreciation of the field in general; and how her commitment to promoting a deeper understanding of Latin American art through museum exhibitions and scholarship has directed her philanthropy, leading her to support the creation of new positions at both large and small museums.

Whether readers of this volume choose to read it cover to cover or pick and choose among the essays here presented, they will be able to appreciate how looking at Latin American art through the lens of collectors and curators offers a new and original perspective to traditional art-historical approaches to the subject, humanizing it through a deeper understanding of the personal preferences expressed by so many energetic and passionate people.

In addition to acknowledging Edward J. Sullivan and the authors of this volume, we are indebted to the staff of the Center for the History of Collecting, Assistant Directors Esmée Quodbach and Samantha Deutch for their invaluable help in editing the manuscript and shepherding the procurement of images and permissions for the illustrations of this book. We are deeply grateful for the financial support we have received for this publication from New York University through the offices of Georgina Dopico, Dean for the Humanities, Faculty of Arts and Science and Thomas Carew, Anne and Joel Ehrenkranz Dean of the Faculty of Arts and Science, and thanks are due as well as to Roberta and Richard Huber, the Institute for Studies on Latin American Art (ISLAA) and its president and founder Ariel Aisiks, and two anonymous donors.

Inge Reist
Series Editor and Director of the Center for the History of Collecting

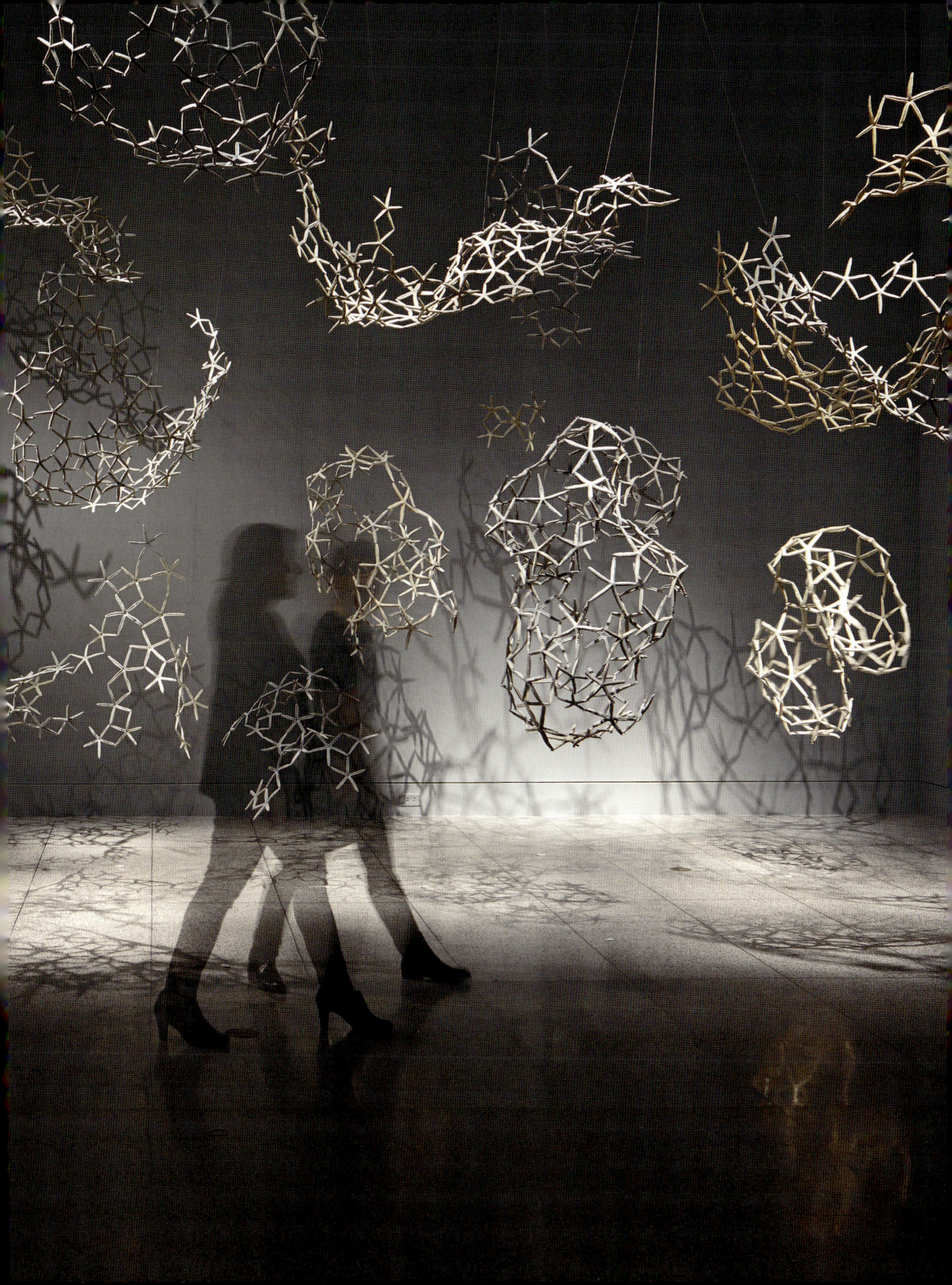

Introduction

Acquisitive Passions
Observations on Collecting the Art of the Americas in the United States

Edward J. Sullivan

2. Andrés López (Mexican, active 1782–97), *Sor Prudencia Josefa Manuela del Corazón de María,* 1782. Oil on canvas, 221.61 cm × 143.51 cm. Hudson, Olana State Historic Site.

Origins of Collecting Art from the Americas

Collecting anything represents its fetishization in the minds and eyes of those who possess the objects they covet. Objects take hold of the imagination. They represent other things, situations, and persons. They carry with them a multitude of associations regarding circumstances and places. Objects may be artifacts that elicit memories, or they may be relics of ownership. Collecting may be as benign as gathering together souvenirs from past trips, or it may be an act weighted with meaning and freighted with memories that evoke desire, possession, and conquest. Collecting must be defined in many categories, from individual gatherings of anything from artifacts or documents to works that connote "artistic sensibility." Collecting comprises the gathering of vestiges of long-disappeared cultures or things that were made yesterday.

In the distant past, what we understand as "collecting" was primarily a private occupation. Individuals used the means at their disposal to gather together objects of interest or rarity value to share with those around them, and to indicate their inquisitiveness as well as their monetary wherewithal to bring together a wide-ranging series of things displayed in discrete spaces that, in the European Renaissance, acquired the term "cabinets of curiosity." At this same time, nation-states made claims to lands beyond their own territories, bolstering their authority and their mandates by bringing together artifacts and works of art that displayed the places and peoples who were conquered or subject to other forms of domination.[1] By the late seventeenth century, museums were created to display such objects together with the fine arts. By the twentieth century, financial entities such as banks and other commercial establishments entered into the quest to accumulate art to serve a variety of purposes, from the simple adornment of their offices to its use as a tool for promoting the accumulation of capital by its customers.

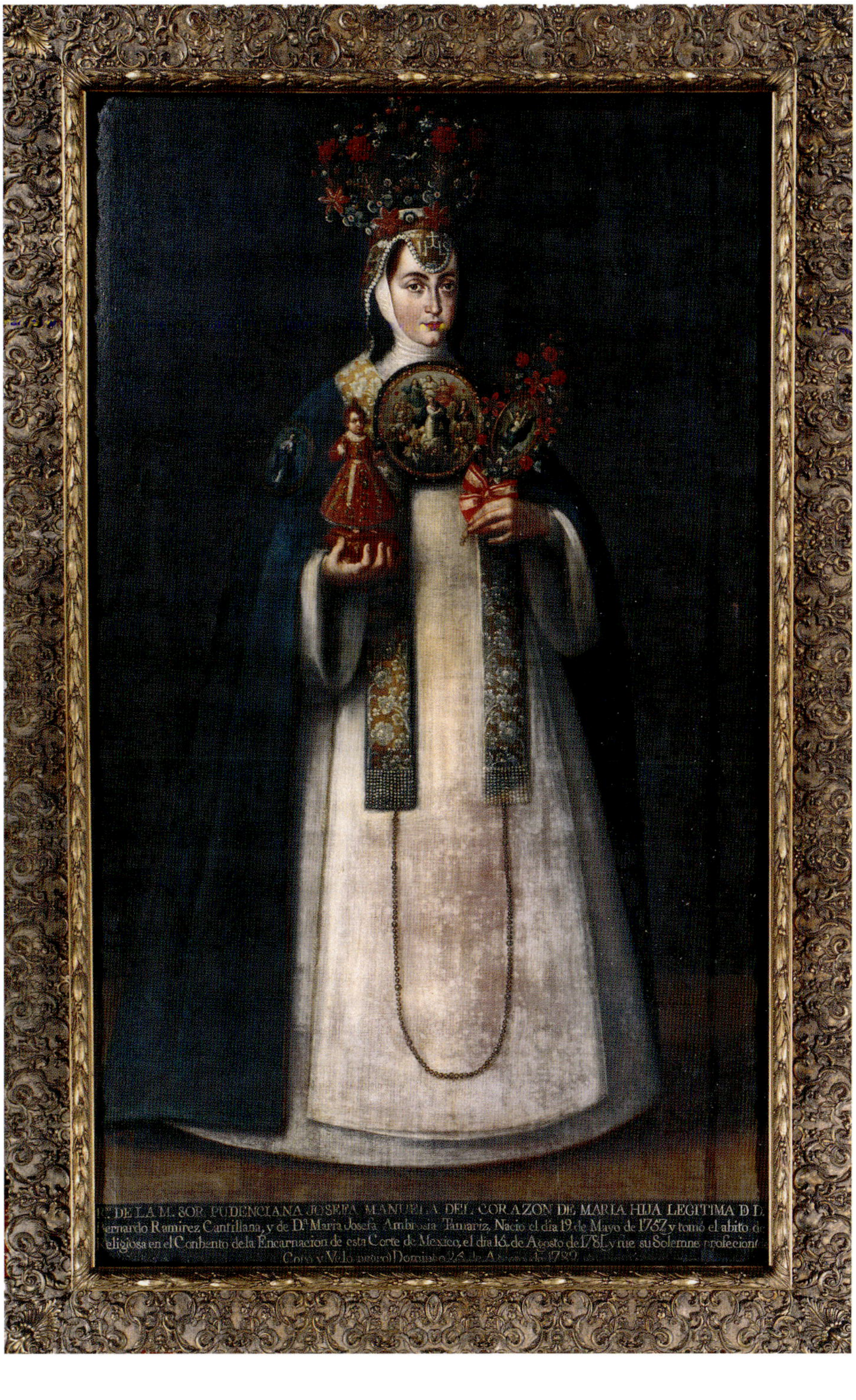
DE LA M. SOR PUDENCIANA JOSEFA MANUELA DEL CORAZON DE MARIA HIJA LEGITIMA D D.
ernardo Ramirez Cantillana, y de Dª Maria Josefa Ambrosia Tamariz, Nacio el dia 19. de Mayo de 1757 y tomó el abito d
eligiosa en el Conbento de la Encarnacion de esta Corte de Mexico, el dia 16. de Agosto de 1781, y fue su Solemne profecion

The above comments represent a very partial definition of collecting in a Western—European and North American—context. This volume is specifically concerned with the collecting of art from the Spanish- and Portuguese-speaking Americas, including the Caribbean, in the United States from the late nineteenth century to the twenty-first. This book forms part of a series of studies about the history of collecting in the United States. But while the other volumes are primarily concerned with art from the so-called Western tradition (Renaissance art, Baroque art, Dutch painting, etc.), this volume deals with the history of collecting objects that, in a sense, form the end point of thousands of years of artistic creation *and* collecting. The arts of the post-Contact era to the period of independence for many of the American nations in the nineteenth century often represented an amalgam of typologies, forms, and styles imported from the dominant powers abroad. Yet colonial art made in the Americas could rarely be mistaken for anything fashioned in Europe. Indeed, we must understand colonial art as a distinct entity or classification within the genealogy of art history, broadly conceived. In our study of the breadth of what constitutes colonial art and architecture within the vast geographical areas that make up the Americas, we are constantly reminded that a large number of cultural forces and tensions from around the globe played into the creation of art from this region from about 1500 to the early nineteenth century.[2]

While this book does not touch on the subject of the collecting of Pre-Columbian art, the collecting of arts from the era before European hegemony over the Americas began is often intertwined with that of more modern time periods. We should also remember that objects of art and material culture that characterized the civilizations vanquished by European powers, from Mesoamerica to the tip of South America as well as the Caribbean, continued to be fashioned after the collapse of the worlds of their creators and continued to be part of the new social and political order well into the sixteenth and seventeenth centuries. This makes it imperative for us to weave this subject into the continuous and nonlinear narrative that is suggested here. I am thinking, for example, of some instances of Taíno spiritual objects called *zemis*; indigenous Mexican (Aztec, Zapotec, etc.) manuscripts, maps, and feather art; Inca *kero* cups specifically for drinking *chichi*, a liquor made from fermented purple corn; and many other examples of what are objects fashioned well after the 1492 moment whose importance survived the ravages of imperial devastation.

In terms of collecting the art of the Americas in the United States, gatherings of Pre-Columbian art in museums and private collections often went hand in hand with those of colonial and modern art from Latin America, especially in the earlier part of the twentieth century. Many institutions began their collections with Pre-Columbian art that was purchased, donated, or came as a result of archaeological excavations financed by museums and universities. The interest on the part of Alfred H. Barr, Jr. (1902–1981), founding director and curator of New York's Museum of Modern Art, in art from the pre-Hispanic past as a foundational touchstone for expressions by twentieth-century artists is well known and serves as an integral link in the chain of relationships between the ancient and the modern in the Americas.[3]

We cannot properly tell the story of collecting art from Latin America (a highly problematic, contested, and insufficient term to define its geographical reach, as has been indicated by many scholars, especially in the past two decades) without signaling that it started with the encounter between Europe and the indigenous peoples of the Caribbean (the quintessential and primal area of "cultural transfer," as Thomas DaCosta Kaufmann might say,[4] or "contact zone," to use the term coined by literary critic Mary Louise Pratt[5]) with the first of Christopher Columbus's four journeys to the Americas, starting in 1492. Throughout the following two centuries numerous written and visual accounts, mostly highly fanciful and mainly created by European artists and writers who had never crossed the Atlantic, show the initial interactions of Europeans and indigenous persons as instances of exchange of objects: jewelry and ritual vessels on the part of the Americans, crosses, rosary beads, and decorative trinkets on the part of the Spaniards. Good examples of this are the famous illustrations by Theodore de Bry (1528–1598), who began to publish his most famous work, *The Discovery of America* (also known as *Les Grands Voyages*), in Frankfurt in the 1580s. This volume represents a substantial compendium of historical information provided by various explorers who had made the journey across the Atlantic. Some of the best-known prints created by De Bry (who had never traveled to the New World) represent Columbus's initial confrontation with the Taíno of the island that became known as Hispaniola as one of greeting and exchange against a background depicting the raising of the cross by Spanish sailors.

The objects brought back to Spain to document and justify the journeys of conquest before the courts of King Ferdinand (1454–1516) and Queen Isabella (1451–1504), and later Charles V (1500–1558), were the beginning of a great wave of imports of things that accrued worth and became objects of fascination for all who observed them. The description by Albrecht Dürer (1471–1528) of the gold of the Americas that he observed at the town hall of Brussels in 1520 is well known.[6] For those who were able to collect the precious metals and stones, images of deities, textiles, manuscripts in the form of codices, and other commodities, they served as testimonies to the collector's wealth and aspirations for global reach, whether in a commercial, religious, or landowning sense. Objects of wonderment from the Aztec, Maya, Inca, and other civilizations formed the bases of royal and noble collections as they were given as gifts from one royal house to another. Among the most renowned of these collections was that of the Medici, which included some of the most distinguished examples of ancient sculpture and other forms of art. Curiously, many of the Medici works, as well as those from other European Renaissance and Baroque collections, were reconfigured or dramatically changed to fit the aesthetic conventions of the time. Stone sculptures or jewelry of ancient American manufacture, for example, were transformed into fanciful objects that reflected the tastes of their European owners.[7]

Collecting of Americana in Europe continued in the eighteenth century as the result of many Spanish expeditions, such as that led by José Celestino Mutis (1732–1808) to the northern coast of South America (1783–1808), during which myriad objects, among them new plant species, were transported back to Iberia. Yet it was the travels to the Caribbean and northern South America of the Prussian polymath Alexander von Humboldt (1769–1859) and his companion the French naturalist Aimé Bonpland (1773–1858) between 1799 and 1804 that forever changed the character of collecting objects of American provenance. As products of the Enlightenment, Humboldt and Bonpland concentrated their efforts on scientific observation. Their collections consisted of thousands of specimens of plants and other forms of natural life that formed, in part, the basis of Humboldt's ample writings about his experiences, published in multiple volumes over the next twenty-one years.[8] Yet Humboldt was also concerned with many forms of American antiquities and described at length the buildings of ancient peoples and indigenous artifacts in his texts.

Humboldt's experiences stimulated further generations of travelers and collectors to journey to Latin America. The subject of traveler artists from both Europe and North America to what Humboldt called the "equinoctial regions" has elicited much interest recently in the form of books and, especially, exhibitions and their catalogues.[9] The theme of traveler-recorders of the landscape, flora, and fauna of virtually every corner of the Americas, from Mexico to Tierra del Fuego, is intimately linked to the subject of this book. By the mid-nineteenth century, many North Americans, especially artists from the United States, began to travel to Latin America and the Caribbean and recorded what they saw in paintings, drawings, and prints to illustrate books for the stay-at-home traveler who was becoming increasingly interested in the world beyond the border between the United States and Mexico. In addition, they also began collecting objects of all types that reflected the fascinating places they had visited. It should be remembered, as scholar Katherine Manthorne has reminded us in her numerous writings on the subject of nineteenth-century traveler artists, that these men, as well as a few women, made their journeys stimulated by the the political rhetoric of the United States, which included the assertion of "American exceptionalism" and the Monroe Doctrine's assumptions regarding the appropriateness of American expansionist aspirations.[10]

Among the best-known travelers and collectors to venture to South America, the Caribbean, and Mexico was Frederic Edwin Church (1826–1900), arguably the most famous artist of the Hudson River School and the promoter of grandly romantic views of sites as far-flung as upstate New York and New England, Jamaica, and the Andes of Ecuador and Colombia. Church was an obsessive collector of "exotica," as he would have described it—objects from both ancient and modern times that attested to his presence in faraway places and his sense of metaphoric ownership of their cultural productions. Church's many winter visits to Mexico after 1882 proved to be especially fruitful for his career as a collector. His grand house, called Olana (now a public museum), located above the Hudson River two hours north of Manhattan, was the venue for his private museum of Americana, among many other things. One may still see there the results of his acquisitiveness, attesting to his interest in Aztec sculpture, colonial painting, and Mexican popular arts of his own day. An impressive example of the colonial tradition of painting nuns on the day of the final profession of vows is included in the Olana collection. Like many works in Church's collection, the eighteenth-century *Portrait of Sor Prudencia Josefa Manuela del Corazón de María* by Andrés López (fig. 2) was "restored" by the artist, and in so doing, he made it look worn and older so as to add a romantic patina of age. Church was also a benefactor of The Metropolitan Museum of Art in New York, to which he donated an outstanding tenth- to thirteenth-century Toltec eagle relief.

The following essay presents a schematic series of ideas to illuminate major aspects of the history of collecting the art of the Americas in the United States. Some of these subjects are developed by the authors of this volume, while others (such as the history of collecting Haitian art, folk or "popular" arts, or corporate collecting) are not touched upon herein.

Collecting in the Americas

Although the subject of this volume is the collecting of Latin American art in the United States, it is important to acknowledge the significance of collecting by Latin American individuals and institutions within the region itself. The history of large-scale interest in amassing public and private assemblages of artworks, by artists from the individual countries and from Europe, also began in the late eighteenth, and especially in the nineteenth, century, just as it had beyond the northern border of the Rio Grande or, as it is called in Mexico, the Río Bravo. One of the principal stimuli for this was the founding of museum-like collections associated with academies. The history of government-supported institutions of the colonial era started with the founding of the Academia de San Carlos in Mexico City in 1781, which was based on the principles, imported from Spain, that had governed developments at Madrid's Academia de San Fernando, created in 1744. Instruction at the academies relied on copying both original works of art and printed reproductions as well as plaster casts of ancient sculptures. The collections of the Academia formed the basis of those of the Museo Nacional de San Carlos (founded in 1968) located in the Neoclassical Palacio de Buenavista in downtown Mexico City.

Other academies founded in the nineteenth century included the Academia das Belas Artes in Rio de Janeiro (1816) and the Academia de San Alejandro in Havana (1818). Like the Mexico City academy, they developed collections of art to aid in instruction. In addition, the nineteenth century witnessed the formation of considerable private collections of international art in various centers of Latin America. Some of these came to form the core of the considerable European and, in at least one case, North American painting collections of the national museums in Buenos Aires and Havana. This story, which can hardly be told here with any completeness, also comprises individual personalities of vast acquisitiveness, such as the German businessman Franz Mayer (1882–1975), who arrived in Mexico in 1905, became a Mexican citizen, and formed one of the most distinguished collections in the Mexican capital of colonial Latin American, European, and modern art. The Museo Franz Mayer is located in an eighteenth-century building facing the historic Alameda Park. An analogous example in Buenos Aires is the collection of Isaac Fernández Blanco (1862–1928), heir to a vast fortune that permitted him, starting in the early 1880s, to amass an immense collection of colonial art from many parts of South and Central America and Mexico. It is now housed in the Neocolonial-style building that constitutes the Museo de Arte Hispanoamericano Isaac Fernández Blanco.

U.S. Collections Begin:
The Early Years, Roots of Collection Practices

Collecting colonial art of Latin America in the United States began in earnest in the nineteenth century with such collectors as Dr. Robert Lamborn (1835–1895), whose Mexican art forms the core of the colonial collection at the Philadelphia Museum of Art, and it gained pace in the first half of the twentieth century, coinciding with a rise in interest in the colonial heritage of the United States itself. This phenomenon might be said to have started with the 1876 Centennial Exhibition in Philadelphia, celebrating one hundred years of the country's existence. Displays of Americana, including objects, furniture, ceramics, and many other examples of colonial material culture, awakened visitors to the accomplishments of the artists and artisans of the period. In the 1920s and '30s, many U.S. collectors enthusiastically embraced American folk art. Electra Havemeyer Webb (1888–1960), daughter of Louisine and Henry Osborne Havemeyer (great collectors of European Old Masters and benefactors of The Metropolitan Museum of Art, whose fortune came from the Caribbean sugar industry), began to buy American folk art shortly after her marriage in 1910. Her collection, which she kept at one of her country homes on the shore of Lake Champlain in Vermont, ultimately became the Shelburne Museum, housing one of the nation's most distinguished gatherings of anonymous popular arts.[11] The art historian Wanda Corn has pointed out the importance of the folk art collections of painters such as Charles Sheeler (1883–1965), whose own sleek, precisionist aesthetic was in part nurtured by the example of the "simple, geometric" lines of the objects that he owned, such as Shaker furniture.[12] The sculptor Elie Nadelman (1882–1946) was highly inspired by the collection of American (as well as European) folk art that he and his wife, Viola Spiess Nadelman (1878–1962), acquired and for which they created their own museum in the Riverdale section of the Bronx, New York, in 1926.[13]

Restored houses and towns also played a role in this growing taste for Americana. In the 1920s, members of the prominent Wells family in Southbridge, Massachusetts, began buying colonial antiquities, including silver, furniture, paintings, and, eventually, entire buildings that were threatened with destruction. The result was one of the country's first "restored colonial towns," Old Sturbridge Village. Much larger and better known is Colonial Williamsburg in Virginia, whose history and restoration as a tourist attraction and "living museum" are intimately linked to the collecting interests of members of the Rockefeller family, who, as we will see in this volume, were also crucial for the development of interest in Latin American art. By 1926 the movement to restore the town had begun, and it opened to the public in its reconfigured state in various phases beginning in the mid-1930s. Among the objects included in the Williamsburg collections were examples of Spanish Colonial furniture purchased by Abby Aldrich Rockefeller (1874–1948).[14]

During the 1920s several major East Coast museums expanded their holdings of American art and opened separate American wings, such as that of the Metropolitan Museum in 1924. The Museum of Fine Arts, Boston, had early strengths in Pre-Columbian and Native American arts as well as some significant colonial paintings. In 1999, they incorporated all of their vast American holdings (redefining the term "American" to include indigenous arts from pre-European times to modern art of the Western hemisphere to 1955) in the Arts of the Americas department. Then, in 2010, a new wing was added to the museum to house all of these collections, thus creating thought-provoking hemispheric juxtapositions. Boston's commitment to examining the arts of the hemisphere in an even wider, global scale was celebrated by a major exhibition, *Made in the Americas: The New World Discovers Asia* (2015–16), curated by Dennis Carr.[15] For contemporary acquisitions, the Leigh and Stephen Braude Fund for Latin American Art, among other funding sources, has been especially active in recent years in providing financial assistance for purchasing works by, among many others, Liliana Porter (b. 1941), César Paternosto (b. 1931), and Eduardo Terrazas (b. 1936).

Walker Evans's many photographs of colonial-era buildings also attest to the growing fascination in the United States with its own preindependence heritage in the years prior to World War II. Painters like Georgia O'Keeffe and members of the Taos School, which flourished during this period, also made a direct link in their art to the heritage of the Spanish settlements in New Mexico and the colonial arts of the United States by depicting the old churches of the state capital, Santa Fe, and smaller northern New Mexican towns such as Taos and Ranchos de Taos. The Museum of Spanish Colonial Art in Santa Fe was established in a 1930 Pueblo Revival building, and the collection grew throughout the 1930s and '40s and beyond to include several thousand objects created in the Southwest when much of this territory belonged to Spain. This is one of many instances in the former Spanish territories of the Southwest and California of Latin American colonial art being considered an integral part of the cultural expression of the formation of U.S. identity. At times these collections play a contested or controversial role in the definitions of cultural patrimony. A visit to the Bullock State History Museum in Austin, Texas, confronts the viewer with the story, among many others, of the siege of the Alamo and features a full-size re-creation of the fort's façade. Its many artifacts and original objects from the period of Spanish hegemony over Texas tell a complicated tale of conflicted loyalties that is never quite resolved in the mind of the viewer.

It is therefore compelling to pose the question of the relationship of the interest in the phenomenon of colonial art in a hemispheric sense. Today, various museums draw upon their permanent collections to link "the Americas" from Canada to the southern tip of South America. This was not so prior to the last ten or fifteen years, yet the shared affinities between the enthusiasm for reconsidering the colonial U.S. heritage in the 1920s and '30s and the parallel movement in Latin America at that time may be fruitfully examined.

The 1930s and '40s were a critical period for establishing private and public collections of both colonial and modern art from Latin America. In some cases, the formation of collections was heralded by large-scale public exhibitions of art that had either already been incorporated into museum collections or would soon be acquired. Among the earliest of such exhibits was the Metropolitan Museum's *Mexican Arts* show of 1930. It included a wide variety of art forms, from ancient sculpture to colonial painting, popular folk arts, and modern works. The Met, however, did not pay serious attention to Latin American modern art until very recently, when Iria Candela, the first Estrellita B. Brodsky Curator of Latin American Art, was appointed to the Department of Modern and Contemporary Art in 2014. The Metropolitan's commitment to the arts of Latin America had been attested to the year before by the appointments of Ronda Kasl (a contributor to this volume) as Curator of Colonial Art (associated with The American Wing) and Joanne Pillsbury to the post of Curator of Ancient American Art.

U.S. Collectors of Latin American Popular Arts

Although none of the essays in this book are solely dedicated to it, collecting "folk" or popular arts from Latin America by U.S. collectors is an important subtheme. Mexico was by far the richest source of acquisitions by American collectors. The art historian James Oles has written extensively about this subject and the impact of Mexican folk arts on both the artistic and popular imaginations of American audiences from the 1920s onward.[16] The story begins earlier, around 1910, during the last days of the dictatorship of Mexican president Porfirio Díaz (1830–1915), when numerous American businessmen came to Mexico City and were attracted by the many forms of art on sale in the shops and from individuals. William Randolph Hearst (1863–1951), for example, owned vast tracts of land in Mexico (later expropriated following the Mexican Revolution) and sought examples of luxury items for his estate at San Simeon, California, with its Spanish Revival theme.

Folk art in Mexico took on a political meaning following the Revolution. The new government sought to bolster an appreciation for popular cultures as part of a campaign of nationalist support of the working classes. Thus, many forms of popular arts were revived and supported by the state. In 1921, the first of several large-scale exhibitions of Mexican folk art opened in Mexico City with the support of the Ministry of Foreign Affairs. Similar shows traveled abroad in order to demonstrate the strength of Mexican traditional arts to foreign audiences. One of the major promoters of Mexican folk art, both to Mexican collectors and especially to foreigners, was the Austrian-born artist, curator, and entrepreneur René d'Harnoncourt (1901–1968), who arrived in Mexico in 1926. He was instrumental in selecting the approximately twelve hundred works of folk art that would be shown in the 1930 Metropolitan Museum exhibition. D'Harnoncourt would later become director of the Museum of Modern Art (1949–67), and his daughter Anne d'Harnoncourt (1943–2008) was a long-time director of the Philadelphia Museum of Art and supporter of Mexican and Latin American art there. While in Mexico, René d'Harnoncourt worked directly with the Morrow family, whose collection of Mexican folk art became one of the most outstanding in the country. Dwight Morrow (1873–1931) served as American ambassador to Mexico from 1927 to 1930. He and his wife, Anne Cutter Morrow (1873–1955), were enthusiastic and knowledgeable about Mexico, spoke Spanish, and eventually amassed their collection to adorn the house they occupied in Cuernavaca, a popular city for foreign residents because of its temperate climate and proximity to the Mexican capital. Called Casa Mañana, it featured colonial and modern Mexican furniture, textiles, and many of the best samplings of popular arts of all kinds. This collection has fortunately remained intact and was ultimately donated to Amherst College, Morrow's alma mater, where it now forms part of the collection of the Mead Art Museum.[17] The Morrows were also instrumental as patrons of contemporary artists in Mexico. Most notably, they provided Diego Rivera (1886–1957) with one of his most significant commissions. In 1930, Dwight Morrow arranged for Rivera to paint a series of frescoes on the history of the country for the colonial monument called the Palacio de Cortés, built for Hernán Cortés in the early 1530s.

Another American collector of Mexican folk art associated with the city of Cuernavaca in more recent times was Robert Brady (1928–1986). A native of Fort Dodge, Iowa, Brady inherited a considerable fortune from his family that allowed him to spend most of his time in leisure pursuits. He conceived a passion for Mexico and in 1961 bought a large house in the center of the city. Built in the sixteenth century, the house, called Casa de la Torre, was restored as a venue to showcase the collector's several thousand ceramics, textiles, masks, ex-voto objects, and paintings, all installed in a setting that preserves the living spaces as he ordered them. It is now a public museum, established in accordance with Brady's will.

Brady's house museum, which also contains a collection of modern Mexican painting and graphic work by such artists as Diego Rivera and Frida Kahlo (1907–1954), is not the only such institution in Mexico owned by Americans to display their collections of popular arts. John Venator (b. 1944) and Dorianne Venator began to travel to Mexico in the 1970s and soon started amassing a collection of folk art, ultimately acquiring more than three thousand pieces from all parts of the country. The Venators decided to settle in the small but historic city of Valladolid in the state of Yucatan in 2000. Like Brady, they purchased a stately colonial building just off the main square, called the Casa de los Venados (House of the Deer). The collection (open to the public on a limited basis) consists mainly of works from the recent past, yet it is comprehensive and gives a clear idea of the range of *artesanías* practiced today throughout the country. Many of these genres had fallen into disuse in the late nineteenth century but were revived as part of the postrevolutionary fervor for Mexican folk art. Others were revived after 1974 with the establishment of the governmental organization known as the Fondo Nacional para el Fomento de las Artesanías (National Fund for the Development of Arts and Crafts), or FONART, which promotes the production and sales of a wide variety of *artes populares*.

Collecting Mexican folk art was one of the many acquisitive activities of various members of the Rockefeller family, as I have suggested above. None perhaps was more enthusiastic in this pursuit than Nelson Rockefeller (1908–1979), whose career was as deeply intertwined with his family's vast business concerns (including interests in Latin American real estate and industry) as it was with his work for the Museum of Modern Art and his own collecting. Mexico was a special focus of Rockefeller's passion for folk art as well as pre-Hispanic and modern art. He made his first visit there as a young man in 1933, encountering some of the most distinguished artists of the day and cementing a long-time association with Frances Flynn Paine, writer and curator, who worked as Rockefeller's consultant in forming his immense collection of some three thousand examples of Mexican popular arts of virtually every type of folk production from every region of the country. The result of this lifelong obsession was displayed in the Rockefeller residences in New York and Washington, D.C., shown in many exhibitions, and seen in 1969 at the Museum of Primitive Art, which Rockefeller founded in 1954 on West 54th Street in Manhattan.[18] After his death in 1979, Nelson Rockefeller's collection was inherited by his daughter Ann Rockefeller Roberts and ultimately divided into two sections. The bulk of the collection was donated to the San Antonio Museum of Art, where it is housed in its own wing. A smaller portion was given to The Mexican Museum in San Francisco. Marion Oettinger, Jr., the noted cultural anthropologist and folk art expert who from 2005 until 2011 was director of the San Antonio Museum of Art, has written the most evocative study of Rockefeller as a collector of Mexican folk art. Oettinger makes clear that Rockefeller the business tycoon was also a man of highly developed sensitivities to the products of both artisans of the past and those of the present, with whom he had intense interactions during his many trips to Mexico.[19]

To end this section devoted to U.S. collectors of Latin American folk art, it is appropriate to cite the outstanding example of Teodoro Vidal (1924–2016). While the bulk of the collecting of Latin American folk art in the United States has focused on Mexico, the Teodoro Vidal Collection, now located at the Smithsonian Institution in Washington, D.C., is the preeminent gathering of Puerto Rican folk arts and material culture in the world. Vidal, a collector, writer, and art historian, was born in San Juan, Puerto Rico, educated at the University of Pennsylvania, and served in the administration of Luís Muñóz Marín, the first Puerto Rican–born governor of the island, a commonwealth or "free associated state" of the United States. He was active on the board of the Institute of Puerto Rican Culture and, starting in the 1950s, traveled around the island in order to collect objects relating to its history and popular culture. Vidal eventually amassed a large collection of maps, documents, works of art by such eminent artists as the Afro–Puerto Rican painters José Campeche (1751–1809) and Pío Casimiro Bacener (1840–1900), and, most notably, over one thousand *santos*, carved wooden images of Christ, saints, and the Holy Family. The *santo* tradition, which began in the sixteenth century, is among the most hallowed folk art modes in the Caribbean as well as in other parts of the Americas, notably in New Mexico, where it continues to flourish today. Although most of the *santos* are by anonymous artists, we know of significant dynasties of *santeros*, including the members of the Espada family from the city of San Germán, who were revered for their artistry.[20] Vidal pursued his collection with immense enthusiasm, and through his examples, many of which are regularly on view at the Smithsonian American Art Museum and the National Museum of American History, the student or any person interested in the autochthonous culture of Puerto Rico may chart its history from the beginnings to its continued vibrancy into the late twentieth century. Vidal's donation to the Smithsonian in 1997 was a surprise for many who would have preferred it to remain on the island, but its presence in Washington complements the strong folk art collections throughout the United States discussed above.[21]

Collecting Becomes More Widespread: 1930s and Beyond

Perhaps the best-known story of collecting art from the region of our concerns is that of MoMA, which began very early in its history and is the focus of several essays in this book. The 1931 Diego Rivera exhibition, held at the museum's then-headquarters on Fifth Avenue and 57th Street in Manhattan, started a long series of both shows and acquisitions

domination. Several splendid examples of sixteenth-century feather mosaics attest to the continuation in the early colonial period of forms that characterized the sumptuary arts of the Aztec court. Baroque paintings collected by the Mayers include examples of some of the classic masters of the genre, such as Alfonso López de Herrera (ca. 1585–ca. 1675), Cristóbal de Villalpando (1649–1714), and Miguel Cabrera (1695–1768). *Casta* paintings, charting the racial blendings of late colonial society in Mexico, are plentiful at Denver thanks to the generosity of the Mayers, who also collected secular arts of colonial textiles and furniture.

Beginning in the late 1990s with the purchase of two small works on copper by the obscure eighteenth-century Peruvian artist José Sánchez, Chicago natives Marilyn and Carl Thoma have amassed a highly distinguished collection of paintings through which the history of colonial Peru, Bolivia, and Ecuador may be studied to advantage. Working with dealers in the United States, South America, Portugal, and Spain, and dialoguing with other collectors and scholars of this material, the Thomas have paid equal attention to the products of the Cuzco School, the lowland Lima workshops, and the ateliers of (mostly unidentified) painters working in other parts of the Andean world. Although most of their collection is made up of religious art, it has some notable examples of secular portraits, including an extremely rare and unusual *Portrait of a Woman in Mourning* by the eighteenth-century Puerto Rican artist José Campeche (mentioned above in my discussion of the Vidal Collection in the Smithsonian Institution). The Thomas, as well as the Mayers and the Hubers, have been active lenders to exhibitions, and their art has been shown to a large public in several collection exhibitions in 2006–8 and 2014–16.[25]

In her introduction to the 2006 exhibition catalogue of the Thoma collection, Marilyn Thoma makes a point of discussing the couple's close cooperation with national and international authorities to ensure that patrimony laws are respected and works of art with questionable provenances do not enter the collection.[26] Questions of national patrimony have become of prime importance in many areas of collecting. In the Americas, special attention has been paid to works of art from pre-Columbian times and the colonial era that have been bought and sold illegally. The same is true for Native American arts and the arts of the First Peoples of Canada, which have recently been subject to very unfortunate sale practices in Europe. Looting has become a sadly common practice in urban, but especially rural, sites where vigilance is poor and the economic situation is precarious at best. In addition, there is a lively market for falsifications of premodern art from Latin America (this is also true for certain sectors of modern and contemporary art), so close attention to the material state of art must be paid. Patrimony issues also pertain in the modern period in some circumstances, such as the law, in existence in Mexico since the 1940s and vigorously enforced by the Instituto Nacional de Bellas Artes (INBA), that prohibits the export of works of art of a group of artists deemed to represent "national heritage." They include Gerardo Murillo, known as "Dr. Atl" (1875–1964), José María Velasco (1840–1912), Saturnino Herrán (1887–1918), Diego Rivera, José Clemente Orozco (1883–1949), David Alfaro Siqueiros (1896–1974), Frida Kahlo, Remedios Varo (1908–1963), and María Izquierdo (1902–1955).[27]

Los Angeles has been a natural venue for collecting Latin American art since the early decades of the twentieth century, due to both its proximity to Mexico and the financial wherewithal of its residents, especially those connected to the entertainment industry. Among film stars and producers who amassed distinguished collections of everything from Pre-Columbian to modernist works were Otto Preminger, Vincent Price, Natalie Wood, and Kirk Douglas. Actor Edward G. Robinson was one of the early collectors of the work of Frida Kahlo, foreshadowing the rage for her art that would later inspire singer-actress Madonna, who acquired several of the artist's best-known works, such as *My Birth* (1932) and *Self Portrait with Monkey* (1940).

The Los Angeles County Museum of Art (LACMA) began as The Los Angeles Museum in 1913. In its early history it acquired a few significant works of modern Latin American art, including Diego Rivera's famous *Flower Day* (painted and purchased in 1925). Yet it was long after the museum, renamed, moved to Hancock Park in the 1960s that further attention was paid to the art of the Americas, from Pre-Columbian to contemporary. A milestone for the modern Mexican holdings was reached in 1997 when the Museum acquired the collection of Bernard and Edith Lewin. Curator Ilona Katzew, a specialist in Mexican colonial art, has done a highly successful job in creating one of California's premier collections of art not only in her own area but in the modern and contemporary field as well.

In some major U.S. arts institutions, Spanish and Latin American art are collected together as natural extensions of one another. The Meadows Museum at Southern Methodist University in Dallas opened in 1965 with a mandate to be a home for choice examples of Spanish Renaissance and early modern art. A highly distinguished collection has resulted, and in the past decade, prompted by the enthusiasm of director Mark Roglán as well as the museum's geographical proximity to Latin America, the Meadows has begun to collect and exhibit Latin American art more aggressively.

The modern states of California, Texas, Arizona, Utah, and New Mexico, as well as parts of Colorado, were part of Spanish America until those lands were annexed by the United States as a result of the Mexican-American War of 1846–48. Louisiana had been part of the Viceroyalty of New Spain from 1762 to 1802, when it was ceded to France. New Orleans was an important trading port of Spanish America, and its Iberian heritage is attested to by the rich collection of colonial art at the New Orleans Museum of Art. Created in 1911 as the Isaac Delgado Museum (named for its founder, the sugar baron who was born in Jamaica and emigrated to the United States), NOMA shares its colonial art with a distinguished Pre-Columbian collection.

New York's Hispanic Society of America is noted for its thousands of Spanish masterworks in virtually every artistic medium, created from Roman times to the twentieth century. Its collecting policy has been expanded over the past several decades to include both colonial and nineteenth-century art from Latin America. One of its most recent acquisitions, the Mexican painter Agustín Arrieta's (1803–1874) *El Costeño* (Young Man from the Coast) of ca. 1843 (fig. 3), is a major work by this highly important genre painter as well as an important testimony to the significance of the Afro-Mexican population of the nation. The institution's chief curator, Marcus Burke, has been especially active in promoting purchases, cataloguing, and lending the Latin American works.

World War II created a special situation for the collecting and study of Latin American art in the United States. Many curators, collectors, and scholars who would normally have turned their attention to Europe were prevented from doing so, and in many cases they looked to Latin America as a source of art for both private acquisition and the development of new museum collections. Art historian Harold Wethey (1902–1984), for example, produced important studies of Peruvian colonial art, even though he is best known for his scholarship on the art of El Greco and Titian. Curator Herbert Spinden (1879–1967) of the Brooklyn Museum took particular advantage of the situation, purchasing impressive examples of (mainly) South American art of the seventeenth to the nineteenth centuries, bought on trips between 1941 and 1943. These he displayed both in the galleries as well as in temporary exhibi-

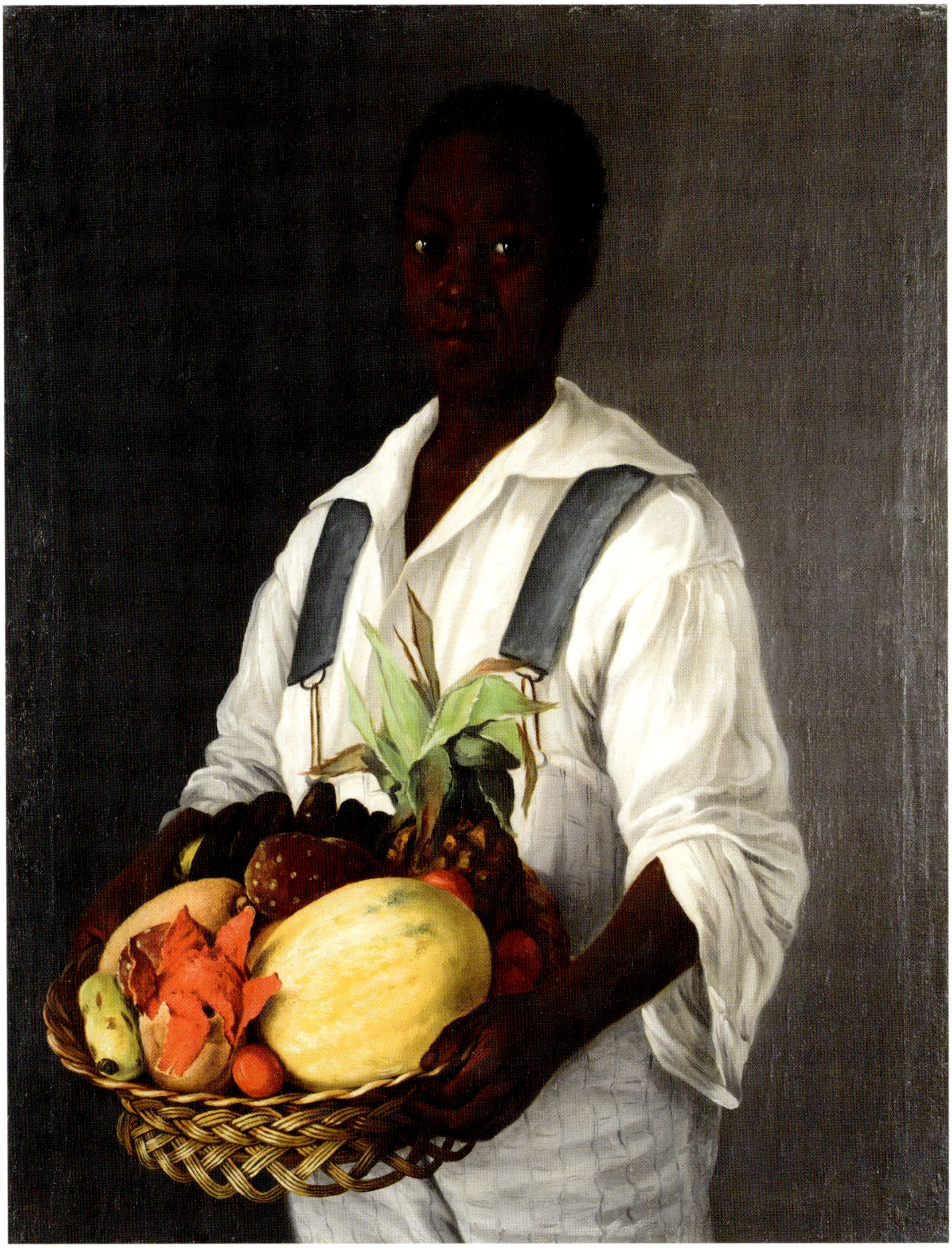

3. José Agustín Arrieta (Mexican, 1803–1874), *El Costeño* (Young Man from the Coast), ca. 1843. Oil on canvas, 89 × 71 cm. New York, The Hispanic Society of America. Courtesy of The Hispanic Society of America.

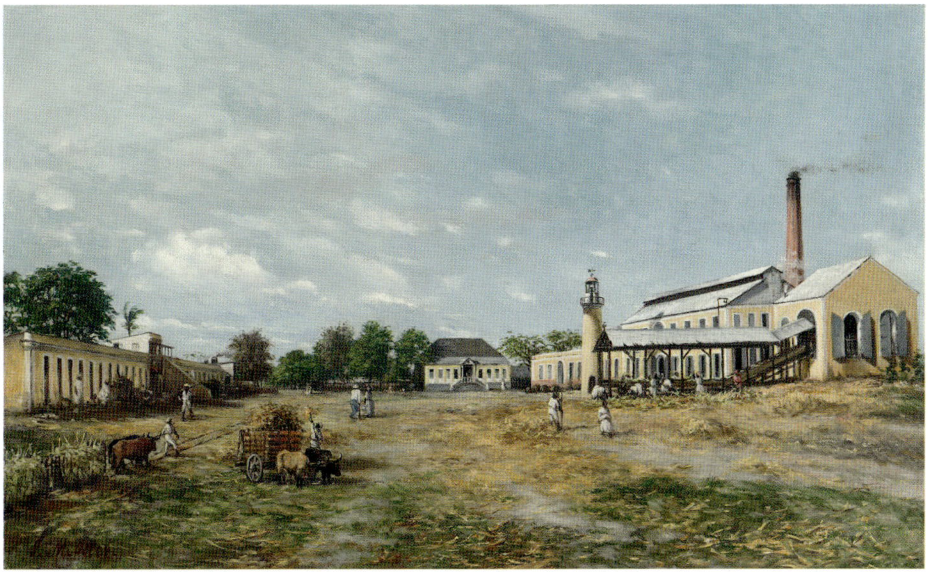

4. Francisco Oller (Puerto Rican, 1833–1917), *Hacienda La Fortuna*, 1885. Oil on canvas, 66 × 101.6 cm. New York, Brooklyn Museum.

tions such as *America South of US* (1941). Brooklyn thus became one of the premier museum collections of colonial art in the 1940s. Due to the vicissitudes of taste, much of the collection remained in storage for decades after the colonial galleries were dismantled in 1956, until Diana Fane, curator of New World Art, began a project to recover of Brooklyn's preeminence in this realm in the early 1990s. Fane's efforts culminated in the monumental exhibition *Converging Cultures: Art and Identity in Spanish America* (1996), which represented a reconsideration of the museum's collections, new scholarship in the catalogue, and, eventually, a reconsideration of the significance of this area for the museum's holdings. Acquisitions have not stopped. Richard Aste, who served as Curator of European Art from 2010 to 2016, had a particular interest in the Caribbean in the eighteenth and nineteenth centuries and made outstanding acquisitions of Spanish colonial art; Caribbean eighteenth- and nineteenth-century painting, including a significant painting by Italian-born, British-trained artist Agostino Brunias (1730–1796); as well as major examples of the art of the Puerto Ricans José Campeche and Francisco Oller (1833–1917), a Realist-Impressionist whose art brought a sense of modernity to the late colonial-era Caribbean (fig. 4).

Collecting Haitian Art

The Figge Art Museum in Davenport, Iowa, was originally called the Davenport Municipal Art Gallery (1878). This eastern Iowa institution has gone through many transformations, and in 2005, renamed in honor of the Figge family of local philanthropic fame, it moved into a new building designed by British architect David Chipperfield. Among its best-known collections is its outstanding selection of Mexican colonial painting.[28] Davenport collector and former mayor Charles August Ficke (1850–1931) donated his collection of European and Mexican art to the city in the late 1920s (after extensive travels in Mexico between 1893 and 1903), and it formed the nucleus of the Davenport Museum of Art's holdings. There are more than fifty examples of significant paintings by such luminaries of the colonial era as Baltasar de Echave Rioja (1632–1682), José de Alcíbar (ca. 1730–1803), and Nicolás Rodríguez Juárez (1675–1728). Yet the Mexican collection is not the only strength of the Figge.

The Figge Art Museum's permanent collection of Haitian art is one of the first and best of several such collections formed in the United States in the mid-twentieth century. While we generally consider only those countries of the Spanish- and Portuguese-speaking traditions as forming "Latin America," Haiti should have a place at the table for many reasons. Geographically it is part of the greater Caribbean and as such forms a unique link in the chain of cultures that constitutes the Americas. Like Spanish, French and Creole are Latin-based languages, even though much of Haiti's visual and literary culture derives in equal measure from African sources. Haiti is one of the oldest republics in the Americas and the first black republic. It has a venerable art-historical tradition from ancient times to today. In the colonial era (which lasted until 1804, the end of the revolutionary phase of its history) it was dominated on the elite side by white, usually French artists imported by the colonial authorities to teach at the art schools of Port-au-Prince and other cities such as Jacmel and Cap Haïtien. This interchange with Europe continued throughout the nineteenth century, though in a diminished mode. The early twentieth century witnessed the development of a distinctive school of "Indigéniste" artists who, while following in the stylistic footsteps of their contemporaries from North America and Europe, developed a mode of representation of the everyday life of Haiti that to a great extent signaled a resistance to the American invasion and presence in the country from 1915 to 1934. The early 1940s, during the so-called Haitian Renaissance, were a period of remarkable efflorescence in the visual arts. Many untrained artists at that time gathered at the newly formed (1944) Centre d'Art in the capital to work, exhibit, and sell their art to the increasing tourist trade.[29] U.S. collections of Haitian art began in the 1940s and continued to be formed, initially as private collections, which were later donated to public institutions. Haitian art was regularly exhibited in shows of Latin American art through the 1960s, and it was often considered a category of many museums' permanent collections of art of Latin America (this is true, for example, at MoMA).

In the case of Davenport, a local medical doctor, Walter E. Nieswanger (1924–2007), first visited Haiti in 1961 and made numerous trips there in subsequent years. He developed a love of the works by self-taught artists who exhibited at the Centre and elsewhere and began amassing an impressive collection that established the foundation of the Davenport Museum's (today the Figge's) collection of Haitian art. Some of the most outstanding artists of the first wave of the Haitian Renaissance, such as Hector Hyppolite (1894–1948), Rigaud Benoit (1911–1986), and Wilson Bigaud (1931–2010), are represented. Bigaud's 1953 painting *Zombies* (fig. 5) is related to the deep interest on the part of many artists of this group in the Afro-Haitian religion of vodou.

The Figge has continued to collect Haitian art, with important acquisitions of the work of Edouard Duval Carrié (b. 1954), perhaps the most recognized contemporary Haitian artist. Now based in Miami, he was given a retrospective show at the Figge in 2005. Yet outstanding as the Figge's Haitian art is, it is by no means the only such collection in a U.S. museum. It is rivaled by the Haitian paintings and sculptures in the Milwaukee Art Museum, whose collection is the product of the enthusiasm of Richard B. Flagg (1906–1994) of the Flagg Tanning Company, one of the largest industries in the city in the early and mid-twentieth century. Flagg began traveling to Haiti in 1973, amassing an outstanding collection that was

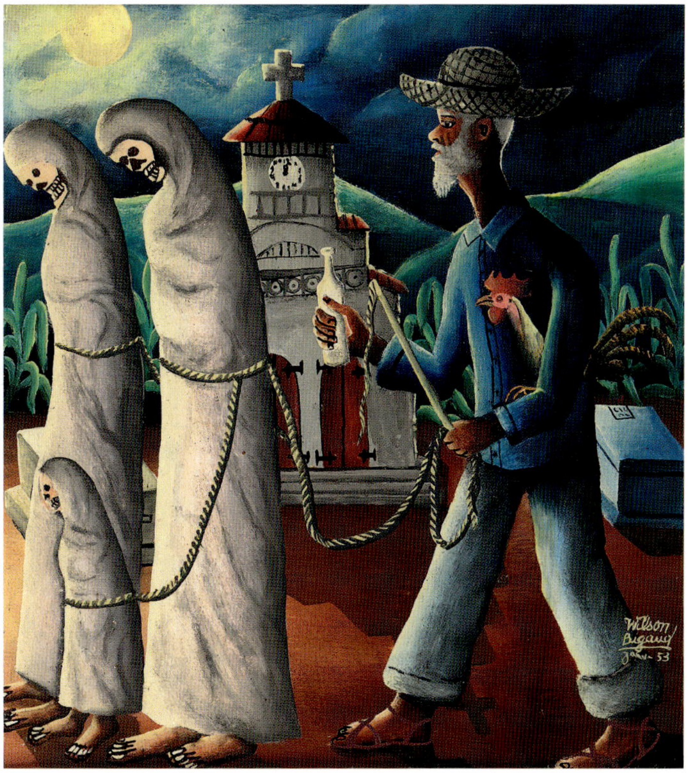

5. Wilson Bigaud (Haitian, 1931–2010), *Zombies*, 1953. Oil on Masonite mounted on wood panel, 24.13 × 21.59 inches. Davenport, Iowa, Figge Art Museum. Image courtesy of the Figge Art Museum, City of Davenport Art Collection.

ultimately donated to the Museum. Another Iowa institution, the Waterloo Center for the Arts, boasts a noted Haitian art collection, established in 1977 with the donation of a large body of work by collectors Dr. and Mrs. F. Harold Freuling.

In the mid-1940s, the distinguished glass and ceramics designer Winslow Anderson, who worked for the Blanko Glass Company in Milton, West Virginia, began traveling to Haiti. The Centre d'Art had just opened, and Anderson fell under the spell of the "exotic and colorful" art, as it was often described, that he found there. He was one of the first collectors of this material, becoming part of a group that included the "high priest" of Surrealism, André Breton (1896–1966), as well as the Centre's second director, the writer, art dealer, and collector Selden Rodman (1909–2002), much of whose collection is now the property of Ramapo College in New Jersey (Rodman also founded the Haitian Arts Center in New York). Taking advantage of both the novelty and the affordability of this art, Anderson began buying during these early trips and eventually amassed an excellent collection of over fifty paintings by virtually all of the most important artists of the first generation of Haitian Renaissance painters. This collection eventually found its way to the largest museum in his area, the Huntington Art Museum in Huntington, West Virginia, which today counts it as one of their points of pride in a highly regarded local encyclopedic museum.

Collecting Since the Mid-Twentieth Century

Many of the premier museums of the Northeast, aside from those already mentioned here and in the texts that follow, have highly regarded Latin American collections. The Guggenheim Museum's exhibition and collecting policies are discussed herein by Delia Solomons, but it is worth commenting further on this institution's engagement with the field. Under the lengthy directorship of Thomas Messer (1920–2013; director 1961–88), the Museum not only organized important, sometimes highly controversial exhibitions of key figures of Latin American modernism, including Joaquín Torres-García in 1970,[30] Jesús Rafael Soto (1923–2005) in 1973, and Rufino Tamayo (1899–1991) in 1979, but it also acquired significant examples of these and other artists' works. Subsequent director Thomas Krens supported Latin American purchases as well, sometimes in connection with major exhibitions such as *Brazil: Body & Soul* in 2001. Richard Armstrong, who became the Guggenheim's director in 2008, has further encouraged the acquisition of contemporary Latin American art for the museum by aligning with UBS Bank and taking advantage of that organization's UBS Bank MAP (Mix, Apply, Propel) Global Initiative to encourage museum acquisitions and fund a curatorship in the field. Pablo León de la Barra, the Mexican-born, Brazilian-based curator from 2013–15, organized an exhibition entitled *Under the Same Sun* in 2014 with contemporary work acquired through his travels and purchases that then entered the museum's permanent collection. Another Manhattan institution, the Whitney Museum of American Art, has also broken through the previously strict definition of "American" as referring to the fifty United States by including work by Latin American–born artists in their permanent collection and, in 2016, organizing a retrospective show of the art of Cuban-born, New York–based painter Carmen Herrera (b. 1915), several of whose geometric abstract paintings were already in the permanent collection.[31] In 2017, the Whitney presented the first U.S. retrospective of Brazilian artist Hélio Oiticica (1937–1980). Entitled *To Organize Delirium*, the exhibition was originally presented in 2016 at The Carnegie Museum of Art in Pittsburgh, whose director, Lynn Zelevansky (formerly of the Los Angeles County Museum of Art), has long demonstrated her support of modern and contemporary arts of South America.

The Art Museum of the Americas in Washington, D.C., was founded in 1976 (the year the country was celebrating its bicentennial). Its parent organization is the Organization of American States (OAS). Located in a 1912 Neocolonial structure near the city center, it features twentieth-century and contemporary art from all of the member states in Latin America and the Caribbean, much of it donations. Although small in physical size, this museum holds a creditable representation of the many styles of painting, sculpture, and graphic arts that developed from the 1920s onward, and its active exhibition schedule reflects the diversity of its holdings. The founder and first director of the Art Museum of the Americas was the Cuban art historian and arts administrator José Gómez Sicre (1916–1991), who had a long history of working with U.S. collections to bolster the presence of Latin American and Caribbean art.[32] Cold War–era politics and the perceived need to bolster positive relationships between the United States and Latin American countries in the era following the Cuban Revolution had a great deal to do with the creation of collections such as that of the OAS museum as well as the organization of several significant exhibitions of Latin American art in the 1960s, as Delia Solomons explains in her essay in this anthology.

Twenty years later, the Museum of Latin American Art (MOLAA) opened in Long Beach, California. Declaring itself to be the single museum in the western United States dedicated to the modern art of the Americas, this institution was created by Robert Gumbiner (1923–2009), a medical doctor who made his fortune as one of the first creators of managed health care organizations. His company was known as FHP International. As he traveled throughout the region for business years before founding his own museum, he collected several hundred examples of principally figurative art from Central and South America. This served as the core of the Museum's collection, which has vastly expanded and shifted its priorities since its founder's death in 2009 to more experimental contemporary forms of visual production.

The 1960s and '70s witnessed the establishment of a number of culturally specific arts institutions that reflected the rise of a growing sense of identity among many ethnic groups in the United States. The Mexican Museum in San Francisco, founded in 1975, and the National Museum of Mexican Art in Chicago, founded in 1982 as the Mexican Fine Arts Center Museum, are chief examples of museums that collect and exhibit art of both Mexican-born and Chicano artists. El Museo del Barrio in New York was founded in 1969 by artists of the Puerto Rican diaspora from the Upper East Side of Manhattan ("El Barrio" or "the neighborhood") as a space for displaying their art at a time when few galleries or museums would represent it. By the 1990s, however, the mission of El Museo was redefined, and it now describes itself as a premier Latin American museum whose collection includes examples of all forms of art, from ancient Taíno to contemporary art from Mexico, Central, and South America and the Caribbean. The now-defunct Museum of Contemporary Hispanic Art opened in downtown Manhattan in 1985 in the era of multiculturalism and, until 1991, played an analogous role to that of El Museo as a place for collecting and displaying work by artists of Latin American heritage. The Bronx Museum of the Arts was founded in 1982 in a borough of New York City that was greatly underserved by cultural institutions. It has since become a premier venue for showing many forms of modern and contemporary art. One of its great strengths has become its permanent collection of Latino/a art by artists from the New York area and far beyond.

The Smithsonian American Art Museum in Washington, D.C., has a long history of commitment to art created by the Latino/a community in all parts of the United States. Collecting Latino/a (or Latinx, as it is also now called to avoid gender binaries) art is a special subcategory associated with this volume's mission. Many scholars and collectors throughout the country have worked for years to build awareness of the diversity of the arts created by Chicano or Mexican American artists, Nuyorican, Dominican American, Cuban American, and many other constituencies of the Latino community. The scholar and arts administrator Tomás Ybarra-Frausto has been a pioneer in this area. As early as 1977, the American Art Museum's director, Joshua Taylor (1917–1981), organized the first nationally touring Latin art exhibition, entitled *Raíces y Visiones* (Roots and Visions). He also encouraged the growth of the Latino art collection at the museum's Washington site. The success of this endeavor is attested by the large-scale exhibition *Our America: The Latino Presence in American Art*, curated in 2013 by E. Carmen Ramos, who was hired by the museum in 2010 to build the Smithsonian's Latino collection into the most representative in the country. In addition, Ramos stated that "I was guided by a single purpose: to ground Latino Art within the art of the United States."[33] A case in point is the work of Olga Albizu (1924–2005), the distinguished Puerto Rican artist, who was trained at the University of Puerto Rico in San Juan by Spanish painter and later member of the first generation of New York Abstract Expressionists Esteban Vicente (1903–2001) and would eventually work with Hans Hoffman (1880–1966) in Manhattan. Albizu's painting *Radiante* (Radiant) of 1967 (fig. 6) was first purchased

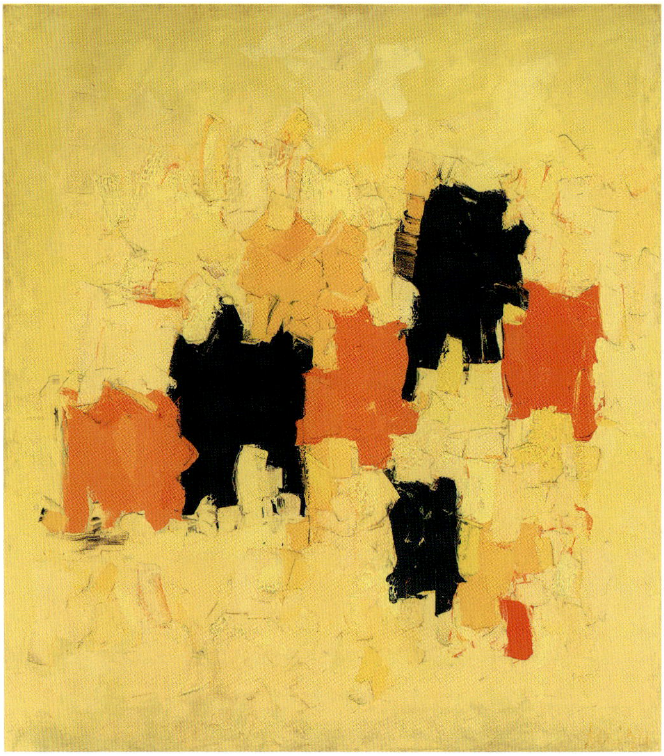

6. Olga Albizu (Puerto Rican, 1924–2005), *Radiante*, 1967. Oil on canvas, 172.7 × 157.5 cm. Washington, Smithsonian American Art Museum.

for the Chase Manhattan Bank collection begun by David Rockefeller (see below) and ultimately acquired as a gift from JPMorgan Chase. Its vibrant color pulsations define a highly personal approach to gestural painting. Rockefeller (1915–2017) was equally influential in collecting Latin American art, as was his older brother Nelson.

College and University Collections of Latin American Art

Within this panorama of institutional collecting of Latin American art, college and university museums also play a critical role. As early as the 1930s, universities became sites of important commissions from Latin American artists, principally, but not exclusively, from Mexico. Diego Rivera's fresco at the San Francisco Art Institute is a key example, as are José Clemente Orozco's frescoes at Pomona College in Claremont, California, the Baker Library of Dartmouth College in New Hampshire, and The New School for Social Research in New York.

The New School, founded in 1929 and home to many artists and intellectuals fleeing oppression in Europe during the Nazi period, as well as many artists from Latin America, became something of a magnet for Latin Americans for several decades. They served as teachers, and many of their works are in the university's extensive art collection. José Clemente Orozco's murals (finished in 1931) are still in situ. They depict allegories of manual labor, social strife, and universal brotherhood. Ecuadorian artist Camilo Egas (1889–1962) headed the school's art department for some twenty-five years and also, in 1932, created an impressive mural on canvas entitled *Ecuadorian Festival* that depicts village holidays in the Andes.[34] Another jewel in the crown of the New School's collection is an enormous untitled 1961 mosaic mural by Uruguayan artist Gonzalo Fonseca (1922–1991), a principal student of Joaquín Torres-García. Like many of Torres's students, including José Gurvich (1927–1974), Julio Alpuy (1919–2009), and Augusto Torres (1913–1992), Fonseca settled in Manhattan in the later part of his life, dividing his time between New York and Italy.

In 1943, Rufino Tamayo painted a monumental mural entitled *Nature and the Artist* for the Hillyer Art Library at Smith College in Northampton, Massachusetts. Highly inspired by Picasso and especially by *Guernica*, which the artist had recently seen on exhibition in New York, this painting was disassembled when the library was expanded and placed on eighteen portable panels so that it could be reconstructed in the new art library that opened at Smith in 1972.

Many of the largest or oldest university museums, including the Yale University Art Gallery, Harvard's Fogg Art Museum, and the Princeton University Art Museum, are in a relatively youthful phase of their emphasis on collecting art from the Americas. Others, however, have established themselves as rivals to the collections of the larger municipal or public museums discussed above. Perhaps the preeminent collecting institution in the field of Latin American modern and contemporary art is the Jack S. Blanton Museum, formerly the Archer M. Huntington Art Gallery, at the University of Texas at Austin. This museum's core Latin American collection was formed in the early 1970s, when the New York art historian and collector Barbara Duncan (1921–2003) and her husband, John, donated over one thousand drawings and two hundred paintings, principally by South American artists whom they knew and collected during their many years living in Chile and elsewhere. Later acquisitions have increased the Blanton's modern holdings to over two thousand works, and a new initiative for collecting colonial painting will continue to add to the number of works in its galleries.

Other college and university museums whose distinguished collections of Latin American art serve their student constituency as well as the general public are the Lowe Art Museum at the University of Miami and the Museum of Art, Rhode Island School of Design (RISD), with the Nancy Sales Day Collection of Modern Latin American Art.

Many college and university art museums that are not generally known for their attention to the art of the Americas have, in fact, created distinguished collections of colonial, modern, and contemporary material. The Latin American and Latino collections in two small liberal arts college museums, Oberlin and Wellesley, are examples of many more such unexpected collections throughout the country. In 1936, the Allen Memorial Art Museum at Oberlin College in Ohio received its first gifts of modern Latin American art. They formed the basis of a steadily growing collection that has, in the recent past, received especially strong curatorial attention. Painting, sculpture, photography, and installations by artists from all parts of the region have been steadily acquired during the directorship of Andria Derstine and former contemporary art curator Denise Birkhofer, whose field of specialization is modern and contemporary Latin American photography. Birkhofer's 2014 exhibition and catalogue *Latin American Art at the Allen Memorial Art Museum* was evidence of a serious commitment to the field.[35]

Several major donors, including Oberlin alumni Christina Delgado and Stephen F. Olson, have been particularly active in donating late twentieth-century and contemporary works to the

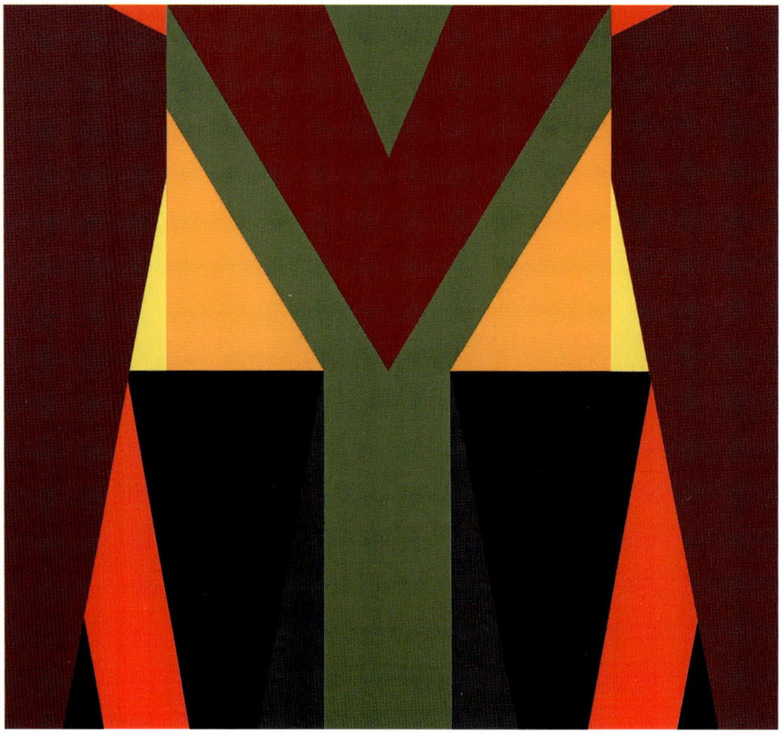

7. Fanny Sanín (American and Colombian, b. 1938), *Acrylic No. 1, 2005*, 2005. Acrylic on canvas, 152.4 × 167.6 cm. Oberlin, Ohio, Allen Memorial Art Museum. © Fanny Sanín. Image courtesy of the Allen Memorial Art Museum.

collection. The collection continues to acquire directly from artists, including the New York–based Colombian painter Fanny Sanín, whose *Acrylic No. 1* (2005) presents a striking example of recent incursions into the form of geometric abstraction, which has been of great interest to South American artists since the 1950s (fig. 7).

The Davis Museum and Cultural Center at Wellesley College, Massachusetts, opened in 1993, but the institution's collections have a longer history behind them. Original works of art were acquired soon after the College was founded in 1875. Wellesley also has the distinction of being one of the first colleges in the United States to offer courses in the history of art. By the end of the century, the Wellesley College Museum was founded in conjunction with what became known as the "Wellesley method" of teaching art history through direct contact with original works. While the early years of the museum witnessed few acquisitions of Latin American art, the 1920s–40s saw important links forged with individuals who certainly planted the seeds of interest in the field. In 1926, Alfred H. Barr was hired as associate professor of modern art. Three years later Barr became MoMA's first director and architect of the first phase of its Latin American collection. Meanwhile, in 1947, MoMA architecture curator John McAndrew (1904–1978) was hired as director of the Wellesley museum. McAndrew had a long-time connection to Mexico. He traveled there often, maintaining close friendships with Mexican artists and members of contemporary art circles in Mexico City, such as the painter Juan Soriano (1920–2006) and the art dealer Inés Amor (1912–1980). He was also close to other American aficionados of Mexico, including Henry Clifford (1904–1991), chief curator at the Philadelphia Museum of Art, who was mainly responsible for the Museum's important collection of Mexican modernist art, acquired in the 1940s.[36] In addition to his job as arts administrator, McAndrew was an architectural historian, and his study of Mexican sixteenth-century architecture remains a volume to consult for students of that subject.

Through the following decades Wellesley acquired significant works by modern masters such as Orozco, Torres-García, Gunther Gerzso (1915–2000), and Roberto Matta (1911–2002). Mexican art scholar James Oles joined the faculty in 1996 and became adjunct curator at the Davis in 2002. Through his astute purchasing the museum has become a notable center for Latin American colonial, modern, and contemporary art. A recent reinstallation of the galleries has placed Pre-Columbian art in its own space and put colonial through contemporary arts throughout the museum in dialogue with art from many other places. Among the most impressive colonial acquisitions made in recent years is the *Portrait of a Young Woman* attributed to the Peruvian artist Pedro José Díaz (fl. 1770–1810) (fig. 8).

Some Latin American collections flourished at specific times due to circumstances of politics. During the temporary liberalization of travel restrictions for Americans to Cuba in the early 1990s, many museum support groups made the trip, especially at the times of the Havana biennial exhibitions, purchasing works for the collections of their institutions of choice (for example, the Department of Drawings of MoMA notably benefitted from this activity). One of the university museums that supplemented their already-strong Latin American collections with Cuban work was the Art Museum of Arizona State University in Tempe, a suburb of Phoenix. Director Marilyn Zeitlin had a particular enthusiasm for the Cuban artists of the 1990s generation and organized exhibitions and artists' residencies and published a lavish portfolio of their prints. She also enhanced the Museum's holdings with work by such artists as Pedro Alvarez (1967–2004), Belkis Ayón (1967–1999), José Toirac (b. 1966), Kcho (b. 1970), and others.

Notes on Corporate Collecting of Latin American Art

Corporate collecting is an important subcategory of this story, and a few examples of some of the most active collections follow. The UBS Bank's collaboration with the Guggenheim Museum in New York has already been mentioned above.

The origins of the IBM collection, perhaps the oldest corporate entity of its kind, date to 1939, when the company's president, Thomas Watson (1874–1956), decided to create an exhibition for the New York World's Fair, which opened in April of that year. Also in 1939, IBM sent another exhibition that included substantial examples of Latin American art to the Golden Gate Exhibition in San Francisco. In New York, the IBM pavilion at the Fair housed one module of a two-part show. The art shared the space with a collection of nascent computer technology. Part two of the exhibition was held at the company's corporate headquarters in Manhattan. IBM commissioned artists from seventy-nine countries to paint one work each, which then entered the corporation's collection.[37]

A great many of the works in the IBM show were from Latin America and the Caribbean. Studying the list of artists and titles is instructive. Most of the painters' names are now obscure, with some exceptions such as Yoryi Morel (1906–1979) from the Dominican Republic, Carlos Mérida (1891–1984) from Guatemala, and Julia Codesido (1883–1979) from Peru. In virtually every case,

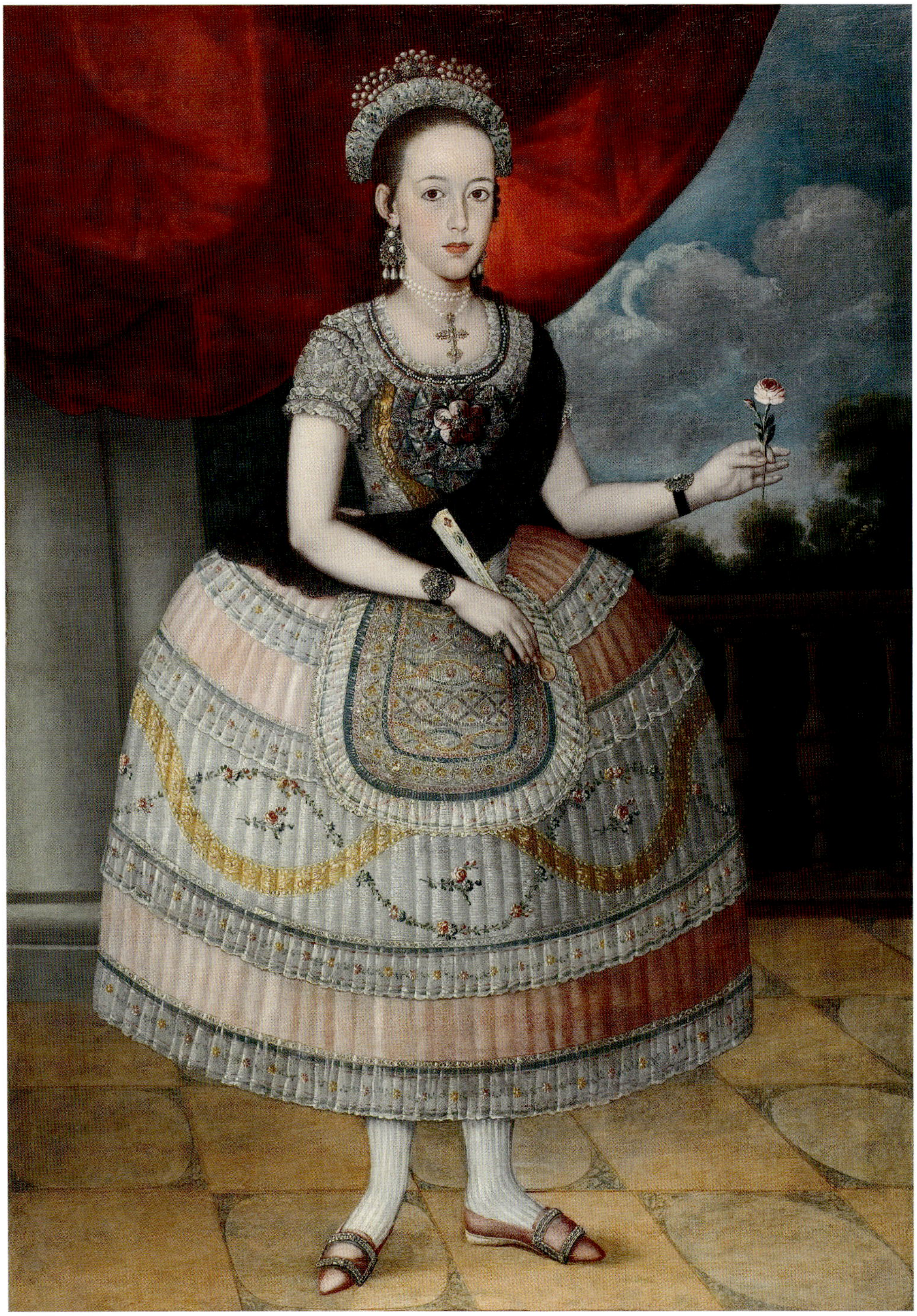

8. Attributed to Pedro José Díaz (Peruvian, active 1770–1810), *Portrait of a Young Woman*, 1795–1810. Oil on canvas, 139.1 cm × 99.7 cm. Wellesley, Massachusetts, Davis Museum.

however, the subjects of the works underscore stereotypical clichés about Latin America. *An Indian Hut*, *The Coffee Picker*, and *The Poet of the Countryside* are just some of the names of the paintings that were shown—and that then entered the IBM collection.

IBM went on to acquire many significant examples of Latin American art for its collection. Two of its most famous pictures were Rivera's 1928 *Dance at Tehuantepec* and Tamayo's 1944 *Flutist*. In 1983, the company opened the IBM Gallery of Science and Art, a below-ground-level space on the corner of Madison Avenue between 56th and 57th Streets in New York. Ultimately, with the economic decline of the mid-1990s, IBM decided to divest itself of the collection and sold it at Sotheby's in 1995. To underscore the vagaries of corporate collecting, we should note that the collection of the Reader's Digest Corporation, whose holdings of Latin American art were as valuable as those in the IBM collection, was also sold at auction at Sotheby's, where it broke price records in 1998.

Chase Manhattan Bank president David Rockefeller enhanced the Chase Manhattan Bank's corporate art collection, which was begun in 1959, by supporting the addition of many examples from Latin America. The collection, now known as the JPMorgan Chase Art Collection, reflecting corporate mergers, has more than thirty thousand pieces, including a large portion of works from all over the Americas.

With almost sixty thousand pieces, the collection of Deutsche Bank is the world's largest corporate holding of art. A listing of all the artists represented may be found on the collection's website, although the exact works cannot be determined. German and American artists dominate the roster, but there are many Latin Americans as well. Brazilian artists are prominent in the list. Amilcar de Castro (1920–2002) and Hercules Barsotti (1914–2010) are included, as are other well-known contemporary artists from elsewhere in the Americas, such as Francis Alÿs (b. 1959) and Gabriel Orozco (b. 1962) from Mexico as well as Carlos Garaicoa (b. 1967) from Cuba. The art is present in the bank's offices throughout the world, serving to create an image of the organization as an entity friendly to artistic creativity. Entire exhibitions of corporate collections have become more and more common in U.S. museums, as recent shows at the Guggenheim and the Bronx Museum of the Arts attested.

Epilogue

If space permitted, a proper end to this discussion would engage with the history of collecting and selling of colonial and Latin American art in the auction houses and galleries that have played crucial roles in the formation of taste for private, corporate, and institutional collectors. Of course, these organizations cater not only to U.S. collectors of Latin American art, but also to those from Latin America itself, Europe, and Asia, all places where the interest for art from the region is growing. However, this key chapter in the history of taste and acquisition deserves recounting in a volume unto itself.

CHAPTER 1

Evolving Taxonomies at The Museum of Modern Art in the 1930s and '40s and the Definitions of the "Latin American Collection"

Miriam Margarita Basilio

9. Dust jacket with chart prepared by Alfred H. Barr, Jr. (1902–1981), of the exhibition catalogue *Cubism and Abstract Art*, 1936. Offset, printed in color, 25.7 × 19.7 cm. New York, The Museum of Modern Art Library. Digital image © The Museum of Modern Art / Licensed by SCALA / Art Resource, N.Y.

An "Evolutionary Pedigree" of Modern Art

Describing Alfred H. Barr, Jr.'s (1902–1981) iconic chart (fig. 9) for the catalogue cover of the Museum of Modern Art exhibition *Cubism and Abstract Art*, Robert Rosenblum wrote, "I still recall vividly its heraldic power, for it proclaimed, with a schema more familiar to the sciences, an evolutionary pedigree for abstract art, that seemed as immutable as a chart tracing the House of Windsor or the Bourbon Dynasty."[1] Excluded from this modernist lineage for decades, what Barr called the Museum's "Latin American collection" was best known through the 1943 exhibition catalogue *The Latin American Collection of The Museum of Modern Art*. The exhibition has been viewed as the peak of his interest, after which these works languished in storage, irrelevant to triumphant narratives of modernist progress.[2] However, works from the "Latin American collection" were shown in the collection display *The First Exhibition of The Museum Collection of Painting and Sculpture* (1945), which encompassed a broad range of artistic tendencies, including figurative art, "popular" art, politically inflected art, and depictions of local landscapes, types, and customs. Barr curated this exhibition with his MoMA colleague Dorothy Canning Miller (1904–2003), who had played a crucial role in the 1943 Latin American exhibition.[3]

Despite its subsequent role as the representation of the Museum's narrative of early modern art, *Cubism and Abstract Art* was just one exhibition in a five-part series presenting modern and contemporary artistic tendencies, both international and local.[4] The others were *Fantastic Art, Dada, Surrealism* (1936), *Masters of Primitive Painting* (1938), *Americans 1943: Realists and Magic Realists* (1943), and *Romantic Painting in America* (1943). In the preface to the *Romantic Painting in America* catalogue, Barr explained that these exhibitions were intended to present "trends, movements or directions of modern art."[5] Their impact on subsequent understandings of the

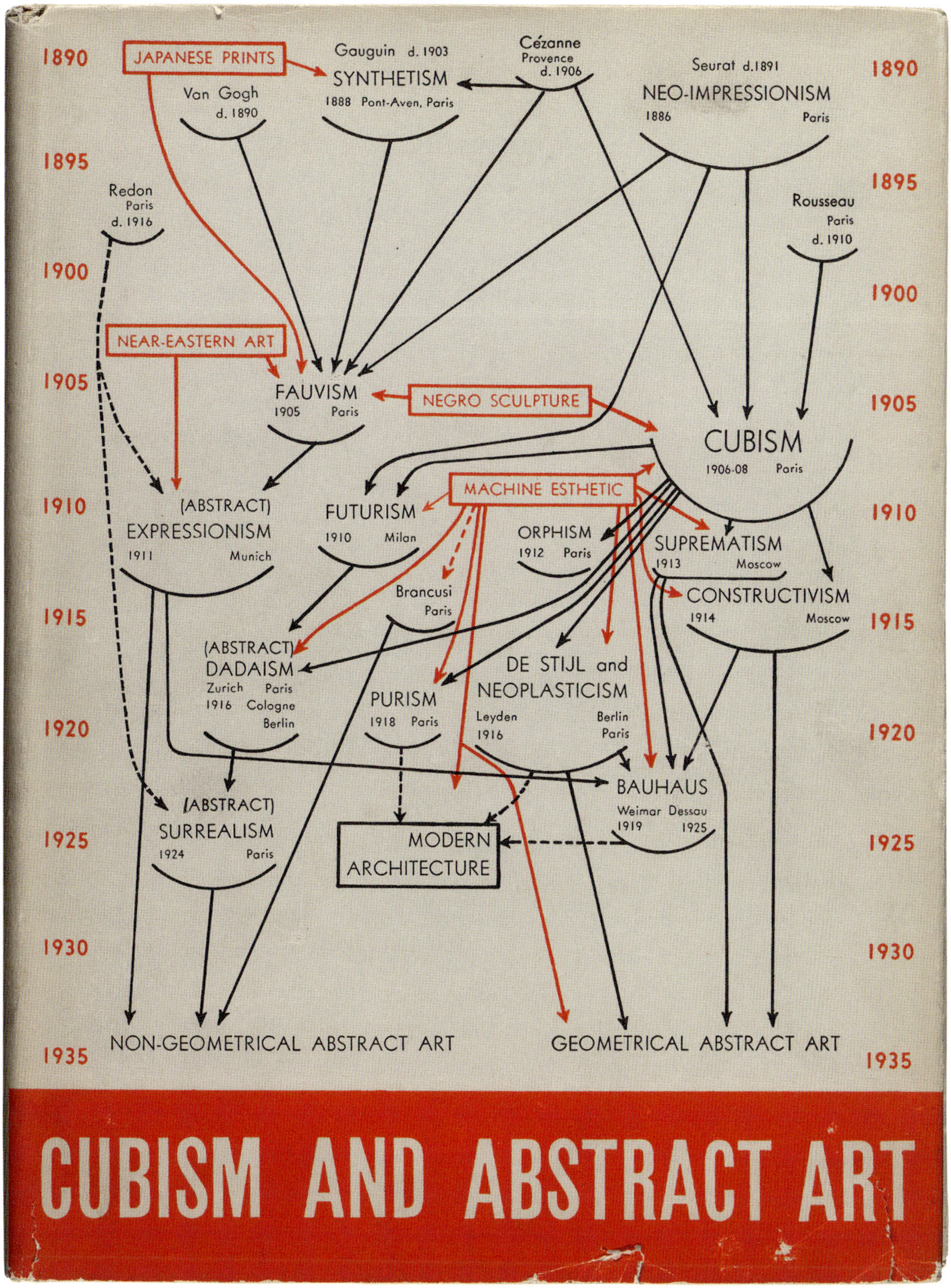
1890
1895
1900
1905
1910
1915
1920
1925
1930
1935
JAPANESE PRINTS
Gauguin d. 1903
SYNTHETISM
1888 Pont-Aven, Paris
Van Gogh d. 1890
Cézanne Provence d. 1906
Seurat d.1891
NEO-IMPRESSIONISM
1886 Paris
Redon Paris d. 1916
Rousseau Paris d. 1910
NEAR-EASTERN ART
FAUVISM
1905 Paris
NEGRO SCULPTURE
CUBISM
1906-08 Paris
MACHINE ESTHETIC
(ABSTRACT) EXPRESSIONISM
1911 Munich
FUTURISM
1910 Milan
ORPHISM
1912 Paris
SUPREMATISM
1913 Moscow
CONSTRUCTIVISM
1914 Moscow
Brancusi Paris
(ABSTRACT) DADAISM
Zurich Paris
1916 Cologne
Berlin
DE STIJL and NEOPLASTICISM
Leyden Berlin
1916 Paris
PURISM
1918 Paris
BAUHAUS
Weimar Dessau
1919 1925
(ABSTRACT) SURREALISM
1924 Paris
MODERN ARCHITECTURE
NON-GEOMETRICAL ABSTRACT ART
GEOMETRICAL ABSTRACT ART
CUBISM AND ABSTRACT ART

collection is evident in the coincidences between the rubrics employed in these exhibitions and those employed in the 1945 collection display. In addition, the Museum acquired some of the works in these exhibitions. Although these surveys were organized according to style, *Americans 1943* and *Romantic Painting in America* were simultaneously part of another series devoted to contemporary U.S. art (the first of that series, *Americans 1942*, included works produced under the auspices of the Works Progress Administration's Federal Art Project). It is also important to note that while these two exhibitions specifically focused on U.S. art, the others examined developments that sometimes included artists originating from or working in Europe and the Americas. The stylistic taxonomies, defined as international or local, shaped the understandings of the Museum's "Latin American collection," its presentation in 1943, and the terms of its inclusion in the 1945 collection display.

Barr originally planned to study paleontology, and in a series of charts he developed beginning in 1925 he examined art-historical periods in a way "similar to the taxonomies of zoologists and botanists."[6] In a 1925 letter to his teacher Paul Sachs (1878–1965), to which he attached a chart detailing the development of prints, he described its purpose: "simplified, it might be of use because it would combine at one glance geographical distributions."[7] The term "geographical distributions" is taken from Charles Darwin's *On the Origin of Species* (1859), and Barr's 1936 chart may be analogized to one of the scientist's phylogenetic charts plotting out the gradual evolution of a species from a common ancestor.[8] Influenced by his interest in theories of evolution, his approach to classification, and his understanding of the local and the international, Barr articulated the place of the Museum's "Latin American collection" during a key period in the development of what became the modernist canon.

Charting "a Pioneer Venture": *The Latin American Collection of The Museum of Modern Art*

From March 31 to June 6, 1943, MoMA presented *The Latin American Collection of The Museum of Modern Art*. The catalogue cover and the opening invitation featured a partial map of the Americas, underscoring the Museum's desire to chart its artistic and geographical ambitions. In his catalogue foreword, Barr stated that although lack of time and wartime travel difficulties meant the collection was incomplete, it was nonetheless extensive and a major part of the Museum's holdings: "the Latin-American division of the Museum Collection is rather more complex than the European—for the Museum now owns more Chilean paintings than British, more Brazilian than Italian; and if certain Latin American countries are not represented, this is also true of European countries."[9] Emphasizing the Museum's preeminent role in assembling a representative collection, he described the catalogue as the first survey of the region's art:

> First of all this is a record of the most important collection of contemporary Latin-American art in the United States, or for that matter in the world (including our sister republics to the south). . . . And, secondly, Lincoln Kirstein's essays on the following sixteen pages may well be the first publication in English of a survey of the pictorial arts of Latin America during the previous three centuries, considered as a whole, and with frequent reference to our own art—a subject so vast, so complex and so unexplored that his short piece takes on the character of a pioneer venture.[10]

Against the backdrop of political debates regarding the United States' Good Neighbor Policy, which had important effects within the Museum, Barr asserted the Latin American collection's importance. He sought to dispel associations between the Museum's interest in the region's art and wartime foreign policy by emphasizing the works' value and importance within the collection. The 1943 Latin American exhibition marked the conclusion of a shopping spree the year before by Lincoln Kirstein (1907–1996), who traveled to Argentina, Brazil, Chile, Colombia, Ecuador, Peru, and Uruguay, and Barr, who visited Cuba and Mexico. During their trips they purchased 293 works.[11] The son of a wealthy Boston entrepreneur, Kirstein had long-standing ties to Barr, Nelson Rockefeller (1908–1979), and MoMA. As a student at Harvard, he was a young poet and artist who promoted modern art and literature, activities that led Barr to invite him to the Museum's new Advisory Committee in 1930.[12] He was hired as consultant for Latin American art in 1942, and, with Miller, curated the second of the U.S. exhibitions and the fourth of the modern art series, *Americans 1943*, held from February 10 through March 21, just prior to the Latin American collection exhibition.

The Museum's purchases of paintings, works on paper, and sculptures were made thanks to the anonymously endowed Inter-American Fund. The donor was Nelson Rockefeller, an influential Museum trustee and son of Museum founder Abby Aldrich Rockefeller (1874–1948).[13] Rockefeller disguised his financial support because in 1940 he had resigned as board president to work for the Office of the President as Coordinator of Inter-American Affairs, a post he held until 1944. This government agency promoted political and economic relationships between the United States and Latin American countries; good relationships with some of these countries benefitted Rockefeller due to his economic investments in the region. Cultural activities intended to persuade Latin Americans to support the Allied cause were an important part of the agency's activities. As Rockefeller spelled out in a 1942 letter to John E. Abbott, then MoMA's executive director, funds for purchases came with strings attached (including hiring Kirstein): "We are of the opinion that his projected trip is of significance to this Office in that he will personally renew his relationships with the intellectual leaders whom he met during his visit to the other American Republics last year, under a project sponsored by the Coordinator's Office. The continuance of these relationships will have a propaganda importance and will be of assistance in our psychological war effort."[14] Rockefeller concluded by stating his keen interest in the possible creation of a Latin American department at MoMA. Besides his ties to Rockefeller and Barr, Kirstein was on friendly terms with Diego Rivera (1886–1957), Ben Shahn (1898–1969), and other artists during the early 1930s, when he was sympathetic to left-wing political causes and published articles in progressive magazines. Kirstein counted David Alfaro Siqueiros (1896–1974) as a close friend and championed his work, publishing articles about his Chillán murals. He also published articles on contemporary Latin American art between 1931 and 1944 in the *Magazine of Art*, *Studio*, and *Town and Country*.

In the above-referenced letter, Rockefeller mentioned Kirstein's previous work for his agency. In 1941, Rockefeller sponsored a goodwill tour by the American Ballet Caravan, which Kirstein, who spoke Spanish, directed (his wife, Fidelma, an artist like her brother, Paul Cadmus, had been taught the language by their mother).[15] During this trip, Kirstein reported to Rockefeller on the political views of local diplomats and artistic figures. In a report sent to W. M. Barclay Harding, a military officer in the American Intelligence Command, he described local political conditions and listed his qualifications, including his language skills, stating that he could "speak and read Spanish and French well, and read Portuguese, speaking it badly."[16] While purchasing works for MoMA in 1942, he again sent reports to Rockefeller about his contacts' political sympathies.

Barr anticipated questions, but ironically the name he chose for this fund inadvertently pointed to its donor. In a slyly humorous memo, he explained that Rockefeller had approved this name:

> The suggestion which came from Nelson's office that we call this fund the American Republics Purchase fund seems pretty unsatisfactory to everyone consulted, including Monroe Wheeler, Lincoln Kirstein, and René [d'Harnoncourt]. The name is ambiguous first, in that it does not distinguish between the Latin American republics from the U.S., second because René thought it would suggest that the American republics had given the fund, and third, and worst, because it seemed to me that a wisecrack might easily be developed out of the suggestion that the fund be used for purchasing American republics.[17]

The last sentence implicitly refers to Rockefeller's substantial business interests in the region and betrays Barr's concern that Museum acquisitions would be attributed to political motives.

Intrinsic to the fund's name, and to how the collection was defined in essays and collection displays, was a tension between presenting art of the Americas as a unified category or as distinctly Latin American. The works were simultaneously compared to those by recognized U.S. and European artists and seen as authentic representations of local life, landscapes, and customs in faraway nations. Despite Rockefeller's aim to promote the idea of a unified "Pan-American" image, Barr distinguished the United States from the rest of the countries in the Americas. In the text he refers more than once to separate geographical categories in the Museum's collection: art of the United States, Europe, and Latin America. As he himself noted, however, the catalogue would present analogies across the Americas. In the catalogue for the 1943 Latin American exhibition, he took care to provide a context to explain the Museum's broad interest in art of the region predating the 1942 purchases. For example, the first works to enter the collection, donated by Abby Aldrich Rockefeller in 1935, were by Mexican artists. This is not surprising given Barr's regard for Mexican art. In 1929, he listed it as one of the Museum's collecting priorities, and in his 1933 and 1941 "torpedo" diagrams, the country was at the forefront of artistic innovation, ahead of the United States. In addition, numerous important works entered the collection after exhibitions such as *Twenty Centuries of Mexican Art* (1940), *Portinari of Brazil* (1940), and *Modern Cuban Painters* (1944) as examples of art in specific countries, but later came to be grouped as "Latin American," a problematic generalizing category.[18]

Barr's mention of the "frequent reference to our own art" in the catalogue raises the question of Kirstein's acquisitions criteria. Kirstein's primary interest at this time was U.S. art, specifically figurative tendencies related to the WPA orbit, realism, magical realism, and American Scene painting. In her important study of the role of U.S. art in MoMA's early collecting and exhibitions, Esther Adler argues that early efforts to classify twentieth-century art as a whole coincided with similar efforts to define U.S. art: "This attempt at rediscovering an American art history may seem unexpected at an institution dedicated to the art of its time but is very much a parallel to Barr's interest in developing genealogies for European art."[19] As Adler explains, Barr worked with MoMA's trustees to develop an acquisitions policy for U.S. art, ratified in November 1938, that stipulated in part that "[w]ork that seems American should be purchased rather than that which shows obvious European influence."[20] Barr's 1938 statement of the collecting priority for U.S. art paralleled criteria for acquisitions of work by Latin American artists, which largely depicted local customs or landscapes. And the work of specialists in U.S. art at the Museum during this period, among them Miller, Kirstein, and Holger Cahill (1890–1960), was doubtless influential: they purchased works for the collection and curated some of the surveys of modern and U.S. art.[21] In the exhibitions preceding the Latin American collection display, Miller, Kirstein, and Cahill proposed that figurative art defined as popular, Magical Realist, or Romantic could represent American political ideals. For instance, in her foreword to *Americans 1943* Miller argued that "Realism has always been a part of the American tradition," calling it "a truly democratic style."[22] This kind of argument is not surprising since Cahill was director of the Federal Art Project from 1935 to 1943.

In his essay for the same exhibition, which included nineteenth- and early twentieth-century precursors to the contemporary artists, Kirstein presented recent figurative tendencies as part of a national tradition that originated during the colonial period. In the catalogue for the 1943 Latin American exhibition, he traced a parallel history of art across the Americas, from the colonial period to the present, in which he emphasized local traditions and landscapes. His preference for figurative art in the United States was a filter through which he understood and judged what he saw in Latin America. As Gustavo Buntinx has argued, Kirstein's secret propaganda mission, which called for emphasizing cultural affinities among the American Republics, and his own taste, shaped his acquisitions: "Ideally, and when the political imperative allowed for it, what Kirstein was looking for was a sort of regional spirit contained in pieces that could not be considered superficially folkloric, but rather 'characteristic.'"[23] In addition, as Barr acknowledged, the brevity of their trips limited the range of work they could study and acquire. They missed important exhibitions and subsequent artistic developments now regarded as essential for understanding modernity in these countries.[24] Despite Kirstein's familiarity with some of these artists' works, his private correspondence evidences his arrogant condescension during his travels. For example, in one of many letters to MoMA colleagues, he described the "primitive" conditions in Ecuador: "I have just returned from a short excursion into the 9th century AD or BC it makes no difference."[25]

In his catalogue essay, organized by country, Kirstein briefly discussed the artists, indicating where they trained and traveled. The section on Mexico, "the strongest school of painting in Latin America," was the most extensive; in contrast to the other countries, he discussed political and historical contexts and the impact of Rivera, Siqueiros, and José Clemente Orozco (1883–1949) in the United States, mentioning the large number of their works in important collections and the role of critics and art dealers in promoting their careers there.[26] He also discussed artists who represented distinct types of figurative painting, such as Antonio Ruíz (1892–1964), described as a "genre painter of solid structure and ironic wit," and identified Frida Kahlo (1907–1954) and Guillermo Meza (1917–1997) as artists linked to Surrealism.[27] When Kirstein mentioned an artist working in a modern style, he qualified it by using geographical terms. (He used condescending gendered terms as well; for example, he mentioned the "individual Cubist style" of Amelia Peláez (1896–1968) but, in the next sentence, added that "her large drawings have an elegance and intellectual piquancy rare in a woman."[28]) For him, Antonio Berni (1905–1981) was "perhaps the Argentine artist who most resembles a North American of the epoch of the W.P.A. and the Treasury Section of Fine Arts." However, as with Mexican artists, Kirstein had a more nuanced view of Berni's work.[29] Similarly, he traced Wifredo Lam's (1902–1982) work to a European catalyst: "while he has felt the harsh and heady influence of Picasso after *Guernica*, [Lam] has nevertheless invented his own subspecies of savage monsters and drawn them with an effective calligraphy."[30] Telling was the use of the term "subspecies," evoking scientific evolution as a correlate to artistic progress. This emphasis on relating artists to European or Mexican "sources," figurative art in the United States, and the preeminence of Mexico shaped how these works were incorporated within the Museum collection as a whole. Thus, the "Latin American collection" was classified according to the categories that Barr, Miller, and their colleagues had devised for the 1936–43 exhibitions, with the vast majority of works fitting into figurative stylistic categories. This is evident in Kirstein's discussion of figurative tendencies in the Latin American works, such as "Magical Realism," that evoked the *Americans 1943* exhibition.

Because of the lack of installation photographs and administrative documents, our knowledge of how the works were displayed in the 1943 Latin American exhibition is drawn from brief reviews. *The New York Times*'s Edward Alden Jewell noted that because Kirstein had been mobilized, Miller installed the show: "For the most part the material has not been arranged on any strict geographical basis, although to certain artists entire rooms have been devoted—Orozco, Rivera, Sequiros [*sic*] etc."[31] Miller's involvement was an important link between the surveys of modern and contemporary European and U.S. art, the 1943 Latin American exhibition, and the 1945 collection display. Jewell divided the artists into two groups: "Much of the work in the present exhibition is very strong and brilliantly 'modern,' as well as indicative of aspects of the lands in which the various artists live." His comments suggest that Miller may have grouped some artists according to formal or stylistic similarities and others according to their depictions of local customs and landscapes. They also suggest that notable artists were shown in separate galleries.

A review published in *Art Digest* linked the works to tendencies in Paris and the United States: "the assemblage reveals that much of the painting going on south of here parallels our own 'modern' developments in almost a ludicrous way. There are Bermans, a Guglielmi, and lots of little Picassos in the group; any number of WPA painters of the 'new realism' variety; surrealists; 'primitives' and a Paul Klee or two. Our neighbors are more than neighbors, it appears. They are practically kissing kin."[32] As we will see, Miller's hybrid categories—stylistic and single-artist—and Kirstein's Pan-American ones established precedents for how these works were shown in subsequent collection displays. Not surprisingly, given Mexican art's critical success in the United States, the depth of the Museum's holdings of works by Rivera, Siqueiros, and Orozco was the "strongest" section, followed by works by Argentine artists, "nearest of all to certain trends in our own painting." Ecuador, Peru, Bolivia, and Uruguay fared less well—the reviewer described the first as "Mexican influenced" and the others as "still fairly backward." Despite the review's overall positive tone, its title, "The Modern Implements Good Neighbor Policy," demonstrates that Barr's efforts to deny that the Museum's collecting was politically motivated failed.

Within the Museum, politics had an impact on trustees' attitudes toward Barr's collecting and exhibition criteria and on his position. In the early 1940s, some trustees questioned the number of Latin American exhibitions, in part because of the perceived political motives of such projects. These internal debates intersected with broader questions about the collection's scope. According to Irving Sandler, Barr disagreed with conservative and influential trustees, particularly Stephen C. Clark (1882–1960), then president and chair of the board, and A. Conger Goodyear (1877–1964), who had served as the Museum's first president before becoming a trustee, over the Museum's mission: would MoMA be a "permanent repository" or "a showplace of new, often problematic and even iconoclastic art?"[33] Some trustees opposed Barr's exhibitions of folk or "modern primitive" artists, while others regarded contemporary abstraction with misgivings.[34] Barr was fired as director on October 15, 1943, and appointed advisory director.[35] Although he continued to present proposals for exhibitions by artists such as Siqueiros after the

1943 Latin American exhibition, by this time the political situation had changed, and funding for the Inter-American Affairs Art Program was cut in June 1943. At an Exhibitions Committee meeting held on October 7, 1943—days before Barr's dismissal—Goodyear opposed the *Modern Cuban Painters* exhibition on the grounds that "that too many ['Good Neighbor'] exhibitions had already been devoted to the region."[36] The term "Good Neighbor" clearly indicates the trustees' association of Latin American art with government propaganda. On September 20, 1943, Barr had written Goodyear to advocate for the exhibition with some caveats: "Cuban painting is on the whole deft and gay with a lot of style. There are no heavyweights of the caliber of Orozco and Siqueiros, but there are several really excellent artists of the middle generation."[37] In the latter category he mentioned Peláez. It is important to note here that Barr purchased in Mexico and Cuba, where local experts based in these countries and the United States advised him, and that he implicitly acknowledged his differences of opinion with Kirstein, who made most of the acquisitions. Also in this letter, Barr admitted that

> perhaps [the Museum was] too generous in accepting several mediocre works . . . but I most urgently recommend that we continue our interest in Latin American art, both through exhibitions and acquisitions. I feel all the more strongly about this because with the successful progress of the War there is now an obvious official tendency to restrict or abandon our efforts to bring about cultural interchange with Latin America. . . . The Latin Americans are no fools and have looked forward cynically to the gradual collapse of the Good Neighbor Policy at least on the cultural level. . . . I hope that we may continue after the War to explore and cultivate Latin American art.[38]

The Museum's contribution to the war effort was addressed in the October–November 1942 issue of *The Bulletin of the Museum of Modern Art*. Titled "The Museum and the War," this issue surveyed MoMA's participation in government programs and war-related exhibitions. The section "United Hemisphere" noted staff collaboration with the Coordinator of Inter-American Affairs while emphasizing that acquisitions and some of the other initiatives related to Latin America predated the war.[39] The last page described the Museum collection as evidence of "freedom of expression." Modern and international art were linked to progressive democratic values, and formal advances were equated with political progress. This contrasted with official art under Hitler, described as "magazine cover realism," chauvinist in content, and propagandistic.[40] The phrase "magazine cover realism," however, also evoked the work of Thomas Hart Benton and some Latin American artists.[41] And the question of internationalism set the stage for a series of associations between local content linked to nationalist sentiment and advanced modern styles adopted by artists in various countries. Three years later the question of the local versus the international, and realist versus modern art, would reemerge as Barr and Miller sought to define the role of Latin American and U.S. art in the Museum.

"National Reputations and International Standards": Locating Latin American Art Within the Museum Collection

The fundamental issue of derivativeness versus originality as the basis for judging the quality of works by artists from Latin America reemerged while Barr and Miller were planning to display the collection. Barr's account of MoMA's interest in Latin American art and his efforts to disavow political motives for collecting surfaced at a conference titled Studies in Latin American Art, sponsored by the American Council of Learned Societies and held at MoMA in May 1945. Barr adroitly alluded to the political motives behind the period's Pan-American discourse: "perhaps we might not have taken any great interest . . . had it not been for the war, the state of emergency, the necessity of establishing closer relations with the countries to the south. I think we were very conscious of the political nature of our interests, and conscious, too, of the somewhat complicating nature of that political atmosphere."[42] He expressed his difficulty in judging work that he viewed as a variant of avant-garde movements or that did not conform to such stylistic trends: "The problem of standards was complicated, I think, not only by a general spirit of haste and emergency, but by a chronic confusion between national reputations and international standards. . . . International standards can be applied to art which is international in style or character. We can easily compare, say, a cubist picture from Chile with a cubist picture from the source of Cubism, namely Paris, and find it lacking. But it is much more difficult to judge values which are national or local in character."[43] His preference for "international" art as the point of reference is implicit. Later he returned to the problems posed by nationalism and "local" art: "The contrast between the international interests of artists and increasingly vigorous nationalistic movements in certain Latin American countries as well as in our own, make[s] a study which would be many times as important if it could be handled on a comparative basis."[44] Attempting to rebut Latin Americans' suspicions that such arguments were "Good Neighbor" propaganda, he proposed that this approach was needed to study an important contemporary art trend. He also pointed to "cynicism in this country where even exhibitions, publications and acquisitions of superior material were often discounted because they were Latin American and therefore supposedly, must have been undertaken for political reasons."[45] Nonetheless, in confidential Museum correspondence, Barr acknowledged the political motives that to a large extent drove Rockefeller's endowment of the Inter-American Fund and predicted that a lessening of MoMA's interest would have a negative impact on the field. Thus, in both public and private, and despite his ambivalence about "local" art, he argued for openness toward acquiring and exhibiting Latin American works after the war. As he put it in 1945, "we have a serious responsibility to justify what we did then in a state of emergency by our continuing interest now that the emergency is past."[46]

A month later, Barr, assisted by Miller, selected "one-third" of the collection for the *First General Exhibition of the Museum Collection of Painting and Sculpture*.[47] They presented Latin American works in both international and hemispheric contexts, as well as within abstract and figurative tendencies.[48] Out of 375 total works, 27 were by Latin American artists—slightly over 7 percent. Although this may seem like a relatively small number, these works were included in various sections of the exhibition, furthering the illusion of inclusiveness. In what follows, I mention selected examples of the Latin American works included to illustrate the terms of inclusion.[49]

In keeping with Barr's claim in the 1943 Latin American exhibition catalogue that the publication was an appendix to the 1942 *Painting and Sculpture in The Museum of Modern Art* handbook, in 1945 the works were integrated within the collection as a whole. On view from June 20 through January 15, 1946, the exhibition took place at a time of internal debates among himself, other staff, and trustees over the Museum's mission. As Kirk Varnedoe argued, at stake was the definition of the "collecting policy, between a desire for breadth and historical, educational inclusiveness on the one hand, and a search for masterpieces of singular quality on the other."[50]

Applying the categories used in the 1938–43 surveys, in the 1945 collection display Barr and Miller created definitions of pre–World War II U.S. and Latin American art that would have implications for years to come. These exhibitions demonstrate that Barr's early taxonomies incorporated a

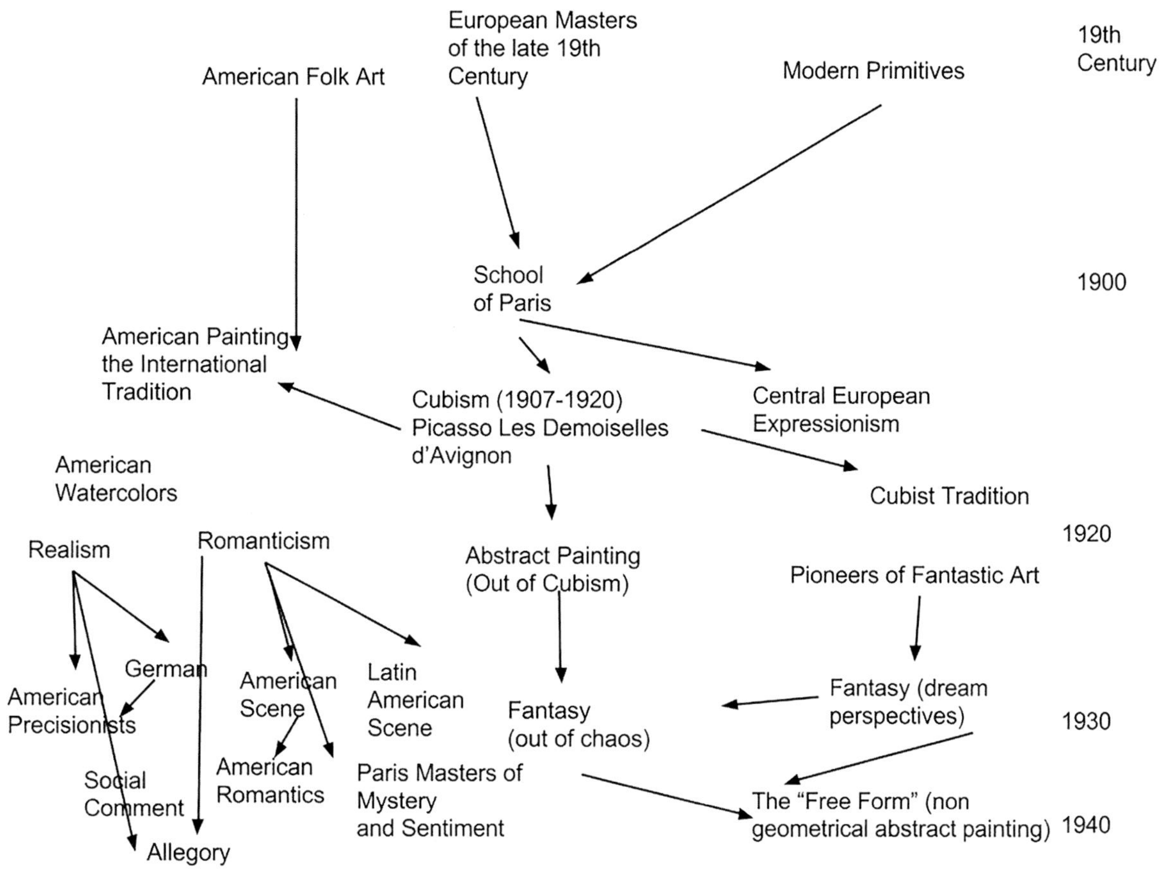

10. Miriam Basilio, chart plotting the evolution of Barr and Miller's 1945 proposed taxonomies. Courtesy of the author.

broad and nuanced repertoire of formal—both figurative and abstract—and thematic categories. However, as we have seen, Barr explicitly or implicitly indicated his preferences for "international" movements. By drawing an imaginary chart plotting out the taxonomies proposed by Barr and Miller in 1945 (fig. 10), I argue that the categories in their evolving schema of modern and contemporary art were far more diverse stylistically and geographically than has been understood. I devised the chart drawing on Barr's terminology in the exhibition announcement as well as the titles given to galleries in the checklist, which correspond to some of the wall texts visible in installation photographs. Despite the range of works on view, as they developed categories to display the collection in 1945, the narratives evolved increasingly toward a binary that distinguished a series of central stylistic movements from certain peripheral figurative stylistic and geographical categories. According to the exhibition announcement, Barr stated that the exhibition's structure was "a complex and challenging problem" and acknowledged the difficulties posed by "its selection and arrangement": "Even were it desirable, it would not have been practicable to follow a strictly chronological order or a systematic division by nationality, school or medium."[51] This difficulty in categorizing works in the collection was already evident in his 1936 flowchart. Barr's narrative in this announcement evidences the tension between stylistic and national categories, and the checklist's headings underscore the difficulties posed by the display. In 1943, the Latin American collection was classified geographically as a totality, rather than as part of the repertoire of styles mapped out in the modern and U.S. art surveys. Barr made it clear that this hanging was not a final and authoritative taxonomy, but rather a preliminary presentation proposing how the collection might be shown—according to temporal progression, nationality, or medium. Much was at stake: by showing the collection as a whole, Barr sought to persuade trustees to help him fill gaps in the Museum's holdings.[52]

As Barr indicated in the announcement, the exhibition opened on the second floor with "Art of the Common Man," divided into two categories: "American folk art," including artists such as Joseph Pickett, and "modern primitives." Thus, despite opposition from some trustees, Barr and Miller included works that Abby Aldrich Rockefeller donated from her U.S. folk art collection in 1939.[53] This section was international in scope, including artists exhibited in *Masters of Primitive Painting* and "modern primitives" such as Henri Rousseau (1844–1910) and the Brazilian Heitor dos Prazeres (1898–1966, whom Kirstein defined as "a young samba player" in the 1943 collection catalogue).[54]

Following this section was "the central international tradition of modern painting," by which Barr meant Paul Cézanne (1839–1906) and the Post-Impressionists, and then the "masters of the School of Paris," such as Henri Matisse (1869–1954) and Amedeo Modigliani (1884–1920). The terms "central tradition" and "masters" became important in the late 1940s and early '50s, when Barr and the trustees debated collecting parameters—specifically, which works fell into a "permanent collection of masterworks."[55] Barr related these "masters" to "related contemporaries or followers elsewhere"; in the checklist these were "Eastern European Expressionists," including Max Beckmann (1884–1950) and Oskar Kokoschka (1886–1980), and artists such as Marsden Hartley (1877–1943) in "American Painting—The International Tradition."[56] Here, we see a pattern in which Barr points to hierarchies among styles and distinguishes between "related" or implicitly derivative groups.

By calling Cubism "the most important movement of the second decade of our century," Barr made it clear that the descendants of the "central European tradition" were the Cubists. He called Picasso's *Les Demoiselles d'Avignon* (1907)—the only work mentioned specifically by name—the origin of Cubism. Here, we see indications of the core movements that would constitute the familiar canon the Museum is linked to today. However, it is important to note that Rousseau—regarded as a "Modern Primitive" in 1945—appeared in the 1936 flowchart as part of the lineage of Cubism and abstraction. And as we will see, in this collection display U.S. artists were shown with those working elsewhere in the Americas, and some international categories included artists from the United States and Latin America. Following works by Picasso (1881–1973), Juan Gris (1887–1927), and Georges Braque (1882–1963) in the Cubist section was "Cubist Tradition." Among the works in this second Cubist group (fig. 11) were Peláez's *Still-Life* (1938), Lyonel Feininger's (1871–1956) *The Steamer Odin II* (1927), and Stuart Davis's (1892–1964) *Summer Landscape* (1930, later deaccessioned). In this case, all three works shared post-Cubist multiple perspectives informed by the artists' studies in Paris. All three also included referential elements, whether still life or landscape, and exemplified hemispheric trends within a broader international tendency. Peláez, included in *Modern Cuban Painters*, was of particular interest to Barr, who in the 1945 press

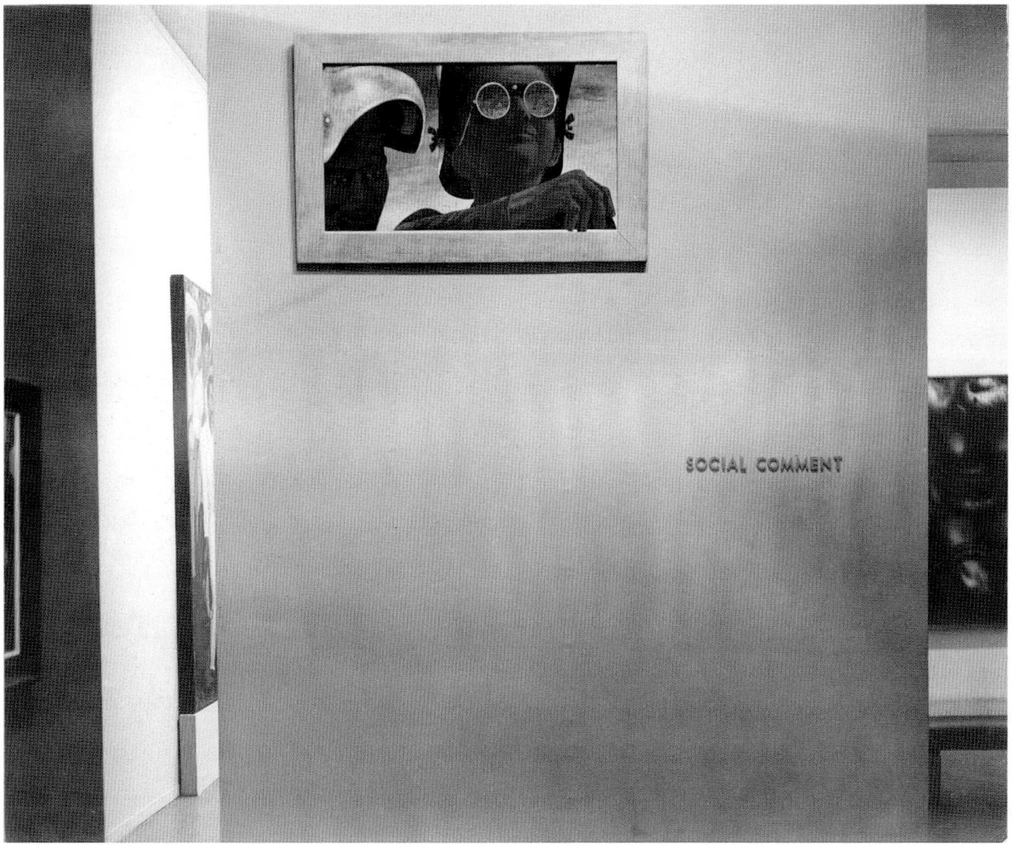

11. Installation view of the exhibition *The Museum Collection of Painting and Sculpture* at the Museum of Modern Art, New York, June 20, 1945, through January 13, 1946, 2nd floor; June 20, 1945, through February 13, 1946, 3rd floor. New York, Photographic Archive, The Museum of Modern Art Archives. Digital image © The Museum of Modern Art / Licensed by SCALA / Art Resource, N.Y.

release named her in the brief list of artists in "Cubist Tradition."

Barr continued to advance international comparisons in the section "Abstract Painting, Out of Cubism," showing Kazimir Malevich (1878–1935), Piet Mondrian (1872–1944), and Picasso. He also grouped paintings from the Americas, such as Bolivian Roberto Berdecio (1910–1996, who was included in the 1943 collection exhibition) and Balcomb Greene (1904–1990).[57] Following this section were galleries that included figurative works "predominantly realistic or romantic in character," American Scene painters Edward Hopper (1882–1967) and Thomas Hart Benton (1889–1975), and the "Latin American Scene." In using the term "scene" for the latter two, Barr associated politically controversial artists such as Benton with Latin Americans. "Realism" echoed the *Americans 1943* exhibition. Here were U.S. precisionists such as Charles Sheeler (1883–1965); Otto Dix (1891–1969), representing Neue Sachlichkeit; along with Latin Americans. For example, Kahlo's *Self-Portrait with Cropped Hair* (1940) and Juan O'Gorman's (1905–1982) *Salt Mines of Tetelpa* (1942) were beside the U.S. artist Peter Blume's (1906–1992) *Landscape with Poppies* (1939), which was shown in *Americans 1943*. Disregarding the content and contemporary international reception, Barr classified Kahlo's work according to formal criteria. "Romanticism" corresponded to the 1943 *Romantic Painting in America* exhibition but added artists such as Mexican Raúl Anguiano (1915–2006) and Cuban Fidelio Ponce de León (1895–1949).

The third floor surveyed two broad tendencies: Social Realism and Surrealism / Biomorphic Abstraction. In the exhibition announcement, Barr argued that these works "spring from two radically different artistic—and human—problems. . . . One, concerned with the relation of man to society, has produced an art of satire, pathos, protest and action, often under Marxian influence: Orozco, Siqueiros, Grosz, . . . Shahn, etc. The other preoccupation springing from the relation of man to his subconscious mind, is more or less inspired . . . by modern psychology and the esthetics of surrealism."[58]

In these sections, Barr privileged content over diverse formal qualities. Thus, in "Social Comment" (fig. 12), Shahn's *Welder* (1943) was paired with three works by Siqueiros, including *Proletarian Victim* (1933), and Rivera's portable mural executed for his 1931 solo show, *Agrarian Leader Zapata*. This tendency to employ figurative styles to depict political content was the subject of *Americans 1942*. However, most FAP works were excluded in 1945, while works from the Latin American collection grouped under this category were included. It may be that Barr regarded these FAP works as lacking originality. In contrast, works that went beyond mimetic figuration were paired, among them Jacob Lawrence's (1917–2000) *Migration Series* (1940–41) and Ruíz's *The New Rich* (1941). Likewise, most works in the *Americans 1943* exhibition were omitted in 1945, but Latin American works linked to these tendencies were shown. This is surprising given Miller's role in the *Americans* exhibitions and suggests that perhaps Barr preferred some of the Latin American works.

It is difficult to ascertain the motives of Barr and Miller, as it is to pinpoint their differences of opinion because Barr was the official spokesman for the 1945 exhibition. However, Miller's important role is clear from internal memos, and Barr promoted her to full curator in 1943. At a time when various types of figuration could still be defined as embodiments of U.S. democracy, while others could be linked to political dissent in the United States or the figurative art championed by Hitler, Barr and Miller sought to classify the collection while negotiating the unstable institutional climate of the Museum, which was largely controlled by powerful trustees.

Although works by Siqueiros were shown in "Social Comment," another facet of his work was visible in "Fantasy out of Chaos," where his *Collective Suicide* (1936) hung alongside the Chilean Roberto Matta (1911–2002), André Masson (1896–1987), Robert Motherwell (1915–1991), and Jackson Pollock's (1912–1956) *The She-Wolf* (1943). This suggests that Barr or Miller noted Siqueiros's and Matta's impact on Motherwell and Pollock. In the third-floor galleries, Mexican artists were shown in ways demonstrating that Barr regarded them as relevant to contemporary artistic trends—both abstract and figurative.[59] Transnational links were also evident in "The Free Form" (fig. 13), an adjacent section featuring Biomorphic Abstraction, where Guatemalan Carlos Mérida's (1891–1985) *Tempo in Red* (1942) was hung alongside Joan Miró's (1893–1983) *The Beautiful Bird Revealing the Unknown to a Pair of Lovers* (1941) and Jean Arp's (1886–1966) *Birds in an Aquarium* (ca. 1920) and *Mountain, Table, Anchors, Navel* (1925). An international grouping appeared in a final paintings gallery, devoted to allegorical works: Lam's *The Jungle* (1945), Matta's *The Vertigo of Eros* (1944), Siqueiros's *Echo of a Scream* (1937), Pavel

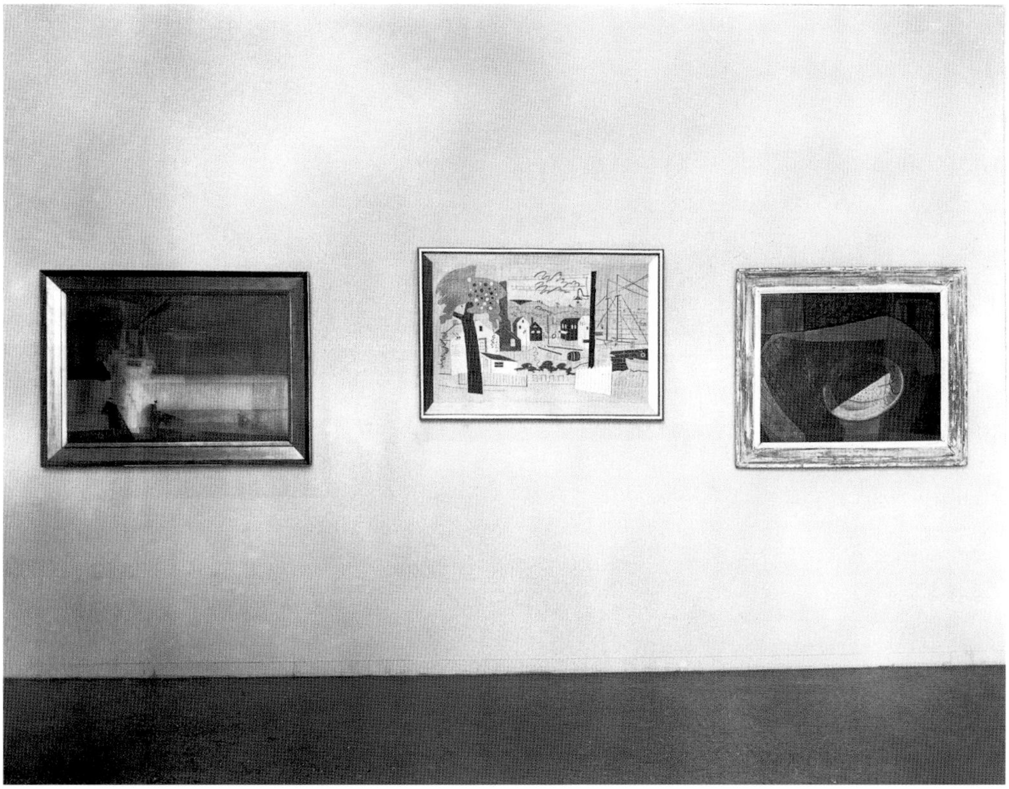

12. Installation view of the exhibition *The Museum Collection of Painting and Sculpture* at the Museum of Modern Art, New York, June 20, 1945, through January 13, 1946, 2nd floor; June 20, 1945, through February 13, 1946, 3rd floor. New York, Photographic Archive, The Museum of Modern Art Archives. Digital image © The Museum of Modern Art / Licensed by SCALA / Art Resource, N.Y.

Tchelichow's (1898–1957) *Hide and Seek* (1942), Beckmann's *Departure* (1932–35), and Blume's *The Eternal City* (1934–37). The exhibition concluded with galleries devoted to sculpture and drawings.

At the 1945 conference, Barr asked how to rank artists' significance and what role their place of origin should play in such distinctions. For him, this judgment was based on a complex balance of style and content. In the 1945 collection display, he and Miller presented works that emerged from networks of artistic relationships internationally—both transatlantic and Pan-American—with others that emerged from local art scenes. Thus, some Latin American works were presented within international categories he plotted in his 1936 flowchart. However, in 1945 there was a broader repertoire of figurative stylistic and thematic categories within which a large proportion of Latin American works could be shown alongside U.S. works. At this time, certain figurative works produced in Europe and across the Americas represented a contemporary artistic tendency. As Barr proposed in the exhibition announcement, "many of the most vigorous and original artists have rebelled in various ways against the vague emotions of expressionism, the dogma of abstraction, and the esthetics of pure form and

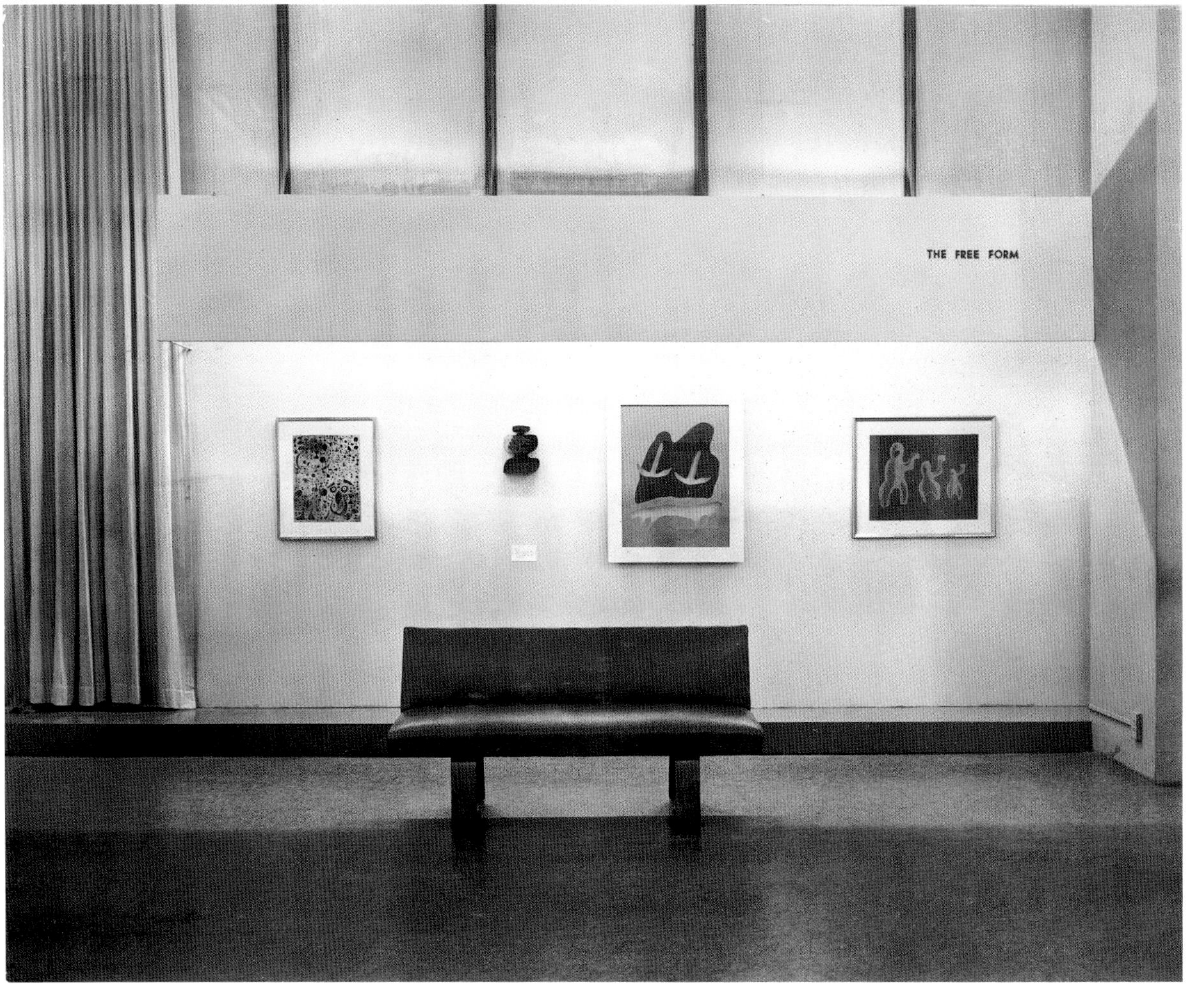

13. Installation view of the exhibition *The Museum Collection of Painting and Sculpture* at the Museum of Modern Art, New York, June 20, 1945, through January 13, 1946, 2nd floor; June 20, 1945, through February 13, 1946, 3rd floor. New York, Photographic Archive, The Museum of Modern Art Archives. Digital image © The Museum of Modern Art / Licensed by SCALA / Art Resource, N.Y.

color."[60] Here, in distinctions between local and international, and in the priority given to form versus content and abstraction or figuration, we see the origins of the eventual exclusion of many of the works by Latin American and U.S. artists from the Museum's canon.[61] In describing most of the Latin American collection, Barr emphasized the "local," thus distinguishing most of the works from the central common ancestor—Cézanne—who appeared in both 1936 and 1945 as the progenitor of international modern artists. Kirstein, too, used the terms "species" and "subspecies" to indicate derivativeness. In this sense, we might regard my imagined 1945 chart to consider how Barr regarded the geographical distribution of the works in the collection. In the evolutionary development of modern art, Latin American artists were largely isolated in their local contexts, relegated to the status of a marginal species, and destined to decadence or possible disappearance over time.

Hot Styles and Cold War

Collecting Practices at MoMA and Other Museums in the Sixties

Delia Solomons

14. Soichi Sunami (American, 1885–1971), installation view of the exhibition *Recent Acquisitions: Assemblage* at The Museum of Modern Art, New York, April 19, 1965, through September 12, 1965. Gelatin-silver print, 18.4 × 24.1 cm. New York, Photographic Archive, The Museum of Modern Art Archives. Works by Marcelo Bonevardi (Argentinian, 1929–1994) in the middle and Jorge Eielson (Peruvian, 1924–2006) on the far right. Digital image © The Museum of Modern Art / Licensed by SCALA / Art Resource, N.Y.

Collecting in Context

In the 1960s, museums in the United States began to collect and exhibit Latin American art with an intensity that had not been seen since the "Mexican art craze" of the 1930s and '40s. This burst of cultural exchange not only introduced new art to new audiences, but also played an important role in inter-American politics.[1] In 1959, the Cuban Revolution established a communist foothold in the Western Hemisphere and amplified Cold War tensions in the Americas. Museums became privileged spaces where one could propagandize cohesion in the face of actual rupture by displaying transnational cultural partnerships and parallel stylistic developments. Shared aesthetics became a useful metaphor for shared cultures, politics, and fates.

The act of collecting Latin American art—and the idea of collecting Latin America itself into an anticommunist hemisphere—played key roles throughout the decade. Purchasing artwork demonstrated the investment of money and prestige beyond that afforded by temporary exhibitions. In fact, collecting proved so critical that the 1960s boom was bookended by exhibitions overtly celebrating U.S. collections of Latin American art. In the summer of 1959, the Art Institute of Chicago mounted *The United States Collects Pan American Art*, the first show of its kind following the Cuban Revolution.[2] Museum surveys of Latin American art began to ebb around 1967, arguably ending with the collection show *Latin-American Art, 1931–1966* (Museum of Modern Art, New York, 1967) and *The Art of Ancient and Modern Latin America: Selections from Public and Private Collections in the United States* (Isaac Delgado Museum of Art, New Orleans, 1968). These exhibitions highlighted the active collecting taking place in the United States by institutions and individuals. The politics behind the prominence of collection-based exhibitions can be interpreted in several ways: at best, a means to better understand

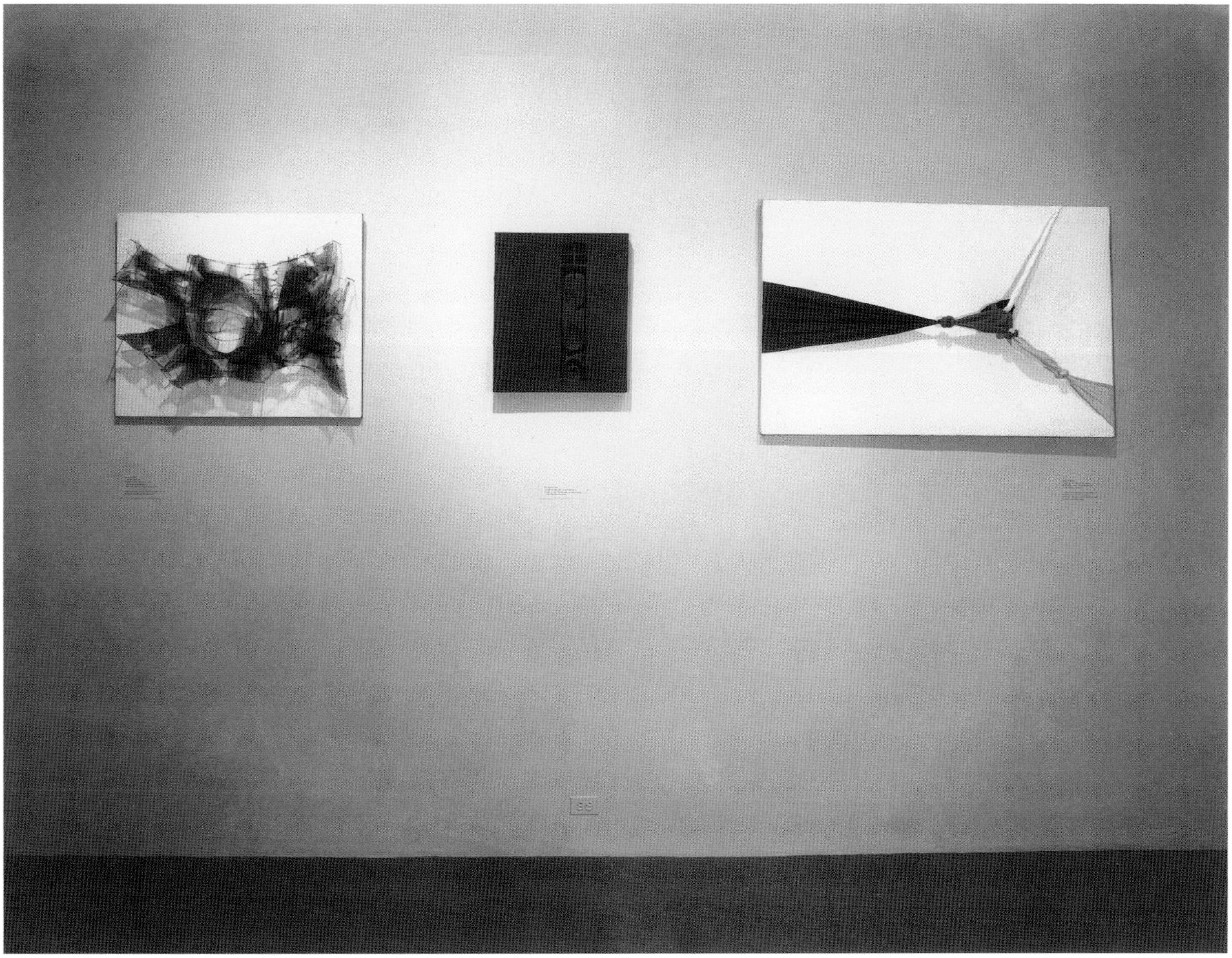

international cultural activity during a period of increased global contact, and at worst, an extension of the desire to possess other regions as one more manipulative measure employed by the United States during the Cold War years.

Several major U.S. institutions initiated or augmented their collections of Latin American art in the 1960s, including the Solomon R. Guggenheim Museum, Walker Art Center, Museum of Fine Arts in Houston, Art Institute of Chicago, and Carnegie Museum of Art. While most exhibitions of Latin American art showcased a variety of contemporary aesthetics, museums' acquisition policies tended to reveal more focused favoritism. For example, the Walker built a small collection of Brazilian Informalist painting after holding *New Art of Brazil* (1962). The selections reflected director Martin Friedman's (1925–2016) taste for Abstract Expressionism, which was frequently displayed at the Walker. The Guggenheim acquired important examples of Argentine Neofigurative art from both *The 1964 Guggenheim International* and *The Emergent Decade* (1965–67). Guggenheim curator Lawrence Alloway (1926–1990) and director Thomas Messer (1920–2013) were predisposed to favor New Figuration (*Nueva Figuración*) even before establishing personal and professional relationships with the artists. Alloway was a world-renowned expert in international Pop, and Messer had conducted prior research on the European COBRA artists. While the Argentine group's intellectual rigor and aesthetic experimentalism cemented their appeal for both Guggenheim leaders, the fact that their work had formal parallels with international styles is also important. Since Alloway and Messer were relatively new to the field of Latin American art, it is no surprise that when both went on their massive expeditions seeking art across the Americas in the mid-1960s, they sought something familiar within the vast, heterogeneous domain.[3]

MoMA: New Tactics at a Cultural Powerhouse

Whereas in the sixties many U.S. museums were turning their attention to Latin America for the first time, the Museum of Modern Art was in a wholly different position. MoMA had been a powerhouse in the field in the 1930s and '40s (as discussed in Miriam Basilio's essay in this volume), with major initiatives dating back to its earliest days, when, in 1931, the fledgling institution devoted its second monograph to Diego Rivera (1886–1957). Despite this storied past, the Museum's collecting practices during the 1960s are practically unknown.[4] The scarcity of scholarship is surprising for several reasons, not least of which is MoMA's position as arguably the U.S. leader in the field of Latin American art in the 1930s and '40s and again since the 1990s; the gap is tantalizingly mysterious. However, research into MoMA's engagement with Latin America during the Cold War has focused largely on the International Council's aggressive policy of sending U.S. and European art (particularly Abstract Expressionism) on extensive tours displaying U.S. economic and cultural power across the Americas. In other words, scholars have focused more heavily on the export rather than import component of the museum's activities. One would also think that MoMA's impressive collection of 1960s artwork from the Americas would attract research into the museum's acquisition activity during that time. However, Neo-Concretism, Conceptualism, and other currents have been more intensively collected and exhibited since the 1990s, as curators now work to fill gaps in the collection and to retroactively construct canons. Due to its particular history of entanglements with Latin American art and the dearth of published material that addresses this phase, the rest of this essay will focus on aspects of MoMA's collecting in the decade following the Cuban Revolution.

When MoMA restarted its Latin American Program in the 1960s, it confronted a very different scene from the one it left in the 1940s. Accordingly, the museum adopted a distinct policy to grapple with the new challenges of a new decade. The 1930s and '40s were characterized by massive collecting expeditions and major loan shows devoted exclusively to Latin American art.[5] In the 1960s, the Museum approached the field more tentatively, instead integrating Latin American artists into theme-based exhibitions and augmenting the collection. Key research was undertaken by curator Elaine Johnson (1928–1979) and collector-scholar Barbara Duncan (1921–2003), and significant financial resources were provided by the Inter-American Fund.

While at the time MoMA built a diverse, eclectic collection of contemporary Latin American art, only a small percentage of that collection was shown in the museum throughout the decade. The styles that did make it onto the gallery walls prove quite revealing. Assemblage and various forms of Kinetic art produced by artists from Latin America were displayed repeatedly and came to dominate the contemporary contingent in the museum's collection show *Latin-American Art, 1931–1966* (1967). These styles correspond to two of MoMA's largest high-profile surveys of the 1960s: *The Art of Assemblage* (1961) and *The Responsive Eye* (1965), both curated by William Seitz (1914–1974). By prioritizing the display of Assemblage and Kinetic art by Latin American artists, MoMA augmented and prolonged the trends heralded in these major exhibitions. This practice served to further internationalize and canonize Assemblage and Kineticism. Although art historians have underscored the importance of both *The Art of Assemblage* and *The Responsive Eye*, they sometimes mistakenly imply that a single blockbuster can secure a style's place in the annals of art history. It is only through repetitive exposure, study, and exhibition that styles actually become widely accepted.[6] This essay examines the role that acquisitions of Latin American art played in extending the reach and visibility of Assemblage and Kinetic art at MoMA, and how this practice represented a new phase in the museum's history of engagement with Latin American art.

Amplifying Assemblage

In 1961, MoMA's *The Art of Assemblage* traced the explosion of collage and *papier collé* into increasingly sculptural and multimedia practices over the first half of the twentieth century. Although dominated by artists from Western Europe and the United States, this major exhibition included some artists with connections to Latin America. Marisol's (Marisol Escobar, 1930–2016) wooden construction *From France* (1960) shared a room with works by H. C. Westermann (1922–1981) and Alfonso Ossorio (1916–1990). Mathias Goeritz's (1915–1990) abstract assemblage of metal, paint, and wood visually rhymed with work by artists ranging from Kurt Schwitters (1887–1948) to Alberto Burri (1915–1995). Marisol and Goeritz themselves might be considered assemblages of national categories. Both accumulated layers of experience across Europe and the Americas; Marisol was born in Paris to Venezuelan parents and resided in the United States for most of her life, and Goeritz was born in Germany but spent the bulk of his career in Mexico. In the show one could also find a wooden construction by Joaquín Torres-García (1874–1949), an Uruguayan artist who made critical sojourns to New York and Europe, and a collage by Eileen Agar (1899–1991), a British artist born in Buenos Aires.

In the years following *The Art of Assemblage*, MoMA extended its engagement with the multimedia accumulative process by adding to its collection assemblages by Latin American artists not included in the landmark show. In 1964, MoMA acquired Marcelo Bonevardi's (1929–1994) *Figure, I* (1964) (see fig. 14), an enigmatic abstract construction made of wood, canvas, paint, and string. The museum also purchased Jorge Eielson's (1924–

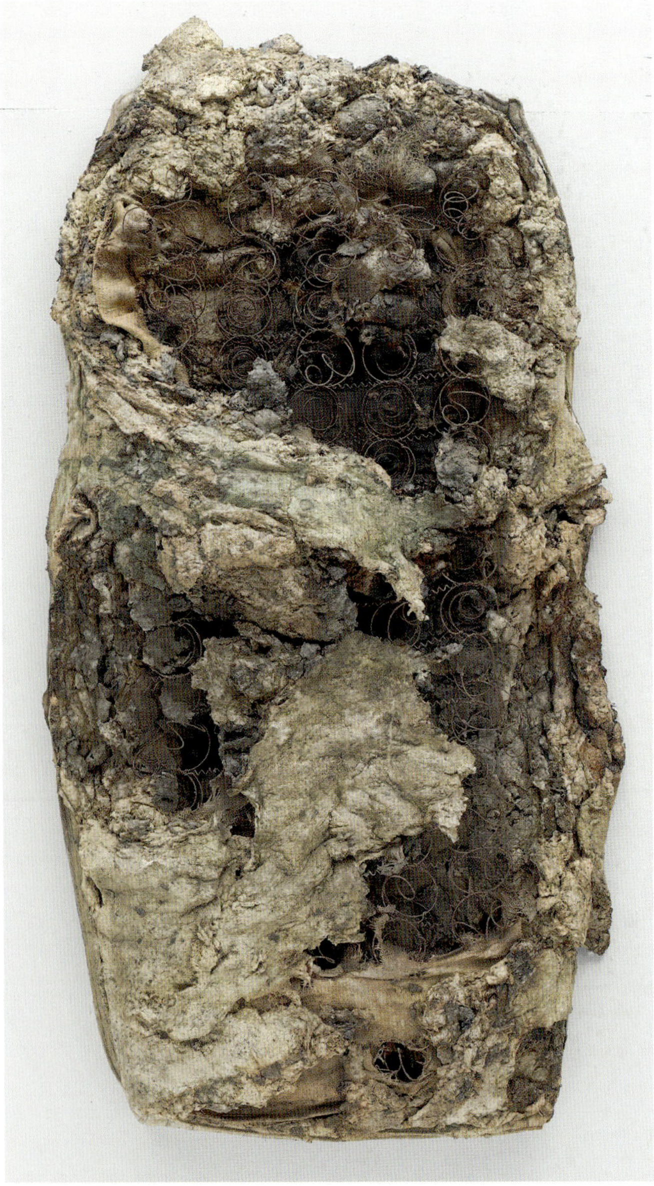

15. Rafael Montañez Ortiz (b. 1934), *Archeological Find, 3*, 1961. Burnt mattress, 190 × 104.5 × 23.7 cm. New York, Museum of Modern Art. Digital image © The Museum of Modern Art / Licensed by SCALA / Art Resource, N.Y.

2006) *White Quipu* (1964) (see fig. 14), which offers a contemporary interpretation of the ancient Andean system of transmitting messages through tied knots. The work invites viewers to contemplate themes of communication, colonialism, and lost traditions. Swiftly after they entered the collection, Bonevardi's and Eielson's assemblages were displayed side by side twice at MoMA in *Recent Acquisitions: Assemblage* (1965) and in *Latin-American Art 1931–1966* (1967). In the mid-1960s, the number of "Recent Acquisitions" shows grew significantly. The 1964 expansion of MoMA's building, designed by Philip Johnson, introduced a special ground-floor gallery devoted exclusively to showing new acquisitions, which in prior years were featured in only one show annually.[7] Fortuitously, at the very moment MoMA renewed its investment in acquiring Latin American art, a gallery opened to connect the public with that growing collection.

In 1963, MoMA also acquired Rafael Montañez Ortiz's (b. 1934) *Archeological Find, 3* (1961) (fig. 15). The piece was exhibited twice in the mid-sixties, in *Recent Acquisitions: Painting and Sculpture* (1965) and in *The Object Transformed* (1966). Ortiz, who would later found El Museo del Barrio, scorched mattresses in a performative process that conflated artistic creation with destruction as well as the fleeting moment with historical recovery. His work exemplifies a gritty, decrepit side of Assemblage not heavily featured in the 1961 MoMA show. In 1964, three newly purchased xilocollages by Antonio Berni (1905–1981) appeared in *Contemporary Painters and Sculptors as Printmakers* (1964). These prints detailed the life of fictional character Ramona Montiel through the detritus of her impoverished urban surroundings. Like Ortiz's deconstructed *objet trouvé*, Berni's xilocollages expanded the repertoire of experimental assemblage techniques showcased in the museum. Finally, after her debut in *The Art of Assemblage*, Marisol's artwork appeared in no fewer than eight exhibitions organized by the museum between 1963 and 1968.[8] By repeatedly exhibiting new acquisitions by Bonevardi, Eielson, Ortiz, Berni, and Marisol, MoMA extended Assemblage's reach in time, across geographic space, and into new styles.

Expanding the Kinetic Experience

Works by Latin American artists that fit loosely into the problematically broad category of Kinetic-Op art propagated by *The Responsive Eye* were even more forcefully showcased than assemblage practices.[9] The exhibit's voguish popularity and the style's immediate commodification into fashion and design upset a number of critics.[10] In the controversial show, alongside Bridget Riley (b. 1931), Victor Vasarely (1906–1997), and Heinz Mack (b. 1931), viewers encountered one of Luis Tomasello's (1915–2014) monochrome serial reliefs, Gego's (Gertrude Louise Goldschmidt, 1912–1994) parallactic metal works, and Carlos Cruz-Diez's (b. 1923) *Physichromies*. Groupe de Recherche d'Art Visuel members Hugo Demarco (1932–1995), Horacio García-Rossi (1929–2012), and Julio Le Parc (b. 1928) were also included in *The Responsive Eye.*

In the years surrounding *The Responsive Eye*, MoMA made key purchases that reflected the show's aesthetics. Gego's *Sphere* (1959) (see fig. 16)—shown in both *The Responsive Eye* and *Latin-American Art 1931–1966*— offers a surprising clash of obdurate materiality and optical dematerialization. As the viewer observes the piece, the static steel lines seem to flicker, shift, and re-form. The museum also acquired three important works by Le Parc, which were included in five exhibitions between 1965 and 1967.[11] The constructions aptly demonstrate the range of Le Parc's approaches to light and movement. *Instability Through Movement of the Spectator* (1962–64) (see fig. 16) features mirrored distortions of bold graphic shapes. Meanwhile, *Double Concurrence—Continuous Light 2* (1961) is a flickering luminous mobile, and *Continuous Instability—Light* (1962) comprises delicate refracted beams of light.

In 1967, MoMA acquired and exhibited Jesús Soto's (1923–2005) *Olive and Black* (1966, see fig. 17), which casts attenuated shadows across the wall as the sculpture's rods oscillate with every slight current of air. Soto had refused to participate in *The Responsive Eye* because he believed that Seitz placed excessive emphasis on Victor Vasarely and Op art.[12] However, only two years later, in a collection show celebrating the 1960s, Dorothy Miller (1904–2003) grouped Soto with Gene Davis (1920–1985) and Bridget Riley (fig. 17). Not only had both Davis and Riley been prominently featured in *The Responsive Eye*, but the work directly adjacent to *Olive and Black,* Riley's *Current* (1964), graced the catalogue's cover. Therefore, Soto's work was placed into a corner physically and conceptually, integrated retroactively into the themes and styles promoted by the blockbuster exhibition he had protested.

The legacy of *The Responsive Eye* loomed particularly large in *Latin-American Art, 1931–1966,* the 1967 collection-based show (fig.18). Here one found work by artists shown in *The Responsive Eye* like Le Parc, Gego, and Cruz-Diez, as well as new additions, including Rogelio Polesello (1939–2014), Alejandro Otero (1921–1990), Victor Magariños D. (1924–1993), and Eduardo Mac Entyre (1929–2014). While many of these artists took highly disparate approaches to line-making, geometry, optics, movement, and the role of the spectator, over half of the works in the room devoted to contemporary art would have been at home with their international colleagues in the very broad spectrum of Op-Kinetic practices corralled into *The Responsive Eye.* For example, Mac Entyre's *Generative Painting: Black, Red, Orange* (1965) (see fig. 18) catalyzes optical vibration and creates the illusion of constant change and self-production. Polesello's *Untitled* (1966) (see fig. 18) shows layers of kaleidoscopic pigment in circular shapes, the smallest of

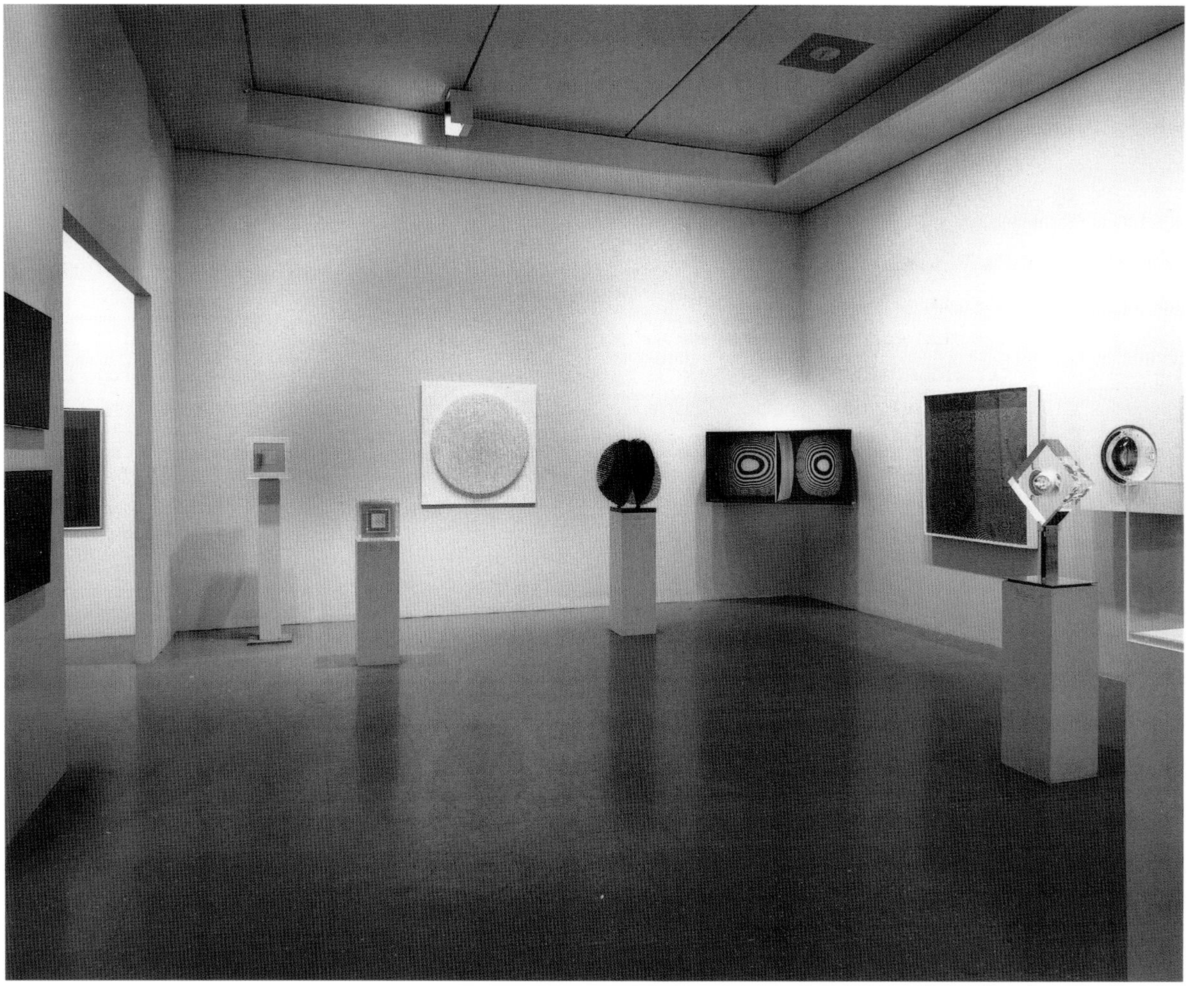

16. Installation view of the exhibition *The Responsive Eye* at The Museum of Modern Art, New York, February 25 through April 25, 1965. Works by Gego (Venezuelan, 1912–1994) and Julio Le Parc (Argentinian, b. 1928) in right corner of the room. New York, Photographic Archive, The Museum of Modern Art Archives. Digital image © The Museum of Modern Art / Licensed by SCALA / Art Resource, N.Y.

which were made by applying industrial spray-paint onto the canvas through an industrial grate, which acts as a ready-made, found pointillist device.

The extremely broad nature of the trends enveloped into *The Responsive Eye* and *The Art of Assemblage* rendered the exhibitions particularly powerful. If Assemblage represents an accumulation of materials, and Kinetic-Op art comprises abstract works that catalyze optical or actual movement, then undoubtedly these categories encompass many disparate practices. Kinetic-Op art, with its emphasis on the universalized phenomenological experience of the viewer, is widely understood to be particularly apt for absorption into such formalist international paradigms. We used to think that the products of Assemblage stamped their geographic origins like a fingerprint (think of the French text in Picasso's *papier collé* and the distinctly German products in Schwitters's Merz pieces). However, as products and material culture became increasingly globalized, the objects incorporated into assemblages perhaps become just as placeless and universal. The themes explored in *The Art of Assemblage* and *The Responsive Eye* were indeed ripe for additions and expansions as the decade progressed. It is then perhaps no surprise that many of the works by Latin American artists that MoMA acquired and exhibited in the mid-1960s articulated the global reach of those styles. This practice retroactively aggregated new artists into these exhibitions and cemented 1960s formalist canons through repeated exposure.

Latin-American Art, 1931–1966: An Institutional Autobiography

MoMA's small collection show *Latin-American Art, 1931–1966*, scheduled to coincide with New York's Pan-American Week in 1967, contributed a visual arts component to the week's dense schedule of conferences, concerts, and other events devoted to inter-American politics, economics, and culture. Assemblage and Kinetic-Op art dominated the room devoted to contemporary art, with assemblages by Eielson, Bonevardi, Emilio Rodríguez-Larrain (1928–2015), and Jorge Damiani (b. 1931) and works engaging with implied or actual movement by Polesello, Gego, Mac Entyre, Otero, Le Parc, Magariños D., and Cruz-Diez. This room did not reflect the

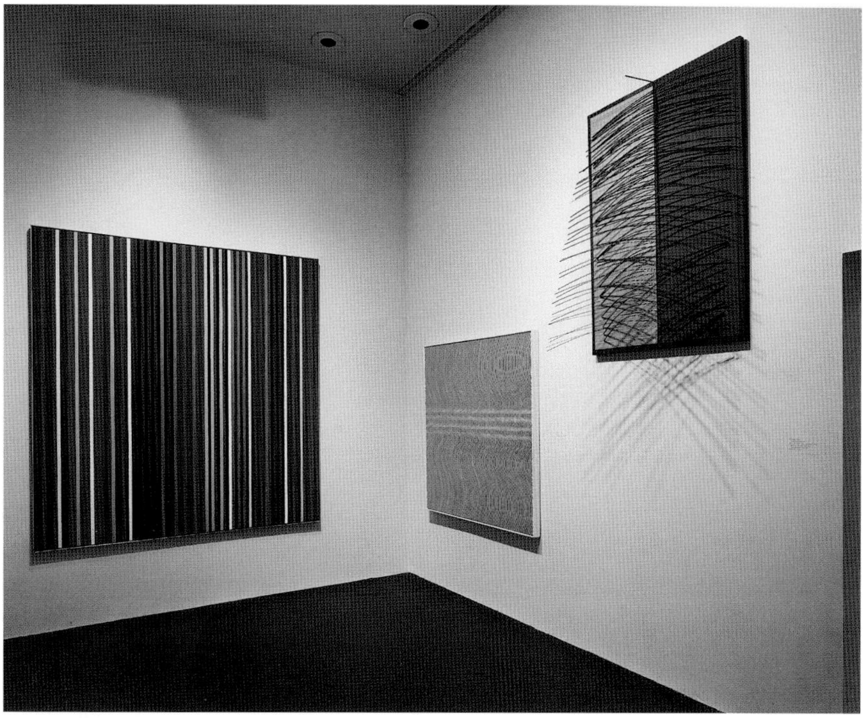

17. Installation view of the exhibition *The 1960s: Painting and Sculpture from the Museum Collections,* at The Museum of Modern Art, New York, June 28 through September 24, 1967. From left to right: works by Gene Davis (American, 1920–1985), Bridget Riley (British, b. 1931), and Jesús Rafael Soto (Venezuelan, 1923–2005). Digital image © The Museum of Modern Art / Licensed by SCALA / Art Resource, N.Y.

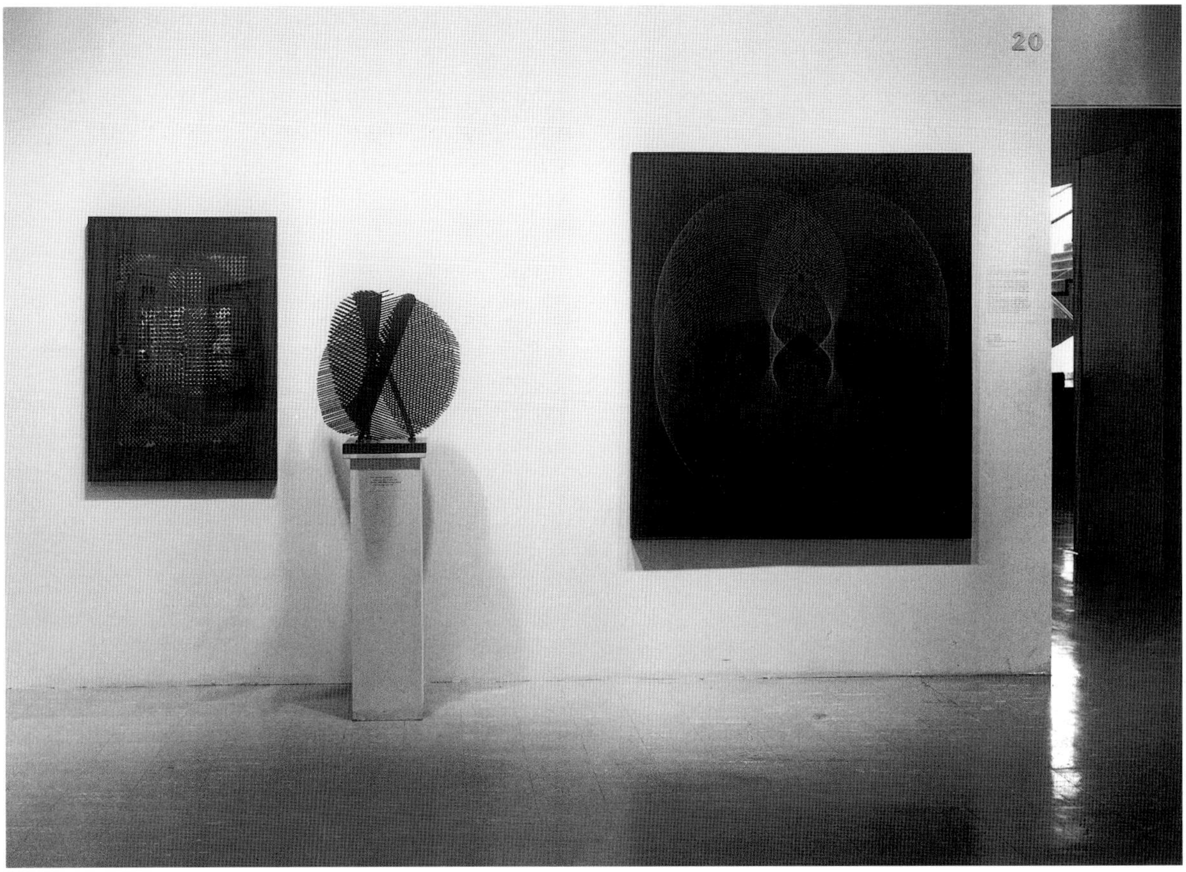

18. Installation view of *Latin-American Art, 1931–1966* exhibition at The Museum of Modern Art, New York, March 17 through June 4, 1967. From left to right: works by Rogelio Polesello (Argentinian, 1939–2014), Gego (Venezuelan, 1912–1994), and Eduardo Mac Entyre (Argentinian, 1929–2014). Digital image © The Museum of Modern Art / Licensed by SCALA / Art Resource, N.Y.

breadth or depth of Latin American artistic production, but rather narrated the very particular way in which MoMA engaged with the field in the 1960s. Since MoMA did not arrange a major loan show of contemporary Latin American painting or sculpture during the 1960s, it did not conduct an extended period of research into the ideas and styles that became prominent in the region.[13] *Latin-American Art, 1931–1966* instead reflected sporadic moments of contact as curators prepared and then extended the concerns of thematic shows such as *The Art of Assemblage* and *The Responsive Eye*. Other works included in the room documented similarly specific interactions. For example, Frans Krajcberg's (b. 1921) *Painting I* (1957) arrived at MoMA as a result of Alfred Barr's (1902–1981) trip to the 1957 São Paulo Bienal, where he served as a juror and infamously secured a prize for Krajcberg, his favorite Informalist, at the expense of the dominant Brazilian Concrete art movement.

The two-room exhibition in Galleries 19 and 20 amounted to an abbreviated autobiography of MoMA's engagement with Latin America not only over the prior few years but since the very inauguration of the museum. Even the press releases and wall texts revealed little about the art itself, instead recounting the museum's own history of involvement in the region. For example, the wall label for Diego Rivera's *Agrarian Leader Zapata* (1931) discussed MoMA's role in the commission more than the artist or subject. The text opened with the words "The Museum invited the artist to New York to paint seven frescoes for an exhibition in 1931."[14] The press releases in Spanish and English similarly underscored MoMA's history rather than the artists, styles, or regions featured in the show.[15]

Where Gallery 20 showcased MoMA's holdings of contemporary art, Gallery 19 celebrated the museum's work in the 1930s and '40s. The room paid homage to MoMA's early years, when Barr and Lincoln Kirstein (1907–1996) championed *los tres grandes*, Surrealism, and other forms of modernist figurative currents in Latin America. It featured oft-exhibited highlights of the collection by Rivera, David Alfaro Siqueiros (1896–1974), José Clemente Orozco (1883–1968), Matta (1911–2002), Frida Kahlo (1907–1954), Cândido Portinari (1903–1962), Rufino Tamayo (1889–1991), and Amelia Peláez (1896–1968). Within the space largely devoted to realisms and surrealisms, two geometric works proved stylistic outliers. Roberto Berdecio's (1910–1996) *The Cube and the Perspective* (1935) and Joaquín Torres-García's *Composition* (1932) each appeared next to wall text. The organizers practically treated these works as graphic design frontispieces for the exhibition. Nearly every work in Gallery 19 had been previously shown in *The Latin-American Collection of the Museum of Modern Art* (1943) and in the museum's collection galleries in the 1950s.[16] Such repetitive installations served to cement this collection in the public imagination.

Visitors to *Latin-American Art, 1931–1966* would have likely seen little connection or causality between the first room's emphasis on figurative painting and the second room's focus on abstract Assemblage and Kinetic art. They perhaps even experienced a shock when moving from one space to the next, wondering if they had wandered into a different show in the abutting gallery.[17] The disconnection reflects at once major shifts in the art world and the relative hiatus in MoMA's active collecting of Latin American art between 1945 and 1959. The stylistic and chronological gap between the two rooms bespeaks the museum's two distinct phases of engagement with Latin America, each characterized by a different methodology. That gap from 1945 to 1959, subliminally narrated in the 1967 collection show, is a critical yet little-explored component of the museum's institutional history and merits extended investigation here.

Confronting a New Decade with Baggage

In 1959, Alfred Barr (founding director of the Museum from 1929 to 1943 and Director of Collections from 1947 to 1967)[18] noted with restrained optimism the sudden renewed attention to Latin American art in the United States. In a letter to the editor of *Art in America*, after congratulating Jean Lipman (1909–1998) on the Fall 1959 issue devoted to "Pan-American Painting," Barr reminded readers of the U.S. history of inconsistent and politicized involvement in the region.[19] Barr relayed his concerns through a conversation he had with an unnamed Mexican historian in the 1940s: "[D]uring the very height of our wartime enthusiasm for Latin America . . . [he] was thoroughly cynical about the whole love affair. You will see, he insisted, that after the war your fractious interest in Latin America will fade. The honeymoon will be over. Politically and economically his gloomy prophecy was all too true. There was also an abrupt decline in Inter-American cultural activities."[20] Barr acknowledged the country's serial history of initiated, abandoned, and then renewed engagement with Latin America. He also warned that too often political interests incentivized cultural initiatives. While he never directly mentioned the Cuban Revolution or the Cold War, he certainly implied that the 1959 upsurge in cultural activity—the "Pan-American Painting" issue of *Art in America* and "the exhibitions in Chicago, Denver and Dallas"[21]—might constitute just another phase in the cyclical problem that unfolded during both world wars. Barr's letter to *Art in America* indeed predicted the swell and ebb of the 1959–68 boom of Latin American art from its very outset.

Fifteen years earlier, at a conference held at MoMA, Barr had used the exact conversation with the Mexican historian he cited in *Art in America*. In the 1945 symposium Studies in Latin American Art, participants largely devoted their lectures and conversations not to specific artists or styles (i.e., the fruits of their research over the prior decades), but rather to taking stock of the state of the field. Barr, George Kubler (1912–1996), Grace McCann Morley (1900–1985), Jean Charlot (1898–1979), Daniel Catton Rich (1904–1976), Philip Goodwin (1885–1958), and others agreed upon the urgent need to invest more time, scholarship, and funds into the nascent discipline. In his speech, Barr identified as a major impediment the inconsistent engagement of the United States with Latin America. He related this problem through the aforementioned anecdotal conversation with the unnamed Mexican historian: "He said that he was old enough to remember our difficulties with Mexico in 1916 and the sudden change in 1917, when we were involved in the war with Germany; how there was suddenly a great deal of excited promotion of goodwill and hands-across-the-Rio-Grande, and how in 1918, the whole thing collapsed suddenly with an extremely disquieting and disillusioning effect on Mexican intellectuals and scholars. I hope this will not happen this time. I think that it will not happen if we can be warned by what occurred then."[22] Despite being "warned by what occurred then," it did happen again. In a cruel irony, the very conference in which Barr expressed that his chief concern was his country's sporadic attention to Latin America actually marked the end of MoMA's first intense phase of collecting and arranging major loan shows of Latin American art. This conspicuously coincided with the end of World War II.

When Barr noted the resurgence of activity in 1959, MoMA found itself confronted with a very different field from the one it helped build prior to the end of World War II. In the 1930s and '40s, the museum had invested in a specific image of Latin American modernism, particularly the one painted by *los tres grandes*. However, in the 1960s, artists like José Luis Cuevas (1934–2017) and curators like José Gómez Sicre (1916–1991), Stanton Catlin (1921–1997), and Thomas Messer vociferously spoke out against the dominance of Mexican figuration in the popular imagination. They resented, in Gómez Sicre's words, U.S. viewers' "expectation of viewing picturesque scenes and types of South America . . . [and] the descriptive realism which was long the exclusive representative of Latin American art in the United States."[23] The picturesque and folkloric images they reference do not accurately reflect the breadth of the work shown at MoMA in the 1930s and '40s. However, the popularity of such tropes at times eclipsed the rest, generating stereotypes that resonated for decades and distorting the image of Mexican art in which MoMA had invested. MoMA and other institutions active in the 1930s and '40s were viewed as at least in part responsible for rendering colorful figuration a problematic metonym for Latin American art.

Barr had also become vocal about his own errors of the 1930s and '40s. He twice confessed the political and methodological problems behind his early work with Latin American art. In 1945, he explained that he and Kirstein "worked in considerable haste. Already, we begin to see that we made errors of policy and taste."[24] In 1959, he again admitted that "a sense of urgency had often made our studies superficial, our judgments hasty. Good will as well as too little learning had handicapped discrimination."[25] Barr's awareness, as well as the shift of his job title to Director of Collections, had a direct impact on the way the museum would approach the field in the 1960s.

With its prior actions deemed problematic and passé, MoMA ventured more tentatively into the field of contemporary Latin American art in the 1960s. The curators did not undertake the massive collecting expeditions or major loan shows that characterized their work the 1930s and '40s. Interestingly, while high-profile loan shows of Latin American art never came to fruition at MoMA in the 1960s, they were originally planned as a crucial facet of the "Five Year Latin American Program" outlined in 1962.[26] The very "core of the proposed program" dictated that the museum organize two exhibitions for circulation in the United States. *Recent Latin American Painting* was intended to open at MoMA before traveling to five other U.S. museums between 1962 and 1968.[27] The second loan exhibition would comprise watercolors, drawings, and prints from Latin America. However, both intended exhibitions were extensively downsized and revised into collection-based rather than loan shows. *Recent Latin American Painting* became the small two-room *Latin-American Art, 1931–1966*, and the exhibition of works on paper became *Latin American Prints from the Museum of Modern Art* (postponed to 1974, restricted to printmaking, and shifted offsite to the Center for Inter-American Relations).

The committee's ultimate decision to abandon plans for the major painting exhibition resulted in part from two pieces of news received in 1964. While traveling separately in South America, Barbara Duncan learned of Stanton Catlin's plans for *Art of Latin America Since Independence* (Yale University and University of Texas at Austin, 1966–67),[28] and Waldo Rasmussen (1928–2013) was informed by Venezuelan philanthropist and developer Hans Neumann (1921–2001) of Thomas Messer's preparations for *The Emergent Decade* at the Guggenheim.[29] Rasmussen, clearly disappointed, stated, "Perhaps, however, something can be salvaged, as I think it would be a terrible mistake for the Guggenheim to take over that show which is so important to the nature of the Latin American program as a whole."[30] The news that two important northeastern institutions—Yale University and the Guggenheim Museum—already had in development large-scale Latin American art initiatives no doubt proved discouraging for MoMA's new Latin American program. By 1964, MoMA was already late to the game.

Conclusion

When MoMA renewed its engagement with contemporary Latin American art in the 1960s, it faced a different cultural and political scene from the one it left in the 1940s. Unlike other contributors to the post–Cuban Revolution activity in the United States, MoMA was saddled with baggage from past decades and thus adopted a distinctive approach. Due to both circumstances and lessons learned from the past, the institution did not host major loan exhibitions that sought to define contemporary "Latin American Art." Instead, curators augmented the collection and utilized Latin American art to prove the global scope and stylistic breadth of the trends they championed, namely, Assemblage and Kineticism. For MoMA this was a decade not of banner statements, massive collection expeditions, or blockbusters devoted to Latin American art, but rather of gradual investment, collection, integration, and repetition. Analysis of these disparate approaches to international styles and international relations is critical to understanding the museum's complex history.[31]

CHAPTER 3

The Philadelphia Story

Joseph Rishel

Philadelphia's first connections with the Hispanic world date back to its time as a bustling colonial port and as the capital of the fledgling American Republic.[1] This moment is perhaps best illustrated by a glorious pair of wedding portraits, now at The Metropolitan Museum of Art, of Don Josef de Jaudenes y Nebot (1764–ca. 1819) and Matilda Stoughton (1778–ca. 1822) by Gilbert Stuart (1755–1828). Don Josef was part of the Spanish delegation sent to treat with the new nation, focusing on major issues such as the status of Spanish Louisiana and trade rights, while Stoughton was the daughter of the Spanish consul in Boston, John "Don Juan" Stoughton, perhaps the most enterprising American in the Caribbean trade. The Metropolitan Museum's portraits were painted in New York following their marriage in the spring of 1794, one year before Stuart, in his pursuit of George Washington, moved to Philadelphia, where Don Josef had resided since 1790. Jaudenes's failure to secure a more permanent diplomatic post in the Americas led to the couple's leaving for Spain, from which they would not return.[2]

Philadelphia's Hispanic relations received another jolt, one with considerably grander social magnitude than poor Jaudenes, with the arrival in 1815 of Joseph Bonaparte (1768–1844), king of Spain and Napoleon Bonaparte's brother. The elder Bonaparte would remain in the United States for twenty-two years, exploring and purchasing large properties in North America and Canada and ingratiating himself to the locals, including the influential Biddle family.[3] He brought with him major works of art, including paintings by Antoine Coypel and Horace Vernet, many of which he gave to local friends. None is more touching than the double portrait of Joseph's daughters Zénaïde and Charlotte by Jacques-Louis David (1748–1825), painted in Brussels in 1821 (now in the J. Paul Getty Museum, Los Angeles), where they themselves were in exile, fondly reading letters from their father marked "de Philadelphia."

19. Miguel Cabrera (Mexican, 1695–1768), *Our Lady of Valvanera*, 1762. Oil on copper, 42.1 × 31.7 cm. Philadelphia Museum of Art. Courtesy of the Philadelphia Museum of Art.

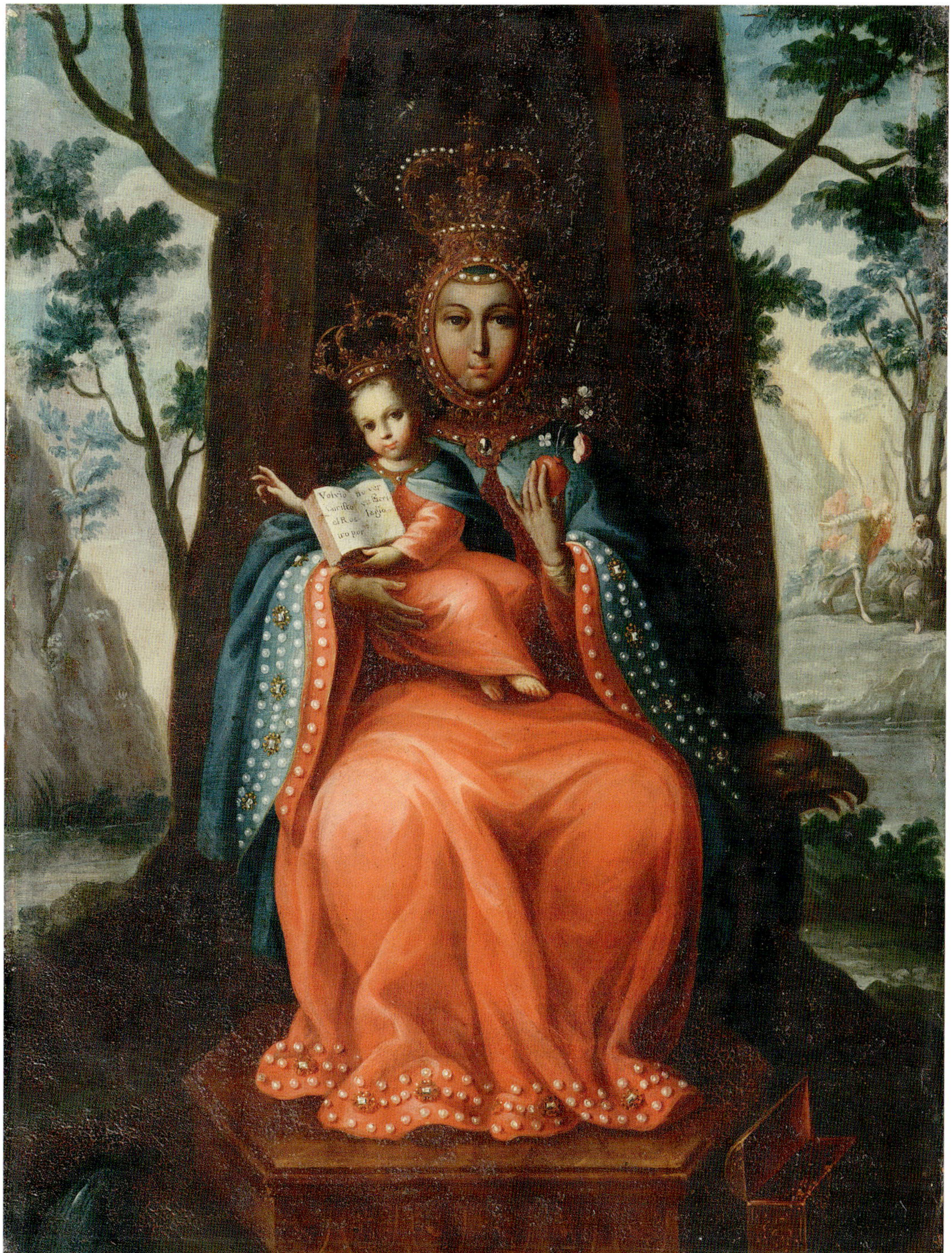
Volvio
tro por

Finally, to come to the subject at hand, Latin America, there was another principal player in Philadelphia's connections to the Hispanic world, Ana María Josefa Ramona de Huarte y Muñiz (1786–1861), empress of Mexico. From a wealthy family in the state of Morelia, she married Agustín de Iturbide (1783–1824), the son of a neighboring landowning family, in 1805. Iturbide built the successful coalition of political and military forces that ended Spanish rule in Mexico in 1821. Proclaimed President of the Regency that same year, Iturbide would a year later proclaim himself Constitutional Emperor, a decision that appears to have been motivated by a complex mixture of patriotism and self-interest. Crowned with pomp and huge public exuberance in the Metropolitan Cathedral in Mexico City, he reigned for a brief time until he was ousted in 1823. After taking his family to Livorno, Italy, and later England, Iturbide returned to Mexico in 1824, having misjudged the political climate as being welcoming to his return. He was arrested shortly after his arrival and then executed by firing squad. His remains would eventually be placed in a large urn, now housed in the chapel of San Felipe de Jesús in the Metropolitan Cathedral, alongside Iturbide's gilded throne.[4]

Empress Ana María, along with her nine children (she was then pregnant with her tenth child), was denied admittance into Mexico. They returned to exile, going northward first to New Orleans and eventually settling in Philadelphia, where the empress remained for the rest of her life. She died in 1861 and is buried in the church of Saint John the Evangelist in Center City. A pair of coronation portraits of the couple in the Philadelphia Museum of Art shows them in their Napoleonic-inspired imperial regalia, important artifacts from this astonishing moment in Mexican history. The coronation portraits came to the museum in 1892 as part of the remarkable collection of Mexican paintings from the colonial era formed by the engineer Robert Henry Lamborn (1836–1893), which is what put the Philadelphia Museum of Art on the map as an institution with interests in Spanish Colonial art, along with museums in Brooklyn, Denver, Los Angeles, and most recently Boston.

Born in Chester County, just west of Philadelphia, in 1836, Lamborn attended the University of Giessen, Germany, where he studied mining and metallurgy, eventually obtaining his Ph.D. He would later take further courses at the École des Mines in Paris. All of this would position him nicely to return in the 1860s to the United States, where the railroad expansion was at its full height. Lamborn amassed a sufficient fortune by 1881 to allow him to become the principal investor and designer in a new rail line from the city of El Paso to the Mexican capital. Over the next two years, during visits to Mexico City, he became a passionate collector and advocate for colonial Mexican art, acquiring for himself eighty works (fig. 19) by "known and unknown colonial artists" from "strange hiding places where they had rested since the secularization of the conventual establishments."[5] These were published in his 1891 text *Mexican Painting and Painters: A Brief Sketch of the Development of the Spanish School of Painting in Mexico*, one of the first books in English with a focus on Spanish Colonial art. In the book he outlines the history of current scholarship with a particularly alert sense of the introduction of European methods as well as the presence of indigenous artistic traditions. Summarizing his admiration for this period of Mexican art, Lamborn writes, "as I compare in my mind the canvases and panels I examined in Mexico with thousands which crowd the galleries of Italy, I am persuaded that students of history will in due season recognize the fact that the repositories of our neighboring republic contain ample material for a treatise which would be honored in the annals of art and form a memorable chapter in the record of human culture."[6] This volume, published two years before Lamborn's death, accompanied the display of his works in Memorial Hall, the huge pavilion intentionally designed to become a permanent art museum following its use as the art gallery for the Centennial Exhibition in 1876. Disregarding Lamborn's declaration of its place in a universal artistic hierarchy, the collection received less attention over time and was eventually placed in storage, until it was reactivated with fresh energy by Anne d'Harnoncourt (1943–2008), who exhibited works from the collection in a show entitled *Mexican Art* in 1968, alongside other Mexican works from the Museum's collection. In 1995, as the Museum reinstalled its European Galleries, Spanish Colonial art was given a permanent gallery space.

Although they narrowly missed each other's time at the Museum, in Edwin Atlee Barber (1851–1916), curator and later director of the Museum from 1901 to 1916, Lamborn would have been pleased to find a fellow enthusiast for Spanish Colonial art. Barber's passion for ceramics was on par with Lamborn's admiration for Mexican Colonial painting.[7] In part governed by the Museum's commitment to provide substantial examples of works from the past to inspire and instruct students of the applied arts in the present, Barber managed in his long career at the Museum to gather one of the richest collections of Mexican ceramics in the United States.

Hopes dating back to the 1900s of creating a new and larger space for the Philadelphia Museum of Art came into full reality in the 1920s, as its new "Greek temple" building opened its doors to the public in 1929, reflecting a new global ambition for collecting. Ironically, among the first victims of this new attention were Lamborn's colonial paintings and Barber's ceramics, which were left behind in Memorial Hall until its closure in the mid-1930s. This hiatus of interest in Spanish colonial material occurred at the same time as a sustained new engagement with later Latin American painting and culture in general, at a moment when Mexican art in particular was capturing attention throughout the United States. All of this was occurring as the ominous cloud of war descended on Europe and Asia.

Among the greatest contributors to this new exploration of Mexican art were two curators who would have a lasting impact on the Museum's future: Henry Clifford (1904–1974), who joined the Museum's staff in 1932, and Carl Zigrosser (1891–1975), who joined in 1941. Clifford was a wealthy collector of modern art, amassing a private collection that contained major works by the Douanier Rousseau and Pablo Picasso, among others. With houses in Florence and Mont Pèlerin-sur-Vevey, Switzerland, Clifford was an avid traveler and, not unlike many in his generation of Americans, was newly attracted to Mexico, where he bought a house in Jonacatepec in Morelos, south of Cuernavaca, in the late thirties. He became a close friend of the painter Juan Soriano (1920–2006) as well as the art dealer Inés Amor (1912–1980), who helped him to begin collecting contemporary Mexican works for his own collection, as well as for the Museum.[8] Clifford also aided and guided purchases for collectors in Philadelphia, encouraging them to eventually donate them to the Museum.

The culmination of Clifford's interest was the organization of *Mexican Art Today* in 1943, a huge exhibition containing 307 works ranging from easel paintings and portable murals to drawings, prints, and photographs.[9] Clifford, with the encouragement and counsel of Amor, embraced a far broader group of modern Mexican artists than had previously been seen in the United States, while at the same time including the works of household names such as Diego Rivera (1886–1957). For the exhibition Clifford borrowed two of the portable murals that Rivera had created for his 1931 retrospective at New York's Museum of Modern Art from the Weyhe Gallery. Both would be purchased by Mr. and Mrs.

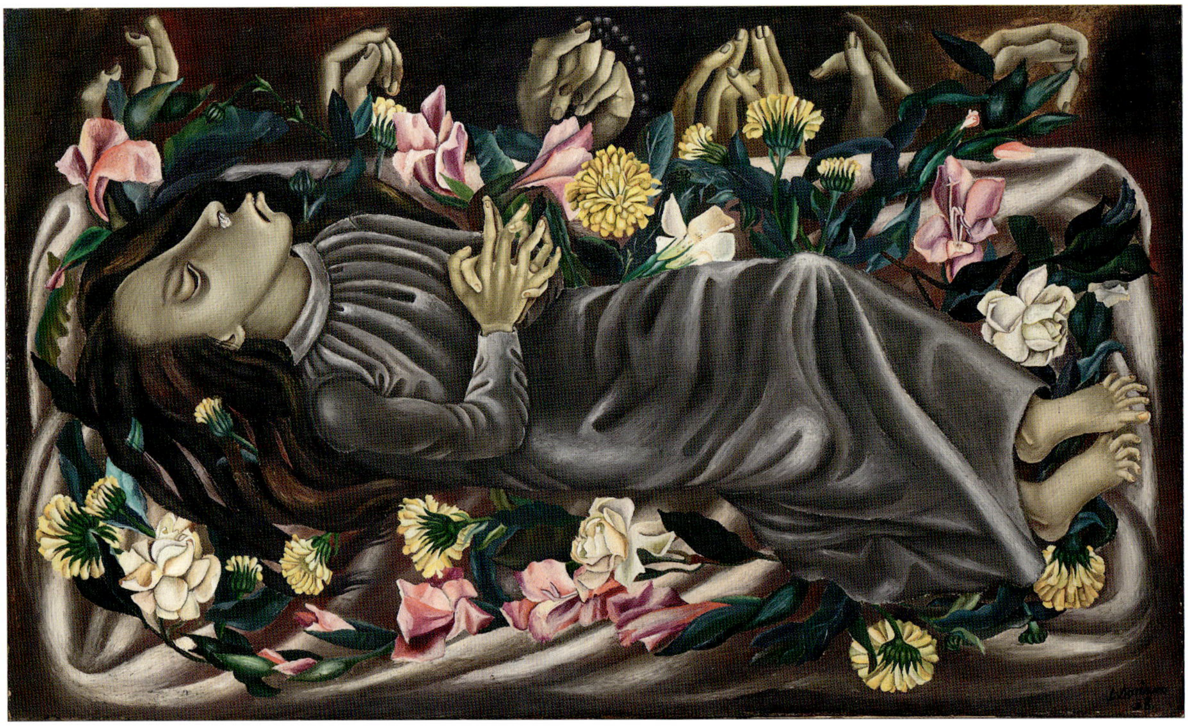

20. Juan Soriano (Mexican, 1920–2006), *The Dead Girl*, 1938. Oil on panel, 47 × 80 cm. Philadelphia Museum of Art. Copyright Fundación Juan Soriano y Marek Keller A.C. Courtesy of the Philadelphia Museum of Art.

Herbert Cameron Morris, who donated the works to the Museum that same year. In looking back through the catalogue for *Mexican Art Today*, it is interesting to see the large number of works that would eventually enter the Museum's collection. Clifford would himself give the eerie *The Dead Girl* by his friend Juan Soriano in 1947 (fig. 20), while his collaborator Inés Amor gave the striking painting *War* by David Alfaro Siqueiros (1896–1974) in 1945 (fig. 21).

Mexican Art Today was a great success, traveling throughout the United States with Clifford coordinating an ever-shifting progression of venues. Clifford's interests, however, were not limited to modern art. In 1944–45, he would organize, along with the Brooklyn Museum, a large monographic show on the celebrated Mexican painter José María Velasco (1840–1912) containing some 55 paintings and 110 drawings.[10] Done in collaboration with the Dirección General de Educación Extra-Escolar y Estética in Mexico, the bilingual catalogue features an opening essay by the Mexican writer and intellectual Carlos Pellicer (1897–1977), nimbly translated by Clifford's wife Esther Rowland Clifford, who also translated the essay by the writer Luis Cardoza y Aragón in the catalogue for *Mexican Art Today*.

In 1941, the Museum's director, Fiske Kimball, hired Carl Zigrosser as the head of the print department. Zigrosser was then working as a print specialist at the Weyhe Gallery, which he had joined in 1919, when it had been a thriving bookstore. How

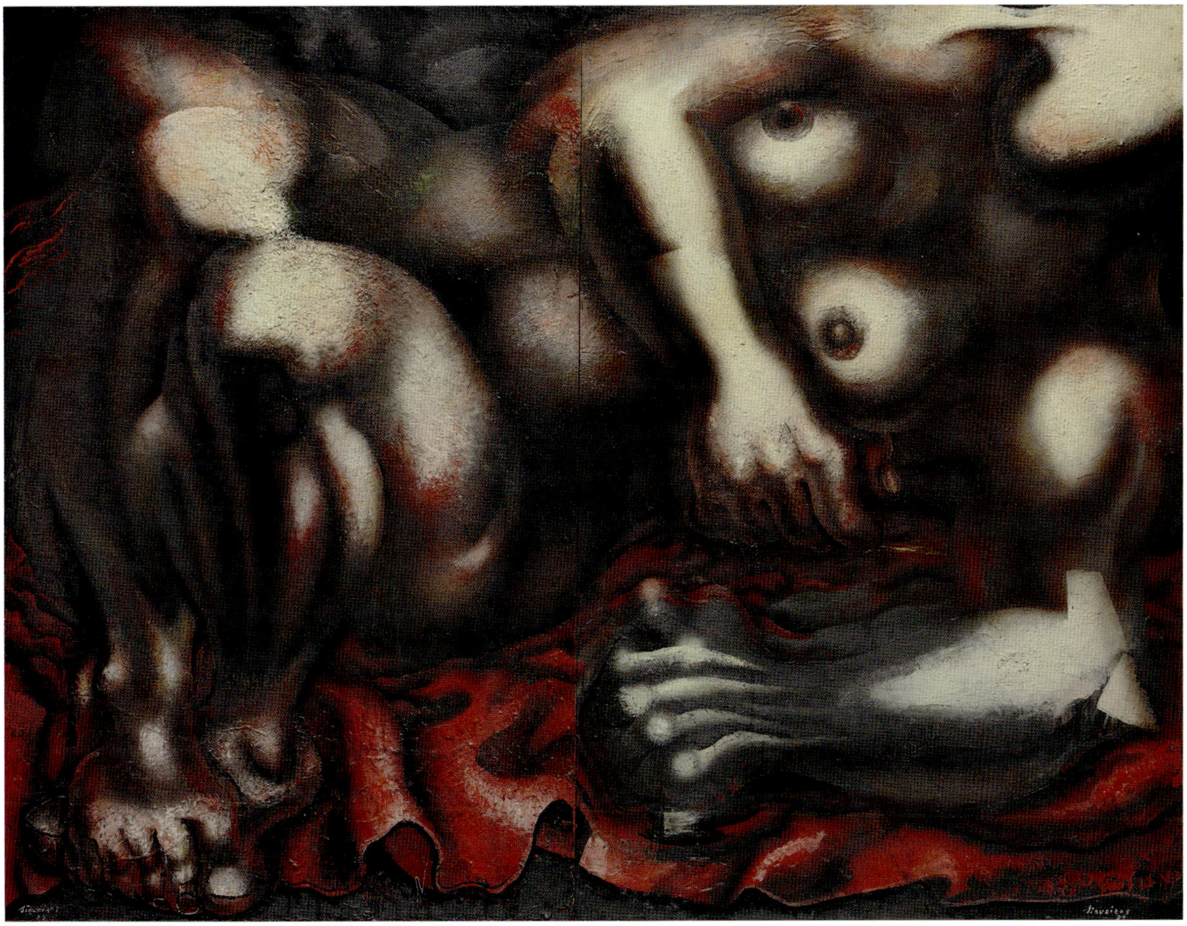

21. David Alfaro Siqueiros (Mexican, 1896–1974), *War*, 1939. Duco on two panels, 123.5 × 162.2 cm. Philadelphia Museum of Art. © 2016 Artists Rights Society (ARS), New York / SOMAAP, Mexico City. Courtesy of the Philadelphia Museum of Art.

much Kimball's decision was guided by Clifford's activities in Mexican art is unclear, but Zigrosser's passion for Mexican art would set the museum on the path to having one of the largest collections of modern Mexican prints in the United States.[11] The collection was recently featured in the masterful exhibition *Mexico and Modern Printmaking: A Revolution in the Graphic Arts, 1920–1950* (2006–7), organized by John Ittmann.[12]

While the Museum at the University of Pennsylvania has long had a superb collection of Pre-Columbian art from throughout Latin America, a much smaller, yet still significant group of works arrived at the Philadelphia Museum of Art in 1950 as part of the collection of Louise (1879–1953) and Walter (1878–1954) Arensberg.[13] Although far better known for their collecting of modern French painting or sculptures by Constantin Brancusi (1876–1957), the Arensbergs peppered their home with works from ancient Mexico. With the arrival of Anne d'Harnoncourt in the late 1960s, bringing with her a great love of Mexican art inherited from her father, René (who lived in Mexico between 1926 and 1933, serving as a dealer and curator of Mexican art before ultimately becoming director of MoMA in 1949), selections of these works were once again integrated with the Museum's display of the Arensbergs' modern art collection.

D'Harnoncourt's exhibition of Mexican art in 1968 marked the beginning of a renewed attention to Latin American art at the Museum, as evidenced by exhibitions such as the retrospective of Diego Rivera's work in 1986 or that of Tina Modotti's (1896–1942) photographs in 1995. This interest would culminate in one of the Museum's most ambitious exhibitions to date, *The Arts in Latin America, 1492–1820*, a sweeping look at art during the colonial era throughout Latin America.[14] This exhibition also marked the beginning of new Pan-American institutional collaborations, with the show traveling first to the Antiguo Colegio de San Ildefonso in Mexico City and later the Los Angeles County Museum of Art.

It was during the making of that show, with much traveling and meeting of new colleagues, that our institution had the fortune to befriend Roberta and Richard Huber. Their collection of primarily Andean paintings and silver, as well as ivories from the Spanish and Portuguese colonies in Asia, became the focus of an exhibition in 2013 entitled *Journeys to New Worlds: Spanish and Portuguese Colonial Art in the Roberta and Richard Huber Collection*.[15] A series of gifts and promised gifts from the Hubers' collection ensures the development of the Museum's South American holdings, creating a balance with the existing collections of Mexican art from the same period (fig. 22).

As the collection grows through gifts like those of the Hubers, it has been aided in recent years by important individual acquisitions, such as *Saint Francis Defeats the Antichrist*, from a series of canvases on the life of Saint Francis of Assisi by the Mexican master Cristóbal de Villalpando (ca. 1649–1714; fig. 23).[16] The Museum purchased its first work from the Spanish colonies in the Caribbean, a refined painting on panel of *The Divine Shepherdess* by the Puerto Rican artist José Campeche (1751–1809).[17] Most recently, at the time of this publication, the purchase of a late seventeenth-century *enconchado* (painting with mother-of-pearl inlay) of *San Diego de Alcalá* connects the Museum's Spanish Colonial works to artistic traditions in Europe and Asia.

It is also worth noting that in recent decades the Museum has renewed its interest in Latin American contemporary art, acquiring such iconic works as Gabriel Orozco's (b. 1962) painted skull *Black Kites* (1997).[18] Or further afield, a joint acquisition with The Art Institute of Chicago of Víctor Grippo's (1936–2002) *Analogy I (2nd version)* (1970–77), an installation that features a long table draped in white cloth and laden with Andean potatoes wired with electrodes that power a string of lightbulbs with electrochemical energy.[19]

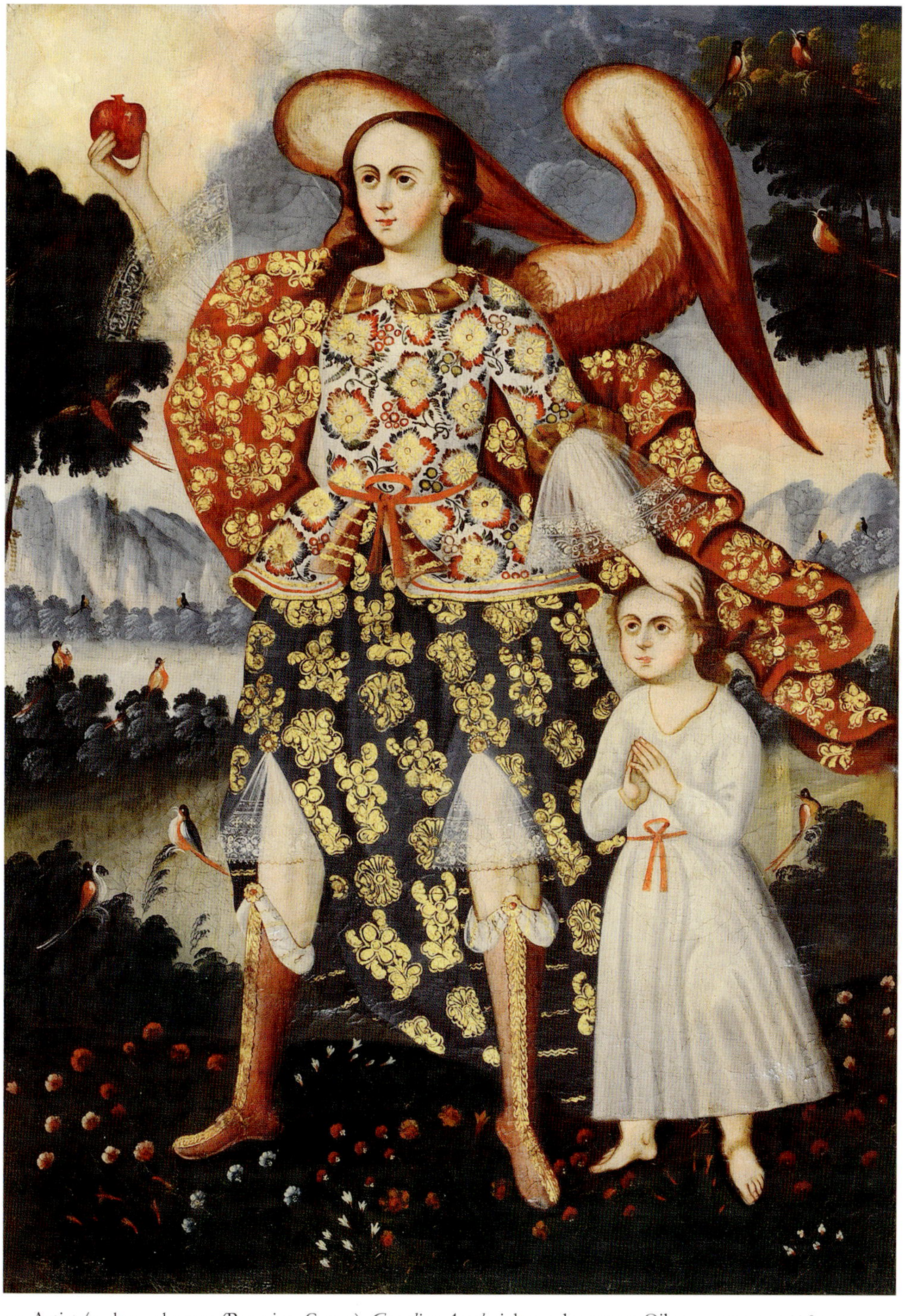

22. Artist/maker unknown (Peruvian, Cuzco), *Guardian Angel*, eighteenth century. Oil on canvas, 122 × 85 cm. Philadelphia Museum of Art. Courtesy of the Philadelphia Museum of Art.

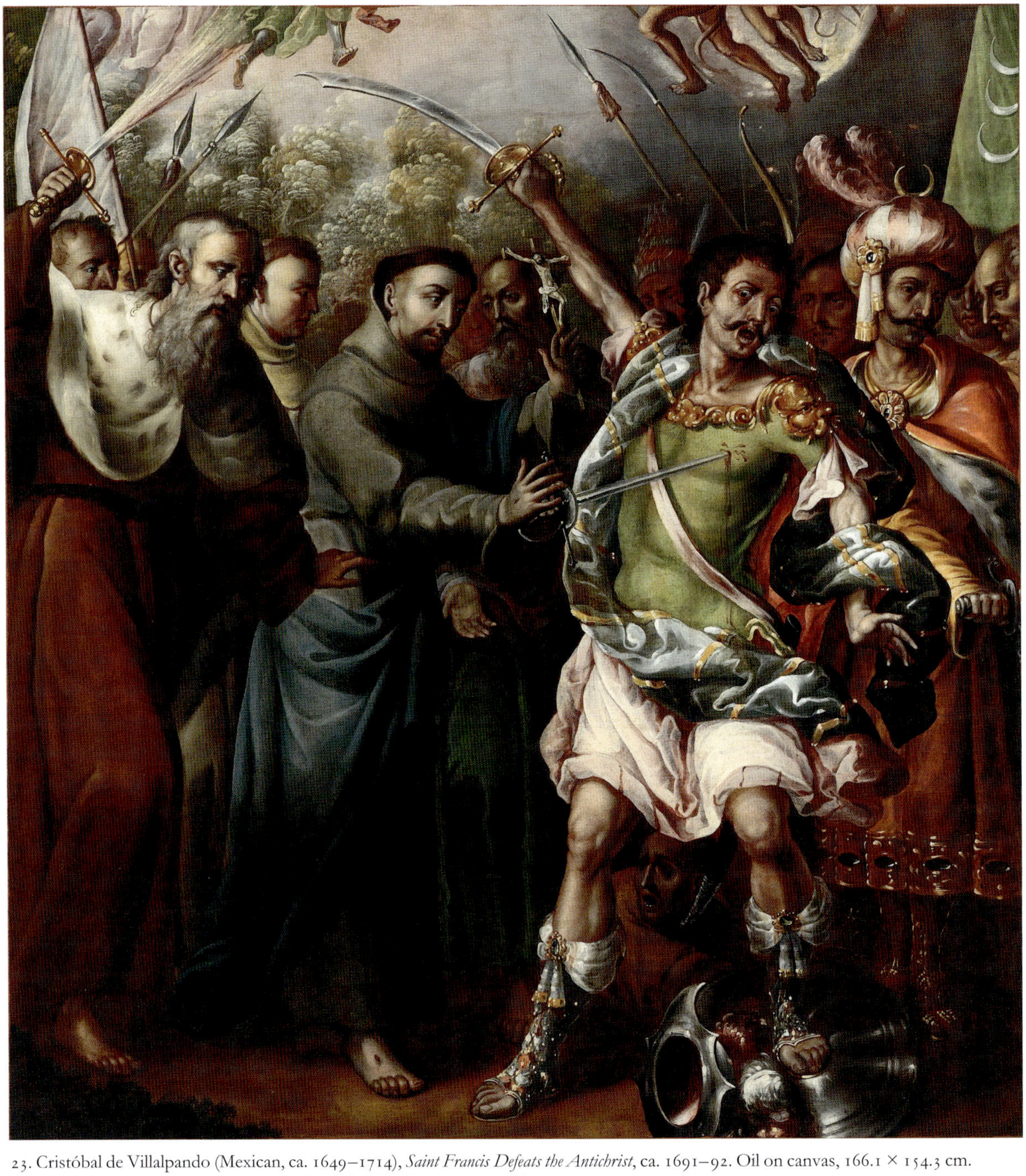

23. Cristóbal de Villalpando (Mexican, ca. 1649–1714), *Saint Francis Defeats the Antichrist*, ca. 1691–92. Oil on canvas, 166.1 × 154.3 cm. Philadelphia Museum of Art. Courtesy of the Philadelphia Museum of Art.

As is often the case, the most innovative ideas build on those of the past, which is the case with the Museum's recent exhibition *Paint the Revolution: Mexican Modernism, 1910–1950*, which opened in the fall of 2016, a major reassessment of modern Mexican art in the spirit of Clifford's 1943 exhibition. Organized in partnership with the Museo del Palacio de Bellas Artes, it built on the Museum's modern collections that Clifford so adeptly fostered and also featured newly acquired works, such as a large preparatory drawing for the sets and costumes of the ballet *H.P. (Horsepower)* by Diego Rivera. With music by the Mexican composer Carlos Chávez (1899–1978) and conducted by Leopold Stokowski (1882–1977), the ballet was performed in 1932 by the Philadelphia Grand Opera Company with the Philadelphia Orchestra, the only known performance of the complete work using Rivera's designs.

CHAPTER 4

Cargadores

Collecting Rivera, Mexican Modernism, and Bearing the Burdens of Historiography

Anna Indych-López

24. Diego Rivera (Mexican, 1886–1957), *The Flower Carrier*, 1935. Oil and tempera on Masonite, 121.92 × 121.29 cm. San Francisco Museum of Modern Art. © 2016 Banco de México Diego Rivera & Frida Kahlo Museums Trust, Mexico, D.F. / Artists Rights Society (ARS), New York.

U.S. interest in Latin American visual culture is part of a long and shifting geographical, temporal, and sociocultural trajectory. While vital, these are fluid, fluctuating, and even contested accounts that, like any historiographic endeavor, allow us to tease out the ways in which the particularities of constructed narratives result from historical tensions and lead to interpretative challenges. Such analyses become all the more critical in the field of Latin American art, which is often driven by the vicissitudes of the marketplace and in which the most visibly advanced and influential knowledge is produced in the curatorial rather than the academic disciplines. Acknowledging this view, I seek to challenge any monolithic understanding of the heterogeneous artistic production of art made in the Americas through a case study of its more well-known arbiters: Diego Rivera (1886–1957) and the example of Mexican Muralism.

In *Muralism Without Walls: Rivera, Orozco, and Siqueiros in the United States, 1927–1940*, I analyzed the circulation of the Mexican Muralists' imagery in the United States through exhibition culture and mediated formats.[1] This collection of essays, which considers the practices of collecting colonial and modern Latin American art in the United States, gives me the opportunity to reflect back on this research to continue my consideration of what has now become a so-called Mexican canon within the broader study of modern Latin American art. Looking to amplify the New York focus of my previous work by incorporating the context of California, I also concentrate here mostly on private collecting and gallery networks as opposed to the better-known institutional histories such as the Museum of Modern Art (MoMA)'s involvement with Latin American art (see the essays by Basilio and Solomons in this volume).

I begin by considering a single image, Diego Rivera's *The Flower Carrier* (1935; fig. 24), a very well-known and oft-reproduced painting that San

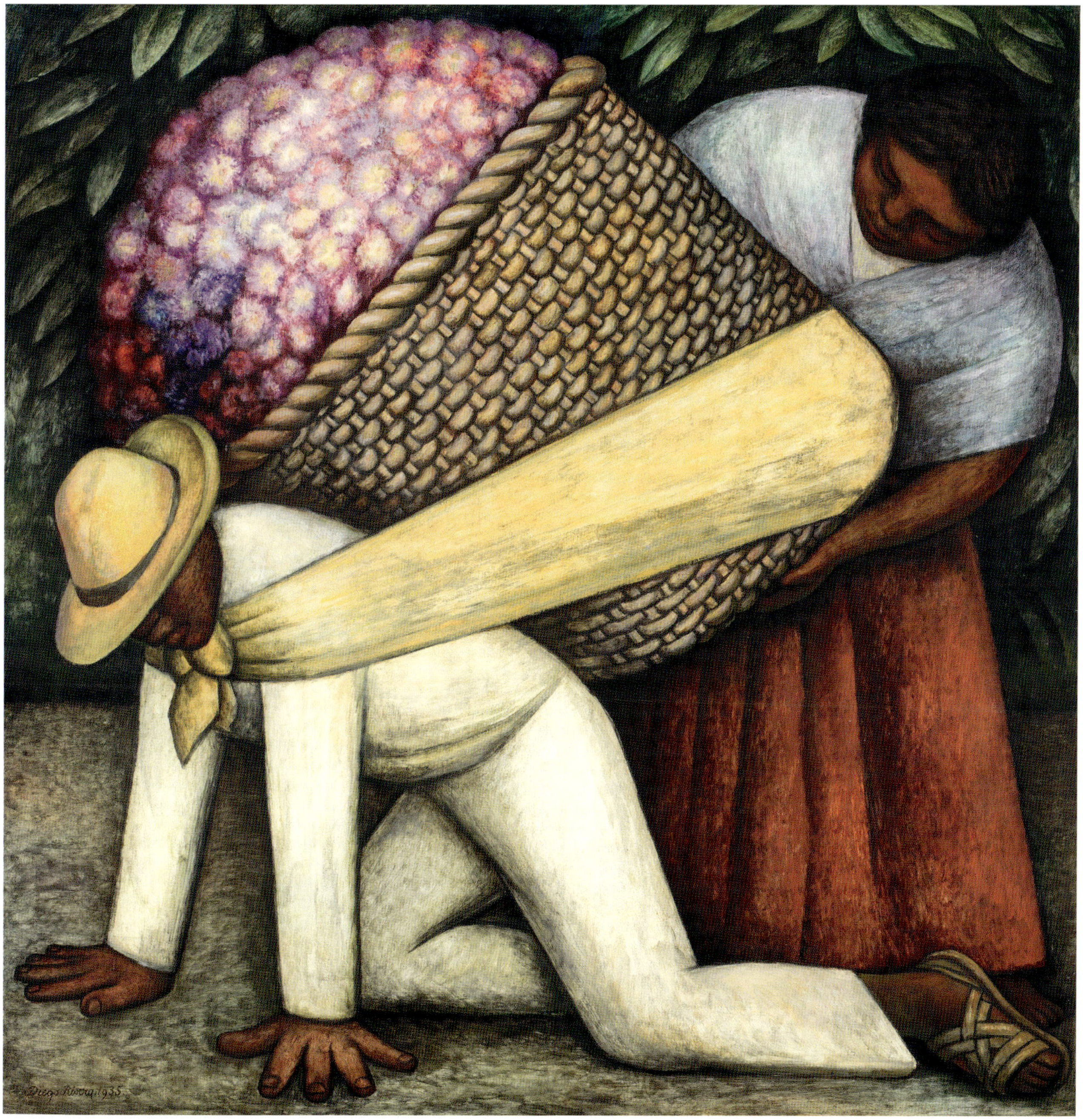
Diego Rivera 1935

Francisco art patron Albert Bender (1866–1941) commissioned specifically for donation to the San Francisco Museum of Modern Art (SFMOMA) in 1935, almost ten years after the collector first began corresponding with the Mexican muralist.[2] Although overshadowed by the collecting practices of perhaps more renowned figures such as Abigail (1874–1948) and Nelson (1908–1979) Rockefeller, Bender was a prominent collector of Mexican art in California and a critical benefactor of SFMOMA who would eventually donate over eleven hundred works to the first museum of modern art on the West Coast. His initial gift of thirty-six works, including Rivera's *The Flower Carrier*, established the initial core of the permanent collection. Significantly, Bender was one of Rivera's first U.S. patrons and played a major role in bringing the muralist to the United States and in securing his first U.S. mural commissions.[3] To be sure, although Bender was most interested in monumental public wall painting and especially the Mexican example, rather than any of the murals Rivera produced in the Bay Area, the most visible expression of his legacy as a collector of Mexican art in the 1920s and 1930s remains *The Flower Carrier*. The somewhat large-scale painting has been reproduced in many major U.S. catalogues and monographs, and its broad circulation in popular culture has turned it into an icon of Mexican art. It is a lens through which we can gauge the salient issues that arise in the collection of Mexican art in the 1930s and canon formation within Latin American art as a whole.

At first glance, *The Flower Carrier* has the trappings of those "folkloric" elements—peasants, pretty flowers—that Rivera often played up in his work to cultivate U.S. patrons seeking seemingly picturesque images. It should be noted that while José Clemente Orozco (1883–1949) and David Alfaro Siqueiros (1896–1974) were extremely wary of the association of their work with the folkloric, they, like Rivera, also altered their imagery and their practice to accommodate new audiences and markets. Artists' own agencies need to be considered in addition to institutional or market mandates in these constructed narratives.

Indeed, in the 1940s Rivera churned out a genre of paintings related to *The Flower Carrier*: copious representations of *female* calla lily vendors posed before impossibly larger-than-life-sized flowers (fig. 25). In all of these works, Rivera derived the contorted poses of the female figures from Aztec stone sculptures, integrating the abstraction and geometric forms found in Pre-Columbian figural conventions into a modern idiom.[4] In his murals, the humble, submissive pose often served as a cipher to indicate colonial or oppressed subject positions, as in a detail from the *Market Scene* panel at the Palacio Cortés cycle in Cuernavaca where an Indian woman offers tribute to a Spanish conquistador. Yet as Rivera continued to paint variations on this theme throughout the decade, the depictions became increasingly eroticized and therefore depoliticized. Feeding a market for noncontroversial, nondidactic "Mexican" imagery, Rivera conflated representations of Mexican peasantry and the indigenous with the fecundity of nature, generating images of excess that have had a long-lasting impact on the perceptions and expectations of Mexican modernism. Yet, while the expectation for the folkloric and Rivera's concomitant assembly-line production are historical realities with which we need to grapple, they do not represent the totality of Rivera's practice, nor are they representative of Mexican modernism as a whole, and therefore have often eclipsed other interpretative models and discourses.

In terms of Bender's interests and the ways in which they intersected with Rivera's practice, the collector played a role in revitalizing the Bay Area art scene and in removing the practice of public wall painting from conservative, academic, and decorative models to more modern concepts of integration. Bender's tastes were not exactly vanguard or progressive, but with his patronage and collecting

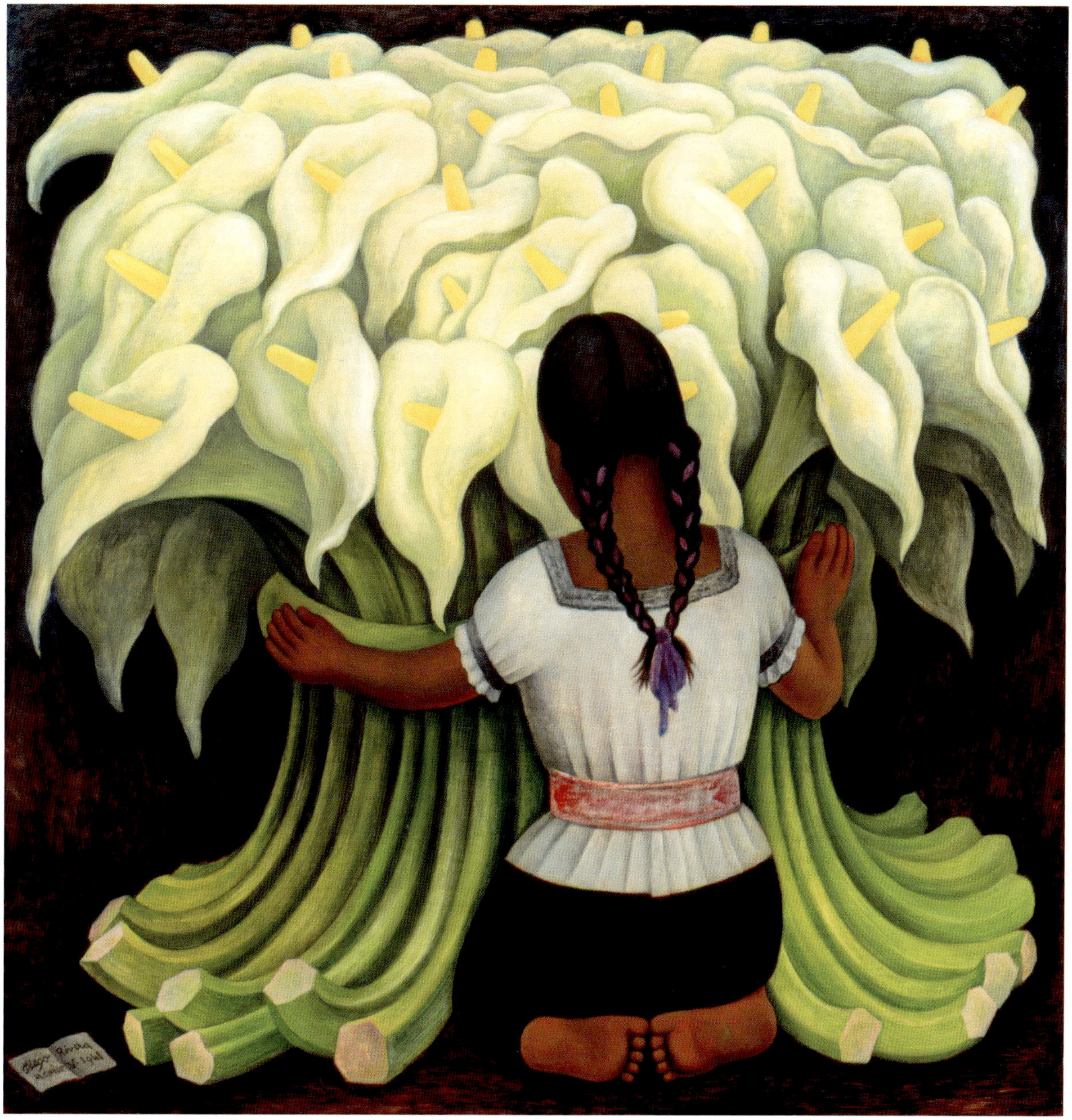

25. Diego Rivera (Mexican, 1886–1957), *The Flower Vendor (Girl with Lilies)*, 1941. Oil on Masonite, 121.9 × 121.9 cm. Pasadena, Norton Simon Museum. © 2016 Banco de México Diego Rivera & Frida Kahlo Museums Trust, Mexico, D.F. / Artists Rights Society (ARS), New York.

practices he helped transform California modernism and significantly looked to Mexico as *the* example forward. In the late 1920s and '30s, as Mexican Muralism became increasingly well known internationally and garnered cultural prestige, its particular staging of the local and the vernacular in the public sphere, combined with its international pedigree and stylistic mixing, made it au courant. Bender, with the key mediation of U.S. artists who had worked with Rivera as assistants in Mexico, turned directly to the Mexican muralist for help with fomenting a new public art movement in the United States. The California collector was by no means left-leaning or even socially engaged, yet works by Rivera associated with Bender, specifically *The Flower Carrier*, are complicated representations of Mexican Muralism that defy the simplistic categorizations often assigned to it and veer away from the crowd-pleasing works others collected. To be sure, Bender's collection included works with controversial and highly politicized imagery, such as Siqueiros's sketch of warriors, part of the Bender Collection at SFMOMA. A study for *América Tropical*, it represents the section of the Mexican artist's mural in downtown Los Angeles that was immediately censored in the 1930s.

In opposition to Rivera's 1940s flower paintings, *The Flower Carrier* is decidedly a painting about labor. Hands splayed out on the floor under the weight of the giant basket held in place by the taut cloth wrapped around his body, the laborer assumes a prone position as a dark-skinned female peasant helps him lift the heavy bundle onto his back. The distilled and abstracted forms of the painting create a graphic and composed simplicity, while the figures completely fill the composition and become monumental—signature traits of Rivera's style, which combined historical and avant-garde aesthetics to reflect Mexican modernity.

The painting no doubt projects an image of a timeless, rural, antimodern Mexico conceivably construed by some as "quaint." Yet it is also in line with scores of related images Rivera produced of *cargadores* (burden carriers or carriers of bundles). Like the figures in the flower paintings, these representations of laborers are based on Pre-Columbian sculptures, such as the ceramic *cargador* from Nayarit (600–900 C.E.) from the Museo Anahuacalli, which houses Rivera's collection of almost 59,400 Pre-Columbian objects.[5] Rivera's images of pathos simultaneously monumentalize indigenous labor in order to ennoble it and critique its concomitant bodily subjugation and oppression through a complex set of associations. The drawings and watercolors on the theme of the *cargador* are either ambiguous in terms of the setting or take place in decidedly urban streets where the vendors would sell their wares. Irrespective of setting, however, these images tackle a theme imbricated in the modernization of the nation, as documented by photo postcards with similar imagery (fig. 26), which were interpretations of the "tipos" tradition and *costumbrismo*.[6] Rivera was no doubt highly aware of these visual cultural precedents and appropriated them strategically. The muralist's works allegorize the rural peasants who migrated and inundated the capital in the 1930s and who formed an integral part of the process of transforming it from an essentially agrarian locale into a sprawling metropolis. Moving forward in time, an artist like Francis Alÿs (b. 1959) clearly intersects with, reconfigures, and updates this tradition of depicting the *cargador* in his *Ambulantes* series: photographs of street vendors and deliverymen pushing, pulling, and carrying their merchandise through the streets of Mexico City.

Both Rivera's flower vendor and burden carrier scenes have their source imagery in the artist's murals at the Ministry of Public Education from the early 1920s. Unlike the paintings and drawings that seek to monumentalize, or universalize, the laboring classes, the murals contextualize the labor of the *cargadores* within very specific local circumstances, such as the economic context of the *tianguis* (local market). At the Ministry of Public Education, French-born muralist Jean Charlot (1898–1979), who was working as one of Rivera's assistants, also depicted *cargadores*, yet in contrast even to Rivera's scenes, Charlot uses figural and compositional distortion to make more evident the theme of backbreaking labor.

The Flower Carrier is a hybrid image based on the series of urban *cargadores*, but related more to the context and social rituals of Santa Anita, where such flower vendors would have been prominent.[7] The small village on the outskirts of the capital, with its characteristic canals, was used to transport produce to the center and was known for its flower festival on the Friday before Palm Sunday, in which all the social classes participated. As James Oles has explicated, Rivera's 1923–24 mural on the theme of Santa Anita, *Friday of Sorrows on the Canal at Santa Anita*, located in the Court of Fiestas at the Ministry of Public Education, reveals the ways in which the locale had already become a tourist attraction in the 1920s, as evidenced by the urban flapper included among the masses.[8] Rivera's inclusion of the cosmopolitan figure also underscores the ways in which the parameters of Mexico City were expanding to include previously "remote" areas. The condensed version of the theme, *Flower Day* (1925), which Rivera had painted for the *First Pan-American Exhibition of Oil Paintings* at the Los Angeles Museum of History, Science, and Art (LACMA's parent institution) and which had won a prize, includes only indigenous figures and eschews the complex issues of modernization and urbanization engaged by the mural version. *The Flower Carrier* and the series of *cargador* images reflect the ways in which artists such as Rivera created surrogates for the murals for distribution in the United States and often accommodated their imagery for these audiences.[9]

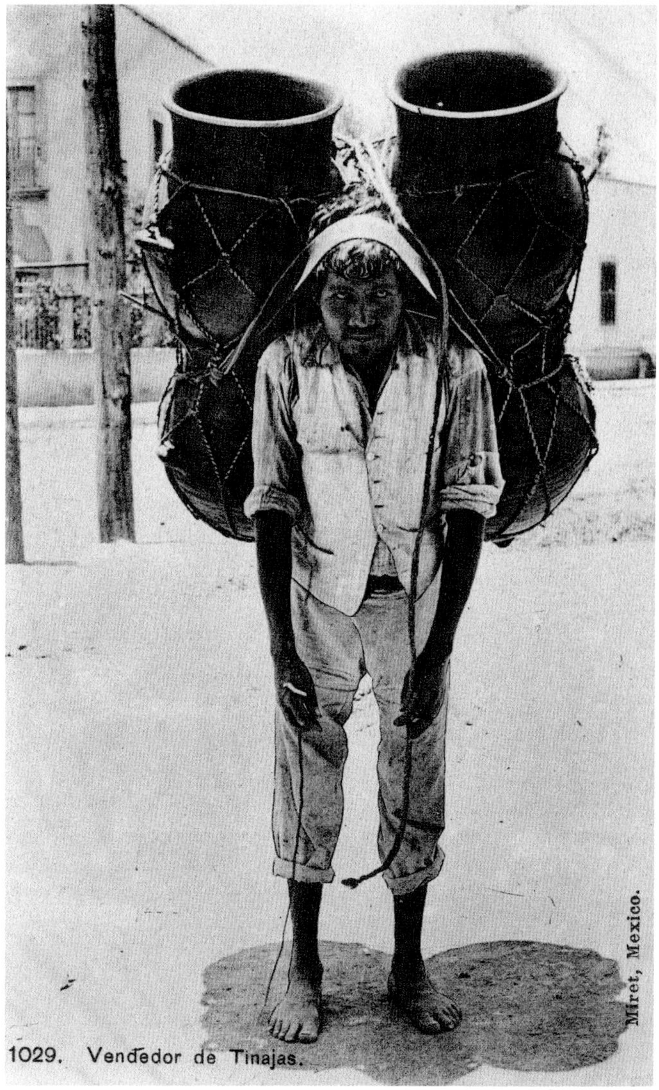

26. Unknown photographer, *Vendedor de tinajas*, early twentieth century. Photo postcard. Angel López Collection.

Yet paintings such as *The Flower Carrier* also served as a counterpoint to the images of industrial and heroic labor that circulated in the United States in the 1930s, and with which Rivera would have been intimately familiar by 1935. Rivera provocatively "Mexicanized" what many viewers would have recognized as an expanding form of communist imagery. Furthermore, by focusing on "subjugated" rather than "heroic" workers, his imagery brought to the fore the unique colonial conditions and racial tensions that informed his vision of alienated labor.

Albert Bender most likely remained unaware of or perhaps did not care for these nuances. Indeed, his support of Rivera was at best ambiguous at first precisely because of the artist's radical politics and associations, and it was only after the collector received confirmation that other prominent cultural figures in the United States were also courting the muralist that he followed suit. Yet his support of Rivera dovetailed with several significant currents. In terms of style, *The Flower Carrier* and all of its precedents are a heady mix of figuration, modern sensibilities—including geometric forms and flattened perspectives—and the historically rooted abstraction found in Mexico's pre-Columbian past, combined into a singular and recognizable socially engaged modern realism. Modern, yet not too modernist; concerned with forging a sense of the local, yet internationalist in terms of its sources and promotion, Rivera's work and the modern art of Mexico provided an American model of regional vanguardism and therefore appealed to a wide array of cultural promoters.

New York–based gallerists, collectors, and promoters involved in one way or another with modern Mexican art, such as Juliana Force (1876–1948), Edith Halpert (1900–1970), and Lincoln Kirstein (1907–1996), sought to promote their own sense of cultural identity and modern art as distinct from European constructs. For these cultural brokers, who also collected U.S. folk art, the Mexican example represented a shared history and a collective interest in forging an autochthonous modern art distinct from Europe. Finding a way to stage and make the local was an international concern at the time. Bender, with his determination to build a local scene in San Francisco, was certainly swept up in this moment as well. Significantly, such images also resonated with staunchly leftist critics such as Elizabeth McCausland (1899–1965), Lewis Mumford (1895–1990), and Anita Brenner (1905–1974), who looked to the monumental public art of Mexico as a model of radically aligned vanguardism. For them, Mexican art represented the viability of Realism as a broader aesthetic and social model. The exhibition culture and collecting practices of the 1930s reveal that as the decade progressed, the association between radical politics and modern Mexican art became increasingly institutionalized.

The afterlife of *The Flower Carrier* in the 1940s and early 1950s bears out this history and alliance. As film historian Frank Krutnik has revealed, at least five different film noirs of the late 1940s prominently featured a small-scale reproduction of *this* painting as an artistic adornment for the bourgeois home (fig. 27).[10] Significantly, the Hollywood filmmakers did not choose the better-known *Flower Day*, Rivera's earliest depiction of a calla lily vendor and the first major painting to enter a public collection in the United States in 1925. While it remains unclear exactly who was responsible for selecting Rivera's *The Flower Carrier*, its strategic appearance in films produced by different companies suggests that it was not merely a recycled prop.[11] Moreover, as Krutnik argues, the prominence of *The Flower Carrier* in particular types of scenes reveals a strategic and discursive deployment of Mexican art and therefore provides us with further insights into the distinct ends Mexican Realism served.

Indeed, the connections between Hollywood and Mexican art are significant, and members of the

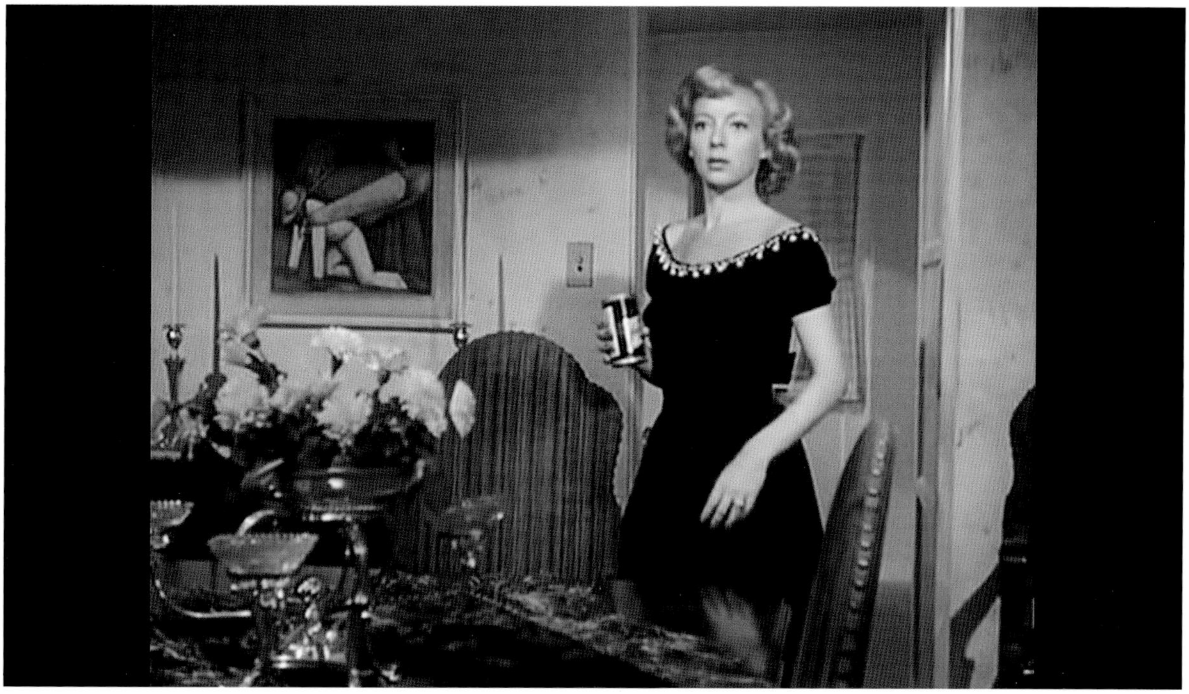

27. Film still with Diego Rivera's *The Flower Carrier* in the background. *The Prowler*, 1951. Directed by Joseph Losey, produced by Horizon Pictures, distributed by United Artists.

film community became noteworthy patrons and collectors. While Hollywood's interest in Mexican art had many entry points and could be characterized as multivalent, Krutnik analyzed the ways in which the makers of these films mobilized Rivera's *The Flower Carrier* as a cipher to denote the defiant morality of the characters that collected them and to suggest political subversion. Rather than stand in as a form of exoticism, folkloric appeal, or mere bourgeois decoration, by the late 1940s modern Mexican art operated as a "coded signifier of left wing political affiliation" in the midst of blacklist-era Hollywood.[12] The films, all released between 1947 and 1951, coincide directly with the beginnings of McCarthyism, the Red Scare, and the Hollywood blacklist. Within this context, filmmakers strategically called upon modern Mexican art, specifically the work of Rivera, as a mechanism for communicating leftist sympathies tied directly to cultural practice. The roots of this understanding of modern Mexican art lie with the exhibiting and collecting practices of the 1930s.

Where would collectors go to buy modern Mexican art in the 1930s? In the 1920s, collectors like Bender directly engaged with artists such as Rivera. Artists were easily accessible, their studios were open to visitors, and few of them had handlers.[13] Things changed dramatically in the 1930s, when several promoters, among them Frances Flynn Paine and Alma Reed (1889–1966), competed to manage artists such as Rivera and José Clemente Orozco. Collectors traveled to Mexico easily, and U.S. artists often served as conduits in transnational exchanges. In the 1930s, there was no formalized, institutional framework for the private acquisition of art within Mexico itself. Artists depended on state, or rather, municipal sponsorship as well as income from work sold in the United States. The 1930s also presented unique political and economic challenges—the aftermath of the stock market crash, the more conservative Calles regime in Mexico, and the nationalization of oil by Cardenas in 1937—all of which impacted the art market in distinct ways.

The first major commercial gallery in Mexico, founded by Carolina and Inés Amor as the Galería de Arte Mexicano, was not founded until 1935, but once it opened it virtually controlled the market and all subsequent promotion of Mexican art in the United States.[14] The majority of their clientele were U.S. patrons. Unofficial, alternative, and mostly artist-run venues for the display of art also existed in 1920s Mexico City, such as Carlos Merida's Galería de Arte Moderno[15] and the Estridentistas' Café de Nadie, but prior to the Galería de Arte Mexicano, collectors, when not dealing directly with artists, turned primarily to book dealers and a network of antique and curio dealers. The Alberto Misrachi Gallery, for example, began as a bookstore in front of the Palacio de Bellas Artes in 1933 and only later moved to the Zona Rosa as a full-fledged gallery.

The lack of a national art market for the majority of the decade meant not only that Mexican artists depended on U.S. patrons for income, but also that U.S. collectors and institutions played major roles in shaping the course of Mexican modern art. When Mexican collectors entered the fray in subsequent decades, they often were already too late to acquire important or representative works from artists. Even Alvar Carrillo Gil (1898–1974), who amassed the most important private collection of works by the artists who would be called the four great masters—Rivera, Orozco, Siqueiros, and Rufino Tamayo (1899–1991)—had trouble merely finding works due to a consolidated art market and the death of artists like Orozco. As Ana Garduño revealed in her study of Carrillo Gil, the collector stated, for example, that in the 1950s "Orozco's works are practically out of the market; rarely am I made aware of the availability of an important work. Furthermore, the prices they have fetched are too high to make it possible to acquire them."[16] Given that Orozco was probably the least successful of the four in terms of securing a presence in the U.S. market, the collector's frustrations provide an indication of the vast changes in the accessibility and availability of modern Mexican art over two decades.

In the United States, Mexican artist Marius de Zayas (1880–1961) was a pioneer in exhibiting Rivera's Cubist-era paintings with Pre-Columbian objects at his Modern Gallery in 1916. The Whitney Studio Club, the Downtown Gallery, and C. W. Kraushaar Galleries were all venues that showed work by the muralists at an early juncture. The Weyhe Gallery was another major source that specialized in prints and therefore approximated the Mexico City model of the bookstore. Modern Mexican artists were not isolated by gallery owners and promoters in 1930s New York, but regularly participated in internationally oriented venues such as the Valentine and Julien Levy Galleries; their works formed an integral part of the circuit of international modernisms at the time. Even Alma Reed's Delphic Studios Gallery, which was often devoted to the work of Orozco, had a broad mission.

In California, a literary-oriented clientele gathered at the exhibits at Jack Zeitlin's bookshop in downtown Los Angeles, while the Stendahl Ambassador Gallery counted George Gershwin, Edward G. Robinson, and Vincent Price as patrons.[17] The Hollywood film community, who became significant patrons of Mexican art, particularly appreciated the work of transplanted Mexican artist Alfredo Ramos Martínez (1871–1946). His paintings of harmonious indigenous Mexicans appealed to his U.S. clients, a group that included screenwriter Jo Swerling;

directors Dudley Murphy, Alfred Hitchcock, and John Huston; and actors Corinne Griffith, Charles Laughton, and Beulah Bondi.[18] Significantly, Albert Bender's SFMOMA collection included one of Ramos Martínez's rare politicized oil-on-canvas paintings, in which he depicted a mass of armed Zapatista revolutionaries.

Examining in more depth the collecting practices of the 1930s allows a reconsideration of the notion of canon formation and interpretative models moving forward. To be sure, proximity, a shared border, economic codependencies, and intertwined colonial histories have made Mexico an obvious point of reference and object of study in the early twentieth century and beyond. Those political expediencies, however, also infiltrated later assessments of artistic practices and the field itself. Pioneers of Mexican art history in the United States, such as Shifra Goldman (1926–2011), delved into the collecting practices of major patrons such as the Rockefeller family to construct by now well-known arguments about the complicity of U.S. cultural policies with geopolitical concerns and economic interests. In the case of the Rockefellers, many scholars have shed light on the connections between Standard Oil, Mexico's nationalization of subsoil rights in 1937, and increased interest in and bilateral promotion of modern Mexican art later in the century with the onslaught of NAFTA.[19] This valuable scholarly and analytical work was groundbreaking and continues to be a significant interpretative model. But others have sought to complement and nuance this line of interpretation. The well-documented appropriation of Latin American, and specifically Mexican, art for political purposes has eclipsed and overdetermined discussions of Mexican modernism. It has also obscured a systematic assessment of the aesthetic practices and networks developed between the two countries and of the cultural valence of socially engaged modernism of the decade. Although political expediencies unquestionably determined the collecting practices of a variety of individuals and institutions, by scrutinizing reception, exhibition culture, the artists' motives, and the works themselves, we can determine that cultural diplomacy and institutional critique are nonetheless often incomplete interpretative frameworks.

While there is no doubt that collectors and promoters in the United States at times used Mexican art as a diplomatic tool, as U.S. viewers grew increasingly aware of socially engaged Mexican art, the task of depoliticizing it, for example, became increasingly more difficult and less feasible.[20] It has therefore become necessary to challenge the assumptions about the hegemony of U.S. cultural institutions and their actual ability to use Mexican culture to serve ideological and political interests in order to reassess the politics and aesthetics of Latin American modernisms. Looking beyond the framework of diplomatic relations helps us to understand more clearly that Mexican art operated within heterogeneous discourses and often signified what today have become unexpected associations.

For example, in 1933 a portfolio of color reproductions of Rivera's mural work from Mexico inaugurated the new MoMA architecture room (fig. 28), which was "installed and decorated as an example of modern interior architecture under the supervision of Philip Johnson [1906–2005]."[21] Replete with furniture designed by Le Corbusier (1887–1965), Pierre Jeanneret (1896–1967, Le Corbusier's less famous cousin), and Charlotte Perriand (1903–1999), and with one wall covered by navy blue raw silk curtains, the room surprises contemporary eyes with its marriage of modernist interior design with the pictorial Indigenism of Rivera's Mexican murals. Such installations remind us that the stylized and abstracted shapes, distilled forms, and shallow spaces of Rivera's compositions not only reverberated with the geometric sensibilities of European modernisms but also, more importantly, were part and parcel of the transforma-

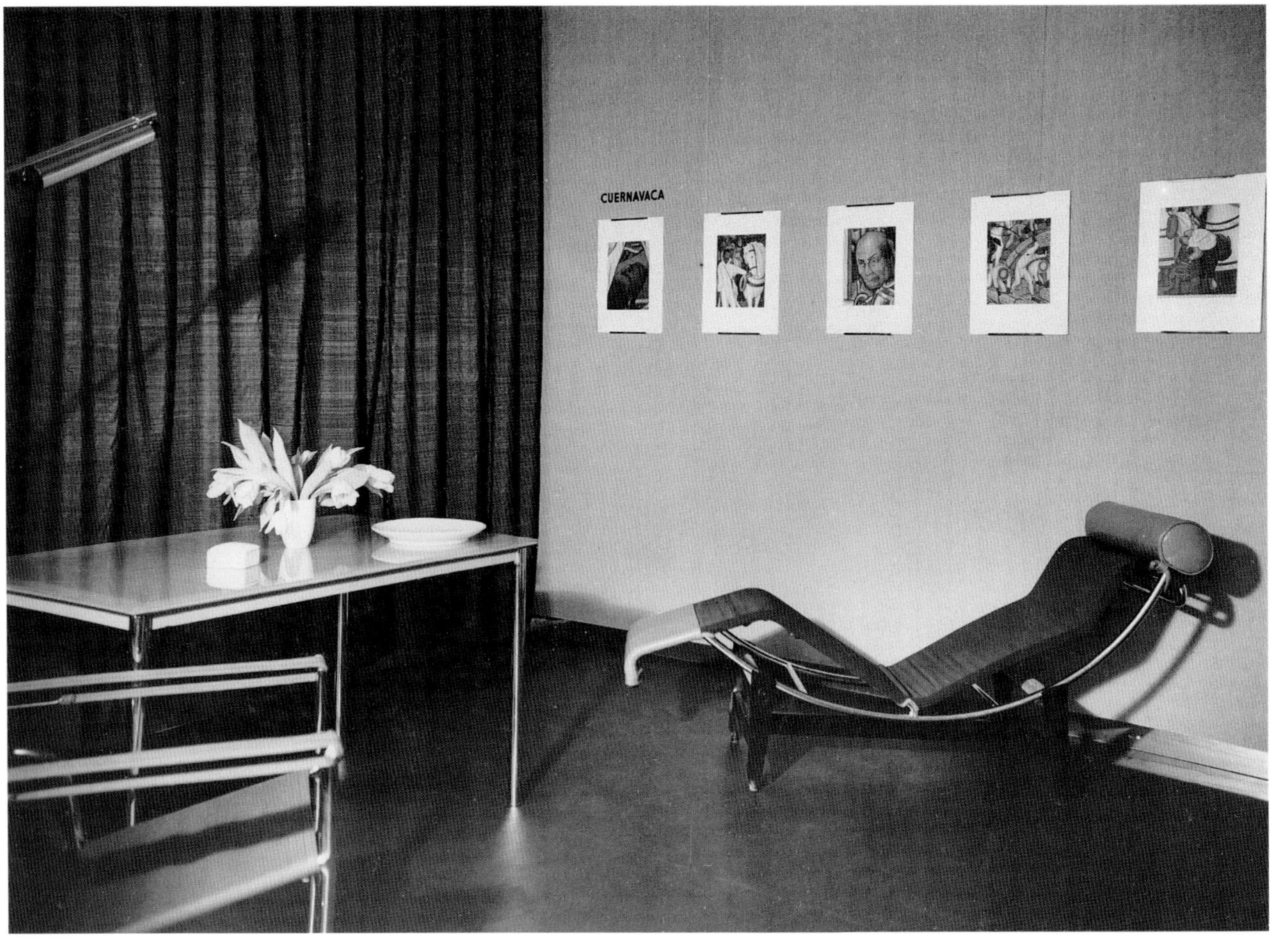

28. *Color Reproductions of Mexican Frescoes by Diego Rivera*, exhibition at The Museum of Modern Art, February 20–March 12, 1933, which inaugurated the new permanent MoMA architecture room installed by Philip Johnson. New York, Photographic Archive, The Museum of Modern Art Archives. Digital image © The Museum of Modern Art / Licensed by SCALA / Art Resource, N.Y.

tive international modernisms of the 1930s. Socially engaged modern public art was not a strange bedfellow to modernist interior decoration, but seamlessly coexisted as a model of radical cosmopolitan art in the built environment. Indeed, only a couple of years later, Indigenist murals by Ecuadoran artist Camilo Egas (1889–1962), head of the art department at the New School, became integral components of the international style architecture of the school's 12th Street building. These examples underscore the necessity of a critical reassessment of the contemporaneity and relevance of 1930s "realisms" as modern stylistic and political currents and as viable vanguard movements.

It would not be an overstatement to suggest that the modern art of Latin America is known in the United States and became a "field" of inquiry *because* of the collection and promotion of Mexican art in the 1930s. It is in many ways the best known and was for decades the most studied period. Mexican art wrongly stood for "Latin American art," more broadly speaking, in the United States and has often erroneously been interpreted solely through the lens of the exotic or the folkloric. Such terms become self-fulfilling or are imposed mandates. Yet when we look back to the 1930s and remember that Mexican art signified that unique juncture of radical politics, social modernity, and artistic modernism for institutions, collectors, artists, and viewers alike, we deepen the study of Latin American art by not falling prey to the vicissitudes of historiography. Instead, we account for the actual modes of operation of a given movement or historical moment. Moreover, placing the collecting practices of modern Mexican art within the broader framework of Latin America has the potential to spur productive dialogue across time periods, borders, artistic practices, and institutional discourses.

CHAPTER 5

An American Museum

Representing the Arts of Mexico at The Metropolitan Museum of Art

Ronda Kasl

In 1911, when Emily de Forest (1851–1942) offered the trustees of The Metropolitan Museum of Art her collection of "Mexican maiolica," she spelled out its rationale: "The collection is important, in my opinion, not only as representing an artistic ceramic development, but, more particularly, as representing such a development in America. It seems to me to form a part of a collection representing the arts of Mexico which I hope will at some time be fully represented in the Museum, as an American Museum."[1] It is a rather unwieldy statement, but its meaning is clear enough. Emily de Forest saw the tin-glazed pottery of Puebla as a North American artistic achievement and envisioned her gift to the Museum as part of a comprehensive representation of the arts of Mexico. Her affirmation that this aim befitted an American museum resonates today, as the Metropolitan commits to collecting and presenting the arts of not only Mexico, but all of Latin America. Beyond the literal meaning of Emily de Forest's statement and its seeming contemporary relevance, her act of generosity and the wording of her letter point to an appreciation of the art of viceregal Mexico that attached fundamental importance to the transfer of artistic traditions from Europe to America. Such a view was commonplace at the time, and de Forest's remarks on the importance of "Mexican maiolica" echo those of Sylvester Baxter (1850–1927), whose landmark study of Spanish colonial architecture, published in 1901, she is likely to have known.[2] Baxter asserted the primacy of Mexican architecture as "not only the first, but the most important development of the depictive arts in the New World under European influences," calling it "the richest aesthetic movement that has yet had its course in the Western Hemisphere."[3]

During the winter of 1904, Robert (1848–1931) and Emily de Forest (fig. 29), and a party of fellow travelers that included Lockwood de Forest (1850–1932), sculptor Daniel Chester French (1850–1931), and their wives, vacationed in Mexico. At the time,

29. Evelyn Beatrice Longman (American, 1874–1954), *Mr. and Mrs. Robert W. de Forest*, 1922, carved 1923. Marble, diameter 26 cm. New York, The Metropolitan Museum of Art. Image © The Metropolitan Museum of Art.

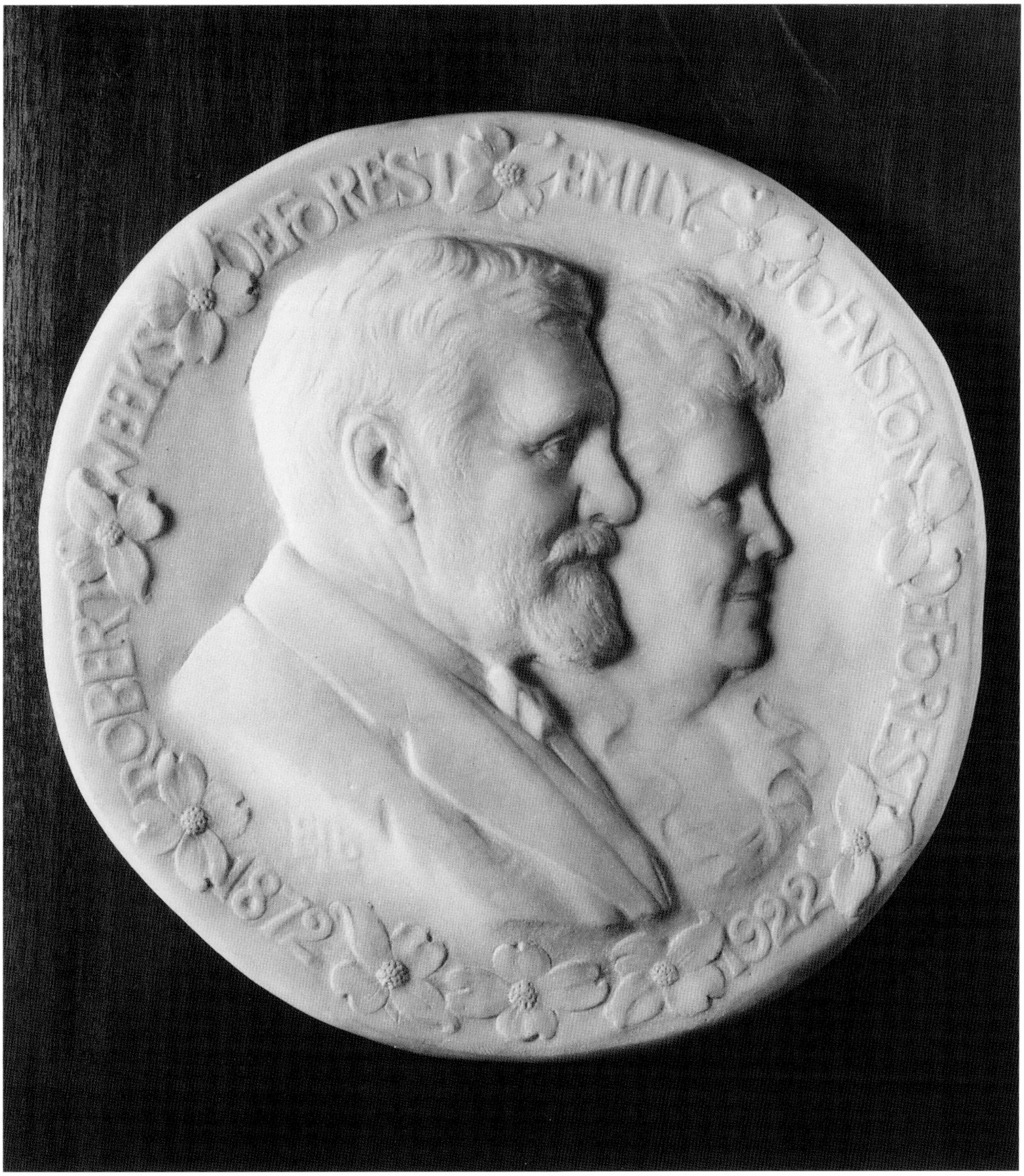
ROBERT W WEEKS DE FOREST
EMILY JOHNSTON DE FOREST
1872
1922

Robert de Forest, a lawyer and philanthropist, was a trustee of the Metropolitan Museum and would soon become its secretary. Emily de Forest was the daughter of the Museum's founding president, John Taylor Johnston (1820–1893).[4] Lockwood de Forest, Robert's younger brother, was a protégé of the landscape painter Frederic Edwin Church (1826–1900) and a designer of Indian-inspired interiors and furnishings. Lockwood recorded his impressions of Mexico, which he visited more than once, in a 1908 article that accompanied photographs by his friend Henry Ravell (1860–1930). He wrote, "There is no country better worth visiting than Mexico. It is very striking, in crossing the border from the United States, to note how completely everything changes. Here there hardly seems anything man has constructed which harmonizes with its surroundings; there everything seems to be entirely a part of the country." Calling it "more foreign than Europe," he said it reminded him of the East: "I could hardly believe that I was not in India." He lauded the natural beauty of the landscape, comparing its colors to those of a Mexican opal, and he observed the picturesque charm of the church towers and tiled domes rising above the towns.[5] Lockwood de Forest's evocation of the twin themes of exoticism and anti-industrialism is not uniquely the view of an Aesthetic Movement designer—it is rooted in a broader discontent with the modern world that not infrequently found an outlet in the appreciation of Mexico and its art. Nor was he alone in discerning qualities he considered to be of Eastern origin in Mexican art. For Sylvester Baxter, Mexico's tiled domes were of "Oriental" origin, "brought to Spain by Arabs who, in turn, acquired the art in Persia."[6]

During the final decades of the government of the *Porfiriato*—the government of Porfirio Díaz (1830–1915)—a rapidly expanding network of modern railways made travel within Mexico increasingly accessible and comfortable. Beginning in the 1880s, passengers like the de Forests rode in American-made parlor cars, on American-financed rails, and read travel literature that described the geography, history, customs, and principal sights of the country. Guidebooks also contained advertisements for shops and services, promoted investment opportunities, and touted the health benefits of the climate. At stops along the way, businesses like the Sonora News Company catered to the demands of American travelers, supplying newspapers, guides, postcards, and stereographs, as well as antiques and curios.[7]

The de Forests' winter retreat in 1904 mirrored the nearly annual trips made by family friend and relative Frederic Edwin Church, who traveled to Mexico fourteen times, primarily for reasons of health, between 1881 and his death in 1900.[8] If, by the last decades of the nineteenth century, the aging painter's fame had waned in the United States, he remained a celebrity in Mexico, where his activities were chronicled in the English-language press and his favored destinations were hailed in popular travel literature. Church traveled widely in central Mexico, but his artistic activity there was limited to sketches and oil studies. He was an avid collector of Mexican antiquities (many of them fake), as well as colonial works of art and contemporary applied arts, which he displayed at Olana, the home and studio he built overlooking the Hudson River Valley.[9] In 1895, in the Mexico City daily *Two Republics*, Edward Garczynski reported, "One of the great delights of Mr. Frederick E. Church, the celebrated landscape artist, when he is in Mexico, is to shop around the bric-a-brac stores seeking what he may purchase. Sometimes it may be a carved bit of jade centuries older than the conquest, a proof, may be, of commerce with Southeastern Asia, a statuette of the Virgin by Tresguerras, sometimes a good bit of pottery, occasionally a book with rare engravings." The article goes on to describe Church's discovery of a portrait of a nun by Andrés López (active between 1763 and 1811; see fig. 2 in Edward J.

Sullivan's introduction in this volume), whose excellence was discerned by his "artistic eye," even though the work was "grimy with dirt and discolored varnish."[10] In 1893, the artist acquired two Toltec reliefs of eagles (fig. 30) and gave them to The Metropolitan Museum of Art, where he was a trustee, declaring, "the pair will add something to the meagre collection of the Ancient Art of the New World in our Museum and I will be on the alert to capture other examples of merit."[11] The reliefs were among the first Pre-Columbian Mexican works to enter the collection.

Frederic Church's travels in Mexico and the discoveries he made were doubtless known to the de Forests, world travelers in their own right, who took a similar delight in hunting and capturing "the good bit of pottery," whether it was from New England or New Spain. It was during their trip south of the border during the winter of 1904 that Emily de Forest became aware of and began to collect what she called "Mexican maiolica," which she considered to be "a phase of Spanish art in Mexico."[12] De Forest was an enthusiastic collector of European and American folk pottery, and it is important to note that when she bought her first pieces of tin-glazed earthenware in Mexico, it was not widely known outside that country and its origins were not well understood. The "discovery" that glazed pottery had been made in Mexico during the colonial period was proclaimed by ceramics scholar Edwin Atlee Barber (1851–1916), who published a brief account of it in 1906. Barber had seen some of the pottery Emily de Forest brought back from Mexico and traveled there himself in 1907 in order to acquire examples for the Pennsylvania Museum.[13]

The pottery de Forest purchased in Mexico in 1904 formed the nucleus of a collection that grew to include 169 works by the time she offered it to the Metropolitan Museum in 1911. After returning from Mexico, de Forest was assisted in her quest by her friend the American archeologist and anthropologist Zelia Nuttall (1857–1933, fig. 31).[14] De Forest acquired works from the Sonora News Company and other shops, but the largest single source was the collection of Albert Pepper, a New York architect resident in Mexico City.[15] She saw the collection during a visit to Pepper's San Ángel home and acquired it a few years later with Nuttall's assistance.[16] Zelia Nuttall hailed from a prominent San Francisco family and was a key figure in the early history of American archaeology and anthropology. In addition to pursuing her own studies of Mexican antiquity, she used her wealth and social connections to advance both disciplines and develop collections in nascent public institutions like the American Museum of Natural History and The Metropolitan Museum of Art. The assistance Zelia Nuttall provided Emily de Forest is comparable to her efforts on behalf of Edwin Atlee Barber, Franz Boas (1858–1942), Phoebe Hearst (1842–1919), and others. Nuttall was also a renowned hostess, and her home in Coyoacán, the historic Casa Alvarado, was a mecca for foreign visitors like the de Forests. A vivid character, she was the model for D. H. Lawrence's Mrs. Norris in *The Plumed Serpent*: "She was an archaeologist, and she had studied the Aztec remains so long, that now some of the black-grey look of the lava rock, and some of the experience of the Aztec idols, with sharp nose and slightly prominent eyes and an expression of tomb-like mockery, had passed into her face. A lonely daughter of culture, with a strong mind and a dense will, she had browsed all her life on the hard stones of archaeological remains."[17] Zelia Nuttall cannot have been pleased with Lawrence's characterization, which emphasized her eccentric appearance over both her scholarly reputation and her social standing.

During the same years when Emily de Forest formed her collection of ceramics, her husband dedicated himself to the difficult and ultimately unsuccessful task of acquiring a Mexican altarpiece

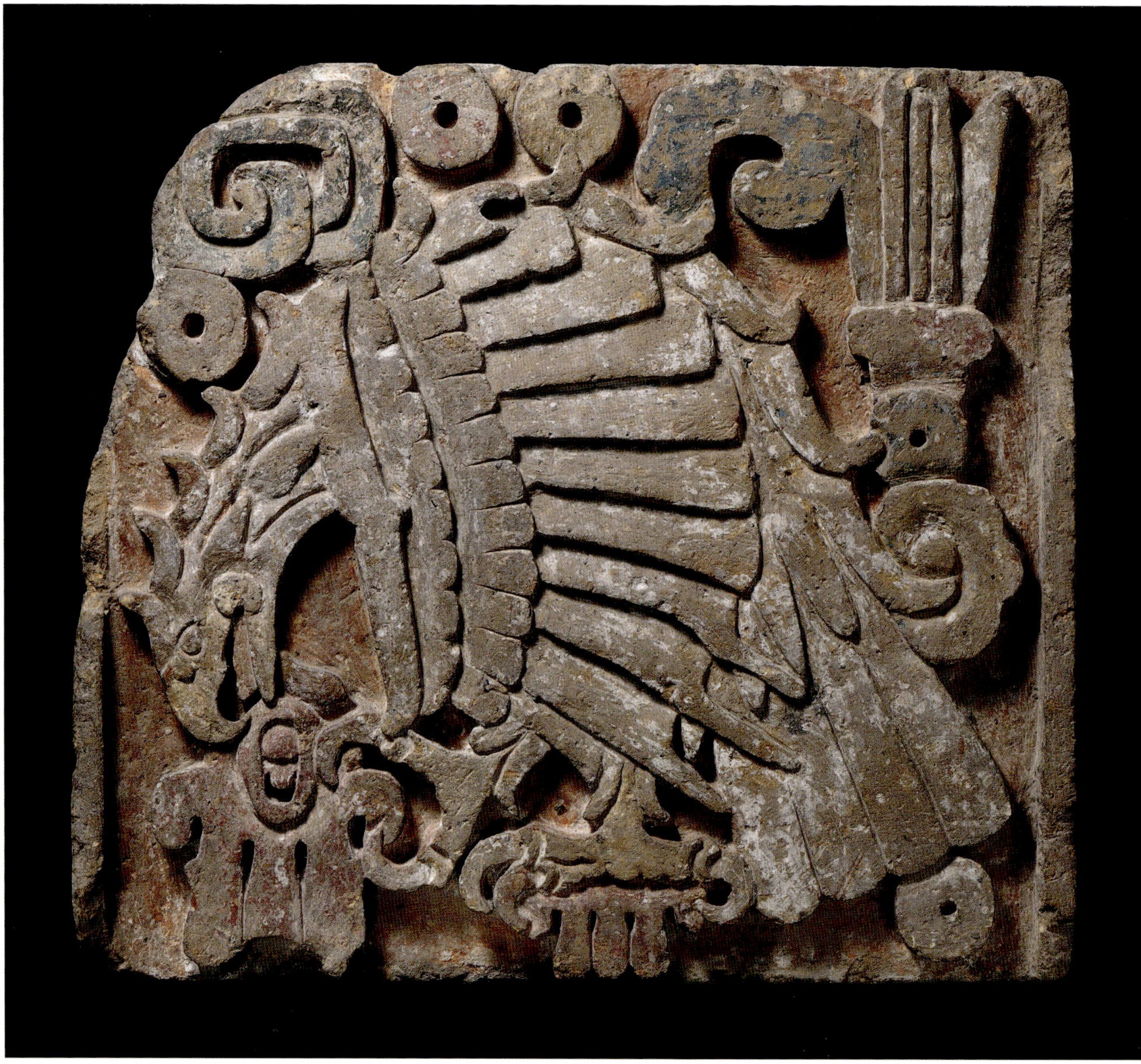

30. Toltec, *Eagle Relief*, tenth–thirteenth century. Andesite/dacite, paint, 62.23 × 77.47 cm. New York, The Metropolitan Museum of Art. Image © The Metropolitan Museum of Art.

for the Museum. This forgotten endeavor was sparked by a request from Sir Caspar Purdon Clarke (1846–1911), who became director of the Metropolitan in 1904.[18] Writing from South Kensington, Clarke informed the Museum's acting director, George Story, of his interest in acquiring Mexican "woodwork" for the collection. "I have expert opinions as to the high merit of the Mexican work but no one seems to know where it was made, whether in situ or sent out from Spain." He recalled having been offered an altarpiece from the Cholula church of Santiago for the sum of 350 pounds two years before and stated that he had since been informed that "there is a great quantity of similar woodwork for sale by church authorities at Cholula and in other Mexican Cathedrals. . . . Would you object to go to Cholula to see any carving if offered?"[19] It is notable that what interested Clarke was decorative wood carving, not figurative painting or sculpture. His knowledge of the subject was doubtless informed by Baxter's *Spanish-Colonial Architecture in Mexico*, which he recommended that Story purchase right away. In it, Baxter quotes his collaborator, the architect Bertram Grosvenor Goodhue (1869–1924), on Mexican wood carving: "The use of wood is marvelous. The Churrigueresque altars are so wonderfully intricate, so elaborate and difficult of design, that it is hard to see how any workman could follow his drawings and harder to comprehend how such drawings could have been made. Carving is excellent—bold and strong, or clear and delicate, as the case may require."[20]

The task of following up on the new director's unusual request fell to the Museum's new secretary, Robert de Forest, and to Daniel Chester French, the sculptor and Museum trustee who had accompanied the de Forests to Mexico in 1904. Robert de Forest turned to Zelia Nuttall for help: "Dear Miss Nuttall: By what the Quakers call 'a leading,' Mr. French and I find ourselves impelled to look for one of those fine, carved, gilded Mexican altars for our Museum

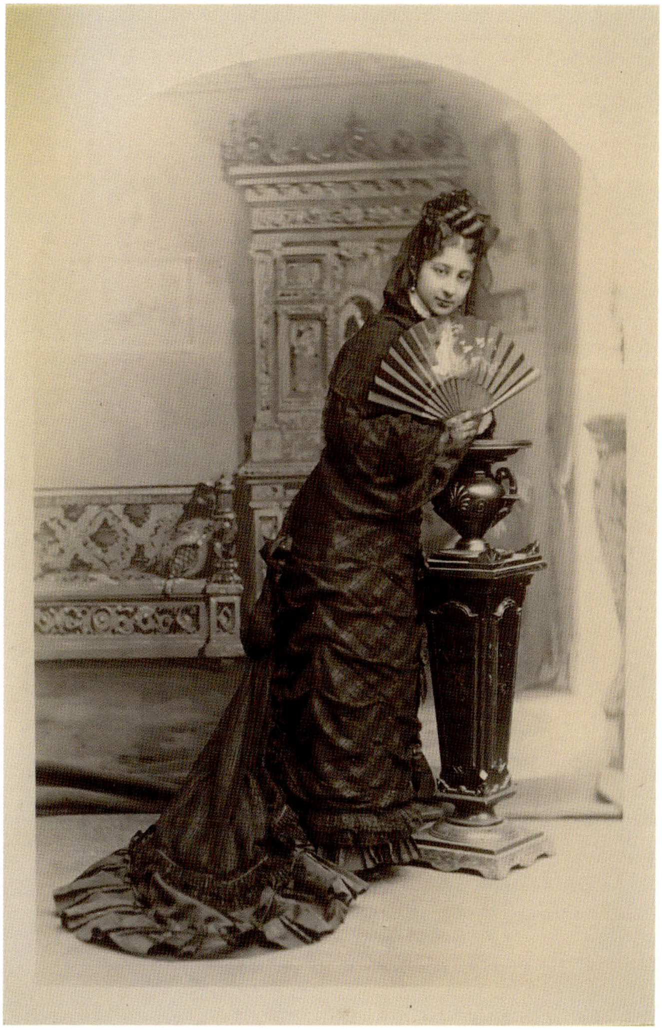

31. Unknown photographer, Zelia Nuttall (1857–1933). Berkeley, University of California. Courtesy of The Bancroft Library.

collection." Enclosing a photograph of the Cholula altarpiece previously offered to the South Kensington Museum, de Forest continued, "[Clarke] suggested (with the delightfully indefinite idea of distance that some of our English friends have) that our Director should make an excursion some week between closing on Saturday and opening on Monday morning, to see what it was like if it was still for sale." He also reported that the Museum had been offered a Mexican altarpiece by someone in California, who had purchased it in Mexico. "All of this seems to point to the proposition that the Museum should have some first class, typical, gold, carved Mexican altar," he wrote, asking Zelia Nuttall whether she would be willing to undertake the task of finding something suitable.[21]

Nuttall accepted de Forest's commission, writing, "The idea of an altar hunt has . . . quite roused me and I now feel quite keen to start for Cholula."[22] She speculated that the altarpiece offered to Clarke was the same one that had been offered to Phoebe Hearst four years before by Sylvester Baxter, who had shown her a photograph of it. De Forest responded, "I should like very much to join in the search myself, and I have no doubt French would do so with even greater eagerness."[23] This exchange of letters marks the beginning of a lengthy correspondence between de Forest and Nuttall, which at times reads like an epistolary novel. Nuttall's frequent progress reports commend her own ingenuity and social connections, providing detailed and often opinionated accounts of her encounters with dealers, politicians, and clerics. De Forest responded with encouragement, instructions, and a line of credit.

Nuttall began the "altar hunt" on May 18, 1905, when she set out for Puebla in the company of Thomas A. Janvier (1849–1913) and his wife, Catherine (1841–1922), who were looking for "literary material."[24] She quickly learned that the altarpiece from Cholula offered to Clarke was no longer available, having been sold to the Sonora News Company, which "had put it several and sundry uses and made furniture out of some of its parts." Guided by a dealer she deemed reputable, Nuttall and the Janviers visited local churches in search of an altarpiece that met de Forest's requirements. One that she considered "a gem" was offered, then withdrawn when the archbishop of Puebla prevented its sale. Negotiations likewise foundered for altarpieces in towns near Puebla and in Xochimilco and Churubusco. Promising to "return to the charge persistently," Nutall wrote, "From all sides I learn that whereas it was easy to purchase altars some years ago, it is a difficult matter now, for there is a reaction against selling church property to heretics."[25]

Robert de Forest responded with more encouragement, declaring that the Museum was prepared to pay a large sum for "a gem" and unwilling to settle for anything less.[26] In her response, Nuttall blamed "ecclesiastical creatures," complaining that she was unable to obtain definite answers from them. Taking note of the growing opposition to the sale of church patrimony to foreigners, Nuttall wrote, "I shall redouble my efforts, but is it not unfortunate that, just at present, the Mexicans should awaken to the fact that if they do not protect their churches foreigners will carry away their best treasures?"[27]

A few months later, Nuttall's progress report was accompanied by a cautionary tale about a failed attempt by the famously profligate Duke of Manchester (William Angus Drogo Montagu, 9th Duke of Manchester, 1877–1947) to purchase an altarpiece in Tlacolula. His representative, a dealer from Mexico City named Ayllón, paid for it, but "[w]hen he and his men proceeded to take possession of the altar a small riot occurred in the village. Its inhabitants rang the church bell, summoning a crowd, and indignantly claimed that the church and all it contained belonged to them and that the priest had no right to sell the altar." Nuttall also reported that a prominent Mexican scholar had been so incensed by the attempt to "despoil" the church that he brought the matter to the president's attention and presented a petition to forbid the export of art from churches.[28] The Tlacolula altarpiece was subsequently offered to Nuttall, along with two others that the priests were willing to sell, albeit without the consent of locals.

Nuttall's suggestion that indigenous people were an obstacle to the enlightened aims of the Metropolitan Museum elicited a stern response from de Forest: "My sympathy is entirely with the Indians. I am glad they intervened and that they intervened successfully. I do not think anything of that kind should be sold out of the churches which the Indians or other local people wish to keep." He cautioned her against any purchase agreement with church authorities that would be unacceptable to either the local residents or the Mexican government: "This may be putting more difficulties in your path, but as a public institution in a free country we could not afford to be parties to anything which seemed like a conspiracy to defraud the people of their sacred things."[29]

The incident in Tlacolula is reminiscent of the uproar caused a few years earlier by rumors that Frederic Church had proposed buying the whole interior of the Querétaro church of Santa Rosa and shipping it to New York. According to Sylvester Baxter, who had been with the painter in Querétaro, "This report had so aroused the populace as to develop in favor of the beautiful interior a public sentiment so strong that the proposition was stigmatized as a sacrilege. When a community realizes that something it possesses is valued in other places, a sense of appreciation is awakened. So, in Querétaro, at that moment, an attempt to carry into effect a proposition to destroy the church would very likely have caused a riot."[30]

The concerns expressed by Robert de Forest caused Zelia Nuttall to seek an altarpiece for the Museum from a private source. After more than a year of fruitless searching—there were no "gems" to be had in haciendas and orphanages—Nuttall once again proposed the acquisition of a work from a church, reporting that she had been offered four altarpieces from the Puebla church of La Soledad.[31] She followed up a few days later, after going to see them: "They are simply magnificent and of the finest I have ever seen. They are in perfect condition, of cedar wood carved and gilded and the paintings are *far* above the average in execution and art. They are exactly what I would wish the Metropolitan Museum to own and preserve as a legacy, for future generations."[32] Calling the proposed purchase "rather a large proposition in every way," Nuttall reported that each of the two largest altarpieces measured 17 × 10 meters meters and contained twenty-eight paintings. The sculptures contained in its niches were not for sale, as the priest wished to retain them for the church. Nuttall proposed installing three of the altarpieces in the Museum in the manner of a chapel, with the best preserved of the large ones in the center, flanked by the two smaller ones. The fourth altarpiece would be resold, thus recovering part of the total purchase price of 12,000 pesos (about $6,000). The photographs Nuttall enclosed with her letter are lost, but there can be no doubt that the altarpieces in question are the ones that still occupy the crossing of the Puebla church of La Soledad.[33]

The same dealer, on the same occasion, offered a lavatory decorated with glazed tiles from the Puebla church of San Francisco. Robert de Forest responded by telegram: "Delighted. Buy lavatory. Buy altars too if immediate action essential to secure them."[34] De Forest was willing to assume the personal financial risk of buying the lavatory and the altarpieces for the Museum without prior approval from the trustee committee on purchases. He ordered photographs and architectural drawings and arranged for his brother Lockwood to travel to

Puebla to examine the altarpieces in situ and advise on the best way to dismantle and pack them for shipment to New York.[35]

Robert de Forest congratulated Zelia Nuttall on the successful outcome of their quest, but one complication after another arose when she sought authorization to export the altarpieces. She was surprised to learn from José Romero, an acquaintance in the foreign office, that they were government property and the church had no legal right to sell them. It would be necessary to petition the government, but it was unclear who had the authority to close the deal. Nuttall was not on good terms with Justo Sierra (1848–1912), Secretary of Public Education, who was charged with oversight of national monuments, and she opted to go around him by asking the Secretary of Finance, José Yves Limantour (1854–1935), to intervene with the Mexican president.[36] Robert de Forest offered, if needed, to ask the Secretary of State, Elihu Root (1845–1937), and even President Theodore Roosevelt (1858–1919), to assist with negotiations.[37]

Zelia Nuttall's interview with Limantour seemed to confirm her judgement regarding the best channel for the Museum's request. The secretary expressed his desire to see the Mexican government make a gift of three altarpieces and offered to take up the matter with President Díaz.[38] A few days later, having spoken to the president, Limantour reported serious, but not insuperable difficulties.[39] After a long silence, and in response to "a rouser" from Nuttall, Limantour wrote that he had not been able to find a way to overcome the prevailing opposition to the export of the country's remaining artistic and historic treasures. The only possible way forward, he suggested, was to exchange the altars for "some objects of importance to Mexico."[40] Limantour apparently had in mind the repatriation of a stone relief from the Mayan site of Palenque, part of the Tablet of the Cross, which had been taken from Mexico by an American diplomat in 1842 and was kept in the Smithsonian Institution.[41] De Forest dismissed the idea that the Washington museum would agree to exchange the Palenque tablet for the benefit of the Metropolitan. Nor was he enthusiastic about exchanging works from the Met's own collection, even though he allowed that there were duplicates in the Cesnola Collection of Cypriot antiquities as well as an abundance of paintings. Instead, he raised the possibility of paying more for the altars or purchasing just two of them. He again reminded Nuttall that Secretary of State Elihu Root was a Museum trustee and that his intervention might help secure the altarpieces.[42]

De Forest was aware of Root's plans to visit Mexico in early October 1907, and, making apologies for mixing museum business with matters of state, he requested the secretary's help. "We have been extremely anxious at the Museum to have one or two Mexican altarpieces to represent this North American art at its best," he wrote. The letter goes on to introduce Zelia Nuttall as his personal friend and the Museum's representative: "If you can spare time when you are in Mexico to give her opportunity of seeing you she can explain the entire situation, and precisely the direction in which you can possibly aid."[43] Not only did Nuttall meet with Secretary Root during his visit to Mexico, but she gave his party a tour of the Grand Hall of Monoliths at the National Museum.[44] Through the efforts of Nuttall and Root, the Palenque tablet in the Smithsonian was repatriated in 1908. The Mexican government reciprocated by presenting a plaster reproduction of the reassembled Tablet of the Cross to the Smithsonian, but permission to export the Puebla altarpieces for the Metropolitan's collection never materialized.[45]

While negotiations to purchase the altarpieces were ongoing, de Forest asked Nuttall to assume that the Museum would construct a Mexican chapel and to buy whatever might be needed to furnish it.[46] In January 1907, Nuttall sent him an account of her purchases to date: a carved pulpit, a Talavera lavatory, a choir book, an ivory page turner, two carved gilded lecterns, an altar frontal, two large Talavera plates, and two vases. Among the items held on approval were two nun's shields (*escudos de monja*), which were eventually purchased from the nuns of La Soledad in Puebla.[47] He arranged to have all of the items shipped to the Museum, and, in a letter addressed to the Committee on Purchases, he described the special circumstances under which he had acquired them, explaining that the decision could not wait for committee action. De Forest clearly expected the Museum to embrace the opportunity to purchase what he had already authorized and paid for himself.[48] He advised the Museum's secretary, Henry W. Kent (1866–1948), to expect the arrival of a shipment of items from Mexico, stipulating that they were his property but that they were intended for the Museum "should the Museum wish to acquire them." He asked to be kept informed "if any such things come (and Lord knows when they will and how they will)."[49] His concerns were justified, as many of his purchases remained in Mexico. In 1927, on Zelia Nuttall's recommendation, de Forest lent some of his unexported works of art to Dwight W. Morrow (1873–1931) to decorate the U.S. Embassy in Mexico City. De Forest prevailed upon Morrow to help with export permits, but the matter was as politically sensitive as ever and it was impossible to contemplate shipping former church property abroad.[50]

It is unclear precisely when Robert de Forest abandoned the idea of acquiring a "Mexican chapel" for the Metropolitan Museum, but any possibility of reaching an agreement with the government of Porfirio Díaz ended with the outbreak of the Mexican Revolution in 1910. During the decade of armed conflict that followed, the de Forests collected a handful of Mexican works outside that country. In 1910, New York philanthropist Mrs. Russell Sage (1828–1918) purchased Mexican and Navajo textiles for both the Metropolitan Museum and the Natural History Museum during a trip to California and the Southwest. She appears to have been carrying out a commission from de Forest, who was her attorney and advisor.[51] In 1912, Emily de Forest bought a mid-seventeenth-century basin, arguably the most important piece in her collection, from a London dealer.[52]

The de Forest collection of Mexican ceramics was first exhibited in 1908 at the opening of the Hispanic Society of America and again, in its entirety, in 1911. The catalogue, written by Edwin Atlee Barber, outlined a taxonomy of forms and decorations, along with a corresponding chronology, thus providing a scientific rationale for the collection.[53] The ceramics were still at the Hispanic Society when she offered all 169 pieces listed in the catalogue to the Metropolitan and triggered an internal debate about how many should be accepted. The curator of decorative arts, Wilhelm R. Valentiner (1880–1958), felt that the maximum number should be about twenty pieces. The Trustee Committee on Decorative Arts initially recommended a selection of about forty pieces, but revised the total to eighty-five in consultation with Edwin Atlee Barber and Daniel Chester French.[54] A few months later, in January 1912, Emily de Forest added two more pieces to the collection, including the basin acquired in London, which was decorated in what Barber called the "Moresque style," the earliest classification in his scheme. Also added was a modern copy of an eighteenth-century jar by Enrique Ventosa, the craftsman credited with reviving Puebla's pottery tradition at the beginning of the twentieth century. With these two gifts, the earliest and latest works in the collection, Emily de Forest declared it complete.[55] Additional gifts followed in 1917 and 1918, when the collection was finally put on view (fig. 32), but almost all had been collected prior to 1911 and were among the 169 pieces previously offered to the Museum.[56] Six years

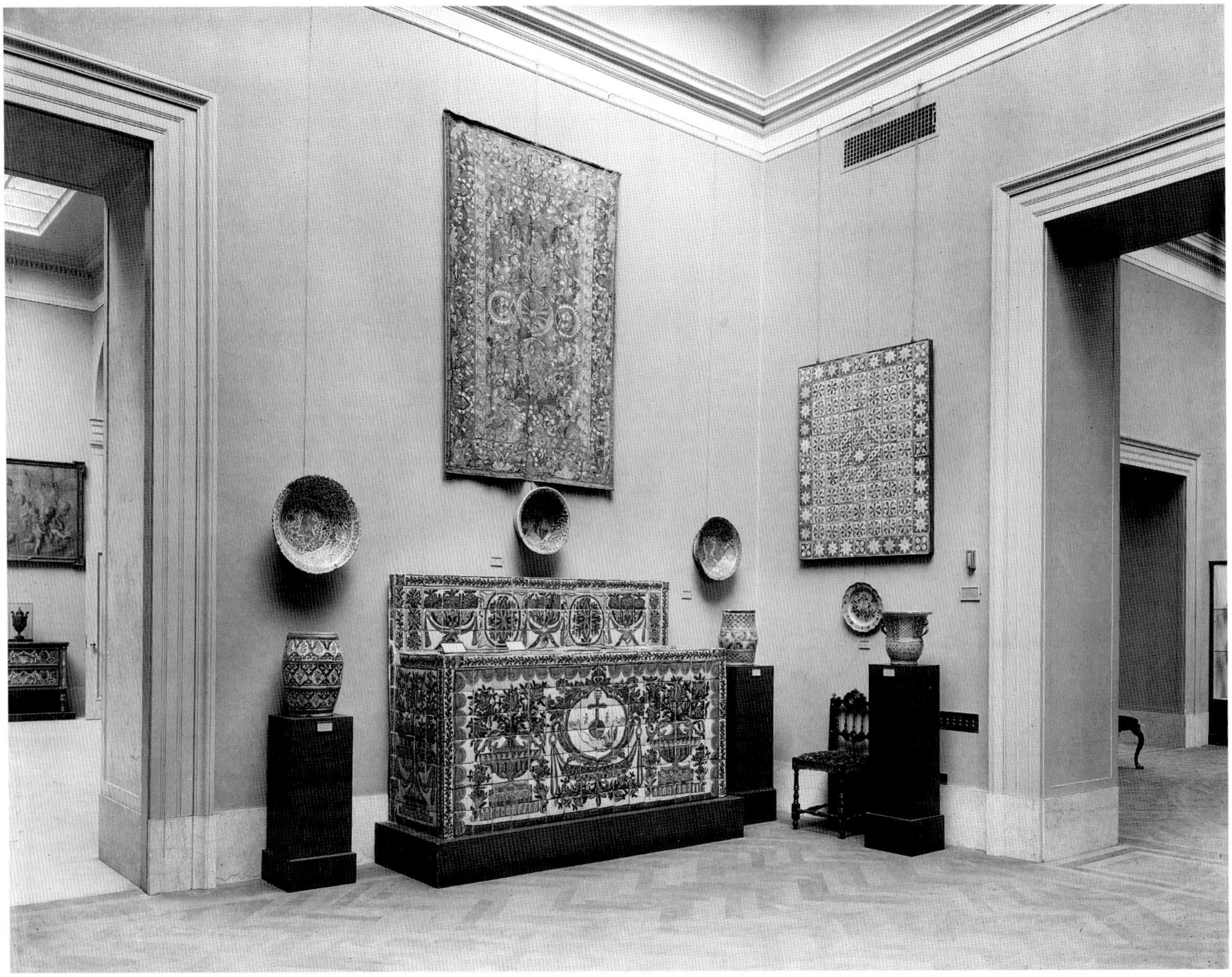

32. Installation of the Emily de Forest Collection of Mexican ceramics, 1926. New York, The Metropolitan Museum of Art. Image © The Metropolitan Museum of Art.

had elapsed since the initial gift when de Forest presented the Museum with the lavatory her husband acquired in Puebla in 1906. She commented, "I have not done so heretofore because I was uncertain how far the Museum was really interested in this particular development of art on our own American continent."[57]

Emily de Forest was right to doubt the Museum's commitment. Edward Robinson (1858–1931), a scholar of classical art who became director in 1910, did not share his predecessor's interest in the art of Mexico. In December 1927, she was informed that the lavatory would be removed from view and the rest of the collection would be incorporated into a gallery of European pottery.[58] Robert de Forest protested: "Is there not some other alternative? . . . The Mexican collection is a natural unit."[59] While it is fair to say that the de Forests' interest in collecting Mexican art waned somewhat after 1910 with the onset of the Mexican Revolution, they never questioned its importance in the scheme of North American art, as they saw it, even as their attention shifted to the founding of the Museum's American Wing at decade's end.

The clearest indication of Robert de Forest's ongoing interest in Mexico was his role in bringing the landmark *Mexican Arts* exhibition to the Metropolitan Museum in 1930 (fig. 33). The impetus for the exhibition was broadly political, and Dwight W. Morrow, the American ambassador to Mexico, was the driving force behind it, along with Homer Saint-Gaudens (1880–1958) at the Carnegie Institute, who organized the effort for the American Federation of Arts.[60] René d'Harnoncourt (1901–1968) was enlisted to curate the exhibition. By showcasing the "spirit and genius of the Mexican race," the exhibition's organizers aimed to promote a positive view of post-Revolution Mexico in the United States and smooth relations between the two countries. In a letter to de Forest, Saint-Gaudens outlined a survey of fine and applied art that privileged works that expressed, both consciously and unconsciously, Mexican national culture.[61] The proposal failed to impress Robinson, and even de Forest, in spite of his deep interest, did not fully endorse it. He questioned the propriety of including items he did not consider to be works of art, citing toys, costumes, and masks. Making a distinction between works of art and items that illustrated "Mexican social development," he proposed excluding the latter from the Metropolitan venue and augmenting the display with material from the de Forest collection of Mexican ceramics. He was also willing to lend works from his personal collection, including "important objects" kept at the U.S. Embassy in Mexico, which he was anxious to recover and present to the Museum.[62]

Edward Robinson's doubts about *Mexican Arts* were confirmed when the show was unpacked. He wrote to de Forest, "I think I ought to tell you that I have now seen all the material submitted as it has been set forth in one of our storerooms, and it is without exception the most atrocious lot of truck I have ever seen offered for a public exhibition. I cannot find that there is one redeeming quality or item in the whole lot. It is certain to bring severe criticism if not ridicule upon the Museum."[63] De Forest did not fully agree with Robinson's harsh assessment. He allowed that the exhibition included things unworthy of display at the Metropolitan, but recommended going ahead as planned, without suppressing anything or adding anything, reasoning that the Museum could not be criticized for a show it had no role in organizing.[64]

When de Forest first learned about the exhibition in 1929, he reminded Dwight Morrow of his long-standing interest in Mexican art and his intention to form a representative collection at the Metropolitan: "This was my original idea and is still my desire."[65] He did not at first perceive that his pan-American rationale for such a collection was irreconcilable with the nationalist cultural agenda of

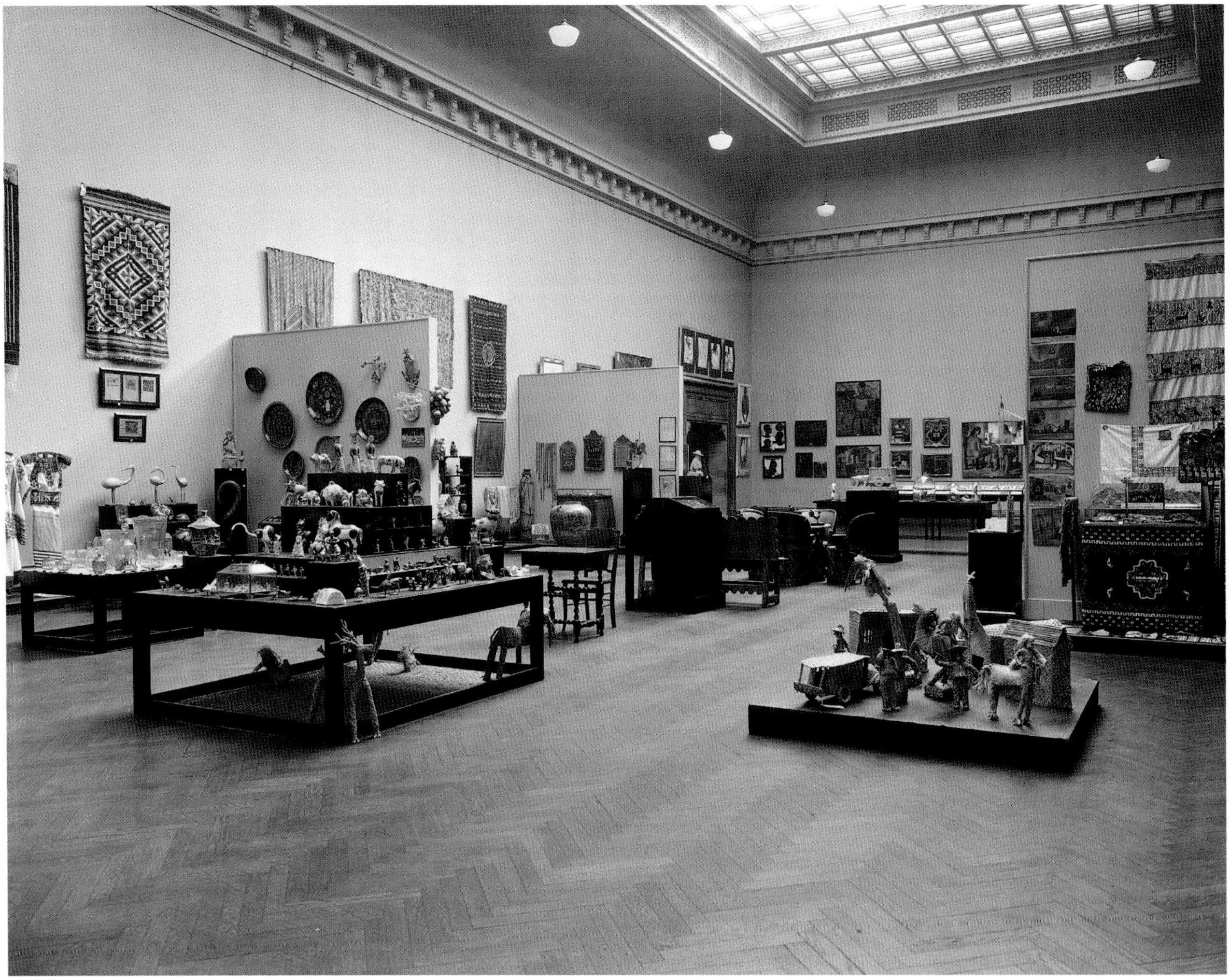

33. *Mexican Arts* exhibition installation, 1930. New York, The Metropolitan Museum of Art. Image © The Metropolitan Museum of Art.

Morrow's exhibition, which privileged the popular and the native as authentic expressions of the Mexican spirit. Excluded from the exhibition were European-influenced artworks of precisely the kind de Forest considered most significant. *Talavera poblana*, the tin-glazed pottery of Puebla, was singled out and disparaged as a foreign art "accidentally practiced on Mexican soil." To paraphrase René d'Harnoncourt's introduction to the exhibition catalogue, it was made in Mexico, but it was not Mexican.[66] In 1930, Robert de Forest was as committed to presenting the arts of Mexico at the Metropolitan Museum as he had been in 1905, but what it meant to do so had changed irrevocably.

CHAPTER 6

Building a Model of Diversity

Grace McCann Morley and Collecting Modern Latin American Art in San Francisco

Berit Potter

34. Photographer unknown, Grace McCann Morley (1900–1985), ca. 1935. San Francisco Museum of Modern Art Archives. Courtesy of San Francisco Museum of Modern Art Archives.

A photograph of the inaugural exhibition of the San Francisco Museum of Modern Art (SFMOMA) in January of 1935 shows a woman in her mid-thirties looking eagerly off-frame. She holds a large painting, representing another young woman with a serious expression, arched eyebrows, and a scarf covering her hair, her arms holding two books (fig. 34). The realist style of the painting and sculptural weight of the embodied figure demonstrate the regional impact of Mexican painter Diego Rivera (1886–1957), who visited San Francisco between 1930 and 1931, where he painted his first murals in the United States. The woman represented in the photograph is Grace Louise McCann Morley (1900–1985), SFMOMA's first director, who had recently taken charge of the museum, then called the San Francisco Museum of Art, and remained its leader until 1958. When Morley became the director of SFMOMA, she was no stranger to San Francisco. Born in Berkeley, California, in 1900, she spent her childhood in rural Sonoma and later attended the University of California, where she earned bachelor's and master's degrees in French and Greek.[1] After completing her education in Berkeley, Morley immediately left her place of birth to continue studying under a fellowship at the Sorbonne in Paris, where she attained a doctorate in art and literature. Morley's time in Paris involved attending the theater nearly every night, visiting the Louvre on Sundays, and frequenting exhibitions of work by Cézanne, Gauguin, and Picasso, all of which would prove to be foundational to her career.

When Morley returned to San Francisco, after serving as the first general curator at the Cincinnati Art Museum, her friend Walter Heil (1890–1973), the director of the Legion of Honor, informed her that the board of SFMOMA was interested in hiring a director. The museum, founded on the heels of art fervor inspired by San Francisco's 1915 Panama Pacific International Exposition (PPIE), had existed in an unstable form, as a venue for traveling exhibi-

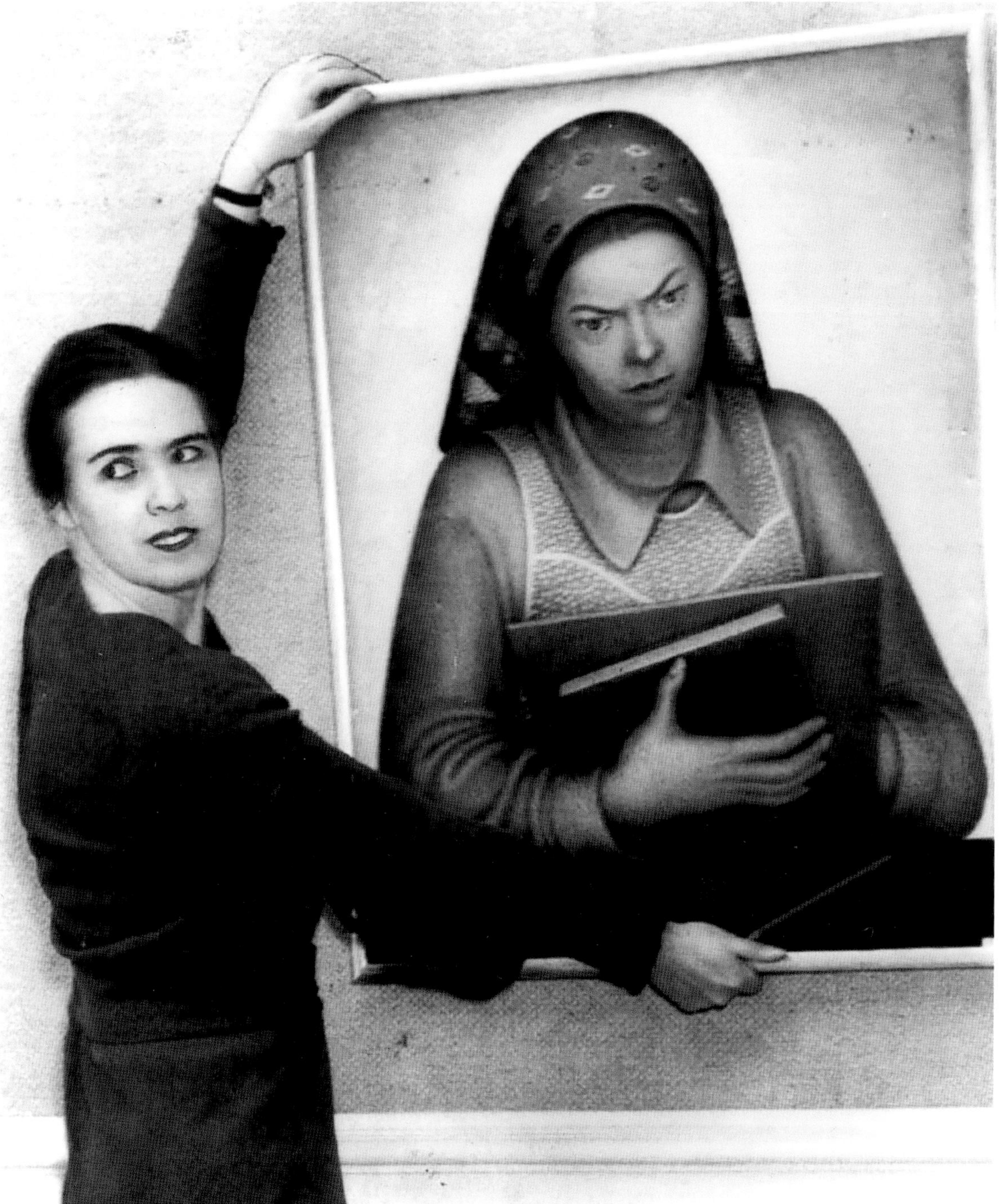

tions housed in the Exposition's decaying Palace of Fine Arts. When Morley approached W. W. Crocker, chairman of the museum's board of governors, about the position, SFMOMA was about to reopen in its first permanent venue on the top floor of the newly constructed Veterans Building across from San Francisco's City Hall. SFMOMA's quarters would include roughly an acre of open space with twenty-seven-foot-high ceilings, topped by a canopy of skylights. The city would allow SFMOMA to occupy the space rent-free and provide the institution with ten to fifteen thousand dollars per year for temporary exhibitions.[2] SFMOMA's permanent collection, however, included only ninety-eight French prints, and there were no funds designated for acquiring new works of art.[3]

At that time, Morley surveyed the cultural landscape of San Francisco and observed little pioneering art activity. Nearly two decades had passed since the PPIE, an event that introduced San Francisco to avant-garde paintings by Oskar Kokoschka and Gino Severini, and still the "City by the Bay" possessed no institution dedicated to the exhibition of modern art.[4] Early on, Morley decided that SFMOMA's exhibitions and programs would support contemporary artists and expose the public to avant-garde art; however, the word "modern" would not be added to the museum's name until 1976.[5] As Morley recounted, when she became SFMOMA's director Crocker asked her, "Well, do you think you can fill the galleries without bothering us?" "I think so," Morley answered. "I'm going to try to anyway."[6] She added, "The problem became rather, as time went on, how to choose from a great number of extremely fine shows."[7] By building upon San Francisco's existing art interests and resources, Morley "turn[ed] San Francisco into one of the nation's most enthusiastic strongholds of modern art," as a *Time* article noted on the twenty-year anniversary of Morley's tenure at SFMOMA.[8]

In light of Morley's education in Paris, it is no surprise that she described San Francisco's art scene as provincial. According to Morley, in the 1930s San Francisco's "artists' group was very strong," but the artists lagged "ten or fifteen years behind the movements of their time, simply because they didn't see enough of what was going on in art," resulting from the lack of institutional support for modern art in the region.[9] The exception, Morley argued, was San Francisco's advanced fresco movement, inspired by Rivera, who was invited to San Francisco in 1930 with his wife, Frida Kahlo (1907–1954), at the behest of art patrons Albert Bender (1866–1941) and William Gerstle (1868–1947). Morley was quick to point out that the "influence of Diego Rivera started in California," where he painted his first U.S. murals, *Allegory of California* at the San Francisco Stock Exchange and *The Making of a Fresco, Showing the Building of a City* in San Francisco's oldest art school, the California School of Fine Arts (now the San Francisco Art Institute).[10] Morley explained, "I think it should be noted that in this particular area you had a more extensive development of mural painting in general, and especially of fresco painting than elsewhere. That was certainly because of Diego Rivera's work here [in San Francisco] and the fact that he had many of the younger artists, who later became more or less prominent, as his helpers."[11] Local artists, including Maxine Albro and Ralph Stackpole (1885–1973), studied with Rivera and served as his assistants both in Mexico City and San Francisco.[12] In addition to training local artists, Rivera inspired many individuals who did not have the opportunity to work directly with him. For example, Dorothy Puccinelli Cravath (1901–1974), who became a prominent artist under the Public Works of Art Project (PWAP), explained that she learned how to paint murals by watching Rivera work on his San Francisco commissions. As Cravath remembered, "I learned about mural technique from Diego Rivera, which is why all these

WPA murals look rather Rivera-ish. I think we all learned about fresco from watching Rivera do the mural at the Art School. . . . We just watched him. I didn't work with him at all."[13] She continues, "As a matter of fact, quite a number of the artists, including myself, had never seen any murals until we started doing them. The first we saw were Diego Rivera's murals at the art school, and that was the big school for the rest of us. We watched him like hawks and observed all the steps of making a mural by a very good technician and then we did likewise, as much as we could."[14] Federally funded projects such as Cravath's murals in the Mother's House building at the San Francisco Zoo and the extensive fresco series created by over forty artists for San Francisco's first PWAP project, Coit Tower, are manifestations of Rivera's influence, which can be found throughout the city.

Regional interest in Rivera and, more generally, Mexican art in the 1930s in San Francisco impacted not only the work of artists but also the collections of local art patrons, including Babette Clayburgh, Leo Eloessor, Elise and Max Honigbaum, Charlotte Mack, Evelyn Mayer, Hattie and Marcus Sloss, and Jeanette Spencer, who collectively owned paintings by Rivera as well as Dr. Atl (Gerardo Murillo Cornado, 1875–1964), Ramón Alva de la Canal (1892–1985), Francisco Díaz de León (1897–1975), Frida Kahlo, Ramos Martínez (1871–1946), Carlos Mérida (1891–1984), Roberto Montenegro (1885–1968), José Clemente Orozco (1883–1949), Máximo Pacheco (1907–1992), Fermín Revueltas (1901–1935), and David Alfaro Siqueiros (1896–1974).[15] The local fervor for Rivera in San Francisco and the availability of representative examples of Mexican art in local collections influenced the early exhibition schedule at SFMOMA.

Rivera's most powerful supporters in San Francisco were William Gerstle, president of the San Francisco Art Association and owner of a San Francisco–based shipping line, and Albert Bender, a prosperous insurance salesman. When SFMOMA opened in the Veterans Building, the museum possessed no funds for establishing a permanent collection, and Morley relied upon generous gifts from both Bender and Gerstle to build SFMOMA's early collection.[16] Bender was particularly interested in establishing Rivera's presence at the museum. As he wrote to Frida Kahlo in 1935, "I am eager to add to Diego's work in the museum. . . . You can well understand that what I have in mind is to emphasize in the public mind the importance of Diego as a great painter and the affectionate regard in which he is held by friends in San Francisco."[17] Between 1935 and 1941, Bender donated eleven hundred objects to SFMOMA,[18] including nearly fifty drawings, oils, pastels, and watercolors by Rivera.[19] In 1936, Bender presented the Museum with Kahlo's important wedding portrait, *Frieda and Diego Rivera*, which she painted in San Francisco in 1931. Bender also gave SFMOMA paintings by Jean Charlot (1898–1979), Leopoldo Méndez (1902–1969), Mérida, Montenegro, and Orozco, as well as works by local artists who assisted Rivera, such as Albro. Gerstle also made generous donations to the Museum, including a series of twenty studies for Rivera's *The Making of a Fresco*.[20]

Morley endeavored to build SFMOMA's exhibitions and programs around San Francisco's established knowledge and interest in modern art. Therefore, when SFMOMA reopened in 1935, Morley dedicated several exhibitions to Rivera and Mexican art, including *Drawings by Diego Rivera*, *Plates of Frescoes by Diego Rivera*, *Rivera Paintings and Drawings*, *Mexican Paintings and Drawings*, and *Work by Mexican School Children: Carlos Mérida Collection*.[21] One of Bender's earliest gifts, Rivera's painting *The Flower Carrier*, formerly referred to as *The Flower Vendor*, served as the focus of a 1938 installation. The exhibition, *Analysis of a Rivera*, was part of a series of didactic installations curated by Morley in the 1930s, including *Analysis of a Picasso* and *Analysis of a Matisse*, which taught museum visitors how to critically

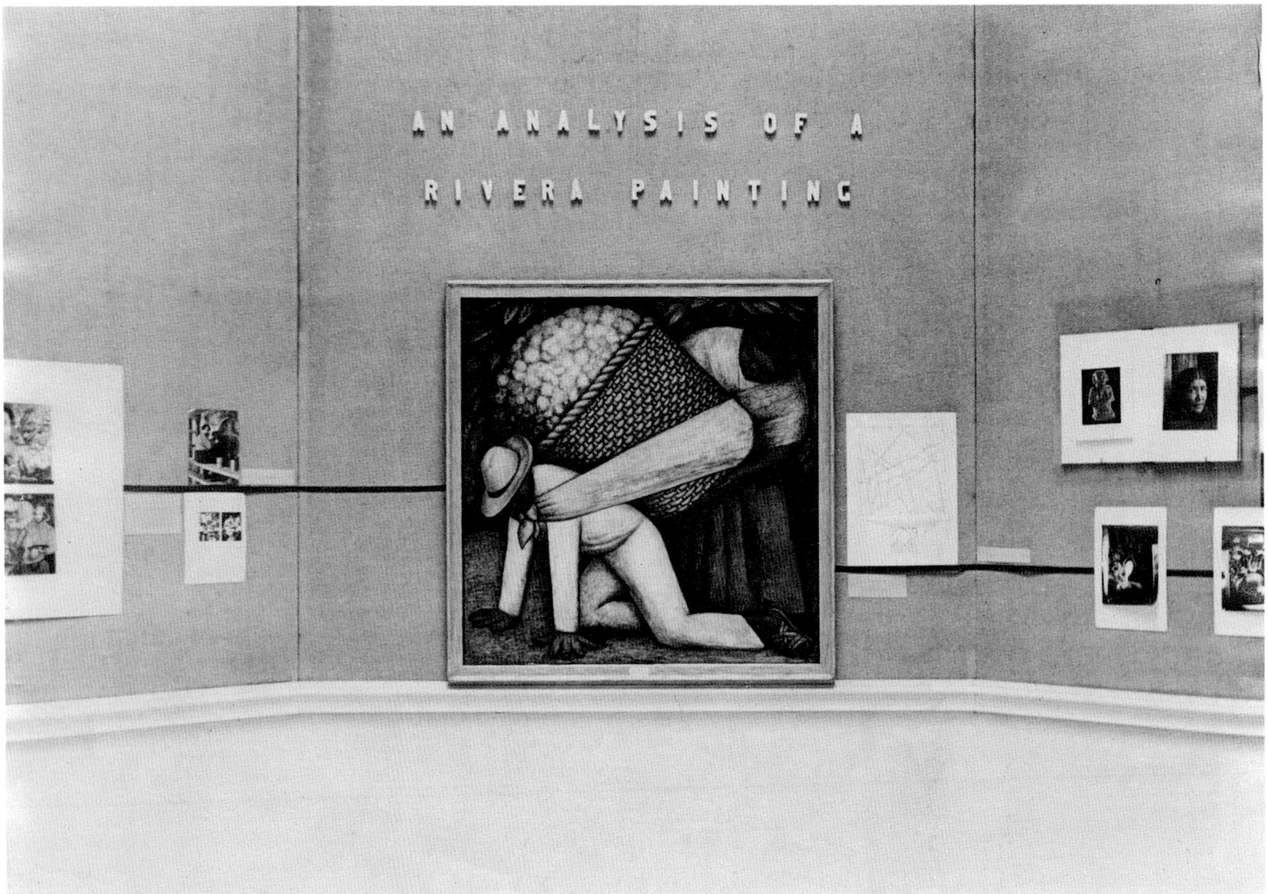

35. Installation view of the exhibition *Analysis of a Rivera*, 1938. San Francisco Museum of Modern Art Archives. Courtesy of San Francisco Museum of Modern Art Archives.

examine modern art. An installation photograph from *Analysis of a Rivera* shows *The Flower Carrier* surrounded by a constellation of supplementary material: explanatory labels, a drawing demonstrating the underlying organizational structure of the painting, a photograph of what appears to be Pre-Columbian sculpture, indicating Rivera's interest in monumentality, a photograph of Rivera sitting on scaffolding in front of a fresco demonstrating his mural practice, and details from his local mural *Allegory of California*. *Analysis of a Rivera Painting* (fig. 35) illustrates how Morley utilized Bender's gift, *The Flower Carrier*, and San Francisco's interest in Rivera to teach viewers the practice of informed looking.

Building upon the exhibitions dedicated to Rivera and Mexican art, Morley expanded SFMOMA's exhibition schedule and the public's interest in Latin American art to include Bolivian, Colombian, and Peruvian artists. For instance, in 1936 Morley dedicated two exhibitions to Peruvian artist Julia Codesido (1883–1979): *Contemporary Peruvian Paintings by Julia Codesido* and *Julia Codesido Woodblocks*. Morley borrowed paintings from Delphic Studios, a New York gallery, which had just arranged the first U.S. exhibition of Codesido's work, *Peruvian Subjects by Julia Codesido*. Notably, Morley changed the exhibition's title from *Peruvian Subjects by Julia Codesido*, as it was referred to by Alma Reed (1889–1966), to *Contemporary Peruvian Paintings by Julia Codesido*, asserting the artist's status as a significant contemporary painter. Delphic Studios was founded by San Francisco native and former *San Francisco Call* journalist Alma Reed to showcase the work of Orozco, but it also arranged important exhibitions featuring Mexican artists such as José Miguel Covarrubias (1904–1957), Roberto Montenegro, and Adolfo Best-Maugard (1891–1964), as well as California photographers Ansel Adams (1902–1984) and Edward Weston (1886–1958).[22] An acclaimed exhibition of Codesido's paintings held in 1935 in Mexico City's Palacio de Bellas Artes may have inspired Reed to organize *Peruvian Subjects by Julia Codesido*. In Mexico City, Siqueiros lauded Codesido's paintings as "all that is indispensable to realize the enterprise of Mexican Revolutionary art."[23] Similarly, in the exhibition brochure for *Peruvian Subjects by Julia Codesido*, a quote from American art critic Waldo Frank affirms that Codesido is "worthy to stand beside the greatest artists of Revolutionary Mexico."[24]

The perceived link between Codesido and Mexican art would have attracted both Reed and San Francisco's public to the artwork of Codesido. When SFMOMA exhibited *Contemporary Peruvian Paintings by Julia Codesido*, Morley celebrated Codesido's relationship with Mexican art, but, unlike Frank and Siqueiros, she was careful not to validate Codesido by linking her with Mexico. In the supplementary text for *Contemporary Peruvian Paintings by Julia Codesido*, Morley describes the artist's work as "authentically Peruvian."[25] She is cautious, however, when comparing Codesido's painting to Mexican modernism. "If anything," Morley allows, Codesido's work "shows a strong relation to the art of Mexico." The qualifying term "If anything" connects Codesido to Mexican modernism, which would have made the Peruvian artist's work accessible to SFMOMA's visitors through familiarity, but at the same time emphasizes difference. While Morley acknowledged that Codesido's paintings were similar to those of Mexican painters like Orozco and Rivera because of their interest in Indigenist subject matter, she argued that Codesido's style was entirely singular. As Morley writes, "Her work is neither delicate nor at all subtle. It is broad and direct, the forms gaining vividness and strength through simplification. . . . They do not lose in decorative value by this penetration, for combined with her uncompromising realism is an equally strong feeling for design and beauty of composition. A fine sense of color makes her canvases even more striking. She can turn the most ordinary scene into a dramatic and vividly told story, and like all good story tellers, she exaggerates to increase the tale."[26] Morley does not reference a specific painting in this text, but her words could describe *Huanca Indian* from 1932, which was featured in the SFMOMA exhibition and on the cover of the Delphic Studios brochure (fig. 36).[27]

In 1936, Morley still lacked funds to develop a permanent collection and was unable to retain a painting by Codesido for SFMOMA. She did, however, extend the presence of Codesido's artwork in California by circulating *Contemporary Peruvian Paintings by Julia Codesido* and *Julia Codesido Woodblocks* through the Western Association of Art Museum Directors (WAAMD), an organization dedicated to sharing exhibitions among museums in the western United States.[28] Between 1935 and 1940, SFMOMA presented numerous Latin American art exhibitions, many of which relied on loans from local collections, including *José Clemente Orozco*, *José Clemente Orozco Prints*, *Selection of Mexican Prints and Drawings from the A. M. Bender Collection*, *Pre-Columbian Art of Peru*, *Guatemalan Textiles*, *Diego Rivera Reproduction Exhibition*, *Oils and Drawings by Ramos Martínez*, and

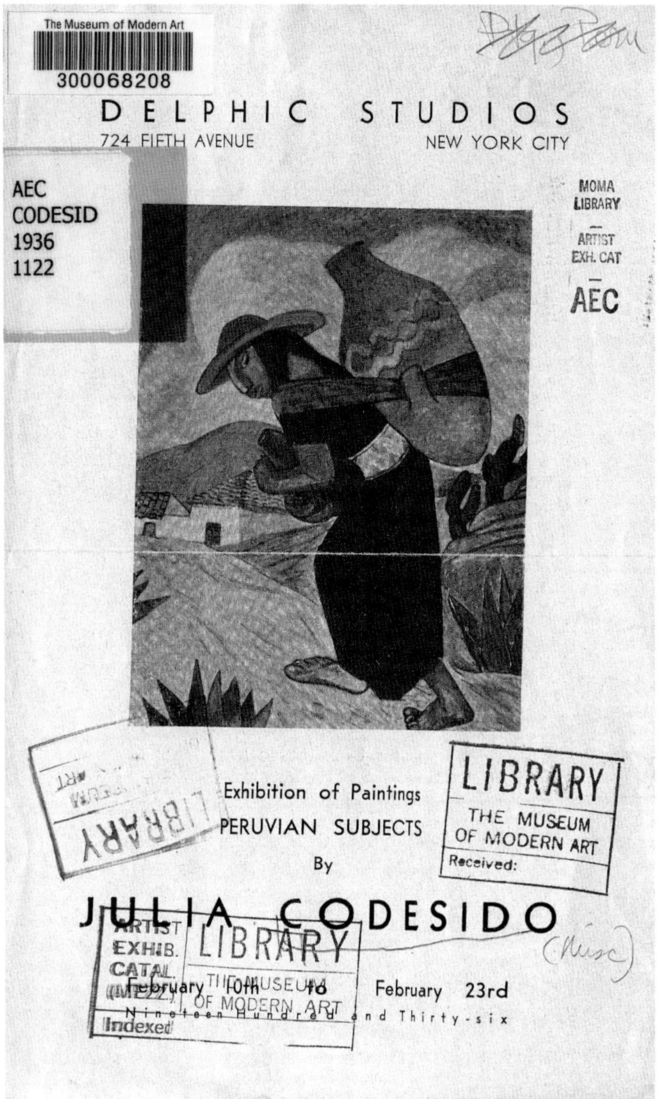

36. Julia Codesido (Peruvian, 1892–1979), *Huanca Indian*, cover, *Exhibition of Paintings: Peruvian Subjects by Julia Codesido*, February 10 to February 23, 1936. New York, Delphic Studios.

Drawings and Watercolors by Diego Rivera from the Collections of the Museum.[29] During this period SFMOMA also organized and circulated exhibitions dedicated to the work of Colombian artist Luis Alberto Acuña (1927–2005) as well as Bolivian-born artists Roberto Berdecio (1910–1996) and Antonio Sotomayor (1904–1985).[30] As a gesture of gratitude, Acuña gave SFMOMA a series of drawings to distribute among the WAAMD institutions that exhibited his work.[31] Morley chose to keep Acuña's drawing *The Annunciation* for SFMOMA's collection.

In 1940, the organizing committee for the Golden Gate International Exposition (GGIE), San Francisco's world's fair, asked Morley to arrange an exhibition of contemporary Central and South American art, and her involvement with this project helped to further develop local collections of modern Latin American art in San Francisco. Acting as consultant for the Exposition's Palace of Fine Arts, Morley spent two weeks traveling throughout Central and South America, borrowing paintings from Chile, Colombia, Costa Rica, Ecuador, El Salvador, and Peru.[32] While traveling, she worked closely with artists from each region, including Codesido, who acted as Morley's cultural liaison in Lima.[33]

Morley's exhibition *South and Central American Art* achieved both popular and critical success. Numerous paintings were purchased by private collectors directly from the exhibition, especially from the Peruvian section, which Morley described as the "nucleus of the exhibition."[34] Morley boasted to her friend Agnes Rindge Claflin (1900–1977), executive secretary for the Office of the Coordinator of Inter American Affairs (CIAA) and member of the MoMA's Advisory Committee, "I am somewhat encouraged too that of the eighteen Peruvian paintings I chose for the Exposition eight were purchased and a ninth would have stayed too had it not been a bit too expensive."[35] Here Morley may be referring to *Andean Landscape* by José Sabogal (1888–1956), leader of Peru's Indigenist movement and director of the Escuela Nacional de Bellas Artes in Lima, which Morley hoped to acquire for SFMOMA's collection. Despite her desire to purchase paintings from *South and Central American Art*, Morley reported to Codesido that there was no "purchase fund from which I could draw."[36] While SFMOMA lacked the financial means for acquisitions, Morley acquired a painting by Codesido, *Landscape, Arequipa*, for her personal collection. After Morley acquired *Landscape, Arequipa*, it spent nearly a decade circulating throughout the United States in several important exhibitions, including the Newark Museum's *Three South American Neighbors: Ecuador, Peru, and Bolivia* of 1941 and SFMOMA's *Contemporary Latin American Art*.[37]

As a curator and museum director, Morley was exacting, self-critical, and the first to acknowledge the shortcomings of her own exhibitions. *South and Central American Art* received considerable acclaim, but Morley admitted its limitations. In the exhibition catalogue, Morley noted that the regions of Central and South America had been given little attention by U.S. museums. She therefore described her exhibition as a "preliminary survey, that should be followed by repeated leisurely and exhaustive examinations of individual countries."[38] In essence, Morley recognized that the exhibition was not comprehensive. Morley aspired to offer more inclusive Latin American art exhibitions at SFMOMA in order to build upon the work she started with *South and Central American Art*. Just after the GGIE closed, Morley began to envision a plan for exhibiting Latin American art at SFMOMA: "What I started on a small scale should certainly be followed up. In the future I should like to be able to hold exhibitions country by country, doing each thoroughly with careful attention to its past, the traditions which have united in its art and with some regard for its popular arts also."[39]

South and Central American Art at the GGIE attracted the attention of Nelson Rockefeller, who asked Morley to serve as Cultural Relations Division Advisor for CIAA.[40] Although Morley's ability to collect and exhibit Latin American art at SFMOMA was enhanced by her connection with CIAA, she was critical of the organization's practices. Morley's first assignment for CIAA involved a two-month trip to Argentina, Bolivia, Brazil, Chile, Colombia, Cuba, Ecuador, Peru, Uruguay, and Venezuela to secure exhibition venues for *La Pintura Contemporánea Norteamericana*, an ambitious traveling exhibition of contemporary U.S. paintings.[41] The exhibition was organized in order to fulfill the primary mission of CIAA: to establish good-neighbor relations between the United States and Latin America and fight Axis sympathies. Even though the exhibition, which featured paintings by artists such as Charles Demuth (1883–1935), Arshile Gorky (1904–1948), and Edward Hopper (1882–1967), was praised in most countries, Morley felt that it was hastily arranged and even ill-conceived. She criticized CIAA members for their lack of knowledge about Latin America.[42] As Stanton Catlin, a young representative for *La Pintura Contemporánea Norteamericana* who later became the first director of the Center for Inter-American Relations (now the Americas Society), admitted, "we were so naïve at that particular time we had no conception of what the size of South America was."[43] Morley similarly noted, "we all have the habit of thinking of [Latin America] as a unity and, in fact, its diversity is the important thing. Each country has developed its contemporary art in its own way, each lies apart from every other, there are complex currents in the countries themselves. In some countries, there are several art centers, not only one, and all those things must be taken into account."[44] Morley advised against the uninformed "cultural export" of paintings through exhibitions like *La Pintura Contemporánea Norteamericana*, and argued that CIAA should take regional interests into account when developing exhibitions for Latin American audiences.[45] Morley argued that CIAA's projects, like *La Pintura Contemporánea Norteamericana*, should be arranged with such diversity in mind, and she endeavored to combat her colleagues' and the public's misconceptions about Latin America's homogeneity through exhibitions and developing a Latin American permanent collection at SFMOMA.

While CIAA's projects were organized in response to the war emergency and primarily considered the immediate future, Morley viewed her own involvement as "the beginning of an exchange" and the first step toward the "continuous contact of professional museum people, artists, art critics and institutions and organizations."[46] Morley used her CIAA-funded trip on behalf of *La Pintura Contemporánea Norteamericana* as an opportunity to develop relationships with Latin American artists and art professionals, and would later call upon their assistance when organizing exhibitions and building a collection of Latin American art at SFMOMA. One example is her relationship with Argentine painter and museum director Emilio Pettoruti (1892–1971). While traveling on behalf of CIAA, Morley met Pettoruti in Buenos Aires. She was equally interested in Pettoruti as a spearhead for the avant-garde in Argentina and as director of the progressive Museo Municipal de Bellas Artes in La Plata. After returning to the United States, Morley organized *Emilio Pettoruti of Argentina*, a comprehensive exhibition of the artist's work which traveled throughout the country in 1942 and 1943.[47] Morley also secured government sponsorship for Pettoruti and his wife, writer María Rosa González (1898–1977), to visit the United States.[48]

Morley's exhibition and relationship with Pettoruti helped to establish a presence for the artist in U.S. collections. The Seattle Art Museum, which served as a venue for *Emilio Pettoruti of Argentina* after SFMOMA, acquired the painting *Intimidad* of 1941, and MoMA in New York purchased *Verdigris Goblet* of 1934. SFMOMA acquired two paintings. The first, *Coparmónica* of 1931, was purchased by the Museum, and Morley personally acquired a second painting, *Quinteto* of 1927, which she immediately presented to the Museum as a gift (fig. 37). As Edward J. Sullivan observes, *Intimidad* and *Quinteto* were "sold at auction in the early 1980s, and acquired by Argentine collections."[49] Only *Verdigris Goblet* and *Coparmónica* remain in the United States.

When Morley returned from her CIAA trip, she was asked to arrange an exhibition of contemporary Latin American art for circulation in the United States on behalf of CIAA. The exhibition, *Contemporary Latin American Art*, was just one part of a much larger traveling show called *Latin American Art*, which featured sections dedicated to Pre-Columbian and colonial art, organized by the Brooklyn Museum. Morley requested permission to make a return trip to South America to loan new artwork for *Contemporary Latin American Art*. "Certainly we shall have to bring some material from South America in order to make the show interesting and important," Morley advised.[50] CIAA wanted to avoid additional costs and hoped to make the exhibition available as quickly as possible, so Morley was forced to build *Contemporary Latin American Art* around established U.S. collections. Morley's correspondence reveals how limited U.S. collections of modern Latin American art were at the start of the 1940s. "We [SFMOMA] do not have a collection of South American paintings. I, personally, own a couple, and friends of mine, a few more," Morley revealed.[51] When Morley wrote to Elodie Courter (1911–1994), head of circulating exhibitions at MoMA, to inquire about borrowing South American art from MoMA's collection, Courter responded, "I am afraid we have very little in our collection."[52]

Even though MoMA and SFMOMA possessed robust collections of Mexican art, in 1941 the institutions owned few paintings from Central America, South America, or the Caribbean. The

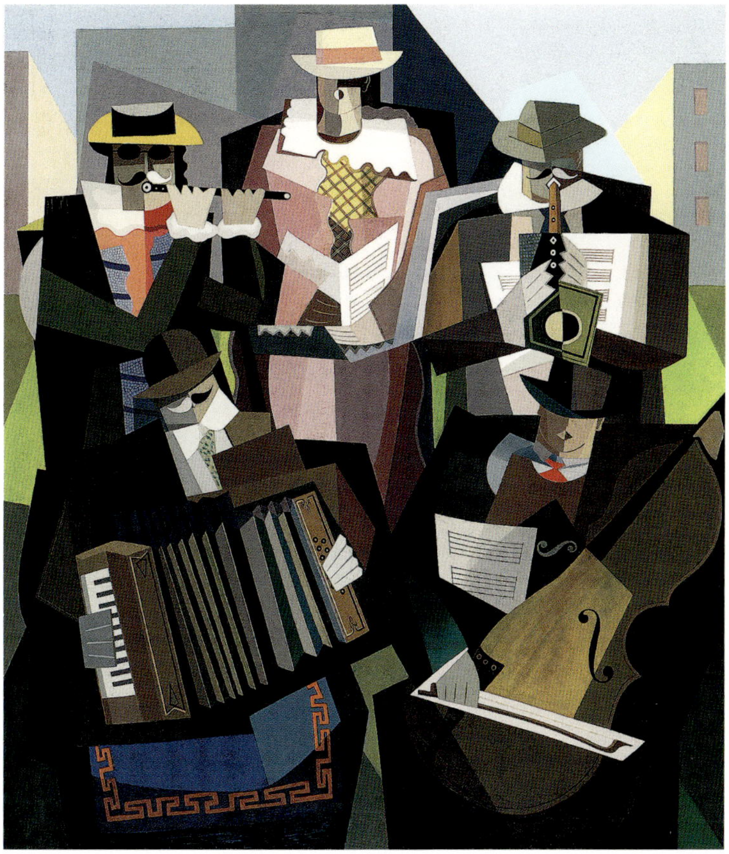

37. Emilio Pettoruti (Argentinian, 1892–1974), *Quinteto*, 1927. Oil on plywood, 149.5 × 131.5 cm. Reproduced in the Pettoruti catalogue, edited by the Pettoruti Foundation in 1995, Buenos Aires, ficha N°255. Copyright Pettoruti Foundation.

scarcity of modern Latin American art in the collections of both museums would radically change during the 1940s, but through very different means. As Miriam Basilio explores in this volume, Nelson Rockefeller's Inter-American Fund helped to establish a Latin American collection at MoMA. SFMOMA, on the other hand, did not have the support of Rockefeller's dollars. Out of her own belief in the importance of establishing a representative collection of Latin American art in San Francisco, Morley developed what she called the Latin American Purchase Fund. After Morley returned from her CIAA trip, she determinedly traveled the United States, giving lectures on Latin American art. Morley used the honoraria she received from such lectures as "Latin America: A Diversity Not Unity in Geography, in People, in Art Background" at the Montalvo Foundation in Saratoga, California, to develop the Latin American Purchase Fund.[53] As Morley wrote, "such fees . . . have gone into a Latin American purchase fund for the Museum, so that whatever comes out of any special knowledge or competence I may have . . . is plowed back into the work."[54] By giving lectures on Latin American art and collecting honoraria to develop a Latin American collection at SFMOMA, Morley was able to share her knowledge and simultaneously acquire new material for exhibitions.

While the survey exhibition *Contemporary Latin American Art* traveled the United States from 1941 to 1944, Morley gradually cultivated SFMOMA's Latin American collection. Beginning in 1942, Morley initiated a "long planned" exhibition schedule dedicated to Latin American art at SFMOMA by utilizing contacts from her GGIE and CIAA trips.[55] Exhibitions such as *Three Artists from Cuba: Enríquez, Orlando, Peláez* in 1942 and *Watercolors by José Perotti* in 1943 focused on specific artists and regions and collectively emphasized the diversity of Latin American art, combatting stereotypes of homogeneity. In an effort to develop a comprehensive collection, Morley tried to retain at least one representative work from each Latin American exhibition held at SFMOMA. In addition to Pettoruti's *Coparmónica*, the Purchase Fund enabled Morley to acquire a still life from 1940 by Cuban artist Amelia Peláez (1896–1968);[56] Cuban artist René Portocarrero's (1912–1985) oil on paper *Cuban Interior*; two prints by Brazilian artist Cândido Portinari (1903–1962), *Figures in a Boat* and *Figures*; Berdecio's painting *Head of a Leader*; a representative example of a *Candombe* painting from 1946–47 by Uruguayan Pedro Figari (1861–1938);[57] Venezuelan artist Héctor Poleo's (1918–1989) 1941 painting *Andean Landscape*; and two watercolors by Argentine artists Héctor Basaldúa (1895–1976) and Horacio Butler (1897–1983), *The Street* and *The Garden*.[58] SFMOMA also received several important gifts during this period: Joaquín Torres-Garcia's (1874–1949) painting *Figures* was donated by the Uruguayan architect Román Fresnedo Siri; Mexican artist Rufino Tamayo's (1899–1991) painting *The Lovers* was purchased with the assistance of W. W. Crocker; and the museum's Women's Board acquired Cuban artist Mario Carreño's (1913–1999) gouache *Afro-Cuban Dancer* of 1943 (fig. 38).[59] José Perotti (1898–1956) gave the museum one of his own terracotta sculptures, called *Earth*.[60] In addition to Pettoruti's *Quinteto*, Morley presented SFMOMA with Eduardo Kingman's (1913–1997) 1945 oil on canvas titled *The Mask*.[61]

While building SFMOMA's collection of Latin American art, Morley simultaneously continued to develop her personal collection. Many of these works remained in SFMOMA's care until Morley left the museum in 1958. Prime examples include the watercolors *Bulls Working* by Carlos Enríquez and *Cuban Tobacco Plantation* by Felipe Orlando from Cuba;[62] Chilean painter Pablo Burchard's (1875–1964) watercolor *Ranch at Night*; Mexican artist Lynn Linares's (Ernesto Butterlin, known as Linares or Lin, 1917–1964) oil painting *God of Growth*; an edition of Mérida's series of lithographs, *Popul Vuh*; a sculpture titled *Head of a Girl* and a drawing labeled *Walking the Drunkard* by Perotti; two drawings by Pettoruti, *Still Life* and *Abstract Head*; a drawing titled *Two Figures* by René Portocarrero; and, finally, a drawing by Sotomayor titled *Spanish Shepherd*.[63] Although Morley often purchased artwork with her own funds in order to add material to exhibitions, she included work as an anonymous lender.[64] In reference to *Contemporary Latin American* Art, Morley alerted Courter, "The examples marked, 'Lent anonymously to the San Francisco Museum of Art' belong to me, but I prefer not to have my name on the loan."[65] Morley used the new acquisitions, from her own collection and SFMOMA's, to reorganize and strengthen *Contemporary Latin American Art* in 1944, which SFMOMA continued to circulate in various forms until at least 1948.[66] Beginning in 1944, the loan fees gathered from *Contemporary Latin American Art* were added to the Latin American Purchase Fund.[67]

Morley strove to develop a comprehensive collection of Latin American art at SFMOMA, but characteristically she was quick to acknowledge the shortcomings of her efforts. Reviewing SFMOMA's Latin American collection, Morley confessed, "Brazil so far is represented only by prints, and Paraguay is not represented at all. These involuntary omissions should some day be repaired to complete the account of South American art."[68] According to Morley, she had simply "tried to provide a foundation for others to build on."[69] This foundation, built with limited outside resources, was quite remarkable. As Catlin observed, Morley "was one of the first collectors of an across-the-board kind, to know the quality, of what was going on in Mexico and South America."[70] In addition to her work at SFMOMA, Morley helped to develop the Latin American collection at MoMA by advising and encouraging Alfred H. Barr, Jr. (1902–1981), to collect South American art when he was reluctant to do so. As MoMA's Latin American collection began to take shape, Morley gloated to Barr, "After all, for good or ill you are now committed to Latin American contemporary art—remember how reluctant and sceptical you were when I first showed you photographs, in 1940 it must have been!"[71] Numerous works which Morley acquired on SFMOMA's behalf, such as *Quinteto* by Pettoruti and *The Mask* by Kingman, were deaccessioned in the 1970s and 1980s, but what remains in SFMOMA's collection, and MoMA's as well, stands today as evidence of Morley's determination to build representative collections of modern Latin American art in the United States.

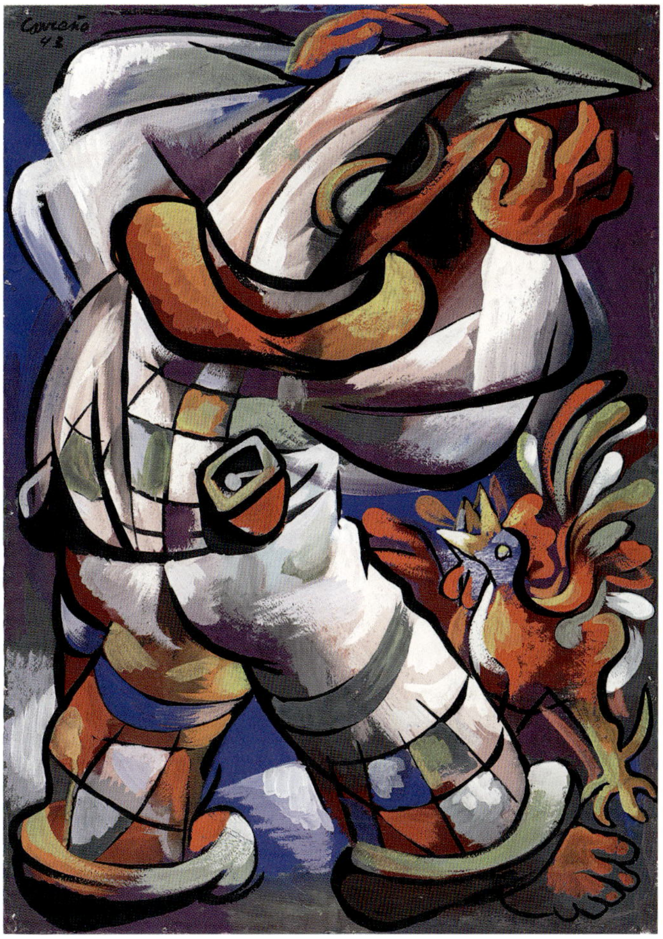

38. Mario Carreño (Cuban, 1913–1999), *Afro-Cuban Dancer*, 1943. Gouache, 85.09 × 62.55 cm. San Francisco Museum of Modern Art. © 2009 Artists Rights Society (ARS), New York / CREAIMAGEN, Santiago de Chile.

CHAPTER 7

Inverted Strategies

An Exhibition as Matrix for a Permanent Collection

Mari Carmen Ramírez

39. Joaquín Torres-García (Uruguayan, 1874–1949), *Estructura en colores puros* (Structure in Primary Colors), 1929. Oil and nails on wood, 22.7 × 11.4 × 4.4 cm. Houston, The Museum of Fine Arts. © Sucesión Joaquín Torres-Garcia, Montevideo, 2015.

Latin American Art in Texas

Permanent collections are museums' most prized assets. They not only justify a museum's existence, but also define it for posterity. However, the project of assembling a comprehensive institutional collection of modern and contemporary Latin American art is one filled with unexpected challenges, ongoing pitfalls, and intrinsic contradictions, as well as unpredictable blunders. In this regard, such an undertaking can be considered a tentative, if not skeptical, experiment; that is to say, a conditional initiative as doubtful as, perhaps, the flawed ideal of a continental community, encompassing the more than twenty countries and hundreds of groups within each country that constitute the multiethnic population of the region.[1] Hampered by complex histories of nationalism, uneven modernization, political repression, economic instability—duly reinforced by an unbelievable (though still-colonized) indifference toward other neighboring nations—not many institutions in Latin America have embarked on such a far-reaching endeavor to gather in one place the most outstanding examples of the art of the continent as a whole. And, until very recently, this included even private collectors. In this regard, it may be time to recognize once and for all that "the idea of collecting modern and contemporary art from Latin America on a comprehensive or continental scale arguably began in the United States in the mid-1940s"[2] at the Museum of Modern Art (MoMA) in New York, under the auspices of Nelson A. Rockefeller (1908–1979) and Alfred H. Barr, Jr. (1902–1981).[3] As a result of these activities, Latin American art enjoyed early on a certain amount of visibility in the New York artistic milieu, a momentum that gradually expanded with the city's rise as the preeminent global center of artistic and market legitimization, later reinforced by the establishment of specialized auctions at Sotheby's and Christie's in the late 1970s and early 1980s.

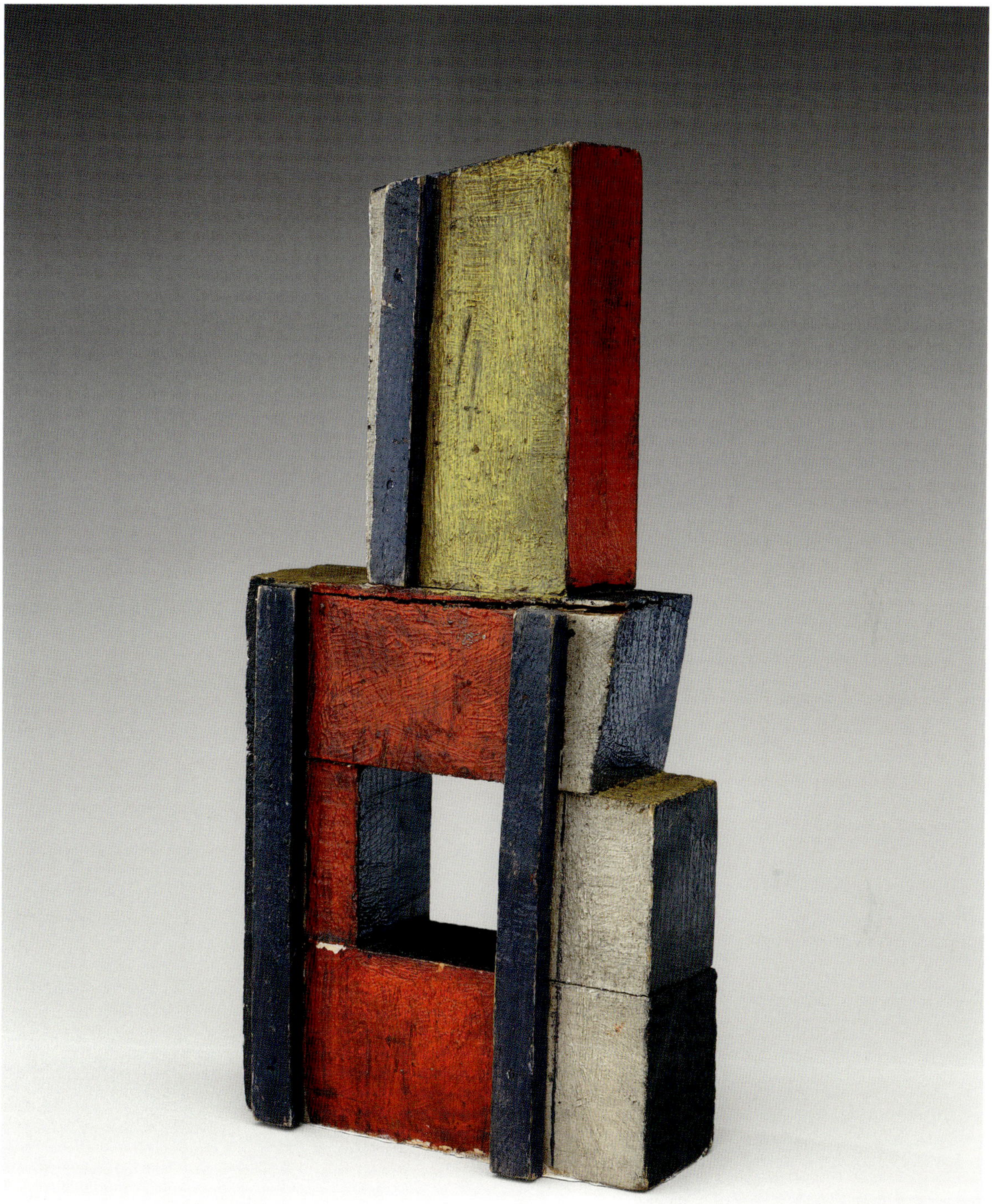

Despite this influential history, however, it was not in the East but in the Lone Star State of Texas that the idea to build all-encompassing collections of Latin American art found fertile ground since at least the second half of the twentieth century. Indeed, the trend can be traced to New York collectors Barbara (1921–2003) and John Duncan, who were attracted early on to the University of Texas at Austin's Archer M. Huntington Art Gallery (now the Jack S. Blanton Museum of Art) in search of a proper place to house their drawings and paintings collection.[4] Today, the Blanton Museum's Latin American art holdings encompass over two thousand modern and contemporary works in all media by more than seven hundred artists from Mexico, South and Central America, and the Caribbean.[5] The University of Texas at Austin is also home to the extensive Nickolas Muray (1892–1965) Collection of Modern Mexican Art, which features, among several hundred works, well-known and reproduced paintings by Frida Kahlo (1907–1954) and Diego Rivera (1886–1957).[6] The vast concentration of scholarly resources at this prestigious academic center, in turn, not only justified the direction that the collection would take but also served as the catalyst for the creation in 1988 of the first position of Curator of Latin American Art in the United States.[7] In a similar vein, since the 1920s the San Antonio Museum of Art (SAMA) has been amassing an extensive collection of Mexican and Latin American paintings, sculptures, works on paper, and decorative arts that spans more than four thousand years.[8] Ironically, these holdings include the large collection of Mexican folk art assembled by another New Yorker, Nelson A. Rockefeller.[9] Last but not least, since the 1930s the Museum of Fine Arts, Houston, has also been actively collecting the art produced south of the Rio Grande. The MFAH's holdings in this area encompass the Glassell Collections of Pre-Columbian Gold[10] and Pre-Columbian art to modern and contemporary works in all media. All in all, the Museum of Fine Arts, Houston, boasts over fifty-three hundred objects from this area, ranging in time from 3300 B.C.E. to the present.

The ubiquity of Latin American art in Texas should not come as a surprise considering this state's territorial history and long-standing historical, political, cultural, and economic links with the countries that make up this geographic enclave, headed by Mexico, to a greater or lesser extent. Undoubtedly, the fact that until 1836 the state of Coahuila y Tejas was officially part of Mexico and the 1,248-mile border that Texas shares with Mexico today attest to a sui generis cultural and political involvement that is completely alien to states in the East, albeit not to California, Arizona, and New Mexico. To this undeniable history must be added the enduring presence since the colonial period of Mexican nationals, Mexican Americans (Chicanos), as well as the continuous influx of immigrants—initially from Mexico, but in the last few decades also from Central and South America and the Caribbean—who have made Texas their home. Nowadays, with more than 40 percent of its population claiming either Latin American, Hispanic, or Latino descent, Texas—like most of the border states (and increasingly the country)—is living proof of the ample, irreversible process of "Latino-ization" of the United States; a reinforced evolution that—as demonstrated by the 2008 and 2012 presidential elections—has the potential to influence the long-term future of the United States as a whole. In this context, the "added value" of Latin American art in Texan museums has less to do directly with artistic fads or market trends. Instead, these initiatives are grounded in the urgent need for these institutions to *reinvent* themselves in light of the cultural demands of these increasingly diverse audiences. Only in this way can Texan institutions ensure their long-term relevance, if not their mere survival.

With a population of over two million,[11] 44 percent of which is Latino,[12] Houston has not been immune to the radical demographic trends that are significantly altering the state;[13] indeed, not only do 38 percent of Houston homes speak Spanish as a primary language[14] but 62.7 percent of Houston's elementary, middle school, and high school population today is of Hispanic and Latino descent.[15] These facts, together with a long tradition of cultural philanthropy grounded in the city's preeminent share of the oil, gas, commercial shipping, and health industries, provided the stimuli for an unprecedented program at the Museum of Fine Arts, Houston, that started with the millennium: one aimed at collecting, exhibiting, researching, and promoting modern and contemporary Latin American and Latino art. The establishment in 2001 of an endowed curatorial department together with a research center—the International Center for the Arts of the Americas (ICAA)—underscored both the financial as well as the ethical commitment of the Museum to this emerging field of scholarship and curatorial expertise. In addition to the intense focus on research embodied by the ICAA and its landmark digital archive initiative *Documents of 20th-Century Latin American and Latino Art*,[16] the most salient aspect of the MFAH's multifaceted program was the mandate to assemble a brand-new collection of modern and contemporary art from Mexico, Central and South America, and the Caribbean as well as outstanding examples of U.S. Latino art. Having started near zero, the collection today encompasses over 180 artists and 700 works of twentieth- and twenty-first-century art in all media.[17] The extensive choice and organization of such a collection illustrate both the challenges and the rewards at the core of what thirteen years ago was still a rather "risky" enterprise, particularly from the perspective of mainstream U.S. art museums. Hence, in what follows, I would like to consider the theoretical and practical issues posed by such an undertaking since its inception.

Inverted Strategies

In 2001, the idea of organizing a permanent collection of twentieth- and twenty-first-century Latin American and Latino art in a major encyclopedic museum such as the Museum of Fine Arts, Houston, represented, at best, an uncharted opportunity; at worst, an extremely challenging enterprise, if not a daunting task.[18] Of the iconic masters of the first half of the century—Diego Rivera, David Alfaro Siqueiros (1896–1974), José Clemente Orozco (1883–1949), Frida Kahlo, Wifredo Lam (1902–1982), and Roberto Matta (1911–2002)—only Matta was represented in the Museum's collection. The majority of the artists from Latin America who contributed to international modernism and, more specifically, to the avant-garde were not only unknown in the United States, but their work had relatively little market presence or even value. Within the complexity and heterogeneity embodied by the operative construct of "Latin American art,"[19] there thus loomed a series of demanding questions. How could the Museum begin to articulate out of nowhere a collection that—in some always incomplete if not fragmentary way—would represent the richness of the art produced in a subcontinental region? And within this focus, how could it avoid the stereotypes and commonplaces with which Latin American art had been pigeonholed until then? How could it insert this art on an equal footing with a larger and more established museum collection that operated within the canonical parameters of an encyclopedic museum? And, anticipating our next step, what kind of "model" could serve as blueprint for this active collection-building effort? Further compounding this scenario is the project for a third Museum building with a specific focus on post-1900 art, where the production of Latin American and Latino artists will be generously displayed for the first time in a permanent and polemical dialogue with their renowned European and North American counterparts. The idea of "polemical" involves, among other issues, the pioneering features of specific works as well as their creative tendency to "invert" trends stemming from the original European avant-garde movements of the 1920s through 1960s.

At the core of this situation lay the particular dilemma confronted by institutional collections at the levels of both organization and display. While private collections are characterized by malleability, museum holdings—even in the most dynamic institutions—are slowly amassed over time in response to market opportunities, critical consensus, patron generosity, and depth of financial resources. As a result, the long and meandering process of building an art museum collection is quite slow and does not always produce a coherent ensemble in the short term. Furthermore, in a period of economic crises and dwindling resources, combined with skyrocketing prices and the intrinsic difficulties that such works in progress entail, museums have frequently opted to dedicate more funds and time to temporary exhibitions than to permanent collections.

In a similar way, permanent collection displays have, for the most part, resisted the radical transformations in exhibition practices of the last decades, remaining stuck in paradigms that favor *synchronicity* as well as *divisions* by media, culture, or geographic locale, all of which lead to pigeonholing artists and movements in preconceived, positivistic, and even biased Eurocentric categories. In my view, this type of paradigm is overtly at odds with contemporary audiences' experience of culture. As Michel Foucault has argued, in an increasingly globalized society, knowledge is enticed by operations that involve "simultaneity," "juxtaposition," "the near-and-the-far," and "the side-by-side." In other words, today we experience the world less in terms of linear, compartmentalized knowledge than on the basis of a vivid network connecting and intersecting with its own skein.[20] Hence, what is at stake is the compelling necessity to find new ways to conceptualize the "moving coordinates" of a permanent collection.

In this context, the temporary exhibition has become a dynamic tool to test all sorts of innovative approaches and "museological models." This situation has led me to raise the following questions: What if the creative development of the collection were to be approached as a comprehensive temporary exhibition? What would happen if—much as we do in temporary displays, where objects from different media, time periods, and cultural or geographic regions are brought together—objects were placed in dialogue with one another in permanent collection displays?[21] The parallel work that the Museum undertook between 2001 and 2004 by means of *Inverted Utopias: Avant-Garde Art in Latin America, 1920–1970*, co-curated by Héctor Olea and myself, suggested a creative way to approach the task of building and consolidating the Museum's permanent collection. Such a comprehensive exhibition showcased approximately 350 works by 63 avant-garde pioneers on the Continent, many of whom, despite the visibility they enjoyed in Latin America, and frequently in Europe, had never or very rarely been shown in the United States. Additionally, *Inverted Utopias* not only brought the work of these creators to the attention of U.S. audiences but also dared to introduce a brand-new exhibition model, based on the notion of *Konstellationen* (constellations), dialectically theorized by Héctor Olea on the basis of Theodor W. Adorno's (1903–1969) *Negative Dialectics*.[22] At the same time, Olea took advantage of ninety-two documents (translated into English) to demonstrate that the importance of these works lay not only in their radical and experimental practice, but also in their solid intellectual contribution to modernism. His essay "Versions, Inversions, and Subversions: The Artist as Theoretician" stresses the relevance accorded to theory by the practitioners of these "changing constellations."[23]

Foregrounding proposals from the 1960s produced under military coups d'état, repressive or colonial regimes in nations such as Argentina, Colombia, Mexico, Venezuela, and Puerto Rico, the constellation of *Play and Grief* exposed the paradoxes at work in such a context. By contrast, *Universal and Vernacular* showcased the production of the generation of avant-garde pioneers represented, among others, by Xul Solar; the School of the South; and the Brazilian Cubist-Nativism of Vicente do Rego Monteiro. *Progression and Rupture*, in turn, encompassed pieces by the now well-known South American Concrete and Constructive art groups: the Argentinean Arte Madi, the Brazilian Concrete and Neo-Concrete groups, as well as forerunners including Joaquín Torres-García (1874–1949) and Lucio Fontana (1899–1968). A fourth constellation, *Vibrational and Stationary*, focused on the idea of motion by unexpectedly pairing the pioneering work of Siqueiros and the artistic teamwork of *Ejercicio Plástico*—the 1933 experimental mural painted in the outskirts of Buenos Aires (represented in the exhibition by a video)—with Venezuelan Constructive and Kinetic artists such as Jesús Rafael Soto (1923–2005), Carlos Cruz-Diez (b. 1923), and Alejandro Otero (1921–1990). As a counterpoint to these investigations, we also positioned Gego (Gertrud Louise Goldschmidt, 1912–1994)—then a relatively unknown artist in the United States—with a group of her early "parallactical" sculptures that dialogued with the Kinetic pieces of Soto and Cruz-Diez. *Touch and Gaze*, a fifth constellation, showcased works that stimulated the senses through interactive works produced in the 1950s and '60s by means of neon lights, pigments, masks, special spectacles or mirrors, colored capes, weights, and water. Finally, *Cryptic and Committed* introduced the highly political conceptual art practices that emerged in South American countries during the 1960s and '70s, at the height of political repression.[24]

Well beyond art-historical parameters, such a constellatory model *condenses*, rather than illustrates, destabilizing themes, innovative approaches, or even antagonistic and regional sensibilities with regard to modernism and its commonplaces. It thus suggests that the idea of "inversion" of the worn-out utopias of high modernism was more a political stance than aesthetic naïveté or an exercise of style, as it had been understood until then by those who considered it "derivative." The theoretical approach grounded in constellations allowed us to assemble works by means of "luminous points"—that is, key developments or singular visions that expose the unbelievable nexus and overt oppositions between these artists, their works, and the specific context of art production as a whole. These developments range from political to religious, from adaptations to innovations, from the questioning of central paradigms and hegemonies, to undeniable assets, unique contributions not only to the region but to twentieth-century art as a whole. The malleability of this "relational/relative model" provokes simultaneous readings of the selected works from comparative perspectives: the ones capable of grasping, in one single glance, historical, cultural, and/or formal traits with no artistic biases or metropolitan hierarchies involved. Moreover, such luminous points can stimulate *material* or *physical* knowledge as compelling as written art-historical accounts—the Official History of Art—thus serving as constellations themselves to orient broader, and much less centralized, navigations and readings of art-historical insights. As Olea states in his essay, the constellatory model "aspires to revolve around an axis, a Pandora's box whose lock responds not to a single combination or key, but to many. Given that we are oriented by constellations in this exhibition, an understanding of the history locked in each object requires a thorough knowledge of the paradoxes in whose negative light the assertiveness of Official History remains concealed and endangered."[25]

From this point of view, both the theoretical parameters handled as well as the malleability at the heart of *Inverted Utopias* suggested a viable blueprint for the long-term development of the Museum's core Latin American art collection, one that in its flexibility and far-ranging scope bypassed the limitations confronted by traditional methods of building institutional holdings. The fact that many of the artists represented in *Inverted Utopias* had, until then, operated on the margins of the mainstream art world ensured that outstanding examples of their production were still available for acquisition. In hindsight, there is no doubt that *taking risks* with artistic manifestations that were still lacking mainstream validation proved to be an efficient strategy.

The Exhibition as Matrix for the Collection

Proceeding from *Inverted Utopias*, the kernel of the collection-building effort became concentrated on pioneers and key exponents of the avant-garde in Latin America. This included independent visionaries and innovators such as Xul Solar (1887–1963), David Alfaro Siqueiros, and Joaquín Torres-García, who—both in theory as well as in practice—set out to push the limits of art: precariousness, experimentation, and figurative abstraction define each case. The idea was to collect, when feasible, the production of these artists in depth and to select works that would allow us to generate either dialogues or tensions in the permanent exhibition space. The fact that at that time the market was being flooded with postwar Constructive and Geometric artworks—trends that had lingered on the margins for decades in search of institutional attention—proved auspicious to this undertaking. Indeed, the first two works that entered the new collection clearly pointed out the direction that the Museum's collecting effort would take. Joaquín Torres-García's *Structure in Primary Colors* (1929; fig. 39), a key example of the master's paradigmatic wood constructions or *maderas* as well as his decisive dialogues with Piet Mondrian (1872–1944) and Theo van Doesburg (1883–1931)—embodied the singularity and diversity of approaches to Constructivism that took hold in Latin American countries from the early 1930s, as did Gego's *Reticulárea* (1975), the last of the series of autonomous stainless steel constructions produced by the artist as offshoots of her Gran Reticulárea environment (Caracas, 1969). Each piece thus functioned to articulate constellatory groupings. Torres-García's *Structure in Primary Colors* served to anchor a series of works by the Argentinean Madí Group that included the *marco recortado* (cutout frame) pieces by Rhod Rothfuss (1920–1969) and articulated structures by Gyula Kosice (1924–2016) and Carmelo Arden Quin (1913–2010), pioneers for more than two decades of a formal equivalent of U.S. artists' "shaped canvas." The same work also set the pace for the accession of a number of *maderas* by Torres-García[26] and his Uruguayan disciples who constituted the so-called School of the South: Julio Alpuy (1919–2009), Gonzalo Fonseca (1922–1997), and Francisco Matto (1911–1995). At the other extreme, Gego's masterwork served as a catalyst for the serial acquisition of a series of constructions by Jesús Rafael Soto, Carlos Cruz-Diez, Alejandro Otero, and the artist herself. This included a representative collection of her extensive drawing and print production—thus far the largest and most comprehensive in any museum or private collection—as well as three-dimensional pieces and drawings-without-paper.

A third group of acquisitions grounded in the *Inverted Utopias* chart of possibilities included Constructive artists who worked with light and water as their primary medium, many of whom were featured through optic-and-haptic proposals in the *Touch and Gaze* constellation. Early on, the Museum was able to get seminal works included in the exhibition by pioneers Julio Le Parc (b. 1928) and Gyula Kosice; these works constituted the basis for a group of light-based structures by, among others,

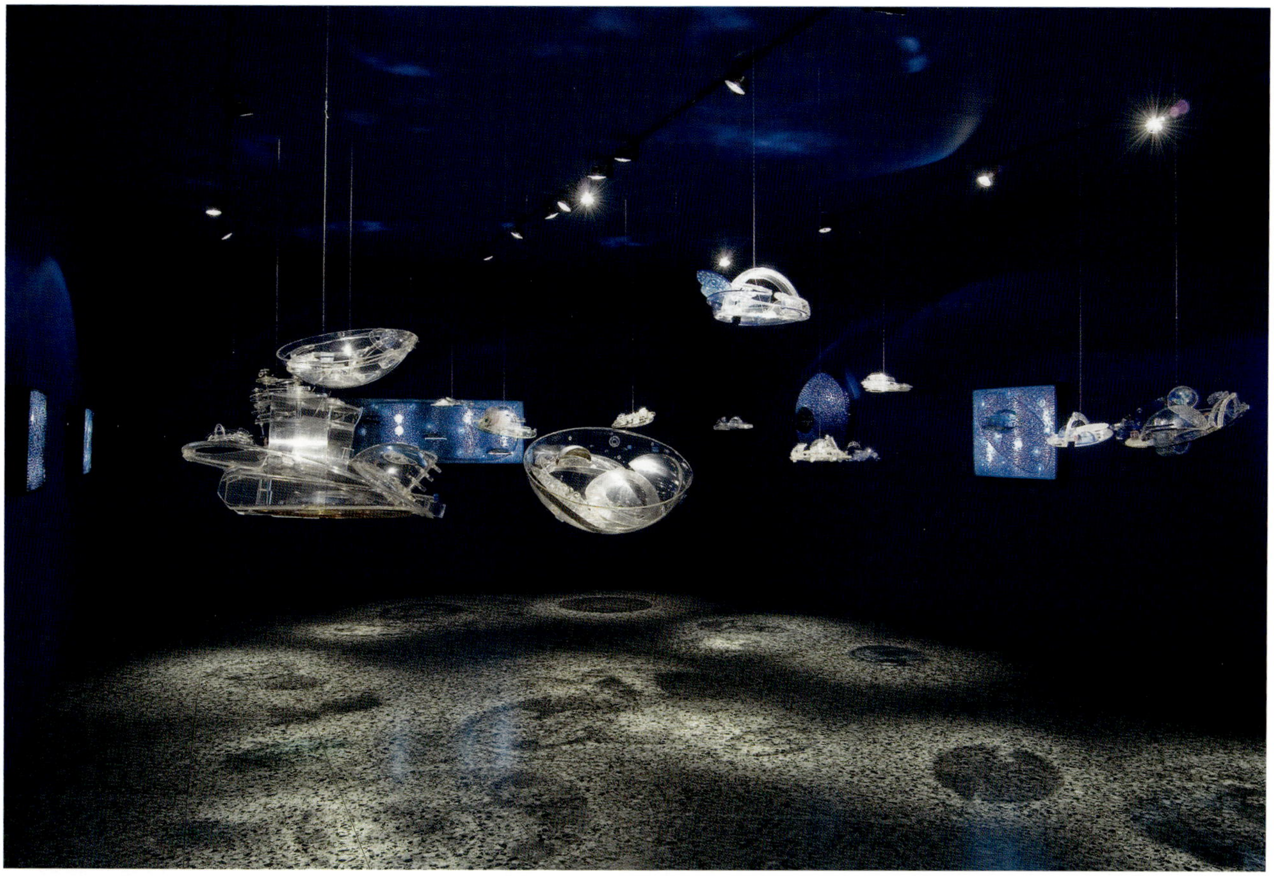

40. Gyula Kosice (Argentinian, 1924–2016), *La ciudad hidroespacial* (The Hydrospatial City), 1946–72. Acrylic, Plexiglas, paint, and light. Houston, The Museum of Fine Arts. La Ciudad Hidroespacial, © Gyula Kosice.

Abraham Palatnik (b. 1928), Martha Boto (1925–2004), and Gregorio Vardánega (1923–2007). At the same time, this type of production is anchored by two paradigmatic installations: Carlos Cruz-Diez's *Chromosaturation* (1965) and Gyula Kosice's *The Hydrospatial City* (1958, acquired later in 2008; fig. 40), a work that stands out not only for its spectacular use of light but, more importantly, for its innovative artistic use of Plexiglas in order to mount poetic—ecological—habitats.

In 2007, the accession of the Adolpho Leirner Collection of Brazilian Constructive Art represented another landmark for the Museum. It allowed us to cover in one fell swoop over one hundred pieces representative of the development of this tendency in Brazil between 1950 and 1962.[27] The collection gathered together paradigmatic examples of Concretismo and Neo-Concretismo—many of which were already represented in *Inverted Utopias*—as well as a broad representation of abstract pioneers and independent artists working in this vein from both cosmopolitan centers: São Paulo and Rio de Janeiro. In addition to this, the Leirner Collection not only expanded the breadth of the Museum's collecting efforts in this area, but also consolidated Constructivism as a major area of strength in the burgeoning

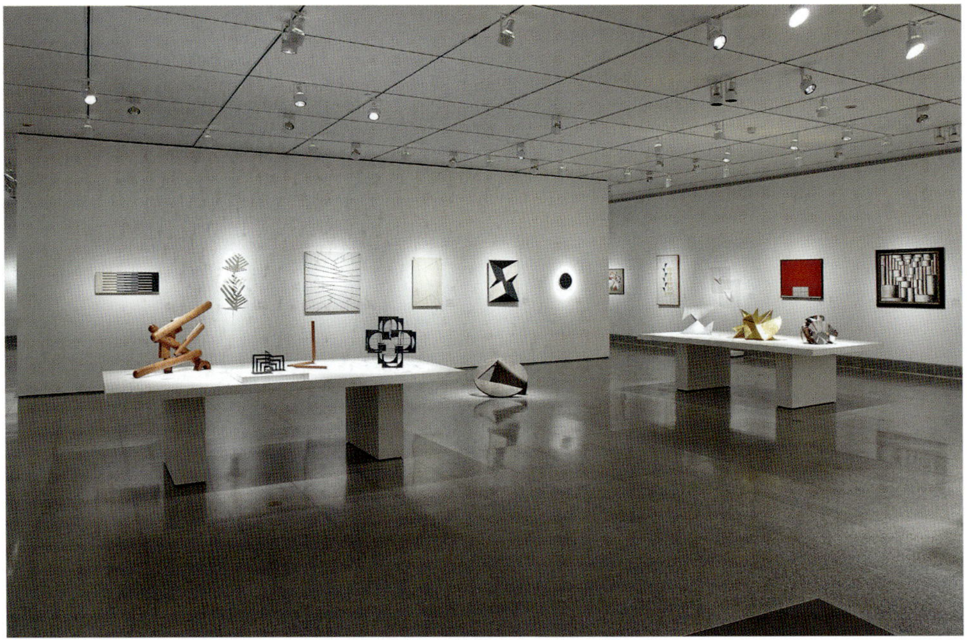

41. Installation view of *Cosmic Dialogues: Selections from the Latin American Art Collection*, May 15–August 23, 2015, at The Museum of Fine Arts, Houston.

MFAH collection, thus allowing us to establish productive dialogues with other Constructive artists represented in the Museum's Latin American holdings (fig. 41). Curiously, this was happening when the mainstream paradigm of Latin American art began to move from figuration and "the fantastic" to the consolidation of a new canon embodied today by Constructive art.

The concentration of Constructive and Geometric art tendencies in the Museum's Latin American art collection strongly established a path that, if pursued in even greater depth, could have determined an exclusive niche for the institution. Yet, given the broad scope of its programming as well as the nature of its audience, the possibility of crafting such a narrow focus for the Latin American collection was not an option for an encyclopedic museum such as the Museum of Fine Arts, Houston. The acquisition at that time of large-scale assemblages and prints by the Argentinean Antonio Berni (1905–1981), together with the illustrated furniture of Colombian Beatriz Gonzalez (b. 1938) and the iconoclastic production of the Argentinean Luis Felipe Noé (b. 1933)—who inverted or distorted his frames in an idiosyncratic manner—served to ground another constellatory ensemble represented by sixties and seventies mixed-media, figure-based avant-garde examples. These include a very precious selection of works by the Argentinean Otra Figuración artists—Luis Felipe Noé, Jorge de la Vega (1930–1971), and Rómulo Macció (1931–2016)—as well as their contemporaries Alberto Heredia (1924–2000) and Juan Carlos Distéfano (b. 1933), all acquired from the prestigious Marion and Jorge Helft Collection in Buenos Aires. Further broadening the selection of artworks from these critical decades is the production of Latino artists like the Chicano Luis Jimenez and Puerto Rican Domingo García (1896–1974),

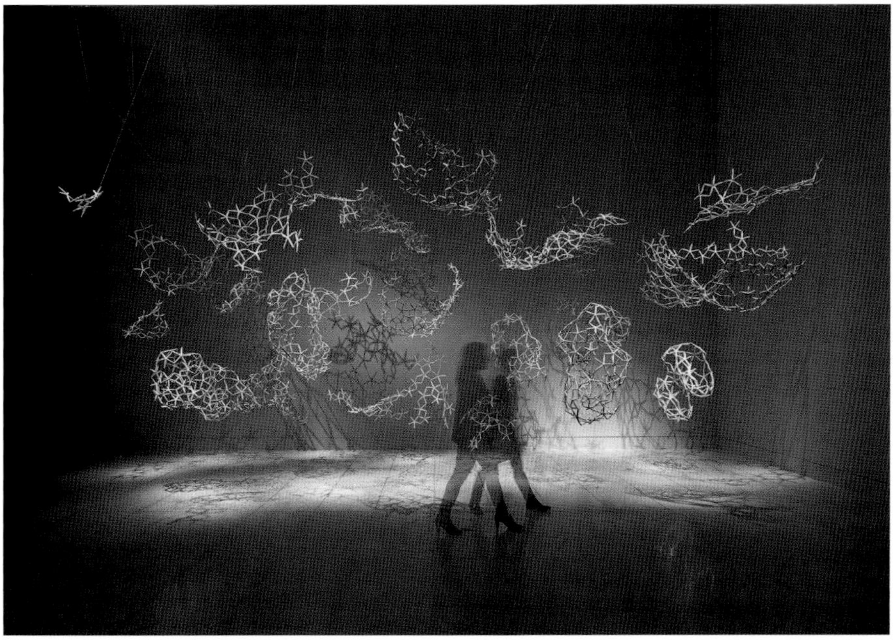

42. María Fernanda Cardoso (Colombian, b. 1963), *Woven Water: Submarine Landscape*, 1994. Dried starfish with metal wire, dimensions variable. Houston, The Museum of Fine Arts. Courtesy of María Fernanda Cardoso.

who combined key aspects of the Pop sensibility with elements from their vernacular cultures to produce *creolized* versions of this international trend.

As evident from the examples discussed so far, the so-called constellatory model—grounded in both unfathomable contradictions and obvious paradoxes—provided by *Inverted Utopias* charted an initial ground plan for building the core collection of Latin American art at the Museum of Fine Arts, Houston. The final idea, however, was not to restrict the collection-building effort to this paradigmatic survey, but to take it as a point of departure and go beyond its chronological and geographic scope. As with any temporary exhibition, the fact that many artists were not represented or were not shown as desired in *Inverted Utopias* was an intrinsic limitation that could only be overcome with a focused long-term collection-building effort. In the meantime, however, the collection has continued to expand significantly into the contemporary area thanks to major acquisitions by well-established or midcareer artists who stand out for their contributions to the medium of installation, video-, or process-based art. Moreover, in 2010 the creation, in a far-sighted partnership with Fundación Gego (Caracas), of a special restricted fund—the Venezuela, Colombia, Central America and the Caribbean Art Fund (Caribbean Art Fund)—allowed the Museum to aggressively collect major examples of the work of contemporary artists from these underrepresented countries (fig. 42).

It must be underscored that the Museum's partnership with Fundación Gego is only one example of a series of innovative, long-term alliances that our institution has established over the last decade with artists' estates or private collections such as MALBA–Fundación Costantini in Buenos Aires, Fundación Cruz-Diez in Houston, and the

Capriles Brillembourg Collection of Latin American Art (Madrid-Miami). These multifaceted enriching partnerships involve collection-sharing, exhibitions, research, publications, and conservation efforts. With the enormous span of the region involved and the variety of production to be encompassed in mind, the rationale behind this type of initiative is that the Museum does not need to own works of art in order to display them or generate programs around them.

Conclusion

As I have argued elsewhere, at the kernel of discussions about permanent collections lies the issue of how museums use space to tell stories for audiences by recharting both the ancient and the immediate artistic past. Current practices for displaying permanent art collections are not only based on "preconceived" notions of how art objects functioned in the past; indeed, they assume that the latter are *frozen* in time and can only be apprehended through a preestablished, already "sanctioned" art-historical account. Ironically, the museum experience then becomes a neutral ground upon which this encounter with an impersonal and remote past should be performed. By contrast, the "inverted strategy" of collection-building pursued by the Museum of Fine Arts, Houston, throughout my tenure as curator of the Latin American area, underscores a basic, though frequently overlooked, principle of exhibition display. The way we place works in the gallery space or in a display case—whether in temporal or in permanent cases—has the capacity to activate a visual, aesthetic, or intertextual nexus or relationship between the works, thus leading to more creative ways of seeing or interpreting them. Such arrangements can thus serve to displace, revise, or generate innovative accounts—obviously going against the grain of hegemonic narratives. As professor Homi Bhabha has recently argued, the traditional approach to permanent collection displays negates the question of temporality that necessarily is embedded at the core of the museum experience. According to this view, the museum can only reconfigure the experience of the past through its awareness regarding the present. And it does so by means of "translating the relational value of its objects and practices" in the exhibition space, that is, by *recognizing* that an axiological issue is at play: the value of these objects is not an absolute but rather hinges on their relevance to our present time. And such a delicate, in-depth, and meandering task demands a proactive mediation involving the intricate refiguring of the past into the present, even "as the present is refiguring itself."[28]

Undoubtedly, the task of building a permanent collection of Latin American and Latino art at the Museum of Fine Arts, Houston, has involved this type of mediation. Moreover, the "constellatory model" introduced by *Inverted Utopias* not only provided guidelines, traces, and hints (a blueprint for the collection), but also contributed to the mainstream sanctioning of artists whose production had remained marginalized for decades. Referring to the commission and execution of the monumental *Houston Penetrable* by the Venezuelan master Jesús Rafael Soto (fig. 43),[29] the *New York Times* recently underscored a key point at stake in this regard: "Few museums would have dedicated its resources to an artist [such as Soto] who, though acclaimed in Latin America and Europe, has little name recognition here."[30] Soto's *Penetrable* is one of the rare cases in which a technically conceived piece under modern parameters allows the audience interplay of touch and gaze that could be considered as belonging exclusively to postmodern approaches to participative art.

This kind of betting on unrecognized or not yet legitimized art and artists to impose those principles and beliefs embedded in long-term research and implementation exemplifies the commitment to innovation regarding selection and

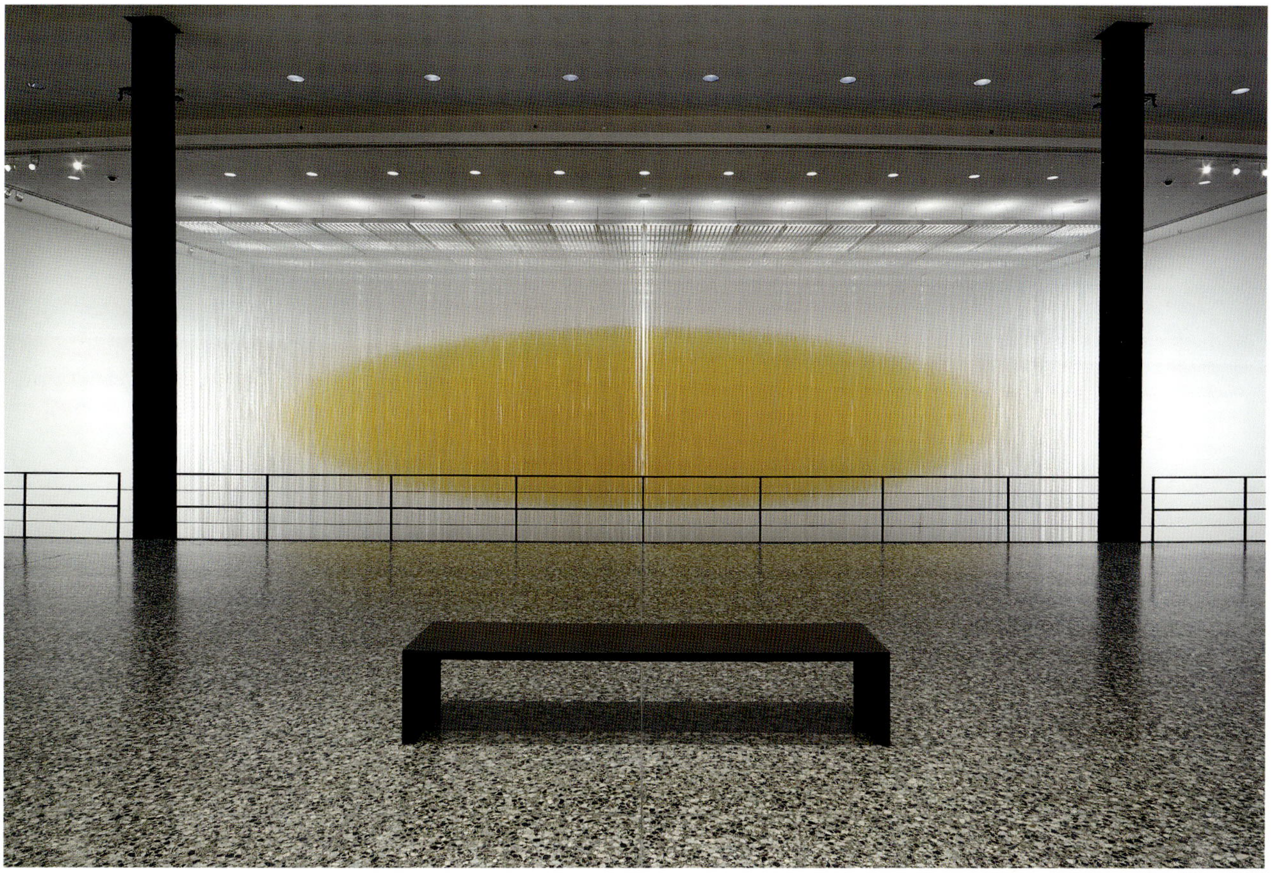

43. Jesús Rafael Soto (Venezuelan, 1923–2005), *Houston Penetrable*, 2004–2010. Lacquered aluminum structure, PVC tubes, and water-based silkscreen ink. Produced by Walter Pellevoisin (La Voie des Arts); produced by Atelier Soto, Paris; installed by The Museum of Fine Arts, Houston. Houston, The Museum of Fine Arts. © 2016 Artists Rights Society (ARS), New York / ADAGP, Paris.

accessions at the Museum of Fine Arts, Houston. To the best of my knowledge, the success or even failure of this "constellatory model" will be tested in the third brand-new building, which is being designed by architect Stephen Holl and is currently slated for completion in 2019. In the meantime, our collection remains a dynamic work in progress and a living testament to the vitality of avant-garde and contemporary artistic manifestations in Latin America: irreverent but well grounded in theory; intriguing and inventive, albeit fully materialized in practice.

CHAPTER 8

Beyond Mexico

The Evolution of the Phoenix Art Museum's Latin American Collection

Vanessa K. Davidson

44. Frida Kahlo (Mexican, 1907–1954), *El suicidio de Dorothy Hale* (The Suicide of Dorothy Hale), 1939. Oil on Masonite with painted frame, 59.7 × 49.5 cm. Phoenix Art Museum. © 2016 Banco de México Diego Rivera & Frida Kahlo Museums Trust, Mexico, D.F. / Artists Rights Society (ARS), New York.

In 2009, the Phoenix Art Museum celebrated its fiftieth anniversary. The Museum opened its doors in November of 1959, but the original, defining moment for the development of the collection came much earlier. In 1915, the Phoenix Women's Club initiated a community art collection by purchasing one work of art from the Arizona State Fair each year. This formed the nucleus of a Phoenix Municipal Collection, and the nature of such acquisitions fostered an early focus on twentieth-century Western American art. Once the Museum itself was founded, however, its permanent collection grew to encompass artworks from Asia created as early as 3500 B.C.E. and from Europe and the Americas from the late fourteenth century to the present day. Remarkably, the great majority of these works were garnered through donations.

The history of the Phoenix Art Museum's collection is a history of reliance on the generosity of donors. Since its inception, the Museum has not consistently had funds slated for the acquisition of artworks. As one Board of Trustees member, Richard Goldsmith, quipped, "We're one of the few museums that became a museum first and the art came later."[1] Over the past fifty-five years, the Museum has built a highly significant permanent collection of over eighteen thousand works, collected piece by piece, primarily though donations or purchased with donated funds. The Museum now features two hundred thousand square feet of exhibition space and seven curatorial departments, including American and Western American Art; European Art; Asian Art; Fashion Design; Photography; Modern and Contemporary Art; and Latin American Art.

Because the Museum has historically lacked funds designated for acquisitions, the tastes of donors have fundamentally shaped its collection. This is especially true for the collection of Latin American art, since the Museum lacked both a curatorial department and a curator for this area for

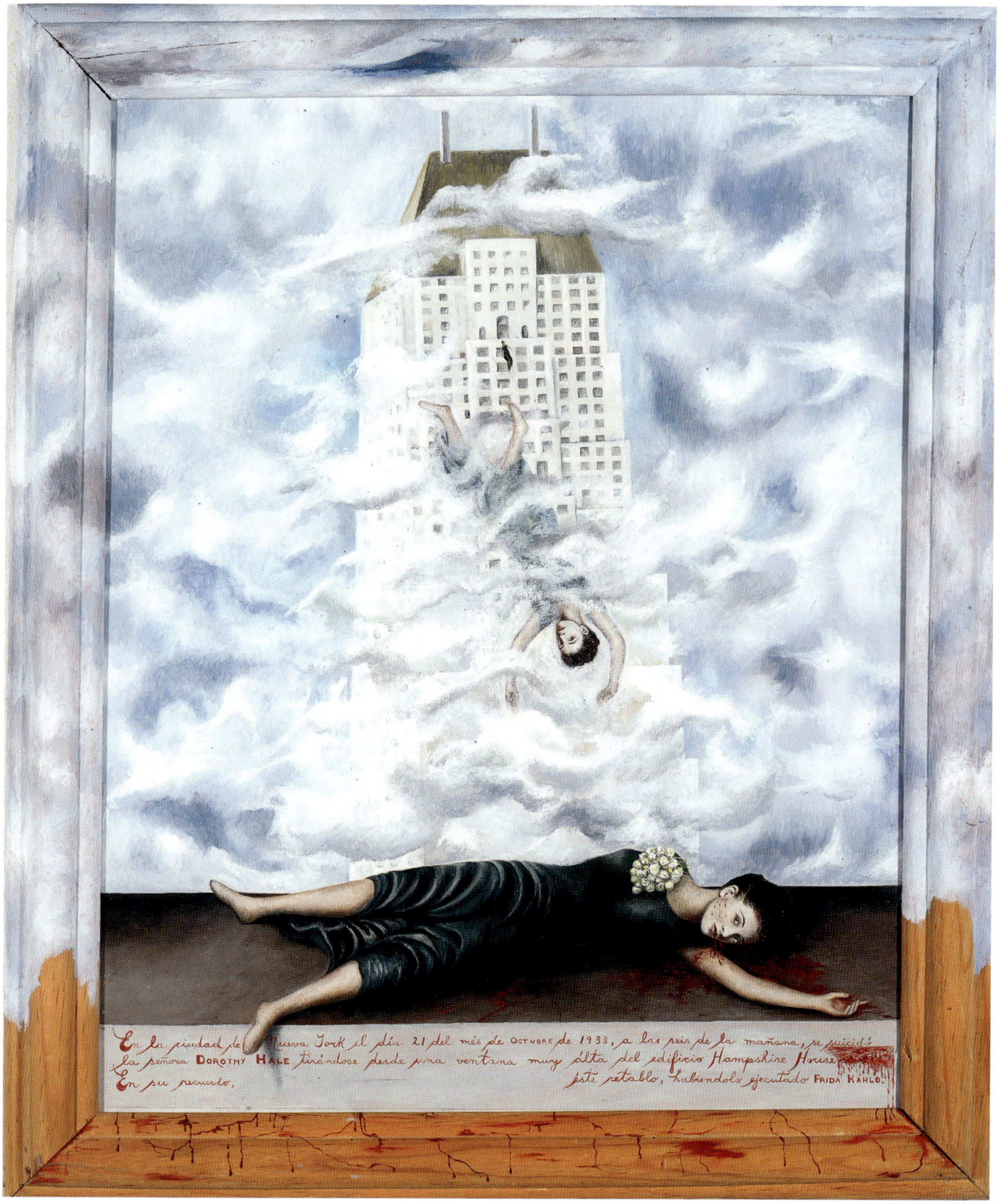
En la ciudad de Nueva York el día 21 del més de OCTUBRE de 1938, a las seis de la mañana, se suicidó
la señora DOROTHY HALE tirándose desde una ventana muy álta del edificio Hampshire House.
En su recuerdo,
éste retablo, habiendolo ejecutado FRIDA KAHLO.

the first thirty-three years of its existence, from 1959 until 1992. During this period, the Latin American art collection had, therefore, been somewhat akin to a rudderless boat. For more than three decades, there was no clear vision for the development of the collection, except for a consistent emphasis on Mexico. Phoenix is situated a mere 175 miles from the Mexican border; on their travels, local benefactors often collected art created there without generally looking further south. Due to the high caliber of Mexican artworks donated by leading patrons, this was in fact a great advantage for the Phoenix Art Museum. Furthermore, the majority of Arizona's significant Hispanic community traces its roots to Mexico, so Mexican artworks have special relevance in Phoenix.

The Museum's Latin American collection has grown over the past six decades to encompass over nine hundred objects acquired through donations, primarily from two sources. These represent two distinct spheres of influence. First are the aforementioned local donors who primarily collected Mexican art, especially important among them the Friends of Mexican Art (FOMA), a pioneering group of local art enthusiasts that has donated many of the iconic works in the Mexican art collection. And second, beginning in the mid-1990s, are vital donations from Museum benefactors Diane and Bruce Halle, whose collecting has focused on a more expansive view of Latin American art, encompassing masterworks from Argentina, Brazil, Chile, Colombia, Cuba, Peru, Uruguay, and Venezuela as well as Mexico. The following pages present an overarching view of Latin American art acquisitions and key exhibitions at the Phoenix Art Museum. The discussion illustrates how the collection began with an almost exclusive focus on Mexico, and how we have been increasingly able to expand our audience's horizons to the great diversity of art produced throughout Latin America in the twentieth century and into the twenty-first.

Exhibitions of Mexican art began at the Museum even before it was officially founded, with a 1957 exhibition entitled *Modern Mexican Painting*. In addition, gifts of Mexican art arrived before the Museum opened its doors, first from Mr. and Mrs. Orme Lewis. Lewis (1903–1990) was a lawyer active in business, politics, and public service. In 1957–58, the Lewises donated David Alfaro Siqueiros's (1896–1974) undated *Apocalipsis* (Apocalypse), Diego Rivera's (1886–1957) *Desnuda sentada con brazos en alto (Frida Kahlo)* (Seated Nude with Raised Arms [Frida Kahlo]) of 1930, as well as a masterful undated still life by Roberto Montenegro (1885–1968). In the 1960s, they continued with gifts of two Rivera drawings as well as the Museum's first South American works: two lithographs by Chilean artist Roberto Matta (1911–2002) and a 1968 intaglio, *Concetto Spaziale*, by Italo-Argentine Lucio Fontana (1899–1968). In the 1970s, the Lewises continued their donations of important Mexican artworks, gifting the Museum works on paper by Rafael Coronel (b. 1931), José Luis Cuevas (b. 1934), Carlos Mérida (1891–1984), Francisco Zuñiga (1912–1998), and our first Rufino Tamayo (1899–1991) print, the 1976 mixografía *Hombre Rojo* (Red Man).

Mr. and Mrs. Lewis laid the foundation for building a significant Mexican art collection. In the midst of their generous donations came another in 1960, a work that is today the most frequently requested painting for loan in the Museum's entire collection: Frida Kahlo's (1907–1954) *El suicidio de Dorothy Hale* (The Suicide of Dorothy Hale) of 1939 (fig. 44). American playwright, author, and ambassador Clare Boothe Luce (1903–1987) commissioned this painting to commemorate her deceased friend,[2] having bought Kahlo's 1937 *Self-Portrait Dedicated to Leon Trotsky* during her travels to Mexico.[3] She expected a conventional portrait in the same vein, but instead received this cinematic, slow-motion rendering of Dorothy Hale's leap from the top of the Hampshire House in New York and its gory end. Boothe Luce was so appalled by the work that she wanted to destroy it "with a pair of library scissors."[4] Fortunately, she kept it at the advice of friends after having her name painted out of the inscription as the person commissioning the work.[5] She donated it to the Museum in 1960 with, as she later related, "the express understanding that it would be listed as the gift of an *anonymous donor*."[6] Over the decades, this painting has become the icon of the Museum's Latin American art collection.

Another decisive moment for the formation of this collection came in 1965, when Mr. and Mrs. Denison Kitchel donated the Museum's first Spanish Colonial artworks. Kitchel (1908–2002) is best known as the campaign manager for Barry Goldwater's 1964 presidential bid against Lyndon Johnson; Mrs. Kitchel (Naomi Douglas Kitchel, 1907–2004) was the Museum's first female trustee. The Kitchels collected colonial works on their travels to Mexico, such as an eighteenth-century *ropero* (wardrobe) created in Michoacán; an eighteenth-century Mexican painting of *Nuestra Señora la Peregrina de Quito* (Our Lady the Pilgrim of Quito); two 1760 Mexican society portraits, *Doña Maria Moreno y Buenaventura* and her companion *Don Juan Mateo Trujillo y Luffo*; as well as a compelling 1720 painting of an *Arcángel con un símbolo de la inmaculada* (Archangel with a Symbol of the Immaculate Conception). (This last painting was felicitously discovered when the overpainting of a *Young Woman Bearing Fruit* was removed from its surface during conservation treatment.) Later, in 1993, the Kitchels also donated our first colonial Peruvian painting: an eighteenth-century Cuzco School *Divina Pastora* (Divine Shepherdess).

The 1960s were important for the Museum's Latin American collection in another regard: in 1963, the Friends of Mexican Art (FOMA) was founded. The group is still active today, and its goals are to encourage and stimulate interest in Mexican art, culture, and heritage and to strengthen cultural ties with Mexico. They have accomplished this through an extensive program of lectures, travels, seminars, and art acquisitions and exhibition sponsorship. Over the past five decades, FOMA has given twenty-six stellar gifts to the Museum, among them José Clemente Orozco's (1883–1949) *Man's Head* (Study for Man of the Sea for Mural in the Dome of the Hospicio Cabañas in Guadalajara), of 1938–39; Alfredo Ramos Martínez's (1871–1946) *La Malinche* (Young Girl of Yalala, Oaxaca) of 1940; Carlos Mérida's *Poma Azul* (Blue Apple) of 1962; Raúl Anguiano's (1915–2006) *Penitentes* (Penitents) of 1963; Arnold Belkin's (1930–1992) *El sueño* (The Dream) of 1964; José Luis Cuevas's 1973 *Retrato del crítico Jose Gomez Sicre* (Portrait of the Critic José Gomez Sicre); Rufino Tamayo's 1973 *Dos figuras en rojo* (Two Figures in Red, fig. 45); Nahum Bernabé Zenil's (b. 1947) *Santísima cena* of 1991; an exquisite *escudo de monja* (nun's shield) of 1690–1710; and Francisco Zuñiga's 1971 bronze relief sculpture *La puerta y la ventana* (The Door and the Window), which is located at the Museum entrance and has become a symbol of the institution.

FOMA's support has been essential for establishing the cornerstones of the Museum's collection of Mexican art. The great majority of these gifts were works of contemporary art at the time they were donated. From the *muralismo* represented by Orozco to the Taller de Gráfica Popular with which Anguiano was associated; from the Generación de Ruptura that Cuevas represents to the Nueva Presencia that Belkin initiated to the Neo-Mexicanismo represented by Zenil: FOMA's gifts have provided the Museum with representative works from many of the most important artistic currents in Mexico during the twentieth century.

In addition, FOMA has collaborated with the Museum on significant exhibition projects that reflect both entities' historical emphasis on Mexican art. Between 1957 and 1992, the Museum held thirty exhibitions of Mexican art. These exhibitions, too,

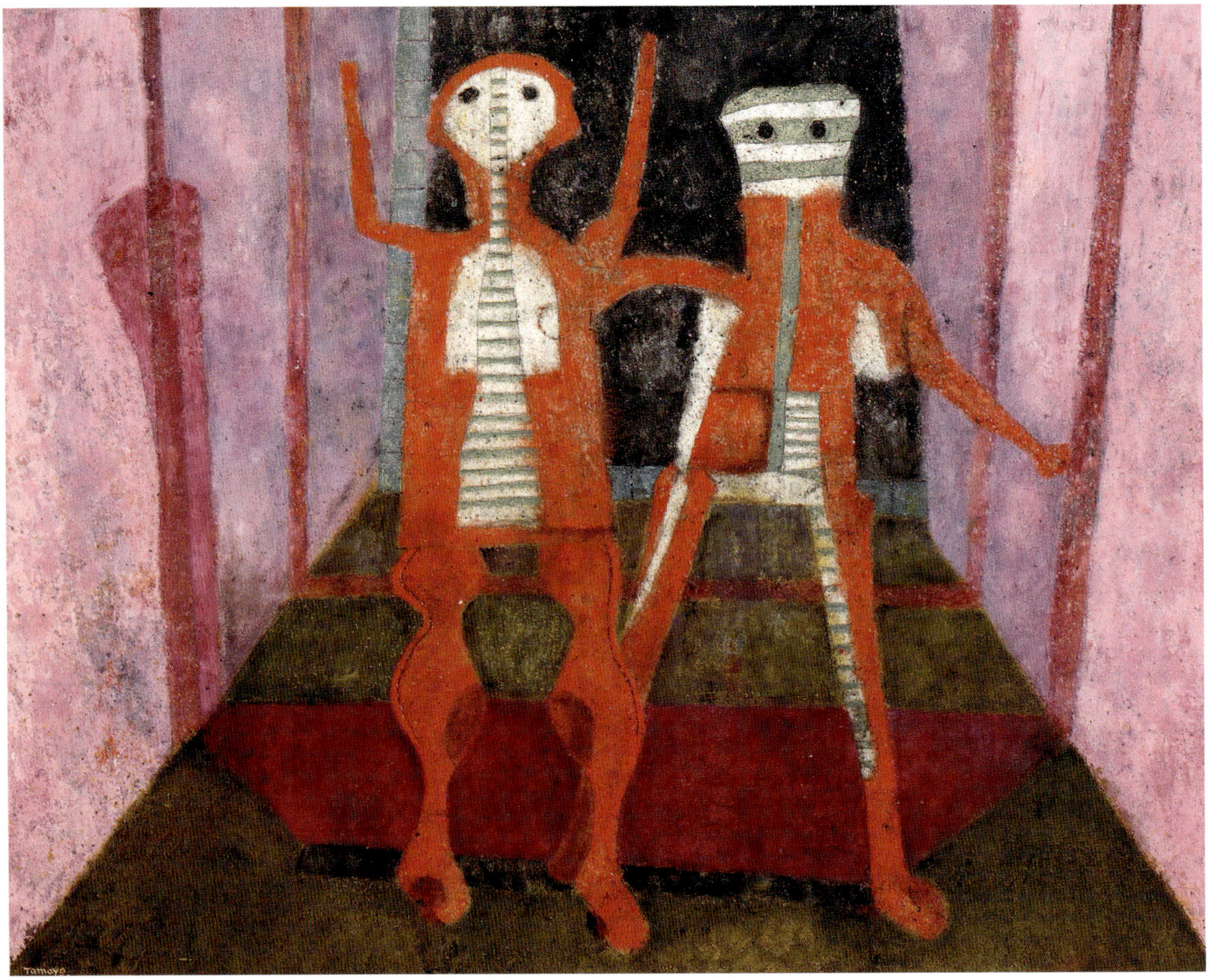

45. Rufino Tamayo (Mexican, 1899–1991), *Dos figuras en rojo* (Two Figures in Red), 1973. Oil on canvas, 110.5 × 140 cm. Phoenix Art Museum. Art © Tamayo Heirs / Mexico / Licensed by VAGA, New York, N.Y.

were predicated on generosity of donors and lenders; the Museum's growing permanent collection was not apt for major exhibitions, although small presentations of works from the collection would be held throughout the years. These exhibitions are of crucial importance for this history of the collection. On one hand, they illustrate how patrons' tastes evolved as they visited Museum exhibitions and learned more about Latin American art. On the other, they serve to highlight how the Phoenix Art Museum rose to prominence as a center for Mexican art through collaborations with institutions in both Mexico and the United States.

Many of these exhibitions were groundbreaking in their day, especially four organized between 1968 and 1984. The first was a 1968 Rufino Tamayo retrospective, a collaboration between the Museum and FOMA that was curated by officials from the Instituto Nacional de Bellas Artes in Mexico. The largest exhibition of Tamayo's work to date in the United States, this show was declared by the Museum's director Hugh Broadly "one of the most important and exciting shows ever to be held at the Phoenix Art Museum."[7] It included 124 artworks drawn from public and private collections throughout Mexico and the United States. In the illustrated catalogue, which included an essay by Tamayo, the artist was described as "a sensualist who creates art out of feeling, instinct, and disorder: a modern primitive."[8] This characterization belies a lack of profound understanding of Tamayo's work, but is nonetheless typical of the lure of the perceived "exoticism" and "primitivism" of contemporary art from Mexico in the United States during this period.

Another high-profile exhibition cosponsored with FOMA came several years later, in 1974: *José Luis Cuevas: An Exhibition of Recent Works*. Organized in collaboration with the Fine Arts Gallery of San Diego and the San Francisco Achenbach Foundation for Graphic Arts: California Palace of the Legion of Honor, this exhibition included seventy-four of the artist's works and traveled to both of these venues after its showing in Phoenix. In the exhibition catalogue, Museum director and exhibition organizer Ronald Hickman described the artist thus: "Intellectual, controversial, literary: all accurate descriptions of José Luis Cuevas and his work. The inquisitive and fertile mind of this prolific artist has produced a legacy of work that places him among the truly great artists of Mexico."[9] The catalogue contains an extensive bibliography of texts on Cuevas's work, including a section titled "Books in Which an Attempt Has Been Made to Defame Cuevas," an indication of the organizers' efforts to elevate this artist's status in American eyes.

The next landmark exhibition organized by the Museum with support from FOMA was a 1978 retrospective of the work of Frida Kahlo. Comprising forty-eight works from sixteen lenders, it was the first major retrospective of Kahlo's work in the United States. It was organized by Judith Russi Kirshner of the Museum of Contemporary Art, Chicago, and traveled from Phoenix to the University Galleries at the University of California, San Diego; the Huntington Gallery at the University of Texas, Austin; the Blaffer Art Museum at the University of Houston; and the Neuberger Museum of Art at the State University of New York, Purchase. Given the renewed interest in Kahlo's work in the 1970s and '80s, as well as the rising tide of multiculturalism in the 1990s, this exhibition was at once groundbreaking and timely. The catalogue accompanying the show included an essay by art historian Hayden Herrera, who would go on to write the bestselling *Frida: A Biography of Frida Kahlo* in 1983.[10]

Kahlo's husband, Diego Rivera, was also the subject of a one-man exhibition at the Museum in 1984: *Diego Rivera: The Cubist Years*. Organized jointly by the Phoenix Art Museum and the Instituto de Bellas Artes, Mexico City, with support from FOMA, the exhibition was curated by Ramón Favela, who had first approached the Museum about the possibility of staging such a show in 1977. With seventy-two works from thirty-six lenders, this was the first exhibition devoted to this seminal aspect of Rivera's work. It constituted a watershed event in the Phoenix community, bringing Rivera's essays in Cubism to an audience that was primarily familiar only with his figurative works. The show then traveled to the IBM Gallery of Science and Art, New York; SFMOMA; and the Museo de Arte Moderno, Mexico City.

Such exhibitions enabled the Phoenix Art Museum to consolidate its emerging status as the premier locus for the research and display of Mexican art in the American Southwest. But in the early 1990s a shift occurred, due to a confluence of several key factors: the quincentennial of the discovery of the Americas; the growing awareness of multiculturalism; and, not least, Arizona's changing demographics. In 1992, James K. Ballinger, the Sybil Harrington Director of the Phoenix Art Museum, decided to found a Latin American curatorial department. This initiative was in itself groundbreaking. The Phoenix Art Museum's was only the second curatorial department of Latin American art founded in a U.S. museum, the first being at the Huntington Art Gallery (now the Jack S. Blanton Museum of Art) at the University of Texas at Austin in 1988.

To establish this new department, Ballinger tapped into a resource already present at the Museum: librarian Clayton Kirking became the first Curator of Latin American Art. Kirking plays the role of linchpin in this narrative. He organized the Museum's first exhibitions of Latin American art beyond Mexico, and, in addition, he was Diane Halle's first cultural ambassador to the art of Latin America. They established a friendship in 1981, when Mrs. Halle became a Museum docent; she would soon become a member of the Museum's Board of Trustees, a position she held for twenty years, serving as Board president in 1993. In the intervening years of the 1980s, Kirking first introduced Mrs. Halle to Latin American art through library books. As she later recounted, it was a combination of her role on the Board and her friendship with Kirking, whose enthusiasm proved contagious, that gave birth to the idea of forging her own collection. As Kirking recalled in an interview, in the early 1990s Mrs. Halle walked into the library and asked, "If I were going to collect something, what would it be?" They both knew the answer would be art from Latin America.

Diane and Bruce Halle began to build their collection in earnest in 1995. From the start, their collecting was conditioned by the desire to use their acquisitions to inspire new understandings of Latin American art in diverse audiences in Arizona and beyond. As Mrs. Halle stated in 2013,

> As I think back, this desire to have the collection be educational related to the years I spent at the Phoenix Art Museum. In the nineties we were talking about museum audiences and about the fact that the Hispanic population of Arizona was growing. So I began to think, what does it mean to me to be in the state across the border from Mexico, and by extension, across the border from all of Latin America? What does that mean to me, and how can I make an impact in Arizona, where an impact [of Latin American art] had never been felt?[11]

In the mid-1990s, the Halles traveled to Monterrey, Mexico, with Kirking to visit private collections and the newly built Museo de Arte Contemporáneo. They also met with Ramis Barquet, who would become an important resource for their collection, helping the Halles to acquire artworks by Guillermo Kuitca (b. 1961), José Bedia (b. 1959), and Julio Galán (1958–2006), among others. Mrs. Halle also engaged Roland Augustine of the Luhring Augustine Gallery in New York as an art advisor, beginning a fruitful relationship that continues to this day.

Another pivotal event of 1995 was the Museum's presentation of the exhibition *Latin American*

Women Artists, 1915–1995. Curated by Gerry Biller and organized by the Milwaukee Museum of Art, this was the first large-scale exhibition in the United States to focus on the role of women in the development of art in Latin America. It included one hundred works by thirty-five artists from throughout the region, from Anita Malfatti (1889–1964) to Raquel Forner (1902–1988), from Beatriz González (b. 1938) and María Magdalena Campos-Pons (b. 1959) to Jac Leirner (b. 1961). This event, too, illustrates the fundamental importance of exhibitions held at the Museum in helping to hone the tastes and collecting practices of benefactors. In this instance, the Halles were first introduced to work by artists who would become the foundation of their burgeoning collection, such as Lygia Clark (1920–1988), Gego (Gertrude Louise Goldschmidt, 1912–1994), Ana Mendieta (1948–1985), and Mira Schendel (1919–1988).

Unfortunately for the nascent Latin American art department, Clayton Kirking moved to New York following this exhibition. He had played a fundamental role in opening the Museum's field of vision to works by Latin American art beyond Mexico, and also in encouraging Mrs. Halle's collecting activities. The department was again without a curator for two years, until Beverly Adams arrived in 1997. Adams continued the Museum's and the Phoenix community's awakening to the rich diversity of art beyond the border, and forged an alliance with Mrs. Halle that mirrored Kirking's friendship with her.

By this time, the Halles had laid the foundations of a formidable collection, and had begun to actively loan works to the Museum. Further, they generously supported traveling exhibitions presented at the Museum, such as the 1999 *Cantos Paralelos: Visual Parody in Contemporary Argentinian Art*, organized by Mari Carmen Ramírez, which began at the Blanton Museum and also traveled to the Biblioteca Centro Cultural Luis Angel Arango in Bogotá and the Museo Nacional de Bellas Artes in Buenos Aires. All the while, Mrs. Halle encouraged the Museum to diversify its Latin American holdings though advocacy on the acquisitions committee. The Halles themselves furthered this goal through a series of generous gifts that began in 2000 with Brazilian artist Jac Leirner's 1992 *Todos os Cem* (All the One Hundreds), a chain of cruzeiro banknotes installed in a serpentine configuration upon the floor, whose title sounds phonetically in Portuguese like *todos os sem* (all those without). In honor of the Museum's fiftieth anniversary in 2009, they donated another outstanding work from their collection, a 1989 triptych by Argentine artist Liliana Porter (b. 1941) titled *El viajero* (The Traveler) that had been on view at the Museum on long-term loan.

From the very start, the Halles were aware of the need to expand the Museum's holdings beyond Mexico, and strategically placed objects in the collection to fortify its points of weakness. Beverly Adams left the Museum in 2001 to become the Curator of the Halle Collection, and with her tremendous knowledge and contacts the Halles further expanded their collection by adding a diverse array of works created in different regions and time periods. Over the past twenty years, they have created one of the most significant collections of Latin American art in the country.

After Adams's departure, the Museum was again without a Latin American curator, this time for ten years, and the Halles focused their efforts on building their own collection. When I began work as the Shawn and Joe Lampe Curator of Latin American Art in 2011, the Halles recognized the Museum's renewed commitment to the promotion and display of art from the region and rekindled their relationship with the institution. Mrs. Halle rejoined the Board of Trustees and also renewed her active role on the acquisitions committee. Over the subsequent three years, the Halles generously gave the Museum five important artworks, further helping to expand

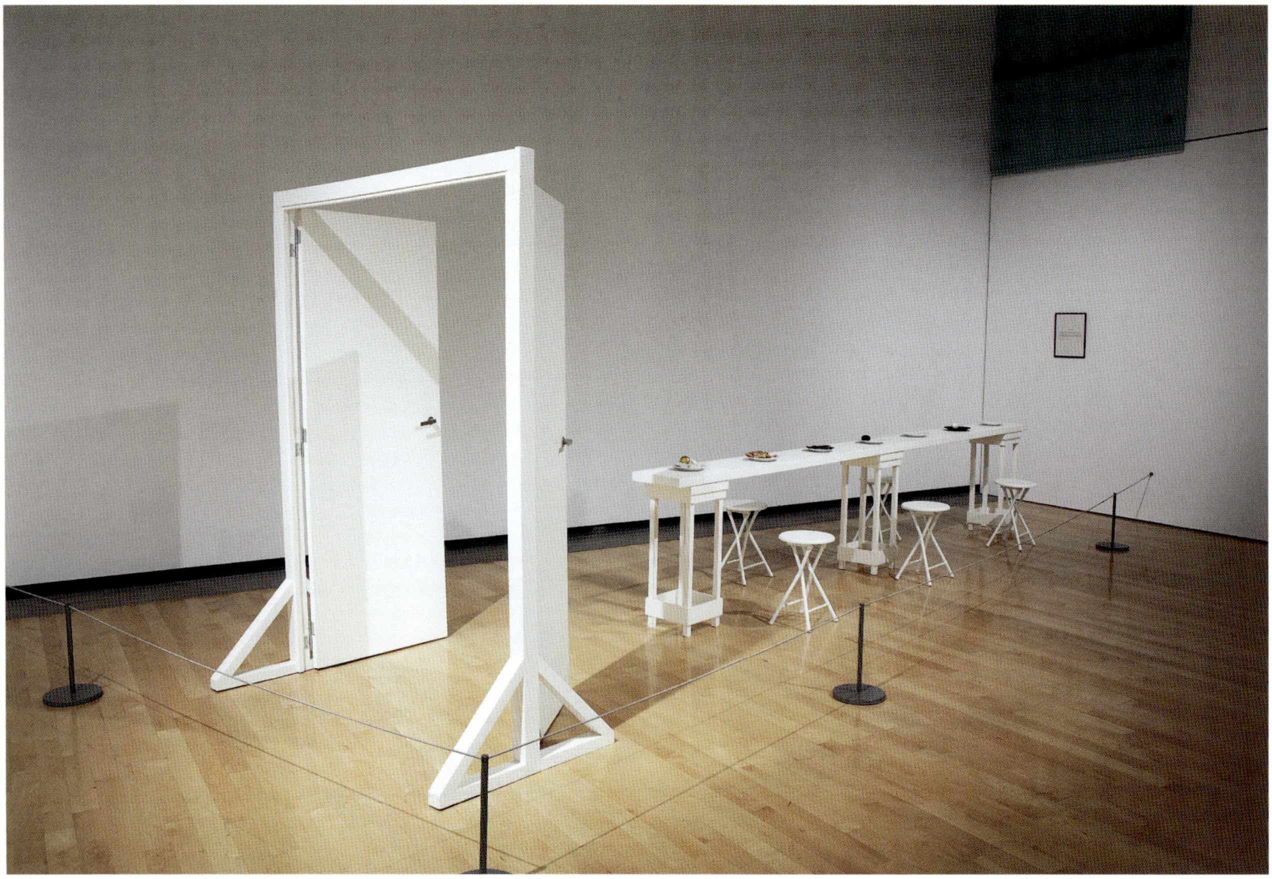

46. Victor Grippo (Argentinian, b. 1936), *La comida del artista* (The Artist's Meal), 1991–2002. Mixed media, 215 × 160 × 550 cm. Phoenix Art Museum. © The Estate of Victor Grippo.

the collection's geographic scope. In 2011, they donated Venezuelan artist Alessandro Balteo Yazbeck's (b. 1972) installation *Unstabile/Mobile* of 2006, and, in 2012, made four additional gifts that bolster the collection of video and installation art: Argentine-Mexican Miguel Angel Rios's (b. 1943) *A morir* (Till Death), a 2003 three-screen video work; British-Mexican Melanie Smith's (b. 1965) *Parres 1* video piece of 2004; Brazilian Rivane Neuenschwander's (b. 1967) *Mapa múndi* slide-projection series of 2005–12; and Argentine Victor Grippo's (1936–2002) *La comida del artista* (The Artist's Meal) of 1991–2002 (fig. 46), another edition of which is in the collection of MALBA–Fundación Costantini in Buenos Aires.

Yazbeck's and Rios's works were featured in the 2013 exhibition of the Halle Collection at the Museum that I co-curated with Beverly Adams, entitled *Order, Chaos, and the Space Between: Contemporary Latin American Art from the Diane and Bruce Halle Collection*. This innovative exhibition featured over fifty artworks created by artists from across the region from the 1960s to the early 2010s, focusing on those who question the nature of the creative process. *Order, Chaos, and the Space Between* was a resounding success. It served to expand our audiences' knowledge of art produced throughout Latin America over the past fifty years and aroused great interest in our community, especially in the Hispanic media.

So, too, had my first exhibition at the Museum, the 2012 *Politics of Place: Latin American Photography, Past and Present.* In this small show, I included Neuenschwander's *Mapa múndi* as a loan from the Halles. This began a trend that has continued over the past several years: the Halles' prescient gifts of works in which the Museum had already expressed great interest. Another example is the Halles' generous purchase of Mexican artist Teresa Margolles's (b. 1963) *La búsqueda* (The Search) of 2015 expressly for the Museum's collection, an installation piece that became the focal point of my 2015 exhibition *Hidden Histories in Latin American Art.* For this exhibition, I also requested the loan of Arizona Chicana artist Annie Lopez's (b. 1958) *Naturalized Citizens* of 2013, a dress made of cyanotyope prints on tamale paper documenting her family's legal status. The Halles not only lent this striking piece for the show, but also donated it to the Museum at its conclusion. In addition, in 2014 the Halles partnered with local benefactors Angela and Leonard Singer, Judy and Samuel Linhart, and Lisa Sette to purchase Venezuelan artist Luis Molina-Pantin's (b. 1969) photographic series *Pooh (Cuenca, Ecuador)* of 2009 for the permanent collection, a compelling work that was immediately put on display and has become a visitor favorite.

The Halles have been extremely savvy about building their collection as a collage of works that can have a tremendous educational impact. As Mrs. Halle remarked in conversation with Mari Carmen Ramírez in 2007 about their collecting practices, "Initially we went with whatever moved us or whatever we wanted to live with. Yet, that has totally changed. Now it is more about the artists that represent the movements, the countries, or a specific period of time. We want to be certain to build from the foundation up. If you're really building a collection that has an educational component to it, you realize that you have to be serious in collecting those people that made the strongest impact on their time and place."[12] This emphasis on education illustrates the Halles' aim that the collection should be made public in the future to educate diverse audiences about the varied histories of art in Latin America.

This educational impetus also dovetails with the Phoenix Art Museum's founding mission: "To be a vibrant destination connecting people to great art from around the world to enrich their lives and communities," and, fundamentally, to educate and inspire. This brings us back to the beginning, a museum founded as an idea before it was filled with artworks, a museum that reflects the community's passions for art because of the great importance of local donations, a museum that strives to inspire audiences with innovative exhibitions. In the Latin American department, we continue to spearhead educational initiatives that make our audience aware of movements, moments, and histories of art in Latin America with which they were previously unacquainted.

It is now clear that the Museum's Latin American art collection is no longer a rudderless boat; rather, it is an increasingly significant cluster of works that continues to grow and evolve. A case in point is the 2013 acquisition of nearly three hundred artworks from colonial Peru and Mexico from the Gerry S. Culpepper collection. This bequest included seventy-four paintings, such as an iconic *Virgen de Pomata* (Virgin of Pomata) (fig. 47) and a monumental *Last Judgment* from the eighteenth-century Viceroyalty of Peru, as well as a masterful *Virgin of Guadalupe* of the same period from the Viceroyalty of New Spain. This acquisition has transformed the Museum's Spanish Colonial holdings in caliber, scale, and geographic

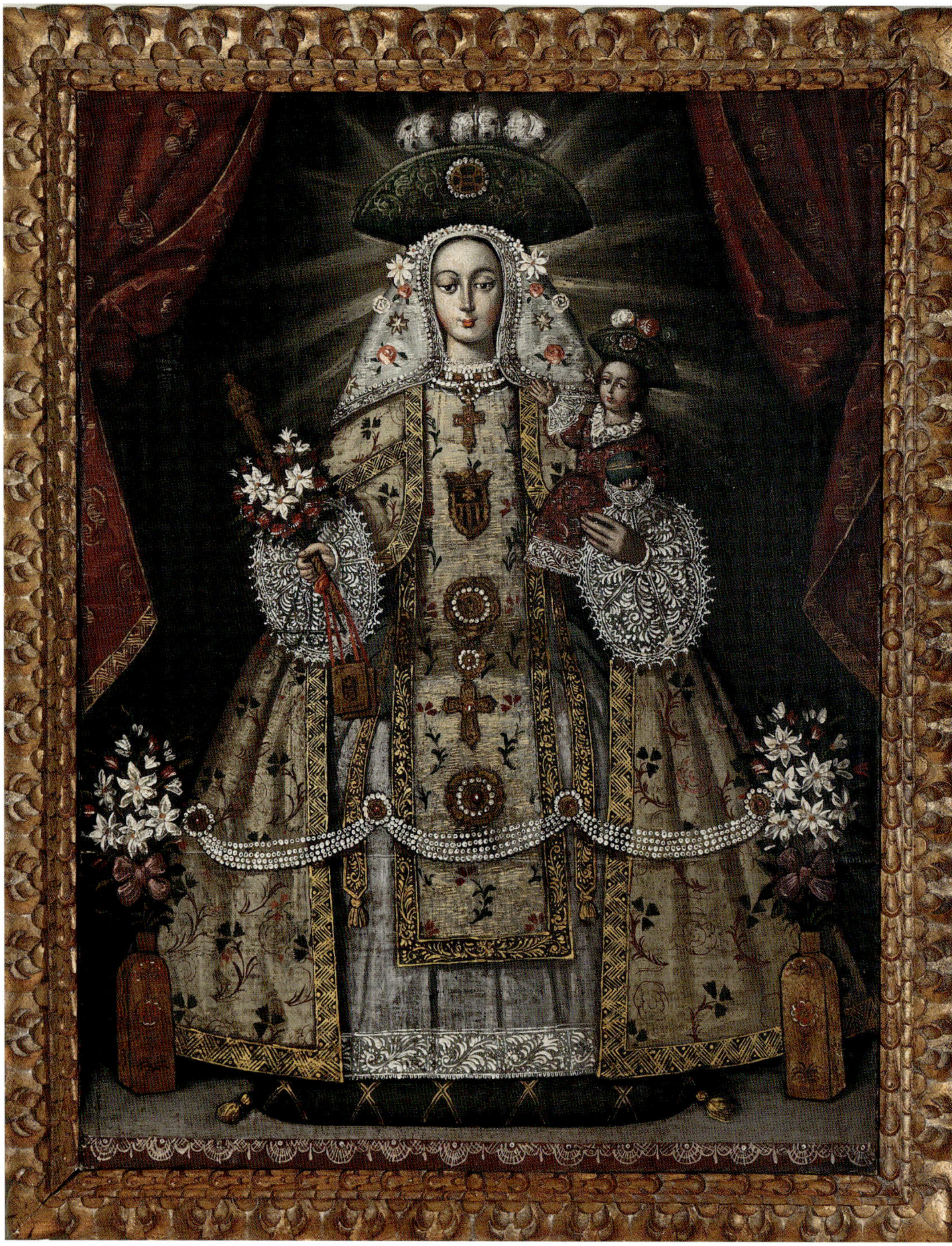

47. Artist unknown (Peruvian, Cuzco School), *Virgen de Pomata* (Virgin of Pomata), eighteenth century. Oil on canvas, 97.8 × 74.9 cm. Phoenix Art Museum.

range, in tandem with eight extraordinary examples of painting and silverwork from colonial Peru, Bolivia, and Guatemala that the Halles donated in 2015. Featured among these are an outstanding 1665 Cuzco School painting of the *Virgen de los Desamparados* (Virgin of the Forsaken), now the earliest work in our colonial collection, and four remarkable silver and gold-vermeil altar plaques depicting *arcángeles arcabuceros* (archangels with arquebuses) (fig. 48).

These most recent gifts serve to illustrate the advocacy of Sybil Harrington Director Amada Cruz and Selig Family Chief Curator Gilbert Vicario, as well as my own advocacy, for expanding the Museum's focus in both its collecting and its exhibitions of art from Latin America. Several exhibitions staged here in recent years reflect this new emphasis, such as the 2014 *Antonio Berni: Juanito and Ramona*, organized by Mari Carmen Ramírez of the Museum of Fine Arts, Houston, and Marcelo Pacheco of MALBA–Fundación Costantini; the 2014 *Paulo Bruscky: Art Is Our Last Hope*, organized in collaboration with Sergio Bessa of the Bronx Museum of the Arts; the 2014–15 *Focus Latin America: Art Is Our Last Hope*, an international exhibition of contemporary mail art featuring submissions from four hundred and forty-four artists from thirty-five countries; and the 2015–16 *Masterworks of Spanish Colonial Art from Phoenix Art Museum's Collection*, which featured many of Culpepper's and the Halles' extraordinary gifts. Additional exhibitions on the horizon through 2018 also reflect redoubled efforts to fortify collaborative partnerships with museums both in Latin America and closer to home, including *Horacio Zabala: Mapping the Monochrome* in 2016, a collaboration with the Museo Colección de Arte Amalia Lacroze de Fortabat in Buenos Aires; a 2017 exhibition of Brazilian art entitled *Past/Future/Present: Contemporary Brazilian Art from the São Paulo Museum of Modern Art* organized in collaboration with the Museu de Arte Moderna de São Paulo; and a major survey exhibition of work by Brazilian-born,

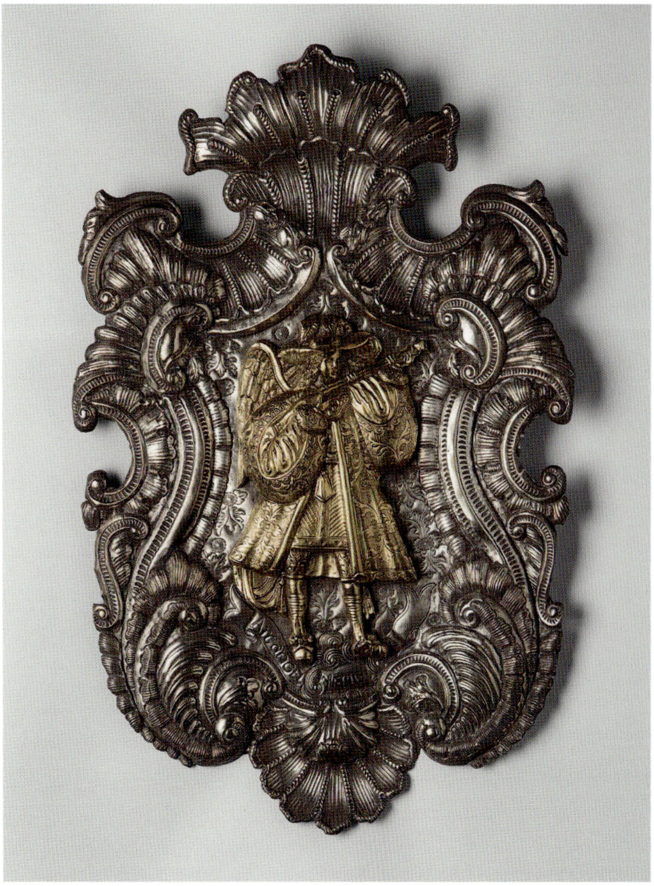

48. Artist unknown (Bolivian), *Arcángel Yeriel* (Archangel Yeriel), ca. 1675–1790. Sterling silver repoussé with gold vermeil, 69.9 × 43.2 cm. Phoenix Art Museum.

Brooklyn-based artist Valeska Soares (b. 1957) organized with the Santa Barbara Museum of Art as part of the Getty Foundation's 2017 *Pacific Standard Time: Los Angeles / Latin America* initiative. These international collaborations reflect the Phoenix Art Museum's expanded vision of Latin American art, in all its richness and tumultuous diversity, and the Museum's engagement with and continued dedication to art created in Mexico and beyond.

CHAPTER 9

Roberta and Richard Huber's Adventures in Collecting

Suzanne Stratton-Pruitt

49. Artist unknown (Peruvian, Cuzco School), *Our Lady of Guápulo*, ca. 1680. Oil on canvas, 149 × 113.3 cm. Collection of Roberta and Richard Huber.

When the Spanish and Portuguese Colonial paintings and objects collected by Roberta and Richard Huber were shown at the Philadelphia Museum of Art in 2013, the exhibition and the catalogue were aptly titled *Journeys to New Worlds.*[1] The "journeys" refer to those of the Spanish and Portuguese explorers whose intrepid feats of navigation can be credited with the first globalization, and to the peripatetic travels of the Hubers themselves.

Dick Huber was reared in the mountains of western North Carolina and educated at Harvard. Roberta Huber was raised on Boston's South Shore and graduated from Wellesley. The couple met at Harvard summer school, dated as undergraduates, and soon after college they were married. In 1962, Dick's employer, the First National Bank of Boston, transferred the young couple to Buenos Aires. Dick had lived in Spain during his Harvard years, studying the chemistry of olive oil production in Seville, but Roberta had never traveled outside of the United States, not even to Canada, so moving to Argentina was an instant adventure. Dick's responsibilities for correspondent banking in South America required considerable travel throughout the continent, including to Bolivia and Peru. In 1967, the couple moved to São Paulo, where Dick was eventually put in charge of all the bank's operations in Brazil. In 1973, Dick left Bank of Boston for Citibank, first in São Paulo and then, in 1974, in Rio de Janeiro. While Dick was working in banking, both he and Roberta became fluent in Spanish and Portuguese and traveled to Córdoba, Mendoza, Rosario, and Misiones in Argentina; to Santa Cruz, La Paz, Sucre, and Potosí in Bolivia, and throughout the vast geography of Brazil. While Roberta was working on a BBC program called *Wildernesses of the World*, she had opportunities to visit undeveloped regions of Brazil. In all, the Hubers spent five years in Argentina and ten years in Brazil, working and raising their three sons.

In 1977, Dick accepted a position as country head for Citibank in Tokyo, and the family moved

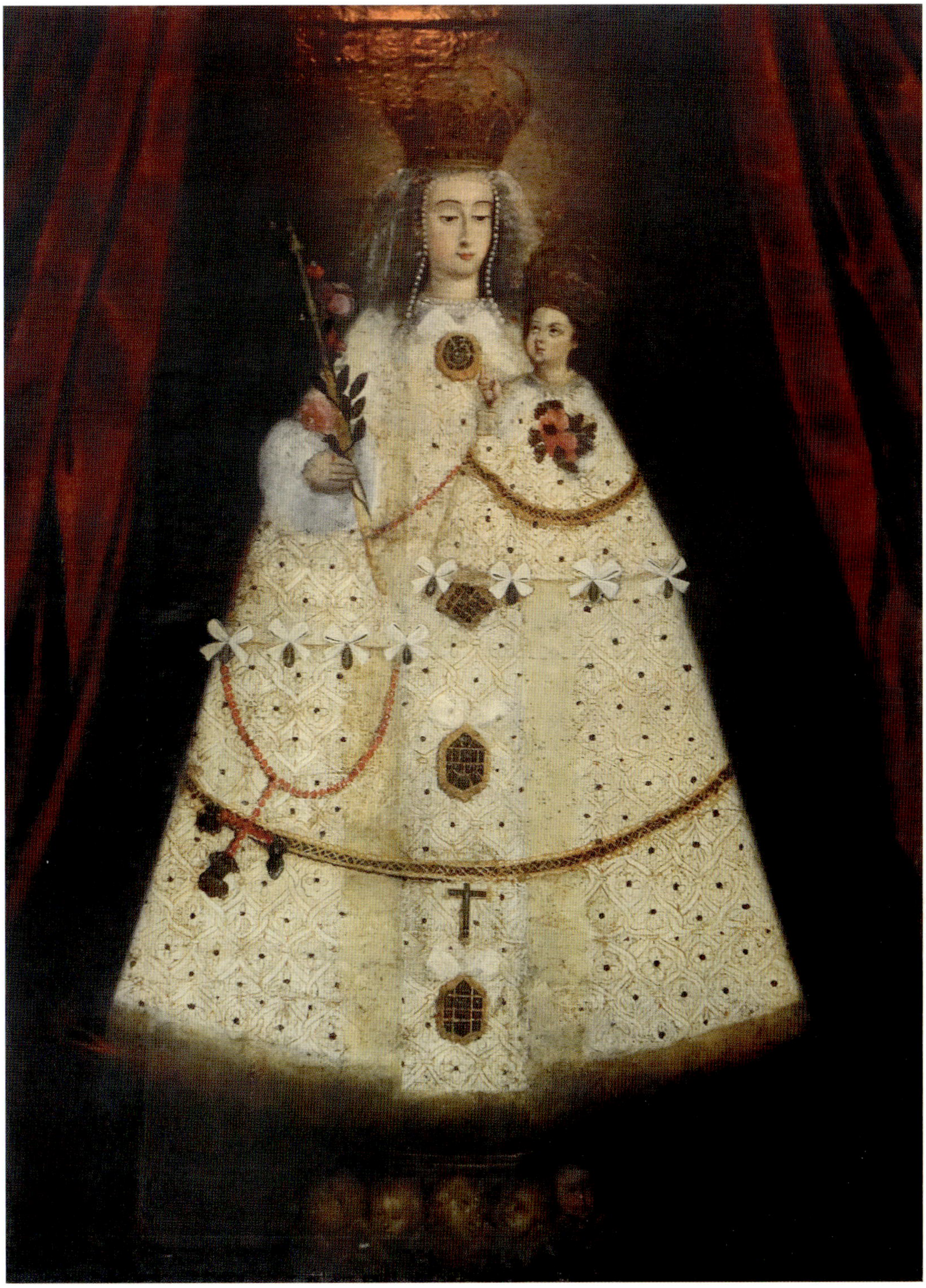

once again. They lived in Japan for five years, relocating in 1982 to New York, where Dick was charged first with Citibank's Asian operations and, after a couple of years, its Latin American operations as well. From 1988, Dick's work at Chase Manhattan, Continental Bank, and Aetna (where he became CEO) brought the family to live in Chicago and then Hartford, but all the while they continued to make trips to South America, before "retiring" to the brownstone on the Upper West Side of New York that houses their collection.

The history and culture of the places they have visited have always informed the Hubers' travels, but their specific interest in the arts of the Spanish and Portuguese colonies blossomed slowly. A visit to the Museo de Arte Hispanoamericano Isaac Fernández Blanco in Buenos Aires in 1963 was a seminal moment, followed by the guidance of a collector-dealer in São Paulo when Dick purchased a few paintings for the bank offices there. It was not until 1973, on a trip to Sucre, Bolivia, that the couple bought their first colonial painting, a small reverse painting on glass representing Saint Augustine that cost $100. It would be a long time before the accumulation of objects purchased from individuals and dealers in South America could actually be called a collection, and an equally long time before Roberta and Dick Huber thought of themselves as collectors.

Naturally, the Hubers had visited the museums of colonial art wherever they traveled, not only the Isaac Fernández Blanco in Buenos Aires, but also the Museo de Charcas in Sucre, Bolivia, and the Museo de Osma in Lima, Peru. However, a series of important exhibitions of colonial art organized by North American institutions in the 1990s also influenced the Hubers' appreciation and deepening understanding of the material. In 1989, the Americas Society Art Gallery in New York exhibited *Paradise Lost: The Jesuit and Guaraní South American Missions, 1606–1767*. (The Hubers' interest in the Jesuit presence and influence in the colonies stimulated a recent return visit to the mission churches of Paraguay.) It was an interest that followed them to Tokyo, where they became fascinated with the history of the proselytizing efforts of the Jesuits in China and Japan, in which imagery played as important a role as it did in the Americas. In 1990, The Metropolitan Museum of Art mounted the groundbreaking exhibition *Mexico: Splendors of Thirty Centuries*, which did not entice the Hubers to extend their collecting to colonial New Spain but did greatly increase general interest in Spanish Colonial art. In 1992, the Americas Society Art Gallery in New York exhibited *Barroco de la Nueva Granada: Colonial Art from Colombia and Ecuador*, and in 1996 the gallery showed *New World Orders: Casta Painting and Colonial Latin America*. Roberta Huber herself worked on the Brooklyn Museum's 1996 *Converging Cultures: Art and Identity in Spanish America*, and she also participated in the organization of the exhibition at the Americas Society dedicated to *Potosí: Colonial Treasures and the Bolivian City of Silver* (1997). Volunteering on these projects enabled her to learn from curators like Diana Fane at the Brooklyn Museum and from the Bolivian conservator and historian Pedro Querejazu, who organized the Potosí exhibition. Beginning in 2003, the Philadelphia Museum of Art undertook a round of research trips through Latin America with scholars and collectors, and Roberta accompanied the group, looking and learning, and occasionally acting as interpreter while Joseph J. Rishel and his team organized the exhibition *Tesoros, Treasures, Tesouros: The Arts in Latin America, 1492–1820*, which opened in Philadelphia in 2006 and then traveled to the Antiguo Colegio de San Ildefonso in Mexico City and the Los Angeles County Museum of Art.

The collection of Roberta and Richard Huber, as a result of their travels and studies, embodies the concept of "globalization," which began in the early Renaissance of Western European time.[2] The paintings, sculptures, worked silver, and carved ivories they have gathered together reflect the seafaring and trading genius of Portugal as well as the mercantile and empire-building goals of the Spanish monarchy. The geographical origins of the objects in the collection are broad: some were made in Spanish America and Brazil by descendants of émigrés from Spain and Portugal, some by upper-class indigenous and mixed-race artists in the colonies, and some by Chinese craftsmen working in the Philippines.

Dick Huber has noted that there are several ways to acquire a collection. The easiest, if not the thriftiest, is to buy a collection amassed by someone else. Another route is to entrust agents/dealers to find available artworks of interest to the collector. The Hubers have taken a third way, pursuing the hunt for themselves in the countries where they have lived and in countries like Spain and Portugal where private collections have long housed artworks from the colonial world. Their "do it yourself" approach has been marked by serendipitous discoveries as well as some of the same obstacles encountered by other private collectors and museums in the market for similar artworks.

Although the Hubers have acquired some Spanish Colonial paintings in recent years from auction houses and dealers in the United States and Europe, many works of art in their collection were acquired while they lived abroad and, later on, from dealers that they had come to know in Buenos Aires and São Paulo. Some were acquired in Bolivia before 1999, when an agreement was reached with the United States intended to halt the export of the colonial patrimony of the country. Some of these acquisitions were serendipitous. In 1996, when Dick Huber was in La Paz, Bolivia, on business, he put out the word that he would like to acquire a painting of an angel, representations of angels being among the best-known and loved creations of the artists of the region. A dealer offered a painting of a guardian angel, but would only sell it as a package with two other works, a "portrait" of Saint Thomas Aquinas and a painting of a "dressed sculpture" from Cuzco. Dick Huber reluctantly bought all three canvases for several thousand dollars. The dirty painting of the "dressed sculpture" was carried around, still rolled up, as the family moved, and, years later, finally cleaned and framed while they were living in Hartford. In 2004, the Hubers were surprised to see the twin of their "dressed sculpture" painting in the exhibition *The Colonial Andes: Tapestries and Silverwork, 1530–1830* at The Metropolitan Museum of Art. They learned that their painting (fig. 49), like the one in the Museum's collection, represents *Our Lady of Guápulo*, a devotion to the Virgin Mary with origins in Quito, Ecuador, that was often painted, always identically, in the workshops of Cuzco, Peru. The Hubers are happy to own this lovely painting that Dick had been forced to buy.

The Hubers have been careful to respect the agreements between Peru (1997) and Bolivia (1999) and the U.S. government designed to protect the cultural patrimonies of those South American countries. However, once works of art have left the countries in which they were created, it is difficult for collectors to rely on the provenances provided to them.

There was an active art market throughout the Viceroyalty of Peru from early colonial times, with paintings created most notably in the artistic centers of Cuzco, Peru, and Quito, Ecuador, shipped in great numbers to Chile and Argentina. Nor did Spanish Colonial paintings, sculptures, silver, and furniture remain in South America. Spanish immigrants often returned to their native Spain (where they were called *indianos*) after having made their fortunes in the Americas in mining, agriculture, or as merchants. Members of the aristocracy who served the Spanish monarchy for a period of years also returned. Portuguese sailors, merchants, and administrators of Portuguese affairs in Brazil and in the "East Indies" also returned to the Iberian Peninsula. All of them took with them their acquisitions, which included art and furnishings, often kept by their descendants for years. Recently, these paintings and beautifully crafted objects in all media have appeared regularly at auctions in Madrid and Lisbon and have been sold by private dealers. The latter was the case with a donor portrait of Joaquín Elorrieta (fig. 50) painted in Quito, Ecuador, in 1777 by José Cortés de Alcocer (active ca. 1750–1803). The inscription details Elorrieta's service to the Spanish monarchy in Mexico and New Granada as the treasurer of the properties taken from the Jesuits when their order was expelled in 1767. It was not unusual for Spaniards living and working in the colonies to commission paintings recalling special devotions brought with them from their hometowns. This painting depicts the sitter kneeling before "Our Lady of the Reedbed" (*Nuestra Señora del Juncal*), a very local devotion to the Virgin Mary established in Irún, a Basque town on the present border between France and Spain. When Elorrieta returned to Spain, he brought the painting with him, and the Hubers acquired it in 2003 from a dealer in Madrid.

Another favorite painting, *Rosa de Salazar y Gabiño, Countess of Monteblanco and Montemar* (fig. 51), was likewise acquired from a Madrid dealer. Doña Rosa was a well-known figure in Peru in the latter part of the eighteenth century, and reportedly the richest woman in Lima at the time. A part of her wealth was the ownership of over one thousand slaves (a shocking fact today but common at the time). Several years ago the Hubers loaned the painting to the Metropolitan Museum, where it was installed in the first room of the new American galleries so that it could be compared to North American portraits of the same period.

One day, just before closing, a small group of tourists from Lima was in the gallery when one of them spotted the Huber painting and identified it as representing one of his ancestors. The gentleman contacted the Hubers and invited them to visit him in Lima. When the Hubers traveled to Lima some time later, they visited the gentleman's home, met a number of members of his family, and were shown a small portrait of Doña Rosa that recorded her appearance when she was older, but still a handsome woman. She was wearing the same earrings as pictured in the Huber painting, and they reappeared in a photo taken of their grandmother a hundred years ago.

It is more difficult for collectors to be sure of the provenance of works of art created in Peru or Bolivia once the objects have left their home regions for other parts of South America. Many colonial works now in Chile and Argentina, as noted above, were introduced there centuries ago. However, in recent decades the collecting of Spanish American colonial art has been tarnished by widespread losses of the historical treasures of colonial churches. The Hubers discovered in 2012 the trap for collectors in unproven provenance of paintings.

When the Hubers' collection was being prepared by the Philadelphia Museum of Art for the exhibition *Journeys to New Worlds*, which would open in 2013, the curator of the exhibition, Joseph J. Rishel, had to break the grim news to the couple that two of the paintings scheduled to be included had appeared on a list of stolen works published by Interpol. All the objects in the planned exhibition were routinely checked by Catherine Herbert, the museum's Coordinator of Collections Research and Documentation. All major museums have staff dedicated to provenance research, prompted by, but not limited to, concerns with Nazi confiscation of private art collections during World War II. All works of art, including Spanish Colonial art, are addressed by the same concerns. According to the Interpol database of stolen works of art, twelve paintings had been stolen from the church of San Martín in Potosí, Bolivia, on June 20, 2002. Two of the Hubers' paintings were identified on that list, a *Flight into Egypt* and *Our Lady of Copacabana*. The couple located an attorney who specialized in

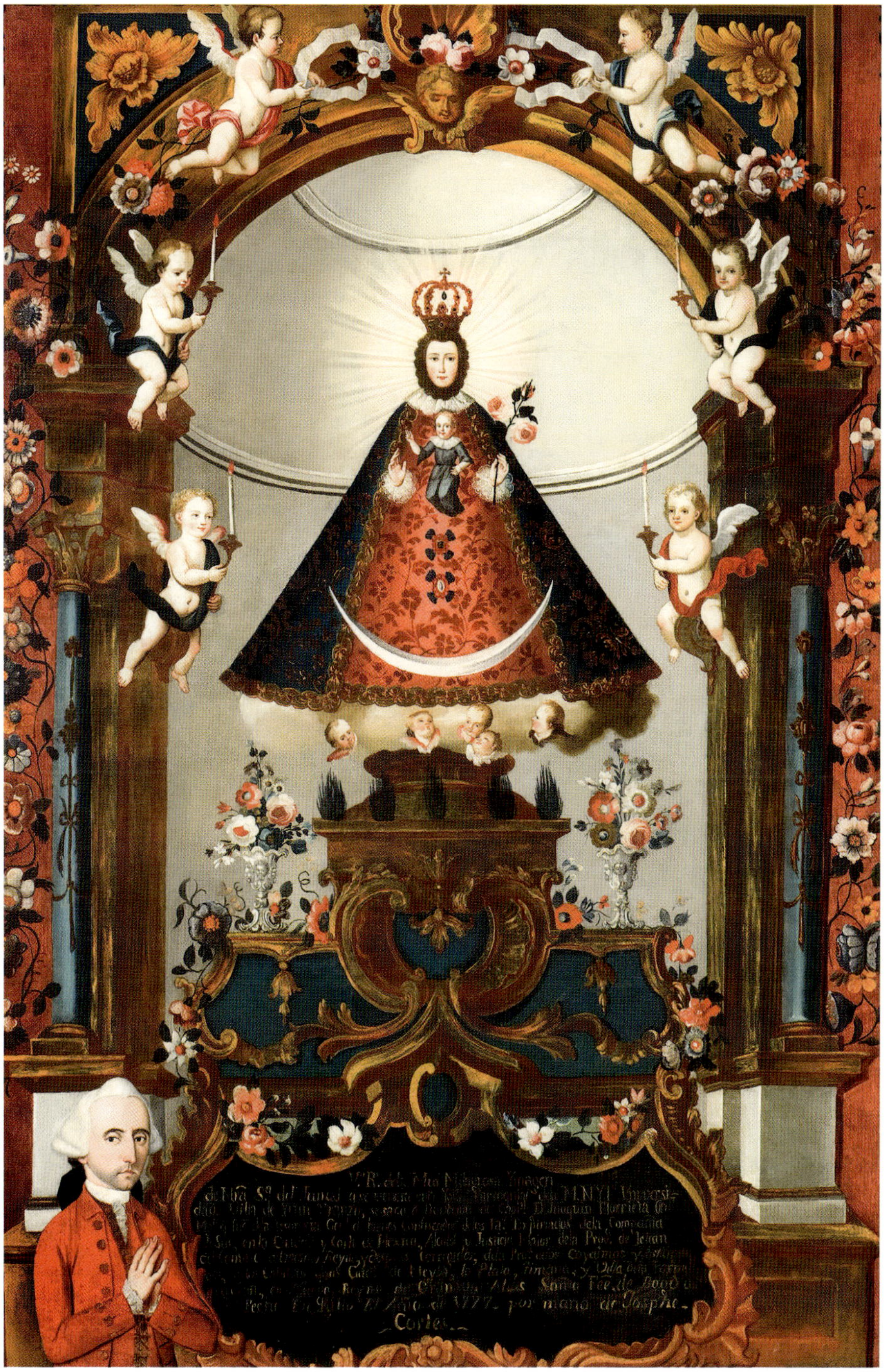

50. José Cortés de Alcocer (active ca. 1750–1803), *Our Lady of the Reedbed of Irún with Donor, Captain Joaquín Elorrieta,* 1777. Oil on canvas, 95 × 64 cm. Philadelphia Museum of Art.

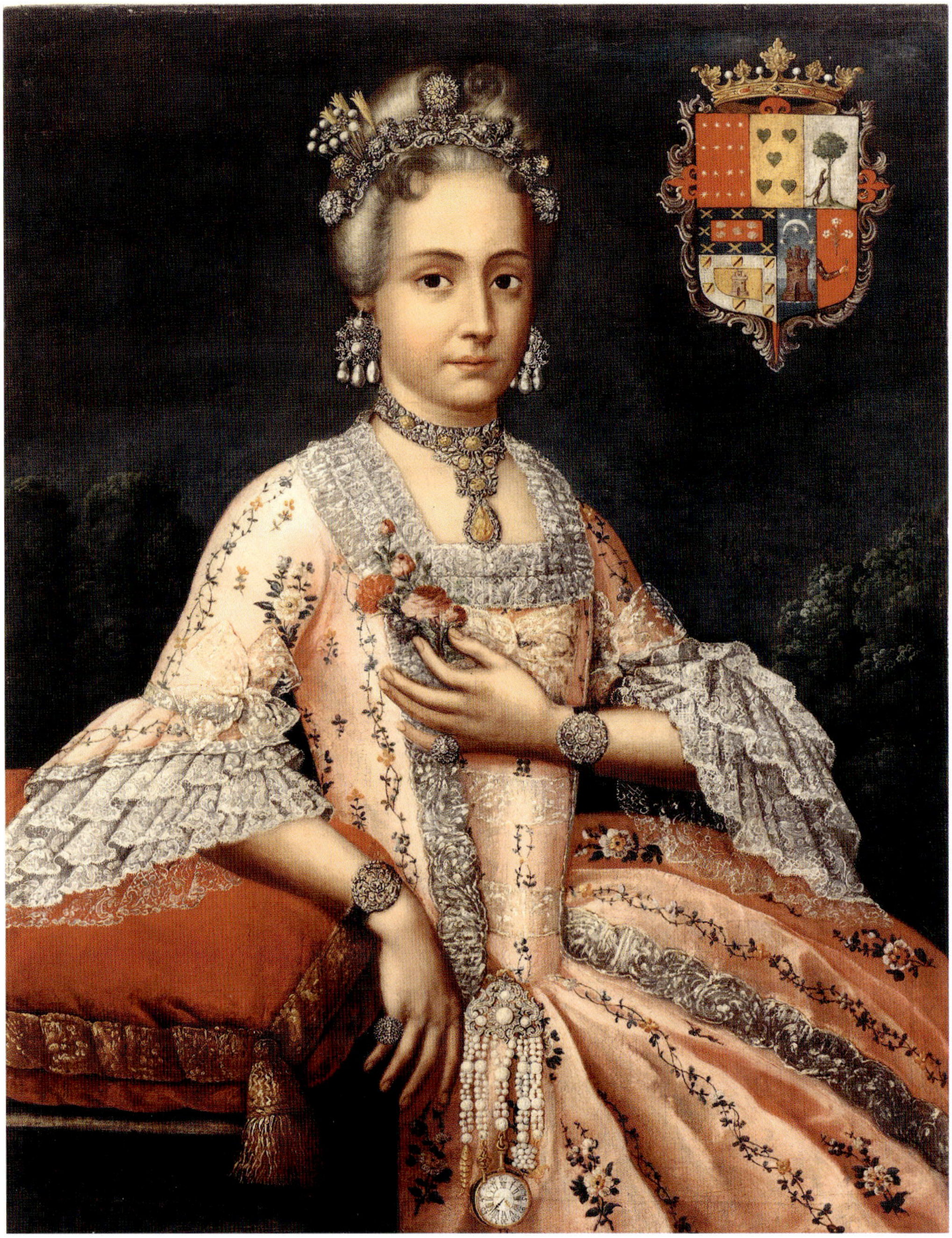

51. Artist unknown (Peruvian, Lima), *Rosa de Salazar y Gabiño, Countess of Monteblanco and Montemar*, ca. 1764–71. Oil on canvas, 96 × 75.6 cm. Collection of Roberta and Richard Huber.

matters of this sort, who in turn contacted the FBI, which is the U.S. partner in Interpol. The paintings were duly registered, so that the Hubers were not in violation of an international treaty, having been innocent as to the origins of the paintings. Some months later, the Hubers received a dossier from the Ministry of Cultures of the Bolivian government identifying the two paintings as having been improperly acquired by the Brazilian dealer from whom they had purchased them. The Hubers wanted to repatriate the works, but found no clear avenue to do so.

Iván Rebolledo, the head of the Bolivia-American Chamber of Commerce, offered to help. He was able to arrange a visit to the Hubers' home in December 2014 by Álvaro García Linara, the vice president of Bolivia, when he was on a visit to New York. Dick Huber showed García Linara the two paintings he and Roberta wanted to return, and they discussed an appropriate path to repatriation. Several months later, the Hubers boarded the presidential plane from New York to La Paz, along with the paintings (now restored and framed at the Hubers' expense), where they were met with a ceremony at the Palacio Quemado (Bolivia's presidential palace), attended by President Evo Morales, the vice president, American chargé d'affaires Peter Brennan, the full cabinet, and a group of Aymara women in their traditional wide skirts and bowler hats and Aymara men in miners' uniforms with shiny helmets. The Hubers received awards describing their good deed as "Vale un Potosí" (Worth a Potosí, i.e., of incredible value). This story thus ends happily, but is a cautionary tale for collectors of Spanish Colonial art.

The depredations of thieves are always sad, and sometimes disastrous. When robbers entered the little church of Achocalla outside of La Paz some years ago, they cut large rectangles of canvas from the two enormous (six meters wide) paintings by the late seventeenth-century master Leonardo Flores (1650–1710). So ignorantly was this cruel mischief done that it is likely the fragments never even found a buyer.

Recently, thieves have turned from paintings to objects from the treasuries of the churches—silver monstrances and other liturgical objects, jewels belonging to cult images of the Virgin Mary, gold crowns garnished with precious stones—taken with the possible intention of extracting the stones and precious metals for their material value, thus avoiding discovery altogether. Of course, many ecclesiastical objects left colonial churches long ago, especially during the years immediately following independence from Spain. In Bolivia, for example, Catholic institutions bore the brunt of abrupt societal changes brought about by efforts to replace religiosity with the rationality of the French Enlightenment. In 1826, the new president of the Bolivian republic, Antonio José de Sucre (1795–1830), closed the Hospital de Belén in Potosí and turned it into the "Colegio de Ciencias y Artes." President Sucre suppressed the Franciscan order in Potosí on November 12 of that year, only to reestablish it on December 14 when he suppressed the Mercedarian order instead.[3]

In 1767, when the Society of Jesus was abolished in Spain and all its realms, the treasures of the Jesuit order were inventoried with exactitude by bureaucrats such as Joaquín Elorrieta working for the Crown. The dispersal of religious paintings, sculptures, and silver pieces in the nineteenth century was undoubtedly far more chaotic, and many ecclesiastical objects on the market today are of provenances lost in time. A missal stand acquired by the Hubers at Christie's New York in 1996 (fig. 52) may well have left a parish church in Peru or Bolivia during the early nineteenth century and thereby have escaped destruction. In 1826, Sucre ordered all the silver in the sanctuary of the Virgin Mary at Copacabana, Bolivia, to be melted down to fund the new government. Silver was also widely

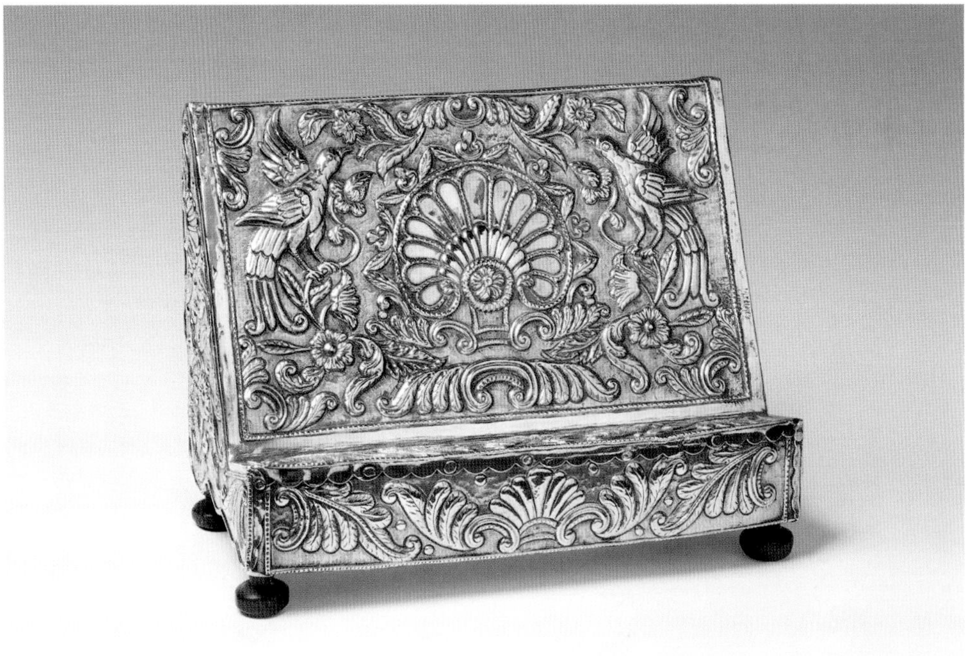

52. Artist unknown (Peruvian or Bolivian), missal stand. Silver, repoussé, chased, engraved, over wood, 30.5 × 38.1 × 21.6 cm. Collection of Roberta and Richard Huber.

used in the homes of the aristocracy and wealthy miners and merchants for extensive sets of tableware. These included plates and cutlery, of course, but also special dishes for sweets, salt cellars, and special sets for serving beverages such as tea, chocolate, and *yerba mate* (called "Jesuit tea" or "Paraguay tea"). A silver box called a *coquera* that was purchased by the Hubers in Santiago, Chile, was intended to hold coca leaves, which have been chewed in the Andes as a mild stimulant since long before the Spanish arrived, or some other aromatic or digestive herbs. Small domestic objects like this rarely have a known provenance.

A unique aspect of the Huber collection is the inclusion of antique ivory carvings of Catholic religious figures created in several "schools" of art: Hispano-Philippine, Indo-Portuguese, and Ceylon-Portuguese. The Hubers were introduced to these antique ivories by their friend James Li, whom they met in Brazil in 1967, though they did not actively begin to acquire works in this category until 2000. When Roberta Huber attended a symposium on Philippine colonial art, held in 2005 at the Ayala Museum in Manila, that included a paper on ivories, she was delighted to learn that the pieces she and Dick had acquired were equal in quality to the works in the Philippine museum: their collectors' "eye" had garnered some fine acquisitions. Roberta Huber was inspired by the scholars at the symposium, especially by the expertise of the Spanish art historian Margarita M. Estella Marcos, to further her own study of these colonial works of art, and their acquisitions continued apace until recently.

Sometimes the lack of competition for these objects has been helpful. Two ivory-and-ebony sculptures of saints (fig. 53) were offered at the famed European Fine Art Fair at Maastricht, the Netherlands. The Hubers loved the works but found them beyond their budget. The pieces did not find a buyer at the art fair, and they were later able to acquire them directly from the dealer. Serendipitously, another pair of these ivory-and-ebony sculptures of saints, apparently from the same workshop, soon appeared in the catalogue of an auction in Lisbon and was acquired by the Hubers to join the other pieces. They later discovered that a fifth piece by the same hands is in the collection of the Victoria and Albert Museum in London.

In 1989, the United States signed the United Nations Convention on International Trade in Endangered Species of Wild Fauna and Flora (CITES). Thereafter, the importation of ivory carvings required documentation attesting that the object was made of ivory culled before 1990. It was sometimes difficult to comply with the requirements of CITES. Four pieces were purchased at auction in Lisbon, all handled properly, export license obtained and CITES permits issued. However, when the sculptures arrived in New York, the Fish and Wildlife officers objected to the fact that line 27, "Quantity / net mass (kg.) actually imported or (re-)exported / Number of animals dead on arrival," a space reserved for customs agents from the shipping country, had been left blank, perhaps because the customs official in Lisbon thought it "Not applicable." The pieces, not just the documents, had to be returned to Portugal, where the customs agents added a number 1 to line 27, and the whole lot was shipped back to New York, where the Hubers, half a year later, were finally able to take it home. Collecting antique ivories was abruptly ended altogether by a 2014 announcement by the Interior Department's Fish and Wildlife Service that banned all commercial imports of African elephant ivory to the United States, including even authentic antiques, in an effort to end the horrific slaughter of elephants in Africa.[4]

This has not, however, prevented the Hubers from continuing to collect objects from the far reaches of the Portuguese colonial world, such as several silver candlesticks that can be assigned on the basis of style to Goa, the city from which Portugal's enterprises in Asia were administered, and a place the couple visited in the fall of 2015. Two of the Hubers' pieces from Goa were acquired at an auction in Austin, Texas, where they were misidentified as Mexican.

Polychromed sculpture, carved of wood and then gilded and painted, was created in both the Spanish and Portuguese colonies. This was the most important aspect of the decoration of colonial churches. Often made to adorn the niches of altarpieces, these sculptures usually represent life-sized figures of saints. Given their size, the altarpieces themselves are usually impossible to include in a private collection, but some smaller examples (called *imágenes* in property inventories) were made for the domestic market, and the Hubers have acquired several of them, originally made in Brazil.

Roberta and Dick Huber live with their collection, and so it is entirely apt that they have acquired colonial furniture such as a handsome cabinet of a type called a *contador*, made in mid-eighteenth-century Lima of wood inlaid with mother-of-pearl, tortoiseshell, ivory, and silver. A large chest of jacaranda wood called an *arca* is from Brazil. Small boxes decorated with ornate inlaid lacquer were made in Colombia. Despite this accumulation, the Hubers' home has a thoroughly domestic feel, without the formal aura of a museum. There are colonial maps of the Indies on the walls of the library. Large paintings hang in the double-height space of the dining room and small ivory saints vie for space on the mantelpieces.

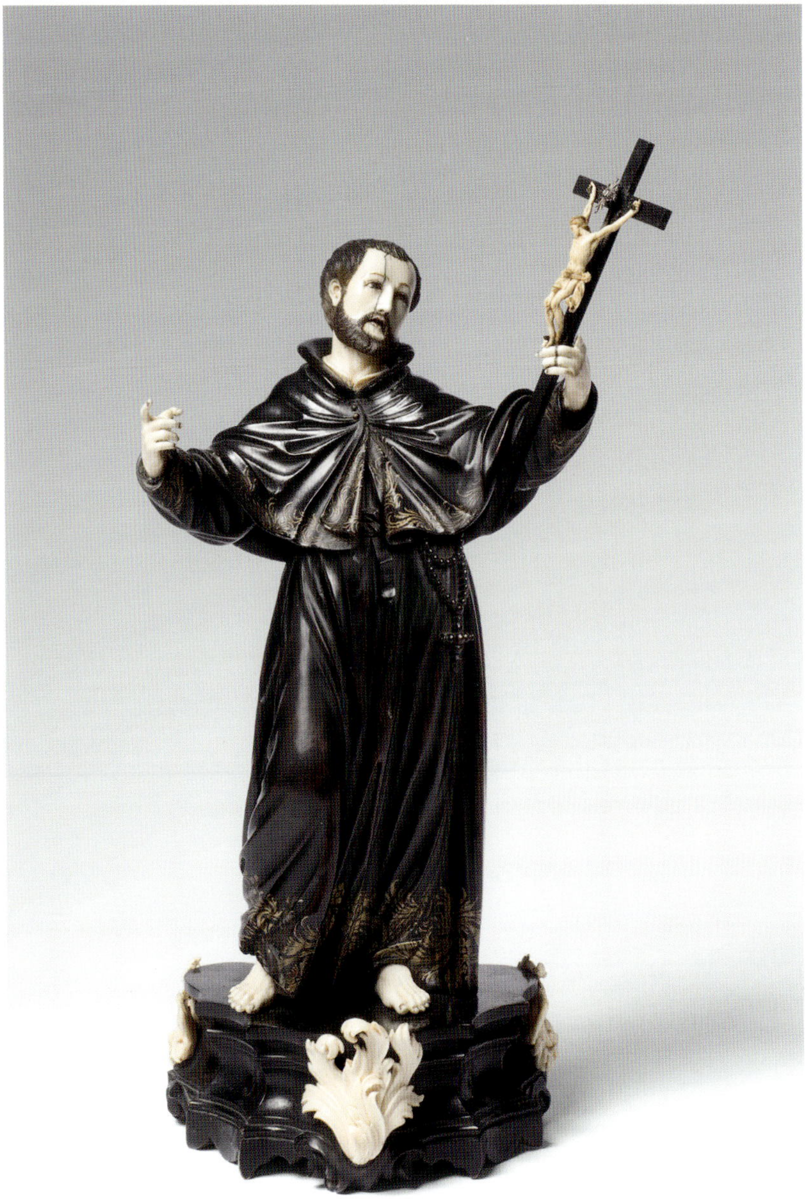

53. Artist unknown (Indo-Portuguese), *Saint Francis Xavier*, second half of the eighteenth century. Ivory with polychromy, ebony, gilding, mounted on wood and ivory base, with wood, ivory, and metal crucifix (possibly modern), height 39.4 cm. Collection of Roberta and Richard Huber.

Roberta and Dick Huber continue collecting, and they are also generous philanthropists who support scholarship in all the areas their acquisitions touch upon. Their collection traveled in 2016–17 to the San Antonio Museum of Art, the Crocker Art Museum in Sacramento, and the Worcester Art Museum. The Huber Family Foundation has contributed to exhibitions and symposia (most recently the New Mexico History Museum in Santa Fe and the Boston Museum of Art). They have for some years sponsored guest lectures at the Institute of Fine Arts of New York University in the series The Roberta and Richard Huber Colloquium on the Arts of Spain and Colonial Latin America, which gives graduate students and the general public an opportunity to hear from scholars working in these fields. The Hubers have also sponsored the restoration of colonial objects in the collection of the Hispanic Society of America, New York.[5] Roberta and Dick Huber are paragons among collectors for their passion for the objects of their desire, their thirst for knowledge, and their support of scholarship and conservation.

CHAPTER 10

Expanding Paradigms

The Colección Patricia Phelps de Cisneros and the Changing Landscape of Latin American Art

Gabriel Pérez-Barreiro

54. Tomás Maldonado (Argentinian, b. 1922), *Desarrollo de 14 temas* (Development of 14 Themes), 1951–52. Oil on canvas, 200.3 × 210.2 cm. Colección Patricia Phelps de Cisneros. © Tomás Maldonado.

Taste, like many other mutable phenomena, often follows something of a bell curve plotted over time, in which knowledge and desire interact in mysterious and often invisible ways. If we try to look for symptoms of a change in taste, we can detect certain patterns. First, a small number of people start to appreciate and understand a previously neglected aesthetic, movement, or style, followed by a slightly larger group of specialists or researchers who are "early adopters." As word gets around, an ever-increasing number of people start to incorporate this repertoire of previously unfamiliar names and works into their awareness. Universities start to teach the material, and eventually museums start to show and acquire it: first on the margins and then in more central places. The market starts to respond, and more collectors express an interest. Eventually, at the top of the curve, the formerly marginal becomes the mainstream, and that taste is accepted unquestioningly and ubiquitously. Once a taste is widely accepted and naturalized, a new generation will inevitably start its own reaction and bell curve with a different aesthetic and implicit questioning of the former values. In this model, the latter part of the curve is slower than the first, as the new value tends to stick around and become part of the collective unconscious in a way it was not at the beginning.

The history of the Colección Patricia Phelps de Cisneros (CPPC) is in many ways illustrative of this bell curve. In its origins, development, and design, it set out to bring awareness of art from Latin America into a system that had largely been ignorant of that part of the world. But perhaps more importantly, it was not just the art of Latin America that was at stake, but a very particular and specific reading of its history, inscribed into a specific historical and cultural sensitivity. To understand the CPPC, we have to consider the history of how the Latin American art field has been constituted, particularly outside of the region itself. Europe and the United States have always understood Latin America within

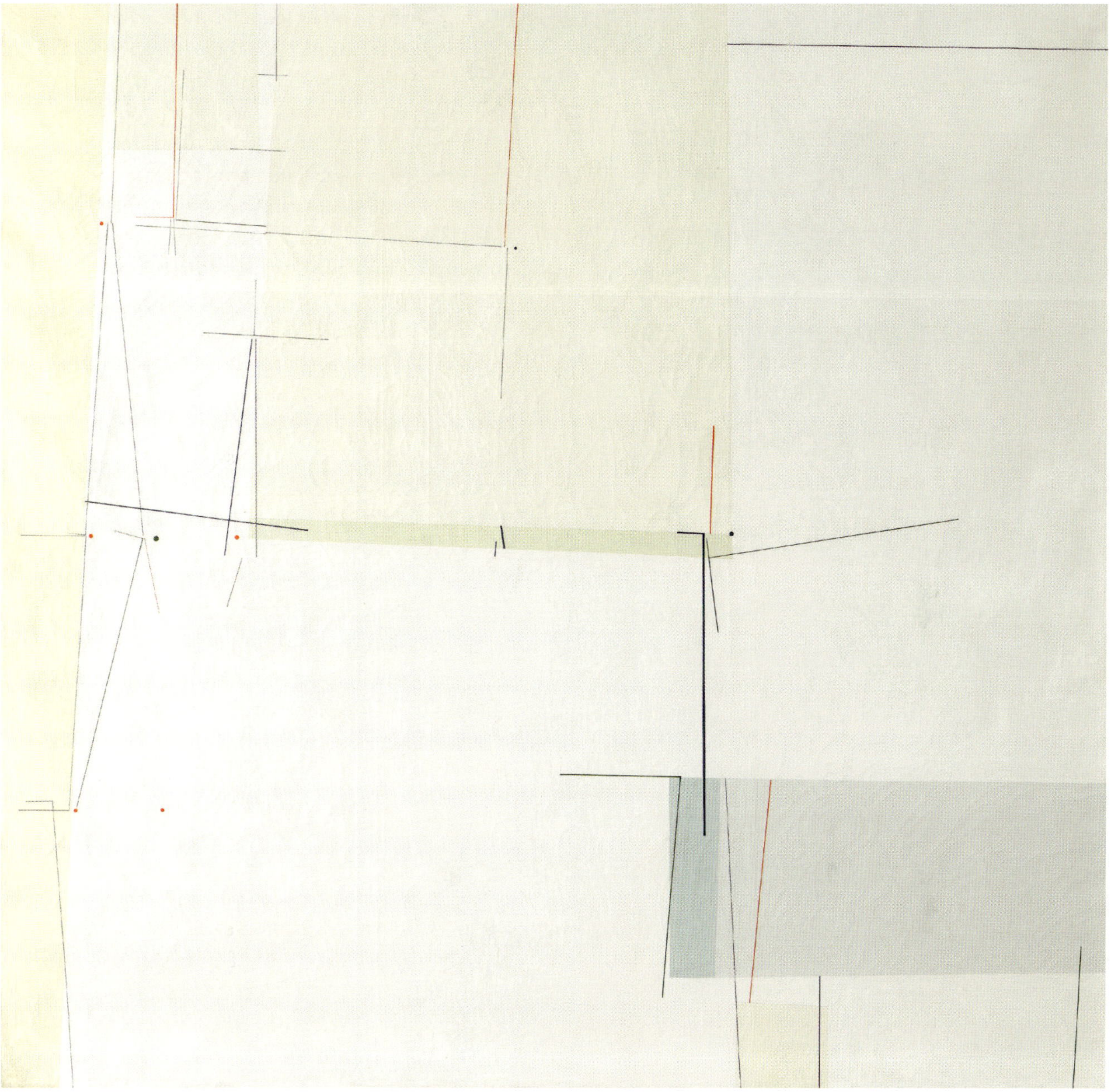

a framework of difference. Although the former Spanish and Portuguese empires were not, at least in one potential reading, fundamentally different from the English, Latin America has come to represent the different, the other, and the exotic in the collective imagination in a way that the United States or Canada has not. One reflection of this is the inadequate terminology often used when discussing Latin America, starting with the very term itself. "Latin America" includes a multiplicity of non-Latin cultures, but excludes the extensive Spanish-speaking population of the United States and, it could be argued, even the French-speaking population of Quebec, which is both Latin and American. The other common distinction made is "Western" vs. "non-Western," which tends, confusingly, to actually mean "Northern" vs. "Southern."

Given this framework of difference, it is perhaps inevitable that the overriding stereotypes applied to Latin America are the exotic, the tropical, the tragic, the political, the passionate. As a result, for most of the twentieth century, the genealogy that was promoted of the region connected Mexican Muralism, magical realism, and *indigenismo* in an image of a region torn by drama and redeemed by passion. Of course, this image played nicely into a false dichotomy that posited the North as the place of reason, formalism, balance, harmony, and political level-headedness.

It was against this panorama of exoticism that Patricia Phelps de Cisneros and her husband, Gustavo Cisneros, started something of a crusade to challenge that stereotype and replace it with a more nuanced and complex version of that history. As Latin Americans with a global outlook (Patricia through her U.S.-Venezuelan family history and Gustavo through his international business interests), they were both concerned with what they perceived to be a limited and limiting view of the region and its place in history. Growing up in the modernist and optimistic city of Caracas in the mid-twentieth century, they had witnessed a more positive version of history in which Latin America played a central as opposed to a marginal role. Patricia's eye and taste gravitated first toward the geometric abstraction that is a key element in Venezuela's history, becoming the visual language of Caracas in a comparable way to Mexico City's Muralism. This recognition of—and taste for—geometric abstraction contained an implicit challenge to the worldview that kept Latin America separate from world history, as its cosmopolitanism and formal sophistication resist a stereotypical reading. In addition, the biographies of the artists included in the early years of the collection—Jesús Soto (1923–2005), Carlos Cruz Diez (b. 1923), and Alejandro Otero (1921–1990)—exemplified a fluid and complex relationship with Paris, the cultural capital of the time, which accepted these artists as part of an international avant-garde that explored formal questions of art, not identity.

In the mid-1990s, what had been a relatively modest collection began to take on a new level of ambition as Patricia and Gustavo traveled extensively around Latin America. Patricia began to visit studios and museums, where she learned about comparable, often earlier movements of abstraction in Brazil, Argentina, and Uruguay. Around this time she hired the first curators who would help her assemble and structure the collection. With the Brazilian Paulo Herkenhoff and the Venezuelans Luis Pérez Oramas and Ariel Jiménez to assist her, she was able to gather together, in a relatively short time, a unique collection that could tell a comprehensive story of the development of abstraction from Joaquín Torres-García (1874–1949) in Uruguay in the 1930s to Gego (Gertrude Louise Goldschmidt, 1912–1994) in Caracas in the 1980s. The modern collection includes many seminal works by artists such as Torres-García, Lygia Clark (1920–1988), Hélio Oiticica (1937–1980), Mira Schendel (1919–1988), Willys de Castro (1926–1988), Soto,

Cruz-Diez, Gego, and many others, and remains unparalleled in private or public collections.

The fact that no museum inside or outside Latin America had comparable holdings raised the question of the uses of the collection and the responsibility of the collectors to the objects in their care. How could these objects best be used to tell their story and influence art history? To answer this question, it can be helpful to think of the collection, and perhaps comparably "activist" collections, in terms of both their tangible and intangible nature. The tangible aspect is manifested in the physically present objects, from which all the meaning ultimately flows. The intangible aspects relate to their implicit historical meaning, the challenge that the objects pose to traditional narratives, and their ability to expand knowledge. Throughout its history, the CPPC has paid at least as much attention to these intangible aspects as to the objects themselves. In fact, Patricia has often rejected the term "collector" as a too simplistic descriptor of an activity that involves much more than just accumulating artworks, but should embrace documentation, research, and study.[1] By the late 1990s and early 2000s the Fundación Cisneros started a series of partnerships with academic institutions, understanding these to be the first agents in a chain that could generate the change in hearts and minds that would ultimately lead to a greater understanding and acceptance of Latin America and the significance of its art. The first academic partner was the University of Texas at Austin. At the Blanton Museum of Art, the Cisneros Seminar for the Study of Latin American Modernism, a joint venture of the University and the Fundación, consisted of a loan of key objects and a speaker and publication series. From this collaboration came the first exhibition of the collection, *Dynamic Oppositions* in 1999. In 2001, the Fundación worked with Harvard University's Fogg Museum to present a more comprehensive exhibition, *Geometric Abstraction: Latin American Art from the Patricia Phelps de Cisneros Collection*. It marked the first time works from Latin America had ever been shown in that museum, in contrast to the Blanton, where Latin America had traditionally been an area of strength. Following these presentations, the decision was made to send the collection on an extensive multinational tour across Latin America. From 2002 to 2006 the modern collection was shown at fourteen museums and cultural institutions in ten countries, in each venue with a slightly different structure and publication, under the curatorial leadership of Ariel Jiménez.

The Latin American tour solidified the notion of a "museum without walls," a collection at the service of its audiences, capable of traveling to different locations in various iterations and responding to local needs and traditions. Implicit in this model was a critique of a phenomenon that was becoming more common during those years: the collector's private museum. While the temptation to exhibit the collection in its own facility must have been great, Patricia and Gustavo early on took the decision to instead use their resources to make the collection travel, and thereby multiply its impact and transformative ability. In addition to these CPPC-organized exhibitions, the collection has traditionally lent very generously to third-party exhibitions around the world, and has made artworks that were previously inaccessible or invisible readily available to curators through professional management and documentation.[2]

At the same time that the collection was touring Latin America, a number of important changes were under way in the United States and Europe that would pave the way for something of a triumphal return. After the Harvard exhibition, the Museum of Fine Arts, Houston, organized a major exhibition, *Inverted Utopias* (see the Ramírez essay in this volume), which presented a complex and nuanced reading of Latin American art that made it legible for a U.S. audience on an unprecedented scale.[3] At the same time, various institutions began to make a long-term commitment to Latin America that would break the cyclical nature of interest that had plagued the field in previous decades. The Museum of Modern Art in New York, the Tate, and the Museum of Fine Arts, Houston, all created curatorial positions dedicated to Latin American art, and although each institution structured its program differently, they had the common purpose of addressing the historical deficits of Latin American art in their collections and exhibitions. At the same time, as the art world became increasingly diverse as a consequence of globalization, and biennials, fairs, and galleries reflected a new reality in which national origin was no longer a determining or limiting factor to the extent it had been, and contemporary artists were breaking through geographic limitations, as they had been for decades.[4]

All of these factors contributed to a shift in context that made the CPPC's next major presentation in the United States have greater impact. In 2007, the Blanton organized *The Geometry of Hope.* As an outgrowth of the original Cisneros Seminar, the exhibition was developed through a graduate seminar and structured using cities as the organizing principle. Visitors to the exhibition started in 1930s Montevideo, passed though 1940s Buenos Aires, 1950s Sao Paulo, 1960s Rio and 1960s Paris, and ended in 1970s Caracas. The exhibition drew attention to the specificity of geography and to the connections between these cities, including Paris as a central location in the narrative. While the exhibition was very well received in Texas by an audience used to seeing this type of art, its presentation later that year in New York at the Grey Art Gallery proved to be something of a turning point.[5] In a glowing review in the *New York Times*, Roberta Smith acknowledged that "Latin American abstraction has tended to be ignored in North America, when not dismissed as fussy, gimmicky, and a tad kitschy. This show of about 105 works by nearly 30 artists invites a reconsideration of such attitudes. Working through its riches is both humbling and thrilling; you encounter your ignorance and have a chance to rectify it."[6] Although many of these works had in fact been seen in New York before in various exhibitions, the timing was such that the audience now seemed ready to understand the exhibition and the history it represented, and the particularity of the geographic locales cited both expanded and concretized viewers' notions of what constituted Latin America's physical and cultural territories.

The Blanton, Fogg, and Grey were all university galleries, and the CPPC exhibitions had in all cases been accompanied by symposia and related academic programming that became important opportunities for emerging scholars in the field to share research and ideas. At the same time, the number of academic courses offering Latin American art increased substantially, and the type of material studied started to gravitate more toward the abstract/Kinetic legacy. As part of this "mainstreaming" of Latin American abstraction, galleries increasingly showed more geometric works, and the Pinta Art Fair, focused on Latin American art, which had been predominantly in the Muralist / Magical Realism mode in its first exhibition in 2007, was almost exclusively abstract by its third exhibition in 2009.

In 2008, the CPPC moved its headquarters to New York, though it still maintained an office in Caracas with activities dedicated primarily to supporting the artistic scene in Venezuela. Based on the sense that the 2007 exhibition had been something of a watershed, marking the achievement of many of the original goals, CPPC programs were refocused more on the generation of knowledge and human capital and on other collection areas beyond geometric abstraction. With this move came a restructuring of the programs to create a more predictable grant program dedicated to artists, curators, and artist-run spaces in Latin America. (For a complete list of CPPC grants, see http://

www.coleccioncisneros.org/grants.) In 2010, the CPPC launched a new publications series, *Conversaciones*, dedicated to book-length interviews with Latin American artists and intellectuals. Although the CPPC had published many books throughout its history, the *Conversaciones* series was aimed at addressing a serious lack of firsthand testimony from artists in the existing literature on art from Latin America, a field dominated by exhibition catalogues. The new programs also marked a certain autonomy between the programs and the objects in the collection. As the collection was becoming better known, the CPPC was able to address the broader field of Latin American art in a more comprehensive way. As an example of this new focus, in 2010 the CPPC signed a five-year agreement with Hunter College to create a new professorship of Latin American art with associated programming, and in the same year the Fundación endowed a position for a Latin American bibliographer at MoMA. In both cases these were initiatives focused on long-term institutional transformation rather than one-off events. Coupled with the new interest from universities and museums, this marked a definitive shift from one-off and cyclical interest in Latin America to its ever-increasing and stable presence within mainstream institutions.

Patricia Cisneros's involvement at MoMA would require an entirely different and longer essay, but it suffices to say here that her championship of Latin American art at the Museum was a key factor in its embracing of Latin American art, made most visible in the reopening of the Manhattan building in 2006, when Latin American art was seamlessly integrated into the collection displays in a way it had not been since the 1940s. Many of the Latin American works on view had been gifted from the CPPC, and its former curator, Paulo Herkenhoff, now working on a three-year contract at MoMA, was instrumental in articulating these new relationships. After Herkenhoff's contract expired, the position was made permanent thanks to a contribution from Estrellita Brodsky, and the Museum hired Luis Enrique Pérez Oramas as its first full-time curator of Latin American art, charged with creating the conditions for dialogue within the Museum to build the collection and programming. Patricia's founding of the Latin American and Caribbean Fund in 2006, the creation of the C-MAP initiative in 2009, and the long-standing Cisneros Fund for Curatorial Travel were all decisive factors in that institutional change, championed from the top by the Museum's director, Glenn Lowry, and his senior management team and enthusiastically embraced by the curatorial staff.

While MoMA was fully engaging in an unprecedented involvement with Latin American modern art, the CPPC began to pay more systematic attention to the other collections under its care. The CPPC consists of five distinct but related collections: modern art (fig. 54), contemporary art (fig. 55), Orinoco (fig. 56, ethnographic objects), colonial (fig. 57), and traveler artists (fig. 58). While the public image of the collection has been dominated by the modern collection, the actual holdings are much more diverse and tell a nuanced and complex story of the history of art and ideas in Latin America, from the original inhabitants to cutting-edge contemporary expressions.

To return to the original image of the bell curve, by 2010 or so the modern collection had reached mainstream acceptance by the academy, museums, and the market. The modern collection had stopped growing, and efforts were focused more on publications (the *Conversaciones* series, as well as the first comprehensive stand-alone book, *A Constructive Vision*) and on two more exhibitions in Europe, outside the academic context, at the Reina Sofia in Madrid and the Royal Academy of Arts in London.[7] In these same years, one could also detect a new interest emerging in the academy for art of the next generation, particularly Conceptual art, marking the arrival of a new tide in taste.

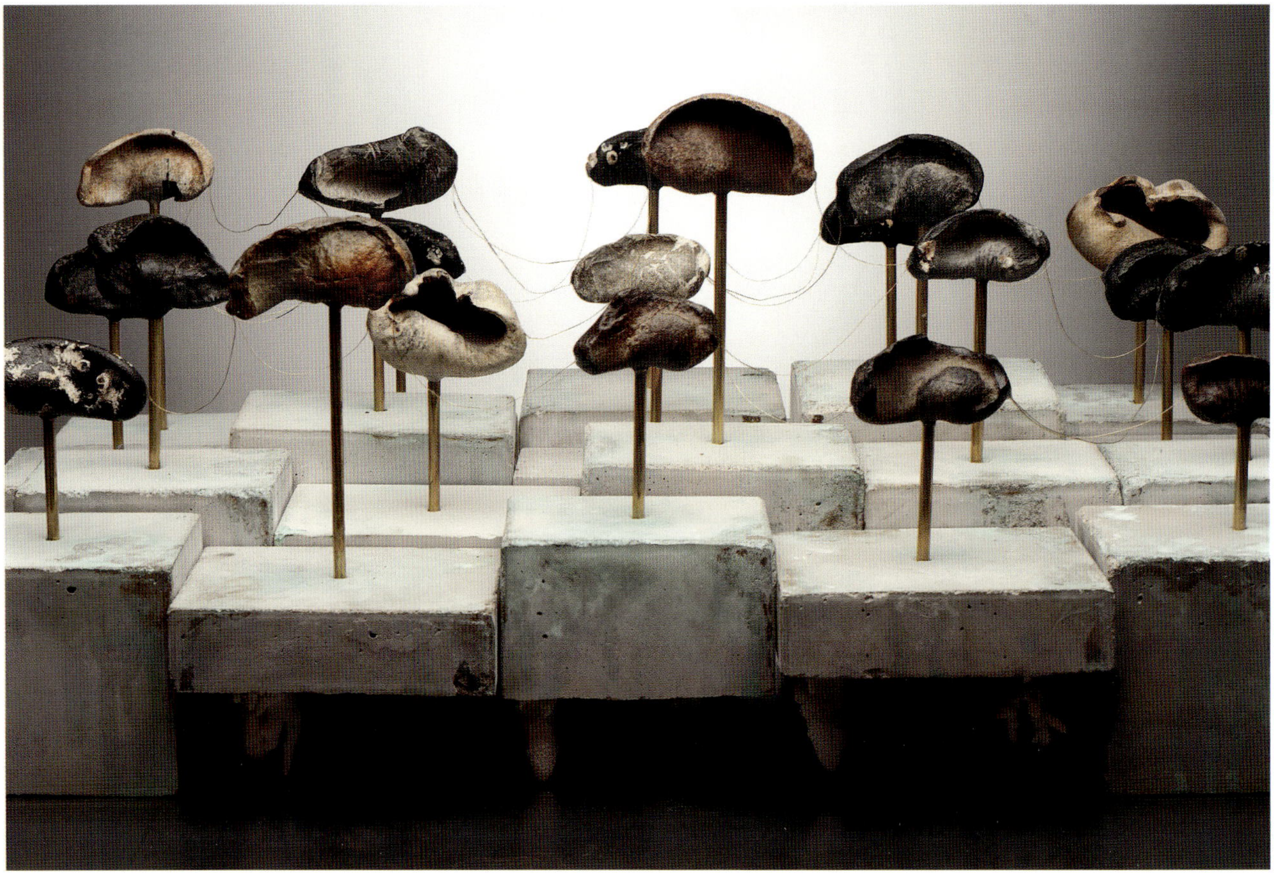

55. Dario Robleto (American, b. 1972), *Fossilhood Is Not Our Forever*, 2014. Fossilized prehistoric whale ear bones salvaged from the sea (1 to 10 million years), stretched audiotape of three centuries of human heartbeat recordings (1865, 1977, 2014), gold paint, concrete, ocean water, pigments, rust, brass, coral, steel, and Plexiglas, 86.36 × 120.65 × 92.71 cm. Colección Patricia Phelps de Cisneros.

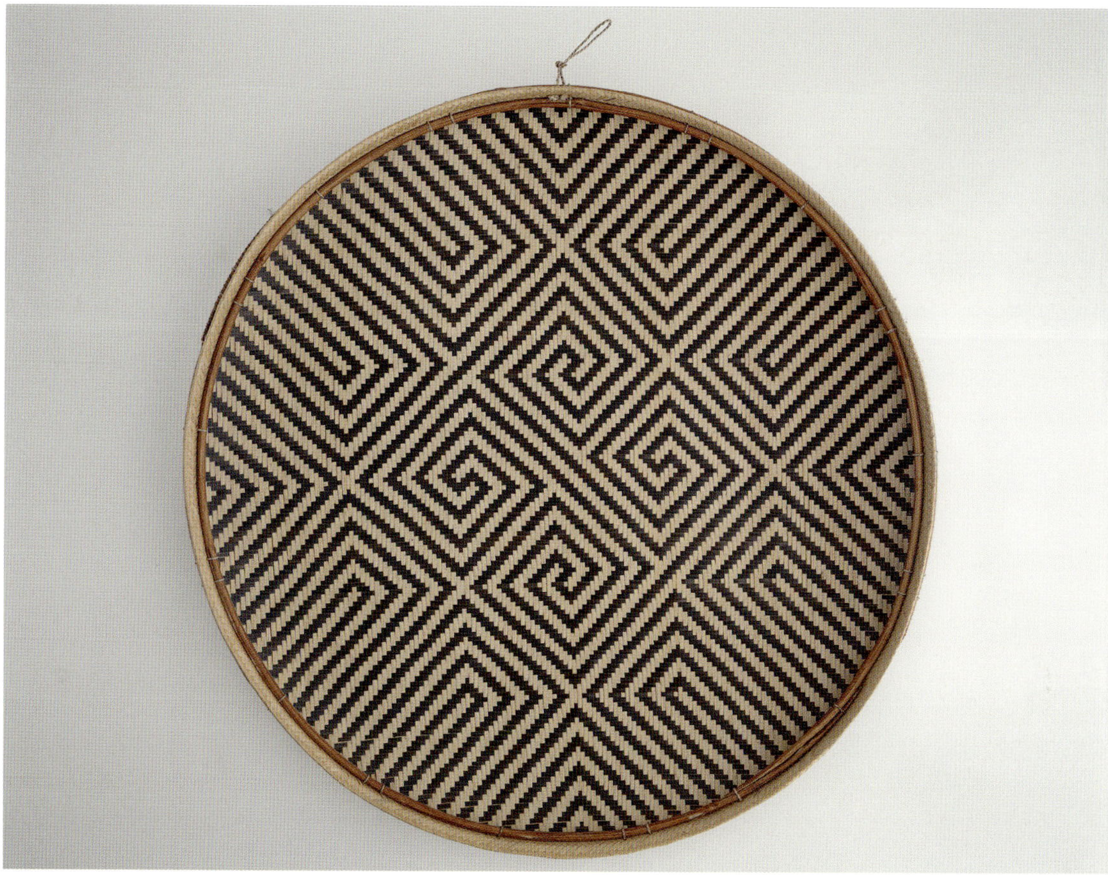

56. Ye'kuana, *Guapa*, Awidi. Tirite bark, reed, curagua fiber, and vegetable dye, 5 × 46.5 cm. Colección Patricia Phelps de Cisneros.

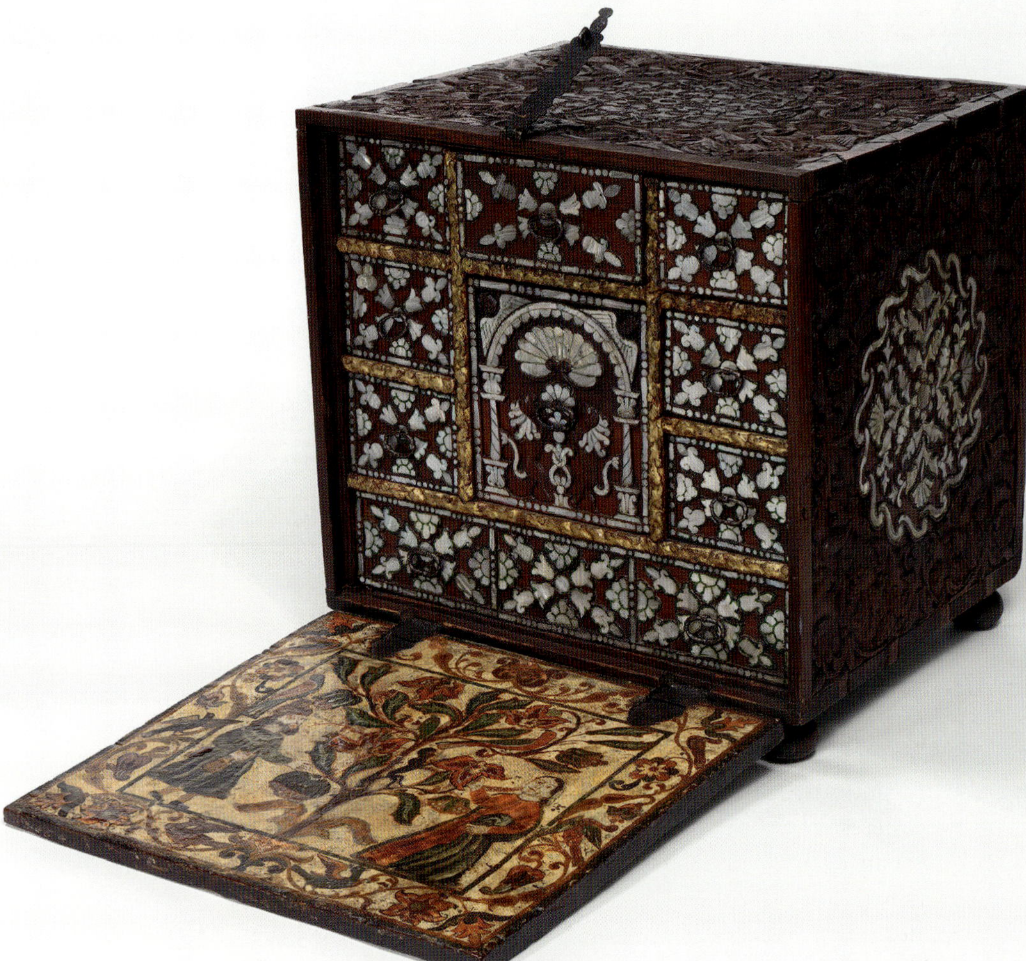

57. Artist unknown, *Escritorios* (Desks), 1752–1767. Wood, mother-of-pearl, iron, and paint, 40 × 33 × 40.6 cm. Colección Patricia Phelps de Cisneros.

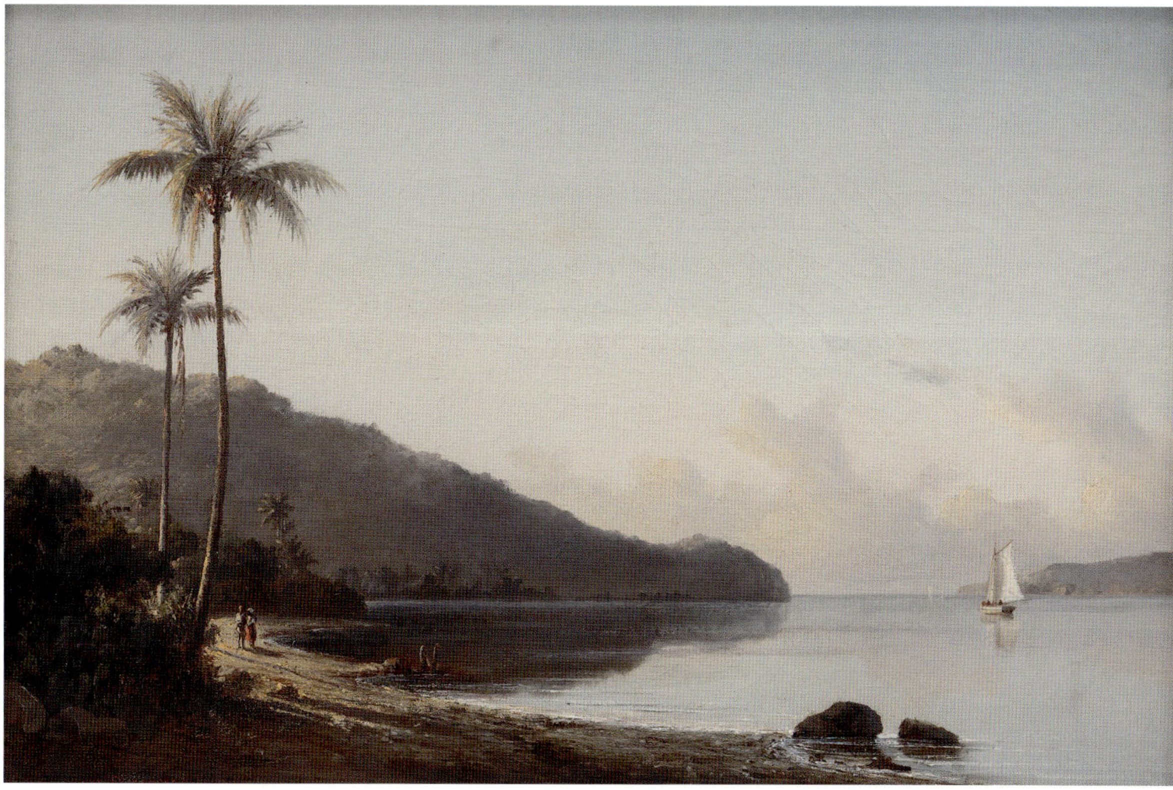

58. Camille Pissarro (French, 1830–1903), *Saint Thomas, Virgin Islands Cove with Sailboat*, 1856. Oil on canvas, 35 × 53 cm. Colección Patricia Phelps de Cisneros.

In many ways, the other collections could be mapped on the same curve, with the (predominantly) nineteenth-century traveler collection starting to attract interest in various places, including The City University of New York (CUNY), New York University (NYU), Crystal Bridges Museum of American Art (Bentonville, Arkansas), the University of Texas at Austin, and other places, in a similar way to how the modern collection had found a small group of specialized enthusiasts in the mid-1990s. As with the modern collection, students had little or no access to the original works of art, so the CPPC started to organize intimate viewings of selected objects for classes, creating essentially a pop-up museum to order—but a museum in which the artworks might be closely scrutinized and even handled. Two institutional collaborations were essential in this process: Katherine Manthorne's graduate seminar on Latin American landscape at CUNY, based on objects in the CPPC, and then Harper Montgomery's practicum seminar at Hunter College, in which her students carried out primary research and also developed a curatorial proposal for the exhibition *Boundless Reality: Traveler Artists' Landscapes of Latin America from the Colección Patricia Phelps de Cisneros*, which opened at Hunter and Americas Society in the fall of 2015. *Boundless Reality* follows a similar model to *The Geometry of Hope* in its involvement with students, supporting them to create and publish new scholarship. The exhibition coincided with a major initiative supported by the Terra Foundation to present American landscapes, North and South, in a major exhibition, *Picturing the Americas: Landscape Painting from Tierra del Fuego to the Arctic*, which toured Canada, the United States, and Brazil. Again, we can find parallels with the rise of the modern collection, built on a comparative model, with art from a number of countries, which makes it different from many collections within Latin America, which are usually focused on a single nation. The nineteenth century in Latin America is further complicated by the fact that many of the artists were European or North American travelers, so the international and networked nature of the art world of the time must be a fundamental factor in its analysis. A similar phenomenon happens with the colonial collection, as scholarship increasingly understands it as the fusion of European, American, and Asian traditions. Although each collection is vastly different in appearance and character, they are united by this cosmopolitan and inclusive vision of culture.

In 2011, the CPPC hired a new curator of contemporary art, Sofia Hernández Chong Cuy, former director of the Museo Tamayo in Mexico City. While the CPPC had collected contemporary art since its origin, with Hernández Chong Cuy's appointment this area was given a new priority. The other collections all have a specific focus defined by ethnicity, historical style, or region, but the contemporary field is of overwhelming complexity, and the new curator was given the challenge of keeping the collection meaningful in an increasingly global context. Her response was to propose a research-based methodology involving extensive travel all over Latin America to visit artists' studios, making it possible to analyze local productions in situ before committing to an acquisition. This approach was a way of recognizing that behind the apparent visibility and integration of Latin America into the global system there are still many artists who work locally and do not have the same access to or even interest in international networks. In this sense, the collection could make a claim to be once again ahead of the curve, following artists who often do not yet have gallery representation or whose reputations may be limited to a local context. The inclusion of these artists in a recognized collection like the CPPC provides a unique platform for visibility for the artists and their work. In addition to the collection itself, the CPPC also organizes events and initiatives to discuss contemporary production and ideas, primarily the Seminario Fundación Cisneros, a one-day multidisciplinary art event presented in Caracas, and the Viewing Room series, in which recently acquired work is presented and contextualized, usually in a single day of viewing.[8]

In 2008, Adriana Cisneros de Griffin was appointed president of the Fundación Cisneros. Under her leadership digital technology was made a priority, as she simultaneously assessed the impact of the Internet on not only the cultural programs but also the core entertainment business of the Cisneros Group of Companies, of which she became CEO in 2013. The Fundación had made early and important forays into technology, most notably through AME, an online teacher-training program in the 1990s, and also through the development of the first CPPC website in 2001 as an ambitious portal containing information on the collection as well as on related art history. By 2008 the Internet was the primary means of accessing information, and a new generation required and demanded open access to knowledge in a radical new way. For the CPPC this presented both a challenge and an opportunity. The challenge was that the collection, like many private collections, had been somewhat shy of keeping too high a public profile and had chosen its audiences strategically, preferring to work directly with a small group of influencers such as curators and professors. The opportunity was to radically expand the "museum without walls" concept to make the artworks and their context (the tangible and intangible aspects discussed above) available to a potentially unlimited audience all over the world, and in real time. The first in-depth engagement with new technology was on the occasion of the exhibition *La invención concreta* at the Reina Sofia in 2013, for which the CPPC developed a mobile website and an app that provided enhanced ways to navigate the exhibition's concepts and artworks, and to share them on social media. That same year the Orinoco collection was given a new website for the exhibition of the collection at the Museo Gaias in Santiago de Compostela, Spain. The Seminario Fundación Cisneros in Caracas was also given a digital push, first by streaming the conferences and, as of 2012, by creating microsites for the event that allowed not only streaming and online registration but also simultaneous participation by speakers and participants from various points across the globe. The publications series was also enhanced digitally by developing sophisticated e-books of the *Conversaciones* series, incorporating videos and archival materials and helping to overcome the traditional difficulties in distributing and importing physical books within Latin America.

In 2014, all these various experiments and initiatives came together in a single platform with the launch of the new CPPC website at http://www.coleccioncisneros.org . This new website was conceived not just as a source of information about the collection and its programs, but also as a kind of magazine that would feature articles and debates about the issues facing the field of Latin American art in general. The site was created to address the lack of a credible online venue for people seeking well-written and researched information about the field, from the ethnographic to the contemporary. Since its launch the website has built and sustained an audience that is global in nature, with visitors from all over the Americas, Europe, and elsewhere, thus realizing, in many ways, the original vision of a collection that could be useful in many different contexts, one that promoted a more inclusive and critical vision of the contribution of Latin America to global culture, and all without building a museum.

CHAPTER 11

Collecting Latin American Art in the United States from New Spain to Today

A Life's Story

Estrellita B. Brodsky

59. Carlos Raúl Villanueva (Venezuelan, 1900–1975), Ciudad Universitaria, Caracas, 1953. View of the lobby of the Concert Hall, with *Positive-Negative*, 1954, by Victor Vasarely (1906–1997). Archivo Fundación Villanueva.

Defined broadly as an act of accumulation or gathering of things, sometimes as a form of obsessive compulsion, collecting is often marked by the personal circumstances and events that have impacted an individual's life over the course of time. These, along with chance meetings and fortunate, sometimes unfortunate, encounters, form the character of a collector as well as that of a historian, guiding choices, even to deciding a field of study to follow. My own choice to study and collect the art of Latin America was the result of these interactions, family dynamics, and the U.S. American environment, in which I often found myself a Latin outsider. They have contributed to my personal commitment to having the accomplishments made by artists from Latin America acknowledged in the United States and abroad.

Whether for personal or institutional purposes, appreciation of Latin American art requires going beyond superficial analogies with or validation through a European-U.S.–based art-historical canon. As a collector of objects, a student of art history, and an independent curator, I believe in a pluralist approach that allows for a multiplicity of views and perspectives while maintaining scholarly standards. And whereas the term "collecting" is defined widely, my goal is to bring together not only objects but also people and institutions to focus on art from Latin America. "Latin American art" need not be considered another essentializing term, isolating the region as an empty category for a region so diverse, but rather one that encompasses a geographical space that continues to change and defy definition.

In many ways, the history of my parents, who both came from South America, reflects that diversity and complexity. My father, Miguel Bograd, left Bessarabia at the age of twenty and settled in Caracas in the early 1920s. There he found an open environment, seemingly devoid of the prejudices he had suffered in Europe. My mother, Beatriz Shep-

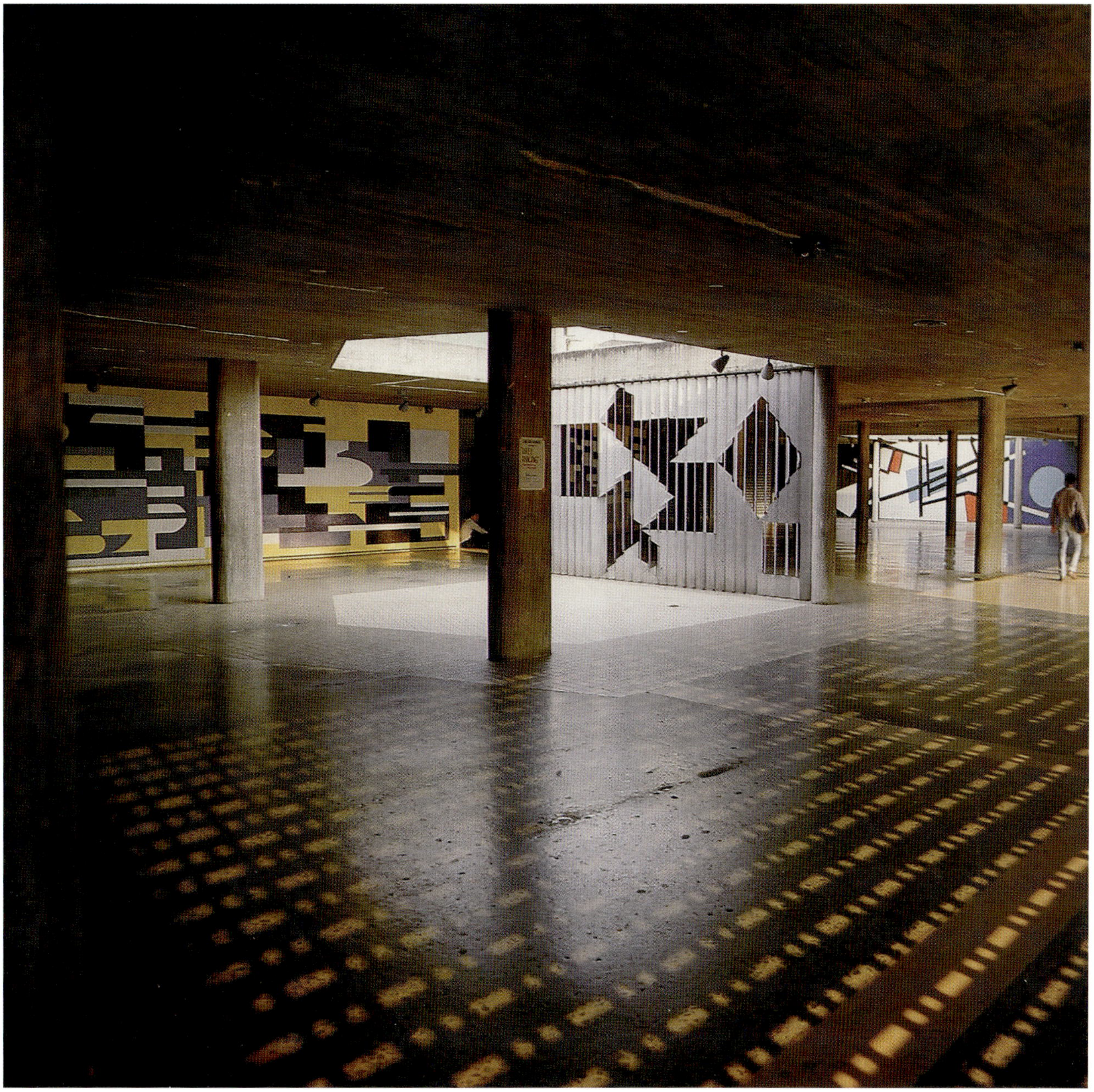

pard Idiarte Borda, was born in Uruguay, where her family had become well established soon after emigrating there from Scotland and the Basque country at the turn of the nineteenth century. By 1945, Uruguay was a politically and economically developed country. Considered the "Little Switzerland of South America," it was the site of the first World Cup in 1930 and had its own set of modest skyscrapers and a richly urbanized society. During the late forties, Venezuela, which had been a tropical, primarily agricultural, country, was just beginning to modernize at a rapid pace thanks to an economic oil boom.

Visiting in the 1950s and '60s, I was struck not only by the abundance of art found in private collections but also by that shown in public spaces, seemingly accessible to all. Venezuela during this period and well into the 1970s offered a stimulating environment where one could find modernist architecture allied to art in public spaces. You could see works by international artists such as Victor Vasarely (1906–1997) and Alexander Calder (1898–1976) at the Ciudad Universitaria (fig. 59), which was completed in 1953 by the Venezuelan architect Carlos Raúl Villanueva (1900–1975). Alongside these artists were public works by local artists such as Alejandro Otero (1921–1990), Jesús Rafael Soto (1923–2005), and Carlos Cruz-Diez (b. 1923). New museums such as the Museo de Arte Contemporáneo de Sofía Imber, established in 1973, highlighted and collected national and international contemporary art. All in all, the city possessed a unique energy that radiated a sense of hope and modernity, encouraging me to believe that everything was possible, that music and art could change the world into a better place for a broader group of society.

While my experiences of Latin America were characterized by either modernity, as in the case of Venezuela, or by Old World values, as in the case of Uruguay, my friends and fellow students in the United States were ignorant of and appeared uninterested in the region. Preferring to study United States or European history and current events, they had no idea about what was going on in Latin America in terms of culture, politics, or anything. Rather, there was a condescending attitude toward the South. The assumption was that the United States was more culturally and economically evolved than Latin America. These early experiences of prejudice against and ignorance of other nations' histories made me profoundly aware of a cultural disconnect. It also fueled my concern that Latin American history be considered from an expanded perspective while providing a local context for its development.

After receiving a master's degree in art history at Hunter College, I became involved working with the curatorial staff and then on the board of El Museo del Barrio. Its mission had recently been broadened to include the arts of all of Latin America as well as the Caribbean. I helped organize the exhibition *Taíno: Pre-Columbian Art and Culture from the Caribbean* (1997), which gave visibility to a culture ignored by most but shared by many within New York City's Caribbean community. Without pandering to the public, the museum held a high standard of educational and artistic quality through the Taíno exhibition as well as the survey show *Re-aligning Vision: Alternative Currents in South American Drawing* (1997), curated by Mari Carmen Ramírez for El Museo de Barrio and the Archer M. Huntington Art Gallery (now the Jack S. Blanton Museum) at the University of Texas at Austin. These two exhibitions at El Museo were followed in 2001 by *Thread Unraveled: Contemporary Brazilian Art*, curated by Fatima Bercht, and the groundbreaking 2004 *MoMA at El Museo*, which brought MoMA's seldom-seen Latin American collection out of storage.

A growing interest in expanding collections and institutional exhibitions of Latin American art in the United States was becoming apparent. The opening of programs focused on Latin American art history, such as at the Institute of Fine Arts (IFA) under Edward J. Sullivan's guidance, also made it possible to study the art of the region in greater depth. I completed my Ph.D. at the IFA in 2009, writing my dissertation on Latin American artists who settled in post–World War II Paris, specifically on Jesús Soto and Julio Le Parc (b. 1928).[1] Both artists investigated ideas of displacement as a vehicle for expressing, directly and indirectly, social and political tensions as well as ideals, which were translated into an aesthetic construct of movement. Latin American Kinetic artists offered individual participants a way of actively participating in the conferring of meaning on a work of art, thereby liberating the viewer and the art object from the historical constraints of cultural elitism. Their ideas echoed those of the Russian Constructivists and Bauhaus utopian theories. And while they shared many of the same principles, the concepts advanced by this and earlier generations of Latin American artists have to be understood as a history and discourse specific to the artists' own political and social context and ideals outside of the commonly accepted Euro-U.S. tenets.

Hoping to avoid the general tendency that validates Latin American artists' production by associating them with better-known European and U.S. artists, I became interested in how these artists exchanged artistic ideas within an international avant-garde while simultaneously reacting to theories shared with their national colleagues. In Paris, Soto developed many of the principles set forth by Los Disidentes, fellow Latin American artists he had known from Caracas in the 1940s. He expanded these concepts while interacting with Latin American artists in Paris similarly relocated there, often for political reasons, such as the Argentine-founded Grupo Madí, and later with European artists of the New Realists and group Zero. Likewise, the Argentine Julio Le Parc arrived with well-founded beliefs about engaging the viewer, concepts established during his student activist years in Buenos Aires, before interacting with Latin Americans and international artists in Paris.

Recognizing the local context in which artists work while simultaneously acknowledging their international significance has been my goal in exhibitions such as *(In)formed by Color: Carlos Cruz-Diez* (2008) at the Americas Society (fig. 60) and *Jesús Rafael Soto: Paris and Beyond, 1950–1970* at the Grey Art Gallery at New York University (2012; fig. 61), rejecting the characterization of these artists as derivative and working on a delayed timeline. In the exhibitions *Julio Le Parc: Uma busca contínua* (2013), shown at the Galeria Nara Roesler in Sao Paolo, Brazil, and *Julio Le Parc: Form into Action* (2016; fig. 62) at the Pérez Art Museum Miami (PAMM), my focus has been on the extraordinarily complex artistic networks the artist Julio Le Parc navigated within a European-based international avant-garde as well as within Latin America. The PAMM exhibition represents a first and long-overdue U.S. museum survey dedicated to Le Parc, a critical twentieth-century Kinetic artist working over six decades transnationally between Europe and Latin America.

Public institutions such as museums and universities can no longer exclude art from Latin America from the art-historical canon. And while my own collecting follows a very private route, one based on individual choice, often enjoying a personal friendship with artists whom I have met and respected through my research, institutional collections should take a different approach from that of a personal collection. They certainly need to tell a story from a well-informed perspective, but at the same time they should take fewer risks, being sensitive to the local social, political, and cultural context but cognizant of a broader institutional narrative.

To do so, international museums as well as specialized museums require dedicated curators with in-depth knowledge of the region. With an understanding of the diverse histories and sensitivity

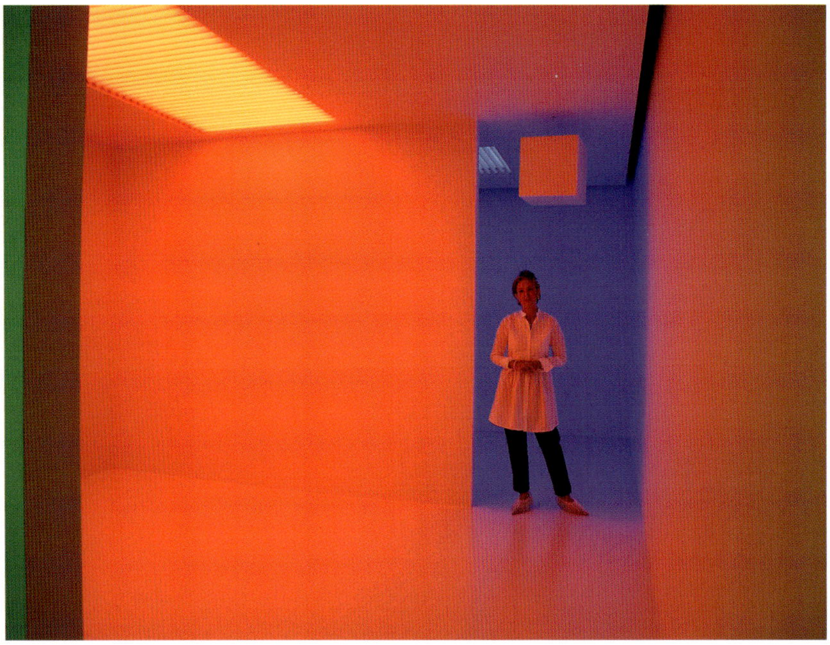

60. Installation view (with Estrellita Brodsky), *Carlos Cruz-Diez: (In)formed by Color*, Americas Society Gallery, New York, 2008. Carlos Cruz-Diez (Venezuelan, b. 1923), *Cromosaturación*, 1965. Courtesy of the author. © 2008 Artists Rights Society (ARS), New York / ADAGP, Paris.

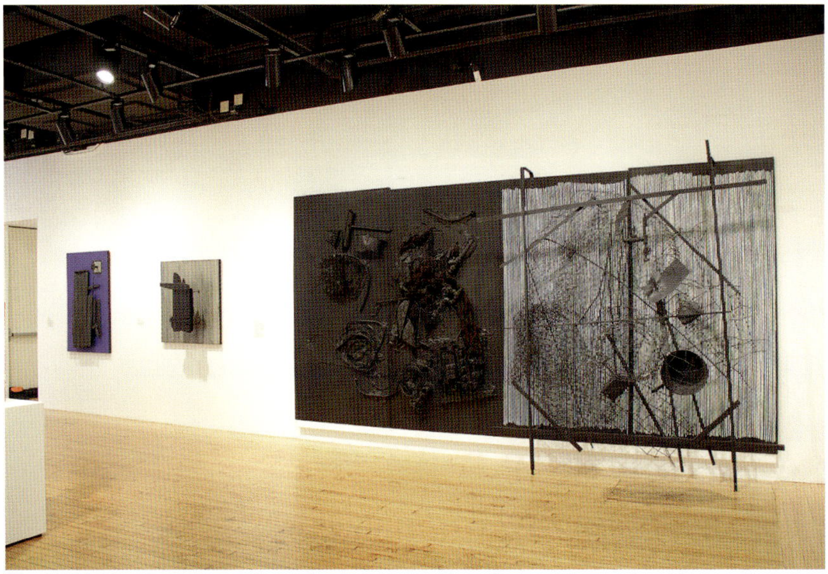

61. Installation view, *Jesús Rafael Soto: Paris and Beyond, 1950–1970*, Grey Art Gallery, New York, 2012. Jesús Rafael Soto (Venezuelan, 1923–2005), *Mural*, 1961. Courtesy of the author. © 2012 Artists Rights Society (ARS), New York / ADAGP, Paris.

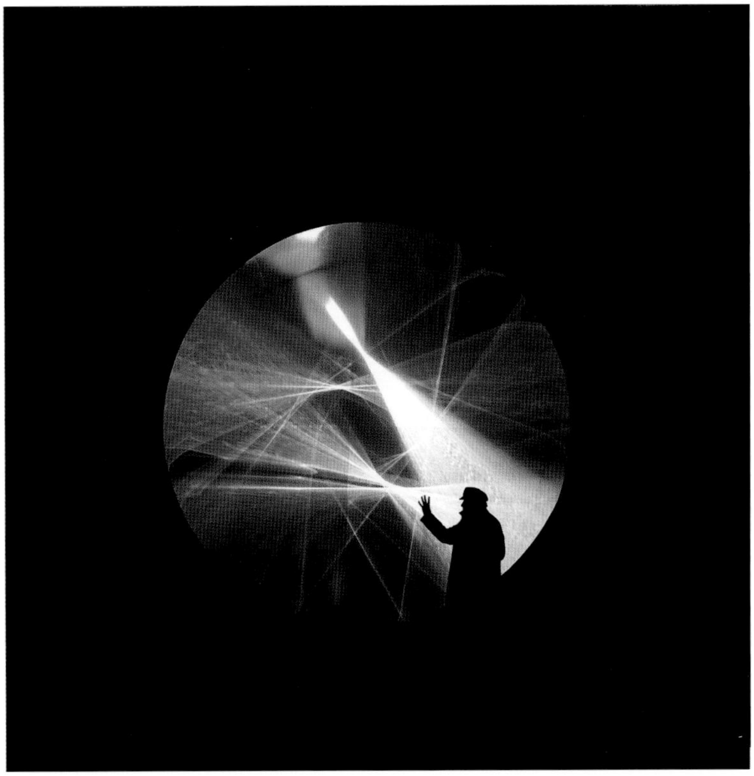

62. Installation view, *Julio Le Parc,* Palais de Tokyo, 2013. Julio Le Parc (Argentinian, b. 1928) in front of *Continuel-lumière cylindre,* 1966 / 2012. Photo © Yamil Le Parc. Courtesy of the artist.

to local contexts and narratives, they can expand the museum collections with intelligent responsibility. For these reasons, I have felt it critical to support the positions of Latin American curators at larger international museums such as the Tate, Museum of Modern Art (MoMA), and most recently The Metropolitan Museum of Art, as well as to underwrite programs of contemporary Latin American art at smaller museums such as El Museo del Barrio. Simultaneously, there is a need to broaden art-historical studies in the field of Latin American art by supporting the work of a growing number of scholars and students through academic initiatives.

Over the last few decades, curators and scholars dedicated to Latin America have already advanced the knowledge and understanding of art from Latin America through collections, exhibitions, and studies. Challenging past misconceptions that ignored individual regions and their artists and saw Latin American art as a homogenized mass, their practices have complicated readings. Furthermore, collections within and without the region are not only desirable but also at times critical to preserving the art and dialectical discourse displaced by turbulent political events that threaten the works' safety. In these situations, global is good, despite what the art historian José Falconi termed the need for a "No Me Token" policy.[2] In Falconi's opinion, acceptance of Latin American art within a broader context within international institutions' collections and exhibition practices implies a demeaning type of "badge of historical progress or validation." But the assumption that the practice of showing Latin American art in international institutions requires a flattening of the continent's uniqueness and its histories actually seems more demeaning and shortsighted. Putting the work in active dialogue and on an equal footing with other art histories should not be considered a simplistic form of ghettoizing.

In 1991, the German-born art historian and professor Benjamin Buchloh (b. 1941) had already questioned the feasibility of a Latin American art in response to the exhibition *America: Bride of the Sun; 500 Years of Latin America and the Low Countries* (1991, Royal Museum of Fine Arts Antwerp). In the exhibition catalogue, he challenged one of the exhibition's organizers, Catherine de Zegher, on what he identified as "the viability and credibility of the current interest in Latin American art, an art world tendency of which your [de Zegher's] exhibition is clearly a part, or to which it inevitably will contribute, if it has not already done so." Buchloh continues, "Is it possible to develop strategies of multi-cultural politics (art world politics, that is) which are not, from the beginning, fostering an already established liberal mode of multi-culturalism in the vein of liberal repressive tolerance? Is it possible to construct a decentered exhibition project that does more than simply expand the territory of control and Western hegemony or if nothing worse, simply alters the current line of art world investment and consumption?"[3]

Buchloh's call for "decentered exhibitions that resist the simple expansion of Western hegemony's control" underscores the dangers of applying simplistic notions of linear influence as yet another form of colonialism. A quarter century later, those concerned about Latin American art's acceptance on a global stage continue to be cautious about that process. Art from Latin America and its history should be approached within the framework in which artists themselves work: an exchange of ideas and challenges without borders.

Toward these goals, I introduced an initiative program called ANOTHER SPACE. A part of the activities of the Daniel and Estrellita Brodsky Family Foundation, ANOTHER SPACE is dedicated to broadening international awareness of art from Latin America. By facilitating substantial grants to museums, universities, and other institutions, ANOTHER SPACE seeks to advance research and produce exhibitions and publications in the field of Latin American art. ANOTHER SPACE also provides a forum for guest-curated exhibitions and educational programs at its Chelsea, New York, location.

I was particularly honored to have as ANOTHER SPACE's inaugural exhibition *Paulo Bruscky: Artist Books and Films, 1970–2013* (2015) organized by Los Angeles–based curator Clara M. Kim (fig. 63). The exhibition and programming focused on the prolific career of Paulo Bruscky (b. 1949, Recife, Brazil, where he lives and works), a critical figure in Brazilian art history, known for his involvement with the international Mail art movement, his extensive Fluxus archives, and his radical experiments with technology. The artist brought a unique perspective to the project by challenging preconceptions about the ways in which art from Latin America is perceived and received. Constantly responding to the local context of Recife, Paulo Bruscky has never lost sight of the communicative challenges of working internationally. He has broken away from stereotypes, whether as an artist both local and international, or with work that defies facile categorizations, using a broad range of techniques and materials, including film, sound, photography, performances, poetry, and public interventions. Throughout all of these activities, Bruscky has maintained a ludic approach grounded in a political and social commitment to challenging absolute authority and a belief in art's ability to overcome adversity.

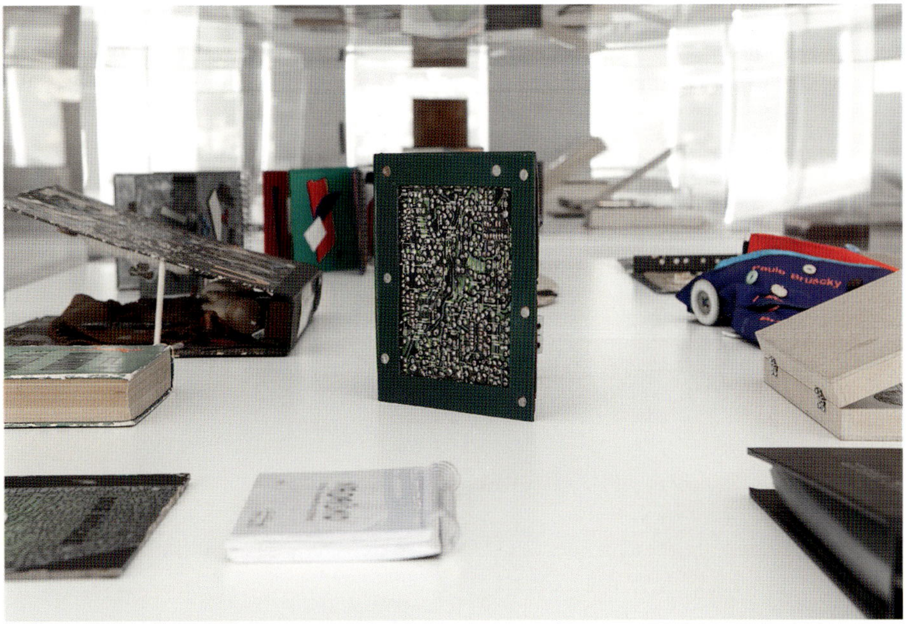

63. Jean Paul Gomez (b. 1952), installation view, *Paulo Bruscky: Artist Books and Films, 1970–2013,* ANOTHER SPACE, New York, 2015. Photo: Jean Paul Gomez. © and courtesy of Paulo Bruscky and Galeria Nara Roesler. Courtesy of the author.

Likewise, the collegial and intelligent approach of the curator Clara M. Kim served as a perfect complement to the artist by introducing a different viewpoint. She focused specific attention on the artist's books and films as a way of intelligently presenting a wide overview of Bruscky's work. By encouraging a critical and open forum in which to examine and discuss Latin American art, the exhibition and its related programming reflected many of the ideas I have supported over the past years. They acknowledged the region's international relevance while understanding the local context in which its art was produced.

Another critical element of the program is the involvement of a younger generation of scholars, Ph.D. students studying Latin American art. Referred to me by colleagues and friends, these students wrote essays for a small publication on Bruscky's work. They were enthusiastic about broadening their knowledge of the artist's work in their writing and guiding others during gallery visits. Having direct contact with artists from the region, they and their colleagues are able to contribute in more meaningful ways to the field of Latin American art.

Ultimately, through collection and curatorial practices, we can redefine broader, interconnected zones of artistic production while still recognizing the specificity of each art object. The specialized and international museums, as well as collectors, can and should provide distinct yet vital perspectives on the representation, preservation, and interpretation of the art produced by artists from Latin America, within and without their respective regions, as a site of mutual cultural respect.

Notes

Introduction

1. A model for the inquiry into imperialism and collecting is Smith and Brown 2015.
2. See, among many other studies, Carr and Bailey 2015.
3. The exhibition *American Sources of Modern Art* opened at MoMA on April 23, 1933. This was during the early phase of Barr's tenure as director of the museum. It featured over two hundred objects of Pre-Columbian art, borrowed principally from New York institutions such as the Museum of Natural History and The Metropolitan Museum of Art. Curator Holger Cahill (and Barr) used this exhibition to suggest that "primitive" art from the Americas was as significant in the eyes of modern European and American artists as was that of Africa, a connection that had long been made by scholars and critics.
4. Kaufmann 2006; see especially n. 35.
5. Pratt 2007.
6. Dürer 1971, 64.
7. An outstanding example is a greenstone mask of Mexican, possibly Aztec origin, set within an elaborate Baroque mount, now in the Museo degli Argenti, Palazzo Pitti, Florence. See Sullivan 2007, 16. This work, like many other similar examples, belonged to the Medici. See Heikamp 1982, 137–39.
8. There is an immense literature on Humboldt's journey to the Americas. For a series of concise essays on this topic, see De Havenon et al. 2014. A recent popular and well-researched biography by Andrea Wulf (2015) also discusses the impact of Humboldt's ideas and exploits on later explorers, artists, and conservationists.
9. See Brownlee, Piccoli, and Uhlyarik 2015; Manthorne 2015; and Sullivan 2014.
10. Manthorne 1989.
11. I am grateful to Mary Cruz for discussing the importance of the Shelburne's collection with me.
12. Corn 1999, 304–5.
13. Hofer and Olson 2015.
14. Oles 2002, 24.
15. See note 2.
16. Oles 1993; Oles 2002; and Oles 2005.
17. See Oles 2002.
18. The museum, across the street from The Museum of Modern Art, was founded in 1954, opened to the public in 1957, and closed in 1976. One of the principal purposes of the museum was to house the vast collections of non-Western art of the Rockefeller family. Its first director was Robert Goldwater, professor of art history at New York University's Institute of Fine Arts and author of the highly influential text *Primitivism and Modern Art* (first published in 1938), which helped shape the discourse on the role of non-Western art in the development of modernism in Europe and the United States.
19. Oettinger 1990. See also O'Neill and Cerny 1984; Espejel, O'Neill, and Roberts 1986.
20. Vidal is the author of numerous studies of Puerto Rican colonial art. Among the best known are Vidal 1994 and Vidal 2006. On the history of Puerto Rican *santos*, see Colón Camacho 2003.
21. For details on the Vidal collection at the Smithsonian Institution, see amhistory.si.edu/vidal (accessed August 3, 2016).
22. Estrellita B. Brodsky has also provided funding for a similar curatorial position in modern and contemporary Latin American art at Tate Modern, London.
23. See Elderfield 2010.
24. Harris, Chambers, and Story 1996, 103–4. See also Pierce 2011.
25. See Stratton-Pruitt 2006. This book was published on the occasion of the 2006–8 traveling exhibition, which began at the Iris and B. Gerald Cantor Center for Visual Arts at Stanford University. Between November 2014 and February 2016 the Art Institute of Chicago presented the exhibition *A Voyage to South America: Andean Art in the Spanish Empire* with paintings and works on paper from the Thoma Collection.
26. Stratton-Pruitt 2006, 10.
27. This prohibition on export pertains to works of these artists still in Mexico; it does not affect those already out of the country at the time of sale.
28. Burke 1998.
29. See Castañeda 2014.
30. This exhibition had originated at the National Gallery of Canada, Ottawa, and, after the New York venue, traveled to the Museum of Art, Rhode Island School of Design.
31. Miller et al. 2016.
32. For a historical analysis of the work of Gómez Sicre and the politics of Latin American art in the United States during the Cold War era, see Fox 2013.
33. E. Carmen Ramos, "Acknowledgments," in Ramos 2013, x.
34. Indych-López 2010.
35. Birkhofer 2014.
36. McAndrew 1965.

37. I am grateful to Delia Solomons and Susanna Temkin for discussing with me the history of the IBM collections.

Chapter 1

This essay's title refers to Kirk Varnedoe's groundbreaking article "The Evolving Torpedo: Changing Ideas of the Collection of Painting and Sculpture of The Museum of Modern Art." See Varnedoe 1995. I thank John Alan Farmer for his helpful suggestions in the writing of this essay. This essay is in memory of Alice Yang.

1.. Robert Rosenblum, foreword to the 1986 edition of *Cubism and Abstract Art*. See Barr 1986, 2–3.

2. Pérez-Barreiro 2005, 133. For the history of collecting and exhibiting Latin American art at MoMA, see Rasmussen 1993; Elderfield 2010; and Basilio 2004. For studies focusing on specific countries, see Indych-López 2009; Paquette 1997, 637–69; Paquette 2006; Greet 2009. The present essay is drawn from the manuscript of a forthcoming book about the development of MoMA's canon and changing definitions of Latin American art, in which I will examine three major collection displays during Barr's tenure and key examples in the 1960s through the 2000s: Miriam Basilio, "Museum Collection Displays and Canon-Formation: The Museum of Modern Art and the Category 'Latin American Art'" (working title; under contract with Routledge Press for publication in Research in Museum Studies series). During the writing of this essay, I received support from the research project "Modernidad(es) Descentralizada(s): Arte, política y contracultura en el eje transatlántico durante la Guerra Fría," funded by Spain's Ministerio de Economía y Competitividad (ref. HAR2014-53834-P).

3. Miller's influential role as curator of the postwar Americans series is rightly recognized. See Zelevansky 1993 and the biographical note at "Dorothy C. Miller Papers in The Museum of Modern Art Archives," The Museum of Modern Art, https://www.moma.org/learn/resources/archives/EAD/dcmillerf (accessed January 29, 2016).

4. I thank Michelle Elligott, Chief of Archives, Library, and Research Collections, MoMA, for bringing this series of exhibitions to my attention. Robert Storr noted the need to study the series and Miller's role in Storr 2000, 65–70 and 83, nn. 50–51.

5. Alfred H. Barr, Jr., "Preface," in Soby and Miller 1943, 5.

6. Kantor 2002, 321. For Barr's interest in Charles Darwin and paleontology, see Marquis 1989, 20, 22; Elderfield 2004; Lowry 2012; and Meyer 2013, 171–83.

7. Kantor 2002, 9.

8. I am indebted to Professor Óscar Cambra-Moo for his useful suggestions, which helped me understand Darwinian evolutionary charts and how Barr may have drawn on them to create analogous artistic taxonomies.

9. Alfred H. Barr, Jr., "Foreword," in Kirstein 1943, 4.

10. Ibid., 3.

11. Basilio, in Basilio et al. 2004, 84.

12. See Duberman 2008, 113–17.

13. See Fox 2013, 45, 117. See also Sadlier 2012.

14. Letter from Nelson A. Rockefeller to John E. Abbott, April 29, 1942. The Museum of Modern Art Archives, Kirstein I.F. Further references to The Museum of Modern Art Archives cited as "MoMA Archives."

15. Duberman 2008, 381. See also "Oral History Interview with Paul Cadmus, 1988 March 22–May 5," Archives of American Art, Smithsonian Institution, http://www.aaa.si.edu/collections/interviews/oral-history-interview-paul-cadmus-12619 (accessed January 29, 2016).

16. Letter from W. M. Barclay Harding, Captain, AUS, Chief, Operations and Contact Section, American Intelligence Command, to Lincoln Kirstein, November 7, 1942, Kirstein I B, MoMA Archives.

17. Memo from Alfred H. Barr, Jr. to Abbot, Dudley, Hawkins, and Wheeler, February 13, 1943, Curatorial Files 224, MoMA Archives.

18. I am grateful to Anna Indych-López for calling attention to this important distinction between the early exhibitions and how the collection was shown in 1943.

19. Adler 2014, 129.

20. Ibid., 132. As Adler notes, this was also due to Barr's wish to avoid overlaps in collecting with The Metropolitan Museum of Art and the Whitney Museum of American Art. Barr's focus on European abstract art was controversial, eliciting complaints from critics and U.S. artists working in similar styles. See ibid., 130, 134–35.

21. Miller had worked with Cahill at the Newark Museum. In 1936, they organized the exhibition *New Horizons in American Art*, which showcased FAP artists, at MoMA.

22. Miller 1943.

23. Buntinx 2005, 189.

24. See Pérez Oramas 2004a.

25. Letter from Lincoln Kirstein to Richard Abbott, September 1, 1942, Cali, Colombia, Kirstein I.F., MoMA Archives.

26. Kirstein 1943, 56.

27. Ibid., 82.

28. Ibid., 47.

29. Ibid., 29. For Kirstein's views on Berni, see Buntinx 2005, n. 24.

30. Kirstein 1943, 47.

31. Edward Alden Jewell, "Shows Modern Art of Latin America: Museum Places on View 224 New Acquisitions Selected by Lincoln Kirstein," *New York Times*, March 31, 1943, 8. On February 4, 1943, Barr sent a memo assigning Miller the task

of installing the exhibition. See Barr, "Exhibition and Catalog of Latin American Exhibition," Curatorial Files 224, MoMA Archives.

32. M. R., "The Modern Implements Good Neighbor Policy," *Art Digest* 17 (April 15, 1943): 9.
33. Irving Sandler, "Introduction," in Sandler and Newman 1986, 28–29.
34. Ibid., 29. See also Sandler 2008, 68. For the connection between some of these exhibitions and Barr's dismissal, see also Storr 2000, 67–68.
35. In 1947, he became director of museum collections.
36. Basilio 2004, 55 n. 28, citing Minutes of the Exhibitions Committee Meeting, October 7, 1943, 65.
37. Letter from Barr to Goodyear, Registrar Files, Exhibition 225, MoMA Archives.
38. Ibid.
39. "The Museum and the War," *Bulletin of the Museum of Modern Art* (October–November 1942): 10.
40. Ibid., 19.
41. Benton's work was politically controversial and associated with right-wing sentiment. See Adler 2014, 130, and Doss 1991, 170–71.
42. Barr 1949, 38.
43. Ibid., 39.
44. Ibid., 40.
45. Ibid., 38.
46. Ibid., 42.
47. "Museum of Modern Art Opens Large Exhibition of Its Own Painting and Sculpture," DCM VII.Add.B.E.1, MoMA Archives.
48. Paquette argues that MacKinley Helm similarly saw Mexican artists as relevant to figurative "international stylistic" and "national characteristics." See Paquette 1997, 654.
49. For a full listing of the twenty-seven, see the checklist Painting and Sculpture 290, MoMA Archives.
50. Varnedoe 1995, 65n52.
51. "Museum of Modern Art Opens Large Exhibition of Its Own Painting and Sculpture," DCM VII.Add.B.E.1, MoMA Archives.
52. According to Varnedoe 1995, 65 n. 52, prior to this Barr and Miller had organized a private exhibition of the collection for the trustees in response to the 1942 "Report of the Committee on Policy."
53. Holger Cahill was acting director during Barr's leave in 1932. He advised Rockefeller in these acquisitions and curated U.S. art exhibitions at MoMA in the 1930s. See Adler 2014, 128–31 and 139 n. 20. According to Adler, Barr sought out the donation. See also Marquis 1989, 104, and Oral History Interview with Holger Cahill, 1960, April 12 and 15. Archives of American Art, Smithsonian Institution, http://www.aaa.si.edu/collections/interviews/oral-history-interview-holger-cahill-11990 (accessed February 14, 2016).
54. Kirstein 1943, 40.
55. See Varnedoe 1995, 14.
56. The second category appears in the checklist. See checklist Painting and Sculpture 290, MoMA Archives.
57. Berdecio disputed Barr's categorization of his work. See Pérez Oramas 2004b, 93–94.
58. "Museum of Modern Art Opens Large Exhibition of Its Own Painting and Sculpture," DCM VII.Add.B.E.1, MoMA Archives.
59. Paquette 2002, 639, argues that in the 1940s Mexican art was still viewed as "intriguingly Mexican but also appropriately modern." Indych-López demonstrates that Rufino Tamayo's work was understood similarly. See Indych-López 2007, 345.
60. "Museum of Modern Art Opens Large Exhibition of Its Own Painting and Sculpture," DCM VII.Add.B.E.1, MoMA Archives.
61. As I will discuss in my forthcoming book, numerous figurative works by Latin American artists acquired in the 1930s and '40s were shown in MoMA's landmark twenty-fifth anniversary collection exhibition, although in markedly geographically distinct groupings. In this way, their relegation to the status of "local" was far more evident.

Chapter 2

1. The institutions, artists, curators, critics, and politics at the heart of this phenomenon are examined in my dissertation, "Installing Latin America for Cold War Culture: U.S. Exhibitions (1959–1967)" (Ph.D. diss., Institute of Fine Arts, 2015), and are the subject of a forthcoming book. This essay draws heavily from the fourth chapter of this dissertation as well as the paper I presented at the Frick Symposium in May 2014.
2. Scheduled to coincide with Chicago's Pan American Games, the exhibition showcased art from Latin America and Canada. U.S. artists were excluded because their nation played host to its neighbors in the Western Hemisphere.
3. Both the Walker Art Center and the Guggenheim Museum have recently revisited the role Latin American art has played in the institutions' ability to claim a global perspective on modern art. The Walker's *International Pop* (2015) referenced its prior show *New Art of Argentina* (1964), and the Guggenheim's *Under the Same Sun: Art from Latin America Today* (2014) was the museum's first major survey show of Latin American art in fifty years.
4. Miriam Basilio's forthcoming book and her essays in this publication as well as in *Latin American and Caribbean Art: MoMA at El Museo* (Basilio et al. 2004) are important exceptions that address this gap in our understanding of

MoMA's history. She elucidates several key components of the museum's activity in the sixties, including the work of Alfred Barr and Elaine Johnson as well as the role exhibitions play in constructing canons. See Miriam Basilio, "Museum Collection Displays and Canon-Formation: The Museum of Modern Art and the Category 'Latin American Art'" (working title; under contract with Routledge Press for publication in Research in Museum Studies series); and Basilio 2004.

5. Major exhibitions included *Diego Rivera* (1931), *Twenty Centuries of Mexican Art* (1940), *Portinari of Brazil* (1940), *Mexican Costumes by Carlos Mérida* (1942), *Brazil Builds* (1943), *The Latin-American Collection of the Museum of Modern Art* (1943), and *Modern Cuban Painters* (1944).
6. James Cutting discusses the role repeated exposure plays in creating and reinforcing Impressionist canons in Cutting 2007.
7. Press Release: Painting and Sculpture from the Museum Collection, May 25, 1964, Museum of Modern Art Archives (hereafter cited as MoMA Archives), Series: Press Releases.
8. MoMA exhibited recent acquisitions by Marisol in *Americans 1963*, *Family Portraits* (1964), *Modern Sculpture: USA* (1965), *The 1960s: Painting and Sculpture from the Museum Collections* (1967), *Frank O'Hara / In Memory of My Feelings* (1967–68), *Recent Acquisitions: Painting and Sculpture* (1968), *The Sidney and Harriet Janis Collection* (1968), and *Word and Image* (1968). I will explore the intricate relationship between Marisol's sculptural development and MoMA's exhibition history in a forthcoming article.
9. Examination of MoMA's mid-1960s exploration of Kineticism, optics, and geometry in Latin American art is timely since, at the time I wrote this essay, El Museo del Barrio was in the midst of planning *The Illusive Eye* (2015), an exhibition that revisited *The Responsive Eye*.
10. On the reception of *The Responsive Eye*, see, for example, Lee 2001; Follin 2004, 171–94; and Villanueva 2009.
11. MoMA's new Le Parc acquisitions appeared in *Recent Acquisitions: Painting and Sculpture* (1965), *The Responsive Eye* (1965), *Recent Acquisitions* (1966), *Latin-American Art, 1931–1966* (1967), and *1960s: Painting and Sculpture from the Museum Collection* (1967).
12. See Brodsky 2009, 195–99.
13. Curator Elaine Johnson invested major research into Latin American printmaking in the 1960s, but printmaking was excluded from the 1967 collection show.
14. Diego Rivera Wall Label, 1967, MoMA Archives (Series: Exhibition Files. Folder: 823 *Latin-American Art, 1931–1966*).
15. Press Release: Museum of Modern Art Shows, *Latin-American Art, 1931–1966*, April 13, 1967, MoMA Archives, Series: Exhibition Files. Folder: 823 *Latin-American Art, 1931–1966*.
16. See Kirstein 1943; and Installation Views of *XXVth Anniversary Exhibitions: Paintings and Sculpture* (IN567.73, 75, 80, 92, 93, 94, and 96), October 19, 1954, through January 23, 1955, MoMA Photographic Archive. Basilio discusses the relationship between the 1943 and 1954 installations in her essay in this publication. Waldo Rasmussen recalled that while the museum maintained a separate room for Latin American art throughout the 1950s, by 1964 it had abandoned this practice. Rasmussen 1993, 13.
17. Galleries 19 and 20 were even installed separately. The prewar gallery was on view from March 17 to April 30, the contemporary room from March 28 to June 4. Checklist, MoMA Archives, Series: Exhibition Files, Folder: 823 *Latin-American Art, 1931–1966*. However, press coverage and MoMA's press releases announced the exhibition run as April 13–April 30, 1967. This opening date marked the start of New York's Pan-American Week, and the closing date indicated the deinstallation of the 1930s–40s room, even though the contemporary gallery would remain on view for an additional month. Press Release: Museum of Modern Art Shows, *Latin-American Art, 1931–1966*, April 13, 1967, MoMA Archives, Series: Exhibition Files, Folder: 823 *Latin-American Art, 1931–1966*.
18. Interestingly, MoMA's two exhibitions of its Latin American collection, held in 1943 and 1967, coincided with the two times Barr left the museum, first when the board asked him to resign as director and then at the time of his final retirement.
19. Alfred H. Barr, Jr., "Letter to the Editor," *Art in America* 47, no. 4 (1959): 10–11.
20. Ibid., 10.
21. Ibid. Here Barr refers to *The United States Collects Pan American Art* (Art Institute of Chicago, 1959), *Latin America: Then and Now* (Denver Art Museum, 1959), and *South American Art Today* (Dallas Museum of Fine Arts, 1959–61).
22. Barr 1949, 42.
23. José Gómez Sicre, "Introduction," in Gómez Sicre 1959, n.p.
24. Barr 1949, 38.
25. Ibid., 10.
26. Preliminary Proposal for a Five Year Program of Cultural Exchange Between the United States and Latin America, June 1, 1962, MoMA Archives, Series: René d'Harnoncourt Papers, Folder: VI.96 Latin American Program 1962–64.
27. Ibid. The committee envisioned *Recent Latin American Painting* as a group exhibition that gave each painter significant gallery space, set up like "a series of small one-man shows featuring 12–16 leading artists." This format had proven successful in MoMA's *Americans* series covering contemporary U.S. art. Since its founding in 1929, the semiannual exhibitions had adhered to the established pattern of "a small number of artists, a sizeable body of work by each." Press Release for *Americans 1963*, May 22, 1963, MoMA Archives, Series: Press Releases.

28. Barbara Duncan in Memorandum on Latin American Trip July–August 1964, MoMA Archives, Series: René d'Harnoncourt Papers, Folder: VI.96 Latin American Program 1962–64.
29. Letter from Rasmussen to René and Eliza d'Harnoncourt, March 12, 1964, MoMA Archives, Series: René d'Harnoncourt Papers, Folder: VI.96 Latin American Program 1962–64.
30. Ibid.
31. Waldo Rasmussen was finally able to organize a major survey exhibition of Latin American art at MoMA in 1993: *Latin American Artists of the Twentieth Century.*

Chapter 3

1. I wish to thank Mark A. Castro for his help with this essay.
2. Barratt and Miles 2004, 125–27.
3. Stroud 2005.
4. Anna 1990.
5. Lamborn 1891, 5.
6. Ibid., 6.
7. Barber 1908.
8. Sullivan 2008. A generous correspondence between Clifford and Amor is part of the Philadelphia Museum of Art Archives.
9. Cardoza y Aragón 1943.
10. Pellicer 1944.
11. It seems worth reiterating that Rivera's two portable murals came to the Museum via the Weyhe Gallery, and that indeed Rivera had a long-standing relationship with Weyhe since they published a set of his lithographs in 1932.
12. Ittmann et al. 2006.
13. Kubler 1954.
14. Rishel 2006.
15. Stratton-Pruitt 2013.
16. Noreika 2014, 253.
17. Ibid., 257.
18. Ibid., 410.
19. Ibid., 376.

Chapter 4

1. Indych-López 2009.
2. Rivera painted it in response to Bender's contributing $500 to SFMOMA for the purchase of a work by the artist. Hurlburt 1986, 91.
3. Lee 1999, 50–51.
4. See Oles 2011, 13–14.
5. See Govan and Magaloni 2016, 220–21.
6. On photo postcards and *tipos*, see Lynda Klich, "Circulating Indigenism in Mauricio Yáñez's Postcards from Mexico," in *Fashioning Identities: Types, Customs, and Dress in a Global Context*, international conference at Hunter College, City University of New York, October 18, 2013.
7. Indeed, *The Flower Carrier* is an invented hybrid by Rivera. While the photo postcards demonstrate that the urban *cargadores* were almost exclusively men, very few images exist of men carrying flowers.
8. Oles 2011, 14.
9. See Indych-López 2009.
10. Krutnik 2007. In their 2011 exhibition *Mex/LA: Mexican Modernisms in Los Angeles*, Jesse Lerner and Rubén Ortiz-Torres created a montage of clips from the various film noirs analyzed by Krutnik in which *The Flower Carrier* appears—*Where There's Life* (1947), *Bury Me Dead* (1947), *The Woman on Pier 13* (aka *I Married a Communist* and *Beautiful but Dangerous*, 1949), *In a Lonely Place* (1950), *The Prowler* (1951). Ortiz-Torres and Lerner 2011, 135.
11. Krutnik 2007, 52. Krutnik consulted the scripts for many of these films, at least those that survive in archives. And while they provide some information about set decoration, they do not mention *The Flower Carrier* by name. Krutnik indicates that on any given film a host of scriptwriters, visual consultants, art directors, prop directors, and set decorators could have been responsible for the choice. Given the climate and that many of the Hollywood Ten worked on these films without screen credit, it is possible that they or someone else entirely may have recommended Rivera's painting. Ibid., 64.
12. Ibid., 78.
13. Oles 2005, 10.
14. See Manrique and Del Conde 1987.
15. Carlos Mérida established the Galería de Arte Moderno in 1929 in Mexico City's Palacio de Bellas Artes (then the Teatro Nacional), which he codirected with artist Carlos Orozco Romero until its closing in 1931. The government provided the funds, but the space was artist-run. See Gilbert 2009, 40.
16. "Las obras de Orozco estan practicamente fuera de mercado, pues muy rara vez llega a mi conocimiento la oferta de alguna obra importante. Ademas, los precios que han alcanzado . . . son muy elevados para poder adquirirlas." Garduño 2009, 124. I would like to acknowledge Dafne Cruz Porchini for making me aware of the publication of this thesis as well as her assistance with other sources and ideas for this essay.
17. For more on Zeitlin, see Dailey, Shivers, and Dawson 2003, 44–55; and Schrank 2009, 43, 46.
18. See Indych-López 2011.
19. Goldman 1994; Paquette 2002.
20. I argue this in relation to the marked contrast in reception to and the display mechanisms of the *Mexican Arts* exhibition that traveled around the United States in 1930 versus *Twenty Centuries of Mexican Art* in 1940. The film noir examples also reveal the ability of Mexican art to resist cooptation at critical junctures.
21. MoMA press release, February 18–19, 1933, for *Color*

Reproductions of Mexican Frescoes by Diego Rivera, MoMA Exh. #24a, February 20–March 12, 1933, http://www.moma.org/momaorg/shared/pdfs/docs/press_archives/113/releases/MOMA_1933_0013_1933-02-18.pdf?2010. The exhibition coincided with Rivera's return to New York City to start his mural for the RCA building in Rockefeller Center and marks the publication of a color portfolio that contains images selected from his Mexican murals. For more on the portfolio, see Indych-López 2009, 153–56.

Chapter 5

1. Emily Johnston de Forest to the Trustees of The Metropolitan Museum of Art, March 29, 1911, de Forest, Mrs. Robert W. (Emily Johnston)—Folk Pottery, 1905–1907, Office of the Secretary Records, The Metropolitan Museum of Art Archives. I would like to thank Barbara File and James Moske for their assistance in the Museum archives.
2. Baxter 1901. Baxter's study comprises ten volumes, nine of which are boxed portfolios containing 150 photographs by Henry Greenwood Peabody. Bertram Grosvenor Goodhue drew the architectural plans that illustrate Baxter's text. The study is dedicated to the memory of Frederic Edwin Church and Charles Dudley Warner, both of whom died in 1900. See Bargellini 2001; Bargellini 1995.
3. Baxter 1901, vol. 1, xi.
4. Robert and Emily de Forest married in 1872, two years after The Metropolitan Museum of Art was founded. Robert de Forest became a trustee in 1889, secretary in 1905, vice president in 1909, and president in 1913. The Museum's American Wing, financed by the de Forests, opened in 1924. See Hijiya 1980; Peck 2000; Frelinghuysen 2000.
5. De Forest 1908.
6. Baxter 1901, vol. 1, 14.
7. Established in 1885, the Sonora News Company operated sales concessions for the Southern Pacific railway. See Oles 1993, 123–27; Ruiz 2014, 10.
8. Carr 1994a, vol. 1, 419–24, 427–30, 437–60, 466–74, 476–92, nos. 609–18, 622–30, 632–56, 658–60, 662–76, 679–80, 683–84, 686–700; Carr 1994b.
9. Bargellini 1991; Davis 1997.
10. Edward Garczynski, "A Forgotten Artist," *Two Republics*, March 16, 1895, 1; reprinted in Bargellini 1991, 136–38. The painting is preserved at Olana State Historic Site.
11. Frederic E. Church to Luigi Palma di Cesnola, July 10, 1893, September 5, 1893; Church, Frederic E., Office of the Secretary Records, The Metropolitan Museum of Art Archives; quoted by Manthorne 1989, 105, 211; Carr 1994a, vol. 1, 474–75, no. 681.
12. Barber 1918, vii.
13. Barber 1906a, 14–16; Barber 1906b; Barber 1908, 3.
14. Alfred M. Tozzer, "Zelia Nuttall, Obituary," *American Anthropologist* 35 (1933): 475–82; Chiñas 1989; Delpar 1992, 5–6, 95–98, 110–11.
15. Pepper is otherwise known for having been the architect of the Edificio Woodrow (1922) in Mexico City.
16. Emily Johnston de Forest, preface to Barber 1918, vii.
17. Lawrence 1926, 28.
18. Sir Caspar Purdon Clarke was recruited by J. P. Morgan to be the second director of The Metropolitan Museum of Art (1905–11), having previously served as director of the South Kensington Museum (1896–1905).
19. Caspar Purdon Clarke to George Story, March 29, 1905; Purchases—Authorized—Woodwork—Altars (Mexican) from Mrs. Nuttall, 1905–7, Office of the Secretary Records, The Metropolitan Museum of Art Archives.
20. Baxter 1901, vol. 1, 39.
21. Robert de Forest to Zelia Nuttall, April 21, 1905; Purchases—Authorized—Woodwork—Altars (Mexican) from Mrs. Nuttall, 1905–7, Office of the Secretary Records, The Metropolitan Museum of Art Archives.
22. Z. Nuttall to R. de Forest, April 29, 1905; Purchases—Authorized—Woodwork—Altars (Mexican) from Mrs. Nuttall, 1905–7, Office of the Secretary Records, The Metropolitan Museum of Art Archives.
23. R. de Forest to Z. Nuttall, May 11, 1905; Purchases—Authorized—Woodwork—Altars (Mexican) from Mrs. Nuttall, 1905–7, Office of the Secretary Records, The Metropolitan Museum of Art Archives.
24. Thomas A. Janvier was the author of the well-known handbook *The Mexican Guide* (New York: Charles Scribner's Sons, 1886), as well as several fictional works about Mexico.
25. Z. Nuttall to R. de Forest, June 9, 1905; Purchases—Authorized—Woodwork—Altars (Mexican) from Mrs. Nuttall, 1905–7, Office of the Secretary Records, The Metropolitan Museum of Art Archives.
26. R. de Forest to Z. Nuttall, June 17, 1905; Purchases—Authorized—Woodwork—Altars (Mexican) from Mrs. Nuttall, 1905–7, Office of the Secretary Records, The Metropolitan Museum of Art Archives.
27. Z. Nuttall to R. de Forest, June 30, 1905; Purchases—Authorized—Woodwork—Altars (Mexican) from Mrs. Nuttall, 1905–7, Office of the Secretary Records, The Metropolitan Museum of Art Archives.
28. Z. Nuttall to R. de Forest, September 13, 1905; Purchases—Authorized—Woodwork—Altars (Mexican) from Mrs. Nuttall, 1905–7, Office of the Secretary Records, The Metropolitan Museum of Art Archives.
29. R. de Forest to Z. Nuttall, September 25, 1905; Purchases—Authorized—Woodwork—Altars (Mexican) from Mrs. Nuttall, 1905–7, Office of the Secretary Records, The Metropolitan Museum of Art Archives.

30. Sylvester Baxter, "A Great Mexican Architect—III," *American Architect and Building News* 55 (March 6, 1897): 75; cited by Carr 1994a, vol. 1, 263. The demolition of the church had been proposed in order to provide for the expansion of a hospital.
31. Vicente Rueda to Z. Nuttall, November 10, 1906; Z. Nuttall to R. de Forest, November 11, 1906; Purchases—Authorized—Woodwork—Altars (Mexican) from Mrs. Nuttall, 1905–7, Office of the Secretary Records, The Metropolitan Museum of Art Archives.
32. Z. Nuttall to R. de Forest, November 15, 1906; Purchases—Authorized—Woodwork—Altars (Mexican) from Mrs. Nuttall, 1905–7, Office of the Secretary Records, The Metropolitan Museum of Art Archives.
33. One of the altarpieces was photographed by Guillermo Kahlo between 1904 and 1908 as part of the commission he received from José Yves Limantour, secretary of public instruction, to create an inventory of churches that were government property. Reg. G. Kahlo no. 573, reproduced in Kahlo 1998, 148.
34. R. de Forest to Z. Nuttall, November 24, 1906; Purchases—Authorized—Woodwork—Altars (Mexican) from Mrs. Nuttall, 1905–7, Office of the Secretary Records, The Metropolitan Museum of Art Archives.
35. R. de Forest to Z. Nuttall, November 23, 1906; November 30, 1906; Purchases—Authorized—Woodwork—Altars (Mexican) from Mrs. Nuttall, 1905–7, Office of the Secretary Records, The Metropolitan Museum of Art Archives. The purchase was authorized by the Committee on Purchases on December 13, 1906.
36. Z. Nuttall to R. de Forest, November 25, 1906; Purchases—Authorized—Woodwork—Altars (Mexican) from Mrs. Nuttall, 1905–7, Office of the Secretary Records, The Metropolitan Museum of Art Archives. Nuttall was on even worse terms with Leopoldo Batres, inspector of monuments, especially after 1909, when he claimed credit for her discoveries on the Isla de Sacrificios. Nuttall 1910.
37. R. de Forest to Z. Nuttall, December 7, 1906; Purchases—Authorized—Woodwork—Altars (Mexican) from Mrs. Nuttall, 1905–7, Office of the Secretary Records, The Metropolitan Museum of Art Archives.
38. Z. Nuttall to R. de Forest, January 15, 1907; Purchases—Authorized—Woodwork—Altars (Mexican) from Mrs. Nuttall, 1905–7, Office of the Secretary Records, The Metropolitan Museum of Art Archives.
39. Z. Nuttall to R. de Forest, January 20, 1907; Purchases—Authorized—Woodwork—Altars (Mexican) from Mrs. Nuttall, 1905–7, Office of the Secretary Records, The Metropolitan Museum of Art Archives.
40. José Yves Limantour to Z. Nuttall, June 8, 1907; Z. Nuttall to R. de Forest, June 10, 1907; Purchases—Authorized—Woodwork—Altars (Mexican) from Mrs. Nuttall, 1905–7, Office of the Secretary Records, The Metropolitan Museum of Art Archives.
41. Rau 1879.
42. R. de Forest to Z. Nuttall, August 8, 1907; Purchases—Authorized—Woodwork—Altars (Mexican) from Mrs. Nuttall, 1905–1907, Office of the Secretary Records, The Metropolitan Museum of Art Archives.
43. R. de Forest to Elihu Root, August 8, 1907; Purchases—Authorized—Woodwork—Altars (Mexican) from Mrs. Nuttall, 1905–7, Office of the Secretary Records, The Metropolitan Museum of Art Archives.
44. Morales and Caballero 1908, 104, 126.
45. *Annual Report of the Board of Regents of the Smithsonian Institution* (1909): 28.
46. R. de Forest to Z. Nuttall, November 30, 1906; Purchases—Authorized—Woodwork—Altars (Mexican) from Mrs. Nuttall, 1905–7, Office of the Secretary Records, The Metropolitan Museum of Art Archives.
47. "The only treasures the poor little nuns had, after all, are two so-called 'escudos' or 'shields' such as the formers wore. These are painted in oils, in miniature, and are framed in tortoise shell, being in perfect condition. . . . Those I saw are to be had for $35 gold and $60 respectively—the last is exquisite—the finest I ever saw and was painted by José Paez." Z. Nuttall to R. de Forest, January 15, 1907; Purchases—Authorized—Woodwork—Altars (Mexican) from Mrs. Nuttall, 1905–7, Office of the Secretary Records, The Metropolitan Museum of Art Archives. The two *escudos* are now in the collection of the Hispanic Society of America.
48. R. de Forest to the Committee on Purchases, April 3, 1908; Purchases—Authorized—Woodwork—Altars (Mexican) from Mrs. Nuttall, 1905–7, Office of the Secretary Records, The Metropolitan Museum of Art Archives.
49. R. de Forest to Henry W. Kent, April 3, 1908; Purchases—Authorized—Woodwork—Altars (Mexican) from Mrs. Nuttall, 1905–7, Office of the Secretary Records, The Metropolitan Museum of Art Archives.
50. Indych-López 2009, 100. See R. de Forest to Homer Saint-Gaudens, November 22, 1929; Loan exhibition—1930—Mexican Art, 1929–30; Office of the Secretary Records, The Metropolitan Museum of Art Archives.
51. Her gifts included a mid-nineteeth-century Saltillo sarape (10.107.9). See Crocker 2008, 232; Goddard 1910.
52. Frederick Rathbone to the Metropolitan Museum, July 28, 1911, de Forest, Mrs. Robert W. (Emily Johnston)—Folk Pottery, 1905–7, Office of the Secretary Records, The Metropolitan Museum of Art Archives.
53. Barber 1911.

54. Trustees of The Metropolitan Museum of Art to Mrs. Robert W. de Forest, acceptance of gift (eighty-five ceramic pieces), May 22, 1911; *Report of Committee on Decorative Arts on Mrs. R. W. de Forest's Gift of Mexican Maiolica*, n.d.; de Forest, Mrs. Robert W. (Emily Johnston)—Folk Pottery, 1905–7, Office of the Secretary Records, The Metropolitan Museum of Art Archives.
55. E. de Forest to the Trustees of The Metropolitan Museum of Art, January 13, 1912; Trustees of the Metropolitan Museum of Art to Mrs. Robert W. de Forest, January 16, 1912, acceptance of gifts; de Forest, Mrs. Robert W. (Emily Johnston)—Folk Pottery, 1905–7, Office of the Secretary Records, The Metropolitan Museum of Art Archives.
56. Trustees of the Metropolitan Museum of Art to Mrs. Robert W. de Forest, acceptance of gift (lavatory), May 21, 1917; acceptance of gifts (33 ceramic pieces, 135 blue and white tiles, and 48 polychrome tiles), June 21, 1917; acceptance of gift (one plate), February 18, 1918; de Forest, Mrs. Robert W. (Emily Johnston)—Folk Pottery, 1905–7, Office of the Secretary Records, The Metropolitan Museum of Art Archives. The only works that are not listed in Barber's 1911 catalogue are the tiles, mounted as panels (accession nos. 17.105.1 and 17.105.2).
57. Emily de Forest to Henry W. Kent, April 25, 1917; de Forest, Mrs. Robert W. (Emily Johnston)—Folk Pottery, 1905–7, Office of the Secretary Records, The Metropolitan Museum of Art Archives.
58. Joseph Breck to E. de Forest, December 28, 1927; de Forest, Mrs. Robert W. (Emily Johnston)—Folk Pottery, 1905–7, Office of the Secretary Records, The Metropolitan Museum of Art Archives.
59. R. de Forest to J. Breck, December 30, 1927, de Forest, Mrs. Robert W. (Emily Johnston)—Folk Pottery, 1905–7, Office of the Secretary Records, The Metropolitan Museum of Art Archives.
60. For an insightful analysis of *Mexican Arts*, see Indych-López 2009, 75–128; also see Delpar 1992, 143–46.
61. Homer Saint-Gaudens to R. de Forest, November 14, 1929; Loan exhibition—1930—Mexican Art, 1929–30; Office of the Secretary Records, The Metropolitan Museum of Art Archives.
62. R. de Forest to H. Saint-Gaudens, November 22, 1929; Loan exhibition—1930—Mexican Art, 1929–30; Office of the Secretary Records, The Metropolitan Museum of Art Archives. In the end, De Forest's personal property in Mexico was not exported with works lent to the exhibition.
63. E. Robinson to R. de Forest, September 11, 1930; Loan exhibition—1930—Mexican Art, 1929–30; Office of the Secretary Records, The Metropolitan Museum of Art Archives.
64. R. de Forest to H. Saint-Gaudens and Frederick P. Keppel, September 18, 1930; Loan exhibition—1930—Mexican Art, 1929–30; Office of the Secretary Records, The Metropolitan Museum of Art Archives.
65. R. de Forest to D. Morrow, August 28, 1929, quoted by Indych-López 2009, 101.
66. Emily Johnston de Forest, preface, Barber 1918, vii; d'Harnoncourt, introduction, American Federation of Arts 1930, xi, xiii.

Chapter 6

1. Morley recalls her childhood, education, and career in Morley and Riess 1960, 1–15.
2. Ibid., 122.
3. Ibid., 34.
4. See, for example, Ackley 2015, 225–57.
5. According to Morley, when the San Francisco Museum was founded at the Palace of Fine Arts, its "allegiance to the art association meant that it was at least to some extent committed to contemporary art." See Morley and Riess 1960, 35.
6. Ibid., 39.
7. Ibid.
8. "Art: Twenty Years of Grace," *Time*, February 28, 1955.
9. Morley and Riess 1960, 107.
10. For a detailed study of Bender's and Gerstle's relationships with Diego Rivera as well as the politics involved in inviting Rivera to San Francisco, see Lee 1999, specifically 47–56.
11. Morley and Riess 1960, 114. Additionally, in a paper read at a luncheon for the American Federation of the Arts, Morley remarked, "The fame of the most successful painters sends an echo beyond the Rocky Mountains but the works of your most gifted are too rarely seen on the Western Coast, exactly as the works of our best artists are sent too seldom to eastern galleries. . . . Fresco painting and sculpture are leading arts in California at present. . . . Fresco painting has enjoyed a veritable renaissance in the West, due to several causes." "Art Resources in California," May 15, 1936, San Francisco Museum of Modern Art Archives and Library, ARCH:ADMIN:001:1:2.
12. For additional information about Rivera's relationships with Bay Area artists, refer to Lee 1999.
13. Cravath collaborated on the PWAP-funded Mother's House murals in the San Francisco Zoo with Helen Forbes, which were completed in 1938. See Lemon 2010.
14. Oral history interview with Dorothy Cravath, 1964, May 13–27, Archives of American Art, Smithsonian Institution.
15. "South American Collections," San Francisco Museum of Modern Art Archives and Library, Unprocessed: C:2.
16. As Morley recounted to Riess, "There is a Latin American

collection of painting and prints which is built partly around the gifts and bequests of Albert Bender and William Gerstle, strong in Mexican material, partly built as the result of an intense cultivation of Latin American interest during the early years of the war and my own knowledge of Latin American countries." Morley and Riess 1960, 42.

17. Albert Bender to Frida Kahlo, September 20, 1935, National Museum of Women in the Arts Archive and Library, Frida Kahlo Papers, Series I:1:1.
18. O'Toole 2009, 83.
19. Barbara Rominski, former head of the research archives and library at SFMOMA, kindly provided me with lists of works donated to SFMOMA by Albert Bender and William Gerstle.
20. Morley 1940, 11–12, discusses the significance of Gerstle's gift.
21. Records for *Exhibition of Plates of Rivera Frescoes* do not exist in SFMOMA's archives. However, the exhibition was most likely borrowed from MoMA. MoMA arranged a traveling exhibition titled *Color Reproductions of Mexican Frescoes by Diego Rivera* (Exh. #24a, February 20–March 12, 1933).
22. For an account of the history of Delphic Studios, see Reed's memoir, Reed 2007.
23. "Exhibition of Paintings: Peruvian Subjects by Julia Codesido," February 10 to February 23, 1936, Delphic Studios, New York. Museum of Modern Art Archives, New York, Artist File: Julia Codesido.
24. Ibid.
25. Grace McCann Morley, "Julia Codesido Exhibition, March 1936," San Francisco Museum of Modern Art Archives and Library, ARCH:EXH:001.3:26.
26. Ibid.
27. For an indispensable study of modern Andean art and its relationship to inter-American diplomacy during the Second World War, refer to Greet 2009.
28. Due to Morley's efforts, Codesido's work was exhibited at the Santa Barbara Art Museum. Morley wrote to Julia Codesido, "Your paintings are at present on an exhibition circuit and have just been shown at Santa Barbara. They are to go to several other cities in the United States, unless you wish us to withdraw them and send them to you as soon as possible." January 6, 1937, San Francisco Museum of Modern Art Archives and Library, ARCH:EXH:001:3:26. Morley also planned to send the exhibitions to the Portland Art Gallery and Seattle Art Museum, but Codesido asked Morley to return her work to Peru. Morley to Alma Reed, April 24, 1936, San Francisco Museum of Modern Art Archives and Library, ARCH:EXH:001.3:26.
29. Jessica Lemieux, Finding Aid to the San Francisco Museum of Modern Art Exhibition records, 1934–ongoing, San Francisco Museum of Modern Art Archives and Library.
30. In addition to organizing an exhibition of Acuña's work, Morley also wrote an article about the artist for *Inter-American Monthly*. See Morley 1942.
31. "[Acuña] left some drawings here and ask [*sic*] us to present them as gifts to a few places in which he was specially interested. Seattle was one, and I know you are interested in contemporary work including Latin America. Acuña's work is good; we own both a drawing and a painting." Morley to Richard Fuller, director of the Seattle Art Museum, October 10, 1944, San Francisco Museum of Modern Art Archives and Library, ARCH:EXH:001:24:2.
32. Morley also traveled to Guatemala, Honduras, Nicaragua, and Panama, but ultimately did not exhibit paintings from these counties.
33. Ultimately, Codesido and Morley developed a close friendship. In a letter to Stanton Catlin, Morley referred to Codesido as "a good friend of mine" and confessed, "I am devoted to her." Morley to Stanton Catlin, August 22, 1941, San Francisco Museum of Modern Art Archives and Library, ARCH:ADM:001:38:11.
34. Morley to Codesido, October 18, 1940, San Francisco Museum of Modern Art Archives and Library, ARCH:ADM:001:32:10.
35. Morley to Agnes Rindge Claflin, August 20, 1941, San Francisco Museum of Modern Art Archives and Library, ARCH:ADM:001.38:11.
36. Morley to Codesido, October 18, 1940, San Francisco Museum of Modern Art Archives and Library, ARCH:ADM.001:32:10
37. Morley lists some of the paintings included in *Three South American Neighbors* while writing to James B. McNaught of Stanford University School of Medicine in order to request the loan of a painting from his collection, Roberto Berdecio's *Chaco Girl*. January 16, 1941, *San Francisco Museum of Modern Art Archives and Library*, ARCH:EXH:001:B:8.
38. Golden Gate International Exposition 1940, 116.
39. Morley continues, "Big group exhibitions are interesting, of course, but I feel are a little too much like presenting art in a vacuum." Morley to Charles Thomson, August 19, 1940, San Francisco Museum of Modern Art Archives and Library, ARCH:ADM:001:31:7.
40. Morley received a Western Union telegram from John Abbott on behalf of Nelson Rockefeller which read, "CAN YOU SERVE AS A MEMBER OF THE COMMITTEE ON ART FOR LATIN AMERICAN [*sic*] AND MAKE A SPECIAL SURVEY OF THE MOST IMPORTANT CENTERS WHICH WOULD GIVE THE COMMITTEE NECESSARY DATA IN SHAPING POLICIES." Abbott to Morley, December 16, 1940, San Francisco Museum of Modern Art Archives and Library, ARCH:ADM:001:34:1.
41. For more information about *La Pintura Contempóranea*

Norteamericana and related projects organized by CIAA, see Sadlier 2012. For information about subsequent Cold War–era Inter-American programs, specifically related to the Pan American Union, see Fox 2013.

42. "My chief worry about the Committee is that no one on it knows the countries to the south and I am fearful of all sorts of ideas that look marvelous from here being adopted—but which aren't feasible or wise from the Latin American point of view. If only they could all go down—with sympathy and see and know for themselves." Morley to John Abbott, April 26, 1941, San Francisco Museum of Modern Art Archives and Library, ARCH:ADM:001:39:1.
43. Oral history interview with Stanton L. Catlin, 1989 July 1–Sept. 14, Archives of American Art, Smithsonian Institution.
44. Morley to Edward Dodd of Dodd, Mead and Company, April 25, 1941, San Francisco Museum of Modern Art Archives and Library, ARCH:ADM:001:40:11.
45. "Preliminary Report," Museum of Modern Art Archives, New York, EMH:II.21.b.
46. Statement from Grace Morley in "Minutes of the Meeting of the Advisory Art Committee, March 19, 1941," Museum of Modern Art Archives, New York, EMH:II.26.
47. For an examination of the political implications of Pettoruti's invitation to visit the United States, see Serviddio 2004.
48. When Henry Allen Moe, head of the Committee for Inter-American Artistic and Intellectual Relations, turned down Pettoruti's request to bring his wife to the United States, Morley argued for her necessity as an important contributor to periodicals in Argentina and Chile: "Mrs. Pettoruti is more than a wife and will actually be coming up in her own right to do her own job." Morley secured travel fare and a per diem for Pettoruti and María Rosa through the Committee for Inter-American Artistic and Intellectual Relations. Morley to Henry Allen Moe, November 26, 1942, San Francisco Museum of Modern Art Archives and Library, ARCH:ADM:001:48:4.
49. Sullivan 2004, 99.
50. Morley to Philip Adams, November 3, 1941, San Francisco Museum of Modern Art Archives and Library, ARCH:ADM:001:38:10.
51. Morley to Robert Drummond, September 12, 1941, San Francisco Museum of Modern Art Archives and Library, ARCH:EXH:001:12:31.
52. Elodie Courter to Morley, January 7, 1942, San Francisco Museum of Modern Art Archives and Library, ARCH:EXH:001.B.16.
53. Morley gave this lecture in August of 1941 along with another lecture titled "European Influences in Latin American Countries and Their Adaptation to Local Conditions." Morley to Agnes Rindge Claflin, January 21, 1942, San Francisco Museum of Modern Art Archives and Library, ARCH:ADM:001:48:6.
54. Morley to Ione Ulrich, November 10, 1942, Museum of Modern Art Archives, New York, EMH:II.4.A.
55. Morley to Alfred Frankenstein, December 22, 1941, San Francisco Museum of Modern Art Archives and Library, ARCH:ADM:001:44:12.
56. San Francisco Museum of Modern Art Permanent Collection Object File: Amelia Peláez, *Still Life*.
57. San Francisco Museum of Modern Art Permanent Collection Object File: Pedro Figari, *Candombe*.
58. Unless otherwise noted, the group of acquisitions listed here was assembled through the document "Permanent Collection List." San Francisco Museum of Modern Art Archives and Library, ARCH:ADM:001:62:9, and Morley ca. 1958.
59. "You will be interested to know that we purchased one of Carreño's large gouaches for the Latin American section of our Permanent Collection. It will be circulated widely in that exhibition which travels on occasions. It is the Afro-Cuban Ceremonial Dancer and a fine and powerful thing." Morley to José Gómez-Sicre, October 20, 1944, University of Texas Libraries, Benson Latin American Collection, José Gomez Sicre Papers, 7:3.
60. San Francisco Museum of Modern Art Permanent Collection Object File: José Perotti, *Earth*.
61. San Francisco Museum of Modern Art Permanent Collection Object File: Eduardo Kingman, *The Mask*.
62. "It will interest you to know that as a result of a loan of watercolors by Orlando and Enríquez for a small exhibition here, two were retained by an anonymous collector who allows us to keep them at the Museum and use them for one of our small circulating Latin American show[s] which goes out into small towns all over the Northern part of California. Just now they are having intensive use with other things that are small and easily transported in the Northwest under the direction of leaders in Latin American affairs." In this letter, Morley is referring to herself as the "anonymous collector." Morley to José Gómez-Sicre, April 12, 1944, University of Texas Libraries, Benson Latin American Collection, José Gomez Sicre Papers, 7:3.
63. Compiled from three documents in the same folder: "Dr. Morley—her *loans* removed from S.F.M.A 1958"; "From Dr. Morley's Collection, on loan to the San Francisco Museum"; "Anonymous Private Collection c/o San Francisco Museum of Art," San Francisco Museum of Modern Art Archives and Library, Unprocessed C#1, Long term loans: Dr. Grace McCann Morley, 1958.
64. For example, when Morley purchased Eduardo Kingman's painting *Procession* (which she later exchanged for *The Mask*),

she immediately included it in an exhibition. Morley wrote to Kingman, "your painting arrived and I at once made good use of it," January 22, 1942, San Francisco Museum of Modern Art Archives and Library, ARCH:EXH:001:B:16.

65. Morley to Elodie Courter, San Francisco Museum of Modern Art Archives and Library, May 5, 1942, ARCH:ADM:001:50:13.
66. Correspondence for *Contemporary Latin American Art*, San Francisco Museum of Modern Art Archives and Library, ARCH:EXH:001, Subseries 2:2, B:23–26.
67. For instance, when Washington State Museum loaned *Contemporary Latin American Art* in 1944, Morley informed Erna Gunther, director of the Washington State Museum at the University of Washington, "the purchase fund allows us to keep on gradually adding to our resources for this service." March 24, 1944, San Francisco Museum of Modern Art Archives and Library, ARCH:EXH:001:B:13.
68. Morley ca. 1958, n.p.
69. Morley to Domingo Santa Cruz, fine arts faculty and dean of the Universidad de Chile, April 13, 1942, San Francisco Museum of Modern Art Archives and Library, ARCH:ADM:48:9.
70. Oral history interview with Stanton L. Catlin, 1989 July 1–September 14, Archives of American Art, Smithsonian Institution.
71. Morley to Barr, May 19, 1943, San Francisco Museum of Modern Art Archives and Library, ARCH:ADM:001:ADM:57:4

Chapter 7

1. For the pitfalls and contradictions involved in this effort from colonial times until the present, see Olea, Ramírez, and Ybarra-Frausto 2012.
2. See Adams 2002, 161–63.
3. See "The United States 'Presents' and 'Collects' Latin American Art," 541–83, and Ybarra-Frausto's introduction to chapter III.4, 531–35, in Olea, Ramírez, and Ybarra-Frausto 2012.
4. John and Barbara Duncan lived in South America (mainly in Peru) in the 1950 and '60s, where they acquired a taste for Latin American art and began to build their modern and contemporary collection. Mrs. Duncan later trained in art history at New York University, where she researched the work of Uruguayan master Joaquín Torres-García. The couple became involved with the Archer M. Huntington Art Gallery (now the Jack S. Blanton Museum of Art) through their friendship with founding director Donald Goodall, who was an early champion of Latin American art and steered the museum into this area during his tenure from the early 1960s until 1978. In 1971, the Duncans donated more than 50 paintings and 100 works on paper to this university museum. Undoubtedly, the Blanton's leadership in this field is rooted both in Goodall's vision and in the Duncans' gift. Over the years, they gave a total of 95 paintings and 225 drawings.
5. See Pérez-Barreiro 2006.
6. The Nickolas Muray Collection of Modern Mexican Art is part of the Harry Ransom Center Art Collections at the University of Texas at Austin. Acquired by the Center in 1966, the Muray Collection includes more than one hundred works by Mexican artists, including three of Frida Kahlo's best-known works: *Self-Portrait with Thorn Necklace and Hummingbird* (1940), *Still Life (with Parrot and Fruit)* (1951), and *Diego and I* (1930), a sketch of herself with her husband, Diego Rivera. Moreover, the Center also owns the magnificent *Portrait of George Gershwin* (1936) by David Alfaro Siqueiros, and a large collection of prints and broadsides by José Guadalupe Posada.
7. I was honored to be the curator who inaugurated such a position and held it from 1988 to 2001.
8. According to Marion Oettinger, director emeritus and curator, "San Antonio's proximity to Latin America and its strong historical and cultural ties to Mexico fed the Latin American collection. Individuals whose families had fled the Mexican revolution and others who moved to San Antonio during the early twentieth century brought colonial paintings, silverware, and furniture that eventually made their way to the museum." See his introduction in Powers and Johnston 2012, 11. In 1998, the Museum inaugurated the Nelson A. Rockefeller Center for Latin American Art, a thirty-thousand-square-foot building dedicated exclusively to Latin American art.
9. The family of Nelson A. Rockefeller donated the Mexican Folk Art Collection to SAMA in 1985. Nelson Rockefeller personally began this collection in 1933 and shepherded it throughout his life. It consists of three thousand objects in all media from all over Mexico, with ceramics making up more than 50 percent of the collection. See Oettinger 1990.
10. The MFAH Pre-Columbian holdings encompass the renowned Glassell Collection, which includes over twenty-five hundred objects that have gold as their primary medium. See Marzio 2012.
11. "City of Houston Planning and Development Department: Ethnicity and Hispanic Report." See website *The City of Houston: Official Site for Houston, Texas*, October 15, 2012, http://www.houstontx.gov/planning/Demographics/docs_pdfs/Cy/coh_ethn_hisp_origin.pdf (accessed March 13, 2015).
12. This cipher represents a 24.5 percent increase since 2000. See "U.S. Census Bureau: State and County QuickFacts," United States Census Bureau, February 5, 2015, http://quickfacts.census.gov/qfd/states/48/4835000.html (accessed March 13, 2015).

13. See Stephen Klineberg, "Shared Prospects: Hispanics and the Future of Houston," Kinder Institute, Rice University, released November 2014, http://issuu.com/kinderinstitute/docs/latinoreportissuu.
14. Ibid.
15. "Houston Independent School District 2012–2013: Facts and Figures Report," Houston Independent School District, http://www.houstonisd.org/domain/7908 (accessed March 13, 2015).
16. See http://icaadocs.mfah.org/icaadocs/.
17. These ciphers reflect the number of works acquired since the establishment of the Latin American Art Department and ICAA in 2001. Before that date, the MFAH had only 23 Latin American art paintings and sculptures, approximately 175 works on paper by Rivera, José Clemente Orozco, Guadalupe Posada, Leopoldo Méndez and the Taller de Gráfica Popular, as well as an indeterminable number of photographs collected by pioneer curator Anne Wilkes Tucker, the Gus and Lyndall Wortham Curator of Photography from 1976 until 2015. These holdings bring the total number of modern and contemporary works in the MFAH collection to approximately 1,300.
18. Ramírez and Papanikolas 2002, specifically Peter C. Marzio's "Foreword" (6–9), and Ramírez's "Introduction" (10–29).
19. In his 1978 doctoral dissertation, "Contribution à l'étude de l'économie rétrospective du Brésil. Essai d'historiographie" (These III, Cycle: Histoire, Université de Paris X), French academic Guy Martinière included a chapter on "The Invention of an Operative Concept: The Latin-ness of America." The author's main contention is that the Latin-ness of America can be as useful as an operative concept in the same vein as other entrenched concepts such as "European," "African," or "Asian." See Martinière 2012. (The English translation of this essay can be consulted at the ICAA Digital Archive, doc. no. 838531, http://icaadocs.mfah.org/icaadocs/.)
20. Foucault 1997, 262.
21. I have dealt with this issue at greater length in Ramírez 2012, 43–46.
22. Adorno 1966; Adorno 1973, see specifically "Constellation"; Adorno 1999, 162–66.
23. Olea 2004.
24. Ramírez and Olea 2004; see specifically Ramírez and Olea's "Prologue" (xv–xvii) and Ramírez's essay "A Highly Topical Utopia—Some Outstanding Features of the Avant-Garde in Latin America" (1–15).
25. See Olea 2004, 443.
26. See Ramírez 2009.
27. See Ramírez 2007; Olea and Ramírez 2009.
28. Homi Bhabha, paper presented at CIMAM 2008 Annual Conference "The Shape of Memory: The Museum and Its Collections," Asia Society and The Museum of Modern Art, New York.
29. The *Houston Penetrable* (2005–14) was Soto's final work—he finished the design in December 2004, a few weeks before his death in January 2005—and the last in the series of site-specific *Penetrables* that he began in 1969. Conceived specifically for Mies Van der Rohe's Cullinan Hall, the *Houston Penetrable* consists of 24,000 PVC tubes that dangle approximately 28 feet from the ceiling to the floor and cover an area of 2,353 square feet, making it his most monumental work. Unlike any of the other *Penetrables* in the series, it has a virtual yellow ellipse painted by hand at the center.
30. See Hilarie M. Sheets, "A Romp in Gossamer, 8 Tons' Worth: An Installation Taxes Ingenuity in Houston," *New York Times*, May 8, 2014.

Chapter 8

1. Cited by Napoleon 2009, n.p.
2. As Clare Boothe Luce recalled in her memoirs, shortly after Dorothy Hale's death she encountered Frida Kahlo at an exhibition of her work at a New York gallery. Kahlo approached her and immediately spoke of Hale's suicide: "Kahlo wasted no time suggesting that she do a *recuerdo* of Dorothy. I did not speak enough Spanish to understand what the word *recuerdo* meant. I thought it meant a portrait done from memory. . . . Suddenly it came to me that a portrait of Dorothy by a famous painter friend might be something her poor mother might like to have. I said so, and Kahlo thought so too. . . . I said 'Go ahead. Send the portrait to me when it is finished. I will then send it on to Dorothy's mother.'" Cited in Herrera 1983, 292.
3. Clare Boothe Luce donated Kahlo's 1937 *Self-Portrait Dedicated to Leon Trotsky* to the National Museum of Women in the Arts in Washington, D.C.
4. As Clare Boothe Luce later related, "I will always remember the shock I had when I pulled the painting out of the crate. I felt really physically *sick*. What was I going to do with this gruesome painting of the smashed corpse of my friend, and her blood dripping down all over the frame? I could not return it—across the top of the painting there was an angel waving an unfurled banner which proclaimed in Spanish that this was 'The Suicide of Dorothy Hale, painted at the request of Clare Boothe Luce, for the mother of Dorothy.' I would not have requested such a gory picture of my worst enemy, much less of my unfortunate friend." Cited in Herrera 1983, 292.
5. In the words of Clare Boothe Luce, "I agreed not to destroy the painting, if the banner proclaiming I had commissioned it would be scrubbed off, and painted over. So Dorothy's

admirer took the painting away and wiped out the offensive legend." Cited in ibid., 293.

6. Clare Boothe Luce, cited in ibid., 478 (italics in original).
7. Lynch 1968.
8. Ibid.
9. Hickman 1974.
10. Herrera 1978.
11. Halle and Augustine 2013, 175.
12. Halle and Ramírez 2007, 217.

Chapter 9

1. Stratton-Pruitt 2013.
2. The other major private collections of colonial art from South America in the United States are somewhat more limited in scope. That of Patricia Phelps de Cisneros is a showcase for paintings, sculptures, and decorative arts of Venezuela, and the Carl and Marilynn Thoma collection has thus far focused on paintings.
3. Chacón Torres 1960, 1.
4. The parameters of the decision are summarized in the editorial "Banning Ivory Sales in America," *New York Times*, February 17, 2014.
5. The writer of this essay is the organizer and editor of *The Art of Painting in Colonial Bolivia* (Philadelphia: Saint Joseph's University Press, 2017), a book that has been generously underwritten by several collectors of Spanish Colonial art, including Dick and Roberta Huber, and by the Carl and Marilynn Thoma Art Foundation.

Chapter 10

1. In a statement published on the CPPC's website, Patricia recalls a public conversation with Edward Sullivan at The Frick Collection on the subject of collecting. She writes, "I wondered aloud if there might not be a term more apppropriate for expressing the responsibilities inherent in collecting; 'collector' has the unfortunate connotation—for me, at least—of a vestigial sense of colonial privilege: the idea that cultural territory is there for the taking; that the pleasure and power of ownership are the focus." She goes on to add, "After the talk . . . a member of the audience approached me and pointed out the contrast between the Spanish term 'coleccionista' and its English counterpart 'collector.' I found it an illuminating observation: the former more nearly approaches the sense of devotion and dedication I feel; the latter seems to point to an almost mechanical process of amassing objects." www.coleccioncisneros.org/editorial/statements/collector-whats-word (accessed August 4, 2017).
2. For a comprehensive list of exhibitions and loans, visit www.coleccioncisneros.org/collections (accessed August 4, 2017).
3. Other important survey exhibitions of this period include Gradowczyk and Perazzo 2001 and Sullivan 2001.
4. The careers of Félix González-Torres and Gabriel Orozco are exemplary in this regard and trod a path for many other artists.
5. In Austin and New York the exhibition was complemented by wide-ranging academic programs that explored the connections across disciplines suggested by the exhibition. See Pérez-Barreiro 2007.
6. Roberta Smith, "Abundant Straight Lines, All Ahead of the Curve," *New York Times*, September 14, 2007.
7. *La invención concreta* (Madrid: Museo Nacional Centro de Arte Reina Sofia, 2013), see Pérez-Barreiro 2013; *Radical Geometry* (London: Royal Academy of Arts, 2014), see Pérez-Barreiro et al. 2014.
8. Information on the contemporary art activities of the CPPC can be found at www.coleccioncisneros.org.

Chapter 11

1. Brodsky 2009.
2. José Luis Falconi, "No Me Token; or, How to Make Sure We Never Lose the * Completely," paper presented at the conference *Between Theory and Practice: Rethinking Latin American Art in the 21st Century*, Museum of Latin American Art, Long Beach, Calif., March 2011. "No Me Token" is a play on the Spanish *no me toques* (don't touch me) and the English "don't tokenize me."
3. Buchloh and de Zegher 1991, 223.

References

Ackley, Laura A. 2015. *San Francisco's Jewel City: The Panama–Pacific International Exposition of 1915*. Berkeley: Heydey.

Adams, Beverly. 2002. "The Challenges of Collecting Latin American Art in the United States: The Diane and Bruce Halle Collection." In *Collecting Latin American Art for the 21st Century*, edited by Mari Carmen Ramírez and Theresa Papanikolas, 157–83. Houston: Museum of Fine Arts and International Center for the Arts of the Americas.

Adler, Esther. 2014. "The Problem of Our American Collection: MoMA Collects at Home." In *American Modern: Hopper to O'Keeffe*, edited by Kathy Curry and Esther Adler, 125–40. New York: The Museum of Modern Art.

Adorno, Theodor W. 1966. *Negativ Dialektik*. Frankfurt am Main: Suhrkamp Verlag.

———. 1973. *Gesammelte Schriften*. Vol. 6. Frankfurt am Main: Suhrkamp Verlag.

———. 1999. *Negative Dialectics*. Translated by E. B. Ashton. New York: Continuum Publishing.

American Federation of Arts. 1930. *Mexican Arts. Catalogue of an Exhibition Organized for and Circulated by the American Federation of Arts*. New York: Southworth Press.

Anna, Timothy E. 1990. *The Mexican Empire of Iturbide*. Lincoln: University of Nebraska Press.

Barber, Edwin Atlee. 1906a. *Tin-Enamelled Pottery*. Philadelphia: The Pennsylvania Museum and School of Industrial Arts.

———. 1906b. "Recent Discovery of Early Maiolica in Mexico." *Bulletin of the Pennsylvania Museum* 4, no. 15, 42–45.

———. 1908. *The Maiolica of Mexico*. Philadelphia: Printed for the Museum.

———. 1911. *Catalogue of Mexican Maiolica belonging to Mrs. Robert W. de Forest*. New York: The Hispanic Society of America.

———. 1918. *The Emily Johnston de Forest Collection of Mexican Maiolica*. New York: The Metropolitan Museum of Art.

Bargellini, Clara. 1991. "Frederic Church, Sor Pudenciana y Andrés López." *Anales del Instituto de Investigaciones Estéticas* 62:123–38.

———. 1995. "Churrigueresco yanqui: Sylvester Baxter y el arte colonial mexicano." In *Los discursos sobre el arte: XV Coloquio Internacional de Historia del Arte*, edited by Juana Gutiérrez Haces, 169–91. Mexico City: Universidad Nacional Autónoma de México; Instituto de Investigaciones Estéticas.

———. 2001. "Los estudios de la arquitectura novohispana: Los avatares de *Spanish Colonial Architecture in Mexico*." In *El Arte en México: Autores, Temas, Problemas*, edited by Rita Eder, 194–216. Mexico City: Consejo Nacional para la Cultura y las Artes.

Barr, Alfred H., Jr. 1949. "Problems of Research and Documentation in Contemporary Latin American Art." In *Studies in Latin American Art: Proceedings of a Conference Held in the Museum of Modern Art, New York, May 28–31, 1945*, edited by Elizabeth Wilder, 10, 37–48. Washington, D.C.: American Council of Learned Societies.

———. 1986. *Cubism and Abstract Art: Painting, Sculpture, Constructions, Photography, Architecture, Industrial Art, Theatre, Films, Posters, Typography*. Cambridge: Belknap Press of Harvard University Press.

Barratt, Carrie Rebora, and Ellen G. Miles. 2004. *Gilbert Stuart*. Exh. cat. New York: The Metropolitan Museum of Art.

Basilio, Miriam. 2004. "Reflecting on a History of Collecting and Exhibiting Work by Artists from Latin America." In Basilio et al. 2004, 52–68.

Basilio, Miriam, et al., eds. 2004. *Latin American & Caribbean Art: MoMA at El Museo*. Exh. cat. New York: El Museo del Barrio and The Museum of Modern Art.

Baxter, Sylvester. 1901. *Spanish-Colonial Architecture in Mexico*. 10 vols. Boston: J. B. Millet.

Birkhofer, Denise, ed. 2014. *Latin American Art at the Allen Memorial Art Museum*. Oberlin: Allen Memorial Art Museum.

Brodsky, Estrellita B. 2009. "Latin American Artists in Postwar Paris: Jesús Rafael Soto and Julio Le Parc, 1950–1970." Ph.D. diss., Institute of Fine Arts, New York University.

Brownlee, John Peter, Valéria Piccoli, and Georgiana Uhlyarik, eds. 2015. *Picturing the Americas: Landscape Painting from Tierra del Fuego to the Arctic*. Exh. cat. New Haven: Yale University Press.

Buchloh, Benjamin H. D., and M. Catherine de Zegher. 1991. "Ver América: A Written Exchange." In *America: Bride of the Sun; 500 Years Latin America and the Low Countries*, by Paul Vandenbroeck et al., 223–41. Exh. cat. Antwerp: Royal Museum of Fine Arts; Ghent: Imschoot.

Buntinx, Gustavo. 2005. "The Missing Link: The Ups and Downs of *Club Atlético Nuevo Chicago*." In *Berni y sus contemporáneos: Correlatos*, edited by Adriana Lauria, 188–96. Buenos Aires: MALBA–Colección Costantini.

Burke, Marcus B. 1998. *Treasures of Mexican Colonial Painting: The Davenport Museum of Art Collection*. Santa Fe: Museum of New Mexico Press.

Cardoza y Aragón, Luis. 1943. *Mexican Art Today*. Exh. cat. Philadelphia: Philadelphia Museum of Art.

Carr, Dennis, and Gauvin Bailey, eds. 2015. *Made in the Americas: The New World Discovers Asia*. Exh. cat. Boston: Museum of Fine Arts.

Carr, Gerald L. 1994a. *Frederic Edwin Church: Catalogue Raisonné of Works of Art at Olana State Historic Site.* 2 vols. New York: Cambridge University Press.

———. 1994b. "Frederic Edwin Church and Mexico." In *Arte, historia e identidad en América: Visiones comparativas*, edited by Gustavo Curiel, Renato González Mello, and Juana Gutiérrez, 2 vols., vol. 1, 253–66. Mexico City: Universidad Autónoma de México.

Castañeda, Luis. 2014. "Island Culture Wars: Selden Rodman and Haiti." *Art Journal* 73, no. 3, 56–69.

Chacón Torres, Mario. 1960. *Notas sobre arte republicano en Potosí.* Potosí: Imprenta de la Universidad Tomás Frías.

Chiñas, Beverly Newbold. 1989. "Zelia Maria Magadalena Nuttall (1857–1933)." In *Women Anthropologists: Selected Biographies*, edited by Ute D. Gacs, 269–74. Urbana: University of Illinois Press.

Colón Camacho, Doreen M. 2003. *Los santos de Puerto Rico: Estudio de la imaginería popular.* Hong Kong: Asia Pacific.

Corn, Wanda. 1999. *The Great American Thing: Modern Art and National Identity, 1915–1935.* Berkeley: University of California Press.

Crocker, Ruth. 2008. *Mrs. Russell Sage: Women's Activism and Philanthropy in Gilded Age and Progressive Era America.* Bloomington: Indiana University Press.

Cutting, James. 2007. "Mere Exposure, Reproduction, and the Impressionist Canon." In *Partisan Canons*, edited by Anna Brzyski, 79–94. Durham: Duke University Press.

Dailey, Victoria, Natalie Shivers, and Michael Dawson. 2003. *LA's Early Moderns: Art, Architecture, Photography.* Los Angeles: Balcony Press.

Davis, Virginia. 1997. "Frederic Edwin Church's Acquisitions of Mexican Textiles." *Studies in the Decorative Arts* 4 (Spring–Summer): 97–109.

De Forest, Lockwood. 1908. "Some Mexican Churches." *Century Illustrated Magazine* 76, no. 4, 28.

De Havenon, Georgia, Christina de León, Alicia Lubowski-Jahn, et al., eds. 2014. *Unity of Nature: Alexander von Humboldt and the Americas.* Exh. cat. New York: Americas Society; Bielefeld: Kerber.

Delpar, Helen. 1992. *The Enormous Vogue of Things Mexican: Cultural Relations Between the United States and Mexico, 1920–1935.* Tuscaloosa: University of Alabama Press.

Department of Fine Arts. 1940. *Art: Official Catalog; Palace of Fine Arts, Golden Gate International Exposition, San Francisco, 1940.* San Francisco: Recorder Printing and Publishing Co.

Doss, Erika. 1991. *Benton, Pollock, and the Politics of Modernism.* Chicago: University of Chicago Press.

Duberman, Martin. 2008. *The Worlds of Lincoln Kirstein.* Evanston: Northwestern University Press.

Dürer, Albrecht. 1971. *Diary of His Journey to the Netherlands: Accompanied by the Silverpoint Sketchbook and Paintings and Drawings Made During His Journey.* Greenwich, Conn.: New York Graphic Society.

Elderfield, John. 2004. "The Front Door to Understanding." In *Modern Painting and Sculpture, 1880 to the Present*, edited by John Elderfield, 8–59. New York: The Museum of Modern Art.

———. 2010. "The Geometry of Change." In *A Constructive Vision: Latin American Abstract Art from the Colección Patricia Phelps de Cisneros*, edited by Gabriel Pérez-Barreiro, 23–33. New York: Fundación Cisneros.

Espejel, Carlos, Annie O'Neill, and Anne Rockefeller Roberts. 1986. *The Nelson A. Rockefeller Collection of Mexican Folk Art: A Gift to The Mexican Museum.* San Francisco: Chronicle Books.

Follin, Frances. 2004. *Embodied Visions: Bridget Riley, Op Art and the Sixties.* London: Thames and Hudson.

Foucault, Michel. 1997. "Of Other Spaces." In *Politics, Poetics. Documenta X: The Book*, edited by Catherine David and Jean-François Chevrier, 262–72. Ostfildern: Cantz-Verlag.

Fox, Claire E. 2013. *Making Art Panamerican: Cultural Policy and the Cold War.* Minneapolis: University of Minnesota Press.

Frelinghuysen, Alice Cooney. 2000. "Emily Johnston de Forest." *Antiques* 157:192–97.

Garduño, Ana. 2009. "El poder del coleccionismo de arte: Alvar Carrillo Gil." Ph.D. diss., UNAM, Mexico City.

Gilbert, Courtney. 2009. "Negotiating Surrealism: Carlos Merida, Mexican Art, and the Avant-garde." *Journal of Surrealism and the Americas* 3, nos. 1–2, 30–50.

Goddard, Paul E. 1910. "Navajo Blankets Recently Acquired." *American Museum Journal* 10, 211.

Goldman, Shifra M. 1994. *Dimension of the Americas: Art and Social Change in Latin America and the United States.* Chicago: University of Chicago Press.

Gómez Sicre, José. 1959. *South American Art Today.* Exh. cat. Dallas: Dallas Museum of Fine Arts.

Govan, Michael, and Diane Magaloni, eds. 2016. *Picasso and Rivera: Conversations Across Time.* Los Angeles: LACMA.

Gradowczyk, Mario H., and Nelly Perazzo. 2001. *Abstract Art from the Río de la Plata: Buenos Aires and Montevideo, 1933–1953.* Exh. cat. New York: Americas Society.

Greet, Michele. 2009. *Beyond National Identity: Pictorial Indigenism as a Modernist Strategy in Andean Art, 1920–1960.* University Park: Penn State University Press.

Halle, Diane, and Roland Augustine. 2013. "Diane Halle and Roland Augustine in Conversation." In *Order, Chaos, and the Space Between: Contemporary Latin American Art from the Diane and Bruce Halle Collection*, edited by Beverly Adams and Vanessa Davidson, 175–86. Exh. cat. Phoenix: Phoenix Art Museum.

Halle, Diane, and Mari Carmen Ramírez. 2007. "Inside a Poetic Universe: A Conversation Between Diane Halle and Mari Carmen Ramírez." In *Constructing a Poetic Universe: The Diane and Bruce Halle Collection of Latin American Art*, edited by Beverly Adams and Mari Carmen Ramírez, 207–29. Exh. cat. Houston: The Museum of Fine Arts.

Harris, Neil, Marlene Chambers, and Lewis Wingfield Story. 1996. *The First Hundred Years: The Denver Art Museum*. Denver: Denver Art Museum.

Heikamp, Detlef. 1982. "Mexiko und die Medici-Herzöge." In *Mythen der Neuen Welt: Zur Entdeckungsgeschichte Lateinamerikas*, edited by Karl-Heinz Kohl, 126–46. Berlin: Frölich und Kaufmann.

Herrera, Hayden. 1978. *Frida Kahlo, 1910–1954*. Exh. cat. Chicago: Museum of Contemporary Art.

———. 1983. *Frida: A Biography of Frida Kahlo*. New York: Harper and Row.

Hickman, Ronald. 1974. *José Luis Cuevas: An Exhibition of Recent Works*. Exh. cat. Phoenix: Phoenix Art Museum.

Hijiya, James. 1980. "Four Ways of Looking at a Philanthropist: A Study of Robert Weeks de Forest." *Proceedings of the American Philosophical Society* 124, 404–48.

Hofer, Margaret K., and Roberta J. M. Olson. 2015. *Making it Modern: The Folk Art Collection of Elie and Viola Nadelman*. Exh. cat. New York and London: New-York Historical Society in association with D Giles.

Hurlburt, Laurance P. 1986. "Diego Rivera (1886–1957): A Chronology of His Art, Life, and Times." In *Diego Rivera: A Retrospective*, edited by Cynthia Newman Helms, 22–115. Exh. cat. New York: Founders Society Detroit Institute of Arts; New York: W. W. Norton.

Indych-López, Anna. 2007. "'None of Those Little Donkeys for Me': Tamayo, Cultural Prestige, and Perceptions of Modern Mexican Art in the United States." In *Tamayo: A Modern Icon Reinterpreted*, edited by Diana du Pont, 343–65. Exh. cat. Santa Barbara: Santa Barbara Museum of Art.

———. 2009. *Muralism Without Walls: Rivera, Orozco, and Siqueiros in the United States, 1927–1940*. Pittsburgh: University of Pittsburgh Press.

———. 2010. "Making *Nueva York Moderna*: Latin American Artists, the International Avant-Gardes, and The New School." In *Nueva York, 1613–1945*, edited by Edward J. Sullivan, 234–55. New York: New-York Historical Society; London: Scala.

———. 2011. "Alfredo Ramos Martínez: Indians, Hollywood, and the *Los Angeles Times*." In *MEX/LA: "Mexican" Modernism(s) in Los Angeles 1930–1985*, edited by Selena Preciado, 44–47. Exh. cat. Long Beach: The Museum of Latin American Art; Ostfildern: Hatje Cantz.

Ittmann, John, et al. 2006. *Mexico and Modern Printmaking: A Revolution in the Graphic Arts, 1920 to 1950*. Exh. cat. Philadelphia: Philadelphia Museum of Art, 2006.

Kahlo, Guillermo. 1998. *La Lente de Guillermo Kahlo en la arquitectura religiosa de México*. Valencia: Consorci de Museus de la Comunitat Academia de San Carlos.

Kantor, Sybil Gordon. 2002. *Alfred H. Barr, Jr., and the Intellectual Origins of The Museum of Modern Art*. Cambridge, Mass.: MIT Press.

Kaufmann, Thomas DaCosta. 2006. "Cultural Transfer and the Arts of the Americas." In Stratton-Pruitt 2006, 19–25.

Kirstein, Lincoln. 1943. *The Latin-American Collection of The Museum of Modern Art*. New York: The Museum of Modern Art.

Krutnik, Frank. 2007. "'A Living Part of the Class Struggle': Diego Rivera's *The Flower Carrier* and the Hollywood Left." In *Un-American Hollywood: Politics and Film in the Blacklist Era*, edited by Frank Krutnik et al., 51–78. New Brunswick: Rutgers University Press.

Kubler, George. 1954. *The Louise and Walter Arensberg Collection*. Philadelphia: Philadelphia Museum of Art.

Lamborn, Robert H. 1891. *Mexican Painting and Painters: A Brief Sketch of the Development of the Spanish School of Painting in Mexico*. New York: Allen, Lane and Scott.

Lawrence, D. H. 1926. *The Plumed Serpent*. New York: A. A. Knopf.

Lee, Anthony. 1999. *Painting on the Left: Diego Rivera, Radical Politics, and San Francisco's Public Murals*. Berkeley: University of California Press.

Lee, Pamela. 2001. "Bridget Riley's Eye/Body Problem." *October* 98 (Fall): 27–46.

Lemon, Isabelle. 2010. "The WPA: The Stimulus Package of Its Day." *Panorama: The Newsletter of the San Francisco Museum and Historical Society* 22, no. 1 (2010).

Lowry, Glenn. 2012. "Abstraction in 1936: Barr's Diagrams." In *Inventing Abstraction, 1910–1925: How a Radical Idea Changed Modern Art*, edited by Leah Dickerman, 358–69. Exh. cat. New York: The Museum of Modern Art.

Lynch, James. 1968. *Rufino Tamayo*. Exh. cat. Phoenix: Phoenix Art Museum.

Manrique, Jorge Alberto, and Teresa del Conde. 1987. *Una mujer en al arte mexicano: Memorias de Inés Amor*. Mexico City: Universidad Nacional Autónoma de México, Instituto de Investigaciones Estéticas.

Manthorne, Katherine. 1989. *Tropical Renaissance: North American Artists Exploring Latin America, 1839–1879*. Washington, D.C.: Smithsonian Institution Press.

———, ed. 2015. *Traveler Artists: Landscapes of the Americas from the Patricia Phelps de Cisneros Collection*. New York: Fundación Cisneros.

Marquis, Alice Goldfarb. 1989. *Alfred H. Barr, Jr.: Missionary for the Modern*. Chicago: Contemporary Books.

Martinière, Guy. 2012. "The Invention of an Operative Concept: The Latin-Ness of America." In Olea, Ramírez, and Ybarra-Frausto 2012, 164–77.

Marzio, Frances. 2012. *The Glassell Collections of the Museum of Fine*

Arts, Houston: Masterworks of Pre-Columbian, Indonesian, and African Gold. Houston: The Museum of Fine Arts.

McAndrew, John. 1965. *The Open-Air Churches of Sixteenth-Century Mexico: Atrios, Posas, Open Chapels, and Other Studies.* Cambridge, Mass.: Harvard University Press.

Meyer, Richard. 2013. *What Was Contemporary Art?* Cambridge, Mass.: MIT Press.

Miller, Dana, et al. 2016. *Carmen Herrera: Lines of Sight.* Exh. cat. New York: Whitney Museum of American Art.

Miller, Dorothy C. 1943. "Foreword and Acknowledgements." In *Americans 1943: Realists and Magic Realists*, edited by Dorothy C. Miller and Alfred H. Barr, 5–6. New York: The Museum of Modern Art.

Morales, Vicente, and Manuel Caballero. 1908. *El Señor Root en Mexico.* Mexico City: Arte y Letras.

Morley, Grace McCann. 1940. *Diego Rivera: Drawings and Watercolors from the Collection of the San Francisco Museum of Art.* San Francisco: San Francisco Museum of Art.

———. 1942. "Return of an Artist: Luis Alberto Acuña." *Inter-American Monthly* 1, no. 8: 26–28.

———. Ca. 1958. *Contemporary Art in America and the Latin American Collection.* San Francisco: San Francisco Museum of Art.

Morley, Grace, and Suzanne B. Riess. *Grace L. McCann Morley: Art, Artists, Museums, and the San Francisco Museum of Art: An Interview.* Berkeley: University of California, General Library, Regional Cultural History Project, 1960.

Napoleon, Landon J. 2009. "The Chronology and Defining Moments in the History of the Phoenix Art Museum." In *Fabulous at Fifty: Phoenix Art Museum.* Phoenix: Phoenix Art Museum.

Noreika, Sarah, ed. 2014. *Philadelphia Museum of Art: Handbook.* Philadelphia: Philadelphia Museum of Art.

Nuttall, Zelia. 1910. "The Island of Sacrifices." *American Anthropologist* 12:257–97.

Oettinger, Marion, Jr. 1990. *Folk Treasures of Mexico: The Nelson A. Rockefeller Collection in the San Antonio Museum of Art and The Mexican Museum, San Francisco.* New York: Harry N. Abrams.

Olea, Héctor. 2004. "Versions, Inversions, and Subversions: The Artist as a Theoretician." In Ramírez and Olea 2004, 443–539.

Olea, Héctor, and Mari Carmen Ramírez, eds. 2009. *Building on a Construct: The Adolpho Leirner Collection of Brazilian Constructive Art at the Museum of Fine Arts, Houston.* Houston: The Museum of Fine Arts.

Olea, Héctor, Mari Carmen Ramírez, and Tomás Ybarra-Frausto. 2012. *Resisting Categories: Latin American and/or Latino?* Critical Documents of 20th-Century Latin American and Latino Art. Houston: The Museum of Fine Arts and International Center for the Arts of the Americas.

Oles, James. 1993. *South of the Border: Mexico in the American Imagination, 1914–1947.* Washington, D.C.: Smithsonian Institution Press.

———. 2002. "For Business or Pleasure: Exhibiting Mexican Folk Art, 1820–1930." In *Casa Mañana: The Morrow Collection of Mexican Popular Arts*, edited by Susan Danly, 11–29. Albuquerque: University of New Mexico Press.

———, ed. 2005. *De artesanos y arlequines: Forjando una colección de arte mexicano.* Exh. cat. Mexico City: Museo Nacional de Arte, INBA.

———. 2011. *Diego Rivera, David Alfaro Siqueiros, José Clemente Orozco.* New York: The Museum of Modern Art.

O'Neill, Annie, and Charlene Cerny, eds. 1984. *Mexican Folk Art from the Collection of Nelson A. Rockefeller.* Exh. cat. New York: Center for Inter-American Relations.

Ortiz-Torres, Rubén, and Jesse Lerner, eds. 2011. *Mex/L.A.: "Mexican" Modernism(s) in Los Angeles, 1930–1985.* Exh. cat. Long Beach: Museum of Latin American Art; Ostfildern: Hatje Cantz.

O'Toole, Erin. 2009. "A Very Human Thing: The Arts Patronage of Albert Bender." In *San Francisco Museum of Modern Art: 75 Years of Looking Forward*, edited by Janet C. Bishop, Corey Keller, and Sarah Roberts, 83–89. San Francisco: San Francisco Museum of Modern Art.

Paquette, Catha. 1997. "US Perceptions of Art Both Mexican and Modern: The Collecting, Publishing, and Curatorial Activities of MacKinley Helm." In *Patrocinio, colección y circulación de las artes: XX Coloquio internacional de historia de arte*, edited by Gustavo Curiel, 637–69. Mexico: UNAM.

———. 2002. "Public Duty, Private Interests: Mexican Art at New York's Museum of Modern Art, 1929–1954." Ph.D. diss., University of California, Santa Barbara.

———. 2006. "Critical Consequences: Mexican Art at New York's The Museum of Modern Art During World War II." In *El proceso creativo*, edited by Alberto Dallal, 529–59. Mexico City: Instituto Superior de Investigaciones Estéticas.

Peck, Amelia. "Robert de Forest and the Founding of the American Wing." *Antiques* 157, 176–81.

Pellicer, Carlos. 1944. *Jose Maria Velasco, 1840–1912.* Exh. cat. Philadelphia: Philadelphia Museum of Art.

Pérez-Barreiro, Gabriel. 2005. "The Accidental Tourist: American Collections of Latin American Art." In *Collecting the New: Museums and Contemporary Art*, edited by Bruce Altshuler, 131–46. Princeton: Princeton University Press.

———, ed. 2006. *Blanton Museum of Art: Latin American Collection.* Austin: The Blanton Museum of Art and University of Texas Press.

———, ed. 2007. *The Geometry of Hope: Latin American Abstract Art from the Patricia Phelps de Cisneros Collection.* Exh. cat. Austin: Blanton Museum of Art; The University of Texas at Austin.

———, ed. 2013. *Invención concreta: Colección Patricia Phelps de Cisneros.*

Exh. cat. Madrid: Museo Nacional Centro de Arte Reina Sofía.

Pérez-Barreiro, Gabriel, et al. 2014. *Radical Geometry: Modern Art of South America from the Patricia Phelps de Cisneros Collection*. Exh. cat. London: Royal Academy of Arts.

Pérez Oramas, Luis Enrique. 2004a. "The Art of Babel in the Americas." In Basilio et al. 2004, 34–43.

———. 2004b. "Joaquín Torres-García's *Composition* and Roberto Berdecio's *The Cube and the Perspective*." In Basilio et al. 2004, 93–97.

Pierce, Donna. 2011. *Companion to Spanish Colonial Art at the Denver Art Museum*. Denver: Denver Art Museum.

Powers, Jessica, and John Johnston. 2012. *The San Antonio Museum of Art: Guide to the Collection*. San Antonio: San Antonio Museum of Art.

Pratt, Mary Louise. 2007. *Imperial Eyes: Travel Writing and Transculturation*. London: Routledge.

Ramírez, Mari Carmen. 2007. *Dimensions of Constructive Art in Brazil: The Adolpho Leirner Collection*. Houston: The Museum of Fine Arts.

———. 2009. *Joaquín Torres-García: Constructing Abstraction with Wood*. Houston: The Menil Collection.

———. 2012. "The Dilemma of 'Activating' the Permanent Collection, or, How to Thaw the Frozen Assets." *Exhibitionist*, no. 5, 43–46.

Ramírez, Mari Carmen, and Héctor Olea. 2004. *Inverted Utopias: Avant-Garde Art in Latin America*. Exh. cat. Houston: The Museum of Fine Arts; New Haven: Yale University Press.

Ramírez, Mari Carmen, and Theresa Papanikolas. 2002. *Collecting Latin American Art for the 21st Century*. Exh. cat. International Center for the Arts of the Americas 1. Houston: Museum of Fine Arts.

Ramos, E. Carmen, ed. 2013. *Our America: The Latino Presence in American Art*. Exh. cat. Washington, D.C.: Smithsonian American Art Museum.

Rasmussen, Waldo. 1993. "Introduction to an Exhibition." In *Latin American Artists of the Twentieth Century*, edited by Waldo Rasmussen with Fatima Bercht and Elizabeth Ferrer, 11–17. Exh. cat. New York: The Museum of Modern Art.

Rau, Charles. 1879. "The Palenque Tablet in the United States National Museum." *Smithsonian Institution Contributions to Knowledge* 22, no. 331: 1–3.

Reed, Alma. 2007. *Peregrina: Love and Death in Mexico*. Edited by Michael K. Schuessler. Austin: University of Texas Press.

Rishel, Joseph J., with Suzanne Stratton-Pruitt. 2006. *The Arts in Latin America, 1492–1820*. Exh. cat. Philadelphia: Philadelphia Museum of Art; New Haven: Yale University Press.

Ruiz, Jason. 2014. *Americans in the Treasure House: Travel to Porfirian Mexico and the Cultural Politics of Empire*. Austin: University of Texas Press.

Sadlier, Darlene J. 2012. *Americans All: Good Neighbor Policy in World War II*. Austin: University of Texas Press.

Sandler, Irving. 2008. "Abstract Expressionism and the Cold War." *Art in America* 96, no. 6, 65–74.

Sandler, Irving, and Amy Newman, eds. 1986. *Defining Modern Art: Selected Writings of Alfred H. Barr, Jr.* New York: Harry N. Abrams.

Schrank, Sarah. 2009. *Art and The City: Civic Imagination and Cultural Authority in Los Angeles*. Philadelphia: University of Pennsylvania Press.

Serviddio, Luisa Fabiana. 2004. "Intercambios Culturales Panamericanos Durante La Segundo Guerra Mundial: El viaje de Pettoruti a los EEUU." In *Arte Argentino y Latinoamericano Del Siglo XX.*, by María Amalia García, Luisa Fabiana Serviddio, and María Cristina Rossi, 55–82. Buenos Aires: Fundación Espigas.

Smith, Alison, and David Blayney Brown, eds. 2015. *Artist and Empire: Facing Britain's Imperial Past*. Exh. cat. London: Tate Modern.

Soby, James Thrall, and Dorothy C. Miller. 1943. *Romantic Painting in America*. Exh. cat. New York: The Museum of Modern Art.

Storr, Robert. 2000. *Modern Art Despite Modernism*. New York: The Museum of Modern Art.

Stratton-Pruitt, Suzanne, ed. 2006. *The Virgin, Saints, and Angels: South American Paintings, 1600–1825, from the Thoma Collection*. Exh. cat. Milan: Skira.

———, ed. 2013. *Journeys to New Worlds: Spanish and Portuguese Colonial Art in the Roberta and Richard Huber Collection*. Exh. cat. Philadelphia: Philadelphia Museum of Art.

Stroud, Patricia T. 2005. *The Man Who Had Been King: The American Exile of Napoleon's Brother Joseph*. Philadelphia: University of Pennsylvania Press.

Sullivan, Edward J. 2001. *Brazil: Body & Soul*. Exh. cat. New York: Solomon R. Guggenheim Museum.

———. 2004. "Emilio Pettoruti: An International Perspective." In *Emilio Pettoruti (1892–1971)*, by Edward J. Sullivan et al., 15–152. Buenos Aires: Fundación Pettoruti, Asociación Amigos del Museo Nacional de Bellas Artes, and La Marca Editora.

———. 2007. *The Language of Objects in the Art of the Americas*. New Haven: Yale University Press.

———. 2008. *Fragile Demon: Juan Soriano in Mexico, 1935 to 1950*. Exh. cat. Philadelphia: Philadelphia Museum of Art.

———. 2014. *From San Juan to Paris and Back: Francisco Oller and Caribbean Art in the Era of Impressionism*. New Haven: Yale University Press.

Varnedoe, Kirk. 1995. "The Evolving Torpedo: Changing Ideas of the Collection of Painting and Sculpture of The Museum of Modern Art." In *The Museum of Modern Art at Mid-Century: Continuity and Change*, edited by John Elderfield, 13–73. Studies in Modern Art 5. New York: The Museum of Modern Art.

Vidal, Teodoro. 1994. *Los Espada: Escultores sangermeños.* San Juan: Ediciones Alba.

———. 2006. *Escultura religiosa puertorriqueña.* San Juan: Ediciones Alba.

Villanueva, Isabela. 2009. "A Kinetic Kraze; or the Rise and Fall of Kinetic Art in the United States, 1964–1974." In *Carlos Cruz-Diez: (In)formed by Color*, edited by Gabriela Rangel, 70–79. New York: Americas Society.

Wulf, Andrea. 2015. *The Invention of Nature: Alexander von Humboldt's New World.* New York: Knopf.

Zelevansky, Lynn, 1993. "Dorothy Miller's 'Americans,' 1942–63." In *The Museum of Modern Art at Mid-Century: At Home and Abroad*, edited by John Elderfield, 56–93. Studies in Modern Art 4. New York: The Museum of Modern Art, 1993.

Contributors

Inge Reist is Director of the Center for the History of Collecting at The Frick Collection and Frick Art Reference Library. She received her Ph.D. from Columbia University and joined the Frick in 1984 as head of its Photoarchive and later Chief of Research Collections and Programs. She has taught at Columbia and Rutgers Universities as well as at Hunter College, has lectured widely on European art at numerous museums and conferences, and her articles have appeared in most major journals. From 2005 to 2011, she chaired the Association of Research Institutes in Art History. Her publications and public lectures focus primarily on art collecting, and, in addition to earlier volumes in this series, they include *British Models of Collecting and the American Response: Reflections Across the Pond* (volume editor; Ashgate, 2014); *Collecting Spanish Art: Spain's Golden Age and America's Gilded Age* (coedited with José Luis Colomer; The Frick Collection with the Centro de Estudios Europa Hispánica and Center for Spain in America, 2012); *Provenance: An Alternate History of Art* (coedited with Gail Feigenbaum; Getty Research Institute, 2012); essays for *Sacred Possessions: Collecting Italian Religious Art, 1500 to 1900*, ed. Gail Feigenbaum and Sybille Ebert-Schifferer (Getty Research Institute, 2011) and for *La circulation des oeuvres d'art / The Circulation of Works of Art in the Revolutionary Era, 1789–1848*, ed. Roberta Panzanelli (Rennes: Presses universitaires de Rennes, 2006). She also maintains her interest in Renaissance and Baroque art, recently writing a chapter for the Blackwell companion series and an essay for *Paolo Veronese: A Master and His Workshop* (Ringling Museum, 2013).

Edward J. Sullivan is the Helen Gould Sheppard Professor of the History of Art at the Institute of Fine Arts and the Department of Art History of New York University. He specializes in modern and contemporary art of the Americas, with an emphasis on the Hispanophone and Lusophone countries. He has published over thirty books and exhibition catalogues on this subject. Among the most recent books are *Making the Americas Modern: Hemispheric Art, 1910–1960* (Laurence King, 2018), *The Language of Objects in the Art of the Americas* (Yale University Press, 2007), and *From San Juan to Paris and Back: Francisco Oller and Caribbean Art in the Era of Impressionism* (Yale University Press, 2014). Sullivan has also organized numerous exhibitions throughout the United States, Latin America, and Europe on the arts and visual cultures of the Americas from the nineteenth century to today. He was chief curator of the Guggenheim Museum's 2001 exhibition *Brazil: Body & Soul*, and co-curated *Concrete Improvisations: Sculptures and Collages by Esteban Vicente* (New York and Segovia, 2011), *Observed: Milagros de la Torre* (New York and Lima, 2012), and *Impressionism and the Caribbean* (Austin, Brooklyn, and San Juan, 2015), among others.

Miriam Margarita Basilio is Associate Professor of Art History and Museum Studies at New York University, where she teaches undergraduate and graduate courses. Her research and teaching interests include visual, print, and exhibition culture, propaganda, cultural property, and national identity in Spain; modern Spanish and Latin American art; the history of collecting and exhibitions of Latin American art in the United States; museums and the art market; histories of global biennials; and art and political activism. Prior to joining NYU, she was a curatorial assistant in the Departments of Painting and Sculpture and Drawings at The Museum of Modern Art from 2001 to 2005. There she co-curated the exhibitions *Tempo* (MoMAQNS 2002) and *Caribbean and Latin American Art: MoMA at El Museo* (co-organized with El Museo del Barrio, 2004) and was part of a curatorial team conducting research on the Museum's Latin American art holdings, new acquisitions, and publications. Her first book, *Visual Propaganda, Exhibitions, and the Spanish Civil War*, was published by Ashgate in 2013 and in paperback by Routledge in 2017. Currently, she is writing a book on the history of MoMA's modernist canon and the idea of "Latin American" art. She has published essays in edited volumes and catalogues published by Museo Nacional Centro de Arte Reina Sofía, Museu Picasso, The Museum of Modern Art, International Center of Photography, and the Cleveland Museum of Art. Her articles have been published in journals including *Art Journal*, *Discourse: Journal for Theoretical Studies in Media and Culture*, and the *Journal of the American Institute of Conservation*. She has lectured at numerous institutions, among them Columbia University, University College, London, Universidad Complutense, University of California Santa Barbara, University of Hong Kong, Universitat de Barcelona, the Museo Nacional Centro de Arte Reina Sofía, Meadows Museum, Fundació Joan Miró, and The Solomon R. Guggenheim Museum. She holds a Ph.D. in Art History from NYU's Institute of Fine Arts.

Delia Solomons is assistant professor of Art History at Drexel University, where she teaches courses in modern and contemporary art. Prior to joining Drexel, she taught at New York University, Tulane University, and The City University of New York. Her research and teaching interests include art's relationship to exhibition practices, activism, revolution, materiality, and inter-American politics. She received her doctorate from the Institute of Fine Arts in 2015. Solomons co-curated the exhibition

Sari Dienes at The Drawing Center in 2014 and has worked as a curatorial and research assistant for exhibitions at the Museo Nacional Centro de Arte Reina Sofía and Grey Art Gallery. She has published essays in the *Journal of Curatorial Studies* (2014) and *In the Distance* (MIT University Press, 2011) and is coediting a themed volume of the *Journal of Visual Culture* (2018) on contemporary art's engagement with gun violence. Her current book project, *Cold War in the White Cube: Latin American Art for U.S. Audiences, 1959–1968* (working title), explores the sudden surge in exhibitions of Latin American art across the United States in the years directly following the Cuban Revolution.

Joseph Rishel, Curator Emeritus, Philadelphia Museum of Art, has written and lectured on a broad range of topics related to European painting and sculpture, and is a noted authority on the French artist Paul Cézanne. He earned his B.A. from Hobart College and his M.A. from the University of Chicago. He has received numerous fellowships and honors, most recently being named the Samuel H. Kress Professor at the National Gallery in 2010 and a Scholar in Residence at the Getty Research Institute in 2015. From 1972 until 2015 he served as The Gisela and Dennis Alter Senior Curator of European Painting and Sculpture before 1900, and Senior Curator of the John G. Johnson collection and Rodin Museum. Exhibitions organized and co-organized by Mr. Rishel have included *The Second Empire* (1978); *Masterpieces of Impressionism and Post-Impressionism: The Annenberg Collection* (1988); *Cézanne* (1996); *The Splendors of 18th-Century Rome* (2000); *Van Gogh: Face to Face* (2000); *Manet and the Sea* (2004); *The Arts of Colonial Latin America, 1492–1820* (2010); *Cézanne and Beyond* (2009); *Van Gogh Up Close* (2012); *Gauguin, Cézanne, Matisse: Visions of Arcadia* (2012); and most recently *Discovering the Impressionists: Paul Durand-Ruel and the New Painting* (2015).

Anna Indych-López is Associate Professor of Art History at The City College of New York and The Graduate Center, CUNY, where she teaches courses on the modern and contemporary art of Latin America, the United States, and Europe. A frequent contributor to exhibition catalogues on modern Mexican and Latin American art, she has also published on contemporary Latino/a artists. She received the College Art Association's Wyeth Foundation for American Art Grant for her book *Muralism Without Walls: Rivera, Orozco and Siqueiros in the United States, 1927–1940* (University of Pittsburgh Press, 2009) and is the coauthor of *Diego Rivera: Murals for The Museum of Modern Art* (MoMA, 2011). Her book on public artist Judith F. Baca for UCLA Chicano Studies Research Center's A Ver series will be published by the University of Minnesota Press in early 2018. She holds a Ph.D. in Art History from NYU's Institute of Fine Arts.

Ronda Kasl is Curator of Latin American Art in the American Wing at The Metropolitan Museum of Art, where she oversees the growth of a new collection area and the planning of related exhibitions. As a specialist in the art of Spain and Spanish America, she is the author of numerous books and articles, including *Sacred Spain: Art and Belief in the Spanish World* (Yale University Press, 2009) and *The Making of Hispano-Flemish Style: Art, Commerce and Politics in Fifteenth-Century Castile* (Brepols, 2014). Dr. Kasl holds degrees in art and art history from the University of Tulsa and the Institute of Fine Arts, New York University.

Berit Potter received her doctorate from New York University's Institute of Fine Arts in 2015 as well as an M.A. from New York University's Program in Museum Studies. She has held positions in several art institutions, including a research fellowship sponsored by the Terra Foundation for American Art at the Smithsonian American Art Museum. She currently teaches art history and museum studies at University of San Francisco and the San Francisco Art Institute. Her research engages with issues including the display and reception of modern art on the West Coast as well as the use of exhibitions as propaganda during World War II. Her current book project examines the career of the San Francisco Museum of Modern Art's first director, Grace McCann Morley, and her pioneering advocacy for global perspectives in the study and exhibition of modern and contemporary art.

Mari Carmen Ramírez is the Wortham Curator of Latin American Art and founding Director of the International Center for the Arts of the Americas (ICAA) at the Museum of Fine Arts, Houston. Prior to that, she was Curator of Latin American Art at the Jack S. Blanton Museum of Art and adjunct lecturer in the Department of Art and Art History, both at The University of Texas at Austin. Ramírez also served as director of the Museo de Antropología, Historia y Arte de la Universidad de Puerto Rico, Río Piedras campus. She received a Ph.D. in Art History from the University of Chicago in 1989. Ramírez has curated numerous exhibitions of Latin American art, including *Inverted Utopias: Avant-Garde Art in Latin America* (with Héctor Olea, MFAH, 2004), which was recognized by the International Association of Art Critics as the "Best Thematic Museum Show Nationally" in the United States. More recently, *New York Times* art critic Holland Cotter declared *Inverted Utopias* one of the two most important exhibitions of the past decade. At the ICAA, Ramírez conceptualized and oversees the continental initiative Documents of 20th Century Latin American and Latino Art: A Digital Archive and Publications Project, dedicated to the recovery and digitalization of primary sources related to the artistic production of the region. In 2005, she was the recipient of the Award for Curatorial Excellence granted by the Center for Curatorial Studies at Bard College. That same year *TIME* magazine named her one of the twenty-five most influential Hispanics in America. She is also the recipient of the 2014 Latino Influencer Award and that same year made the One Hundred Most

Powerful Women in the Arts list. Ramírez has been widely published on a broad range of topics, such as the relationship of Latin American art to the avant-garde, identity politics, multiculturalism, globalization, and curatorial practice. She has also written extensively about modern and contemporary artists from the region, including Joaquí Torres-Garcí, Gego, Hélio Oiticica, Carlos Cruz-Diez, and Antonio Berni.

Vanessa K. Davidson received a B.A. in Hispano-American Literature from Harvard University and studied Latin American and Pre-Columbian art and Argentine poetry at the Universidad de Buenos Aires, Argentina, as well as Portuguese at the Universidade de São Paulo. She has worked at the Museum of Fine Arts, Boston, on the Pre-Columbian and Spanish Colonial Collections, and also at The Metropolitan Museum of Art on the groundbreaking exhibition *The Colonial Andes: Tapestries and Silverwork, 1530–1830*. She was awarded a Fulbright-Hays Fellowship to conduct dissertation research in Argentina and Brazil in 2009, and in 2011 she received her Ph.D. in Twentieth-Century Latin American Art History from the Institute of Fine Arts, New York University. Since starting work at the Phoenix Art Museum as Shawn and Joe Lampe Curator of Latin American Art in 2011, she has organized many exhibitions, including *The Politics of Place: Latin American Photography, Past and Present* (2012); *Order, Chaos, and the Space Between: Contemporary Latin American Art from the Diane and Bruce Halle Collection* (2013); *Rufino Tamayo, Master Printmaker (2013); Paulo Bruscky: Art Is Our Last Hope* (2014); *Focus Latin America: An International Exhibition of Contemporary Mail Art* (2014); *Hidden Histories in Latin American Art* (2015); *Masterworks of Spanish Colonial Art from Phoenix Art Museum's Collection* (2015); and *Horacio Zabala: Mapping the Monochrome* (2016). Upcoming projects include an exhibition of Brazilian art organized in collaboration with the São Paulo Museu de Arte Moderna entitled *Past/Future/Present: Contemporary Brazilian Art from the Museum of Modern Art, São Paulo*; and the exhibition *Valeska Soares: Any Moment Now*, a project organized with the Santa Barbara Museum of Art as part of the Getty Foundation's 2017 *Pacific Standard Time: Los Angeles / Latin America* initiative.

Suzanne Stratton-Pruitt received her Ph.D. in 1983 from the Institute of Fine Arts, New York University. For over a decade she was curator of the gallery of The Spanish Institute on Park Avenue, organizing exhibitions on a broad selection of themes, from Spanish polychrome sculpture to modern Spanish photography. As an independent scholar, Dr. Stratton-Pruitt has edited two anthologies for Cambridge University Press: *The Cambridge Companion to Velázquez* and *Velázquez's "Las Meninas"* (both 2002) and curated a traveling exhibition, *Bartolomé Esteban Murillo (1682–1681): Paintings from American Collections* (2003). Soon thereafter, Dr. Stratton turned her attention to Spanish colonial art, participating in a series of exhibitions, such as *The Virgin, Saints, and Angels: South American Paintings, 1600–1825, in the Thoma Collection* (Stanford University, 2006, and other venues); *The Arts in Latin America, 1492–1820* (Philadelphia Museum of Art, 2006, LACMA and the Colegio de San Ildefonso, Mexico City); *Beyond Closed Doors: Art in the Spanish American Home, 1492–1898* (The Brooklyn Museum, 2013, and other venues); *Journeys to New Worlds: Spanish and Portuguese Colonial Art in the Roberta and Richard Huber Collection* (Philadelphia Museum of Art, 2013); and *Painting the Divine: Images of Mary in the New World* (New Mexico History Museum, 2014). She edited and contributed to *The Art of Painting in Colonial Quito* (Saint Joseph's University Press, 2012) and *The Art of Painting in Colonial Bolivia* (Saint Joseph's University Press, 2017).

Gabriel Pérez-Barreiro is Director and Chief Curator of the Colección Patricia Phelps de Cisneros in New York and Caracas, and Curator of the 33rd Bienal de São Paulo (2018). He was Curator of Latin American Art at the Blanton Museum of Art, University of Texas at Austin, and Director of Visual Arts at The Americas Society, New York. In 2007, he was Chief Curator of the 6th Mercosur Bienal in Porto Alegre, Brazil. He has a Ph.D. in Art History and Theory from the University of Essex and has published and lectured widely on modern and contemporary art from Latin America.

Estrellita B. Brodsky received her Ph.D. in Art History from the Institute of Fine Arts, New York University (2009), where she completed her dissertation, "Latin American Artists in Post–World War II Paris: Jesús Soto and Julio Le Parc." A graduate from Sarah Lawrence College (1973), she went on to receive a master's degree in Art History from Hunter College (1996). She co-organized the 1997 exhibition *Taíno: Pre-Columbian Art and Culture of the Caribbean* at El Museo del Barrio in New York City, and later served as the museum's co-chairman. Her curatorial and academic work has focused on post–World War II Latin American artists. Dr. Brodsky's curatorial projects include the first U.S. retrospective exhibition on the Venezuelan Kinetic artist Cruz-Diez, *Carlos Cruz-Diez: (In)formed by Color* at the Americas Society in 2008; *Jesús Soto: Paris and Beyond, 1950–1970* at the New York University Grey Art Gallery in 2012; *Una Búsqueda Permanente: Julio Le Parc* on the Argentine Kinetic artist in São Paulo in 2013; and jointly curating *Bearing Witness: Art and Resistance in Cold War Latin America* at the John Jay College for Criminal Justice in 2014. In 2015, she inaugurated a not-for-profit program for Latin American art, ANOTHER SPACE, where she presented *Paulo Bruscky: Artist Books and Films, 1970–2013* and in 2016 *Marta Minujín: Arte agrícola en acción—Toronjas, 1977–2016*. Most recently, she curated *Julio Le Parc: Form into Action* (2016–17), the artist's first U.S. museum survey, which covered six decades of Le Parc's work at the Pérez Art Museum Miami.

Index

Locators in italics signify illustrations.

Typeset by
BESSAS & ACKERMAN

Printed and bound by
PACOM

Composed in
MONOTYPE GARAMOND
AND FRUTIGER NEXT PRO

Printed on
HANSOL MATTE ART

Bound in
SAIFU